AFTER SCHOOL
NIGHTMARE

Story and Art by
SETONA MIZUSHIRO

(5)

go!comi

Translation – Christine Schilling
Adaptation – Mallory Reaves
Lettering & Retouch – Eva Han
Production Manager – James Dashiell
Editor – Brynne Chandler

A Go! Comi manga

Published by Go! Media Entertainment, LLC

Houkago Hokenshitsu Volume 5
© SETONA MIZUSHIRO 2006
Originally published in Japan in 2006 by Akita Publishing Co., Ltd., Tokyo.
English translation rights arranged with Akita Publishing Co., Ltd.
through TOHAN CORPORATION, Tokyo.

Visit us online at www.gocomi.com
e-mail: info@gocomi.com

ISBN 978-1-933617-47-3

First printed in October 2007

1 2 3 4 5 6 7 8 9

Manufactured in the United States of America.

Koukoku Senior High School

Table of contents

AFTER SCHOOL NIGHTMARE

Our Story So Far

High schooler Mashiro Ichijo's body is half female and half male. One day, he's called down to a secret infirmary to participate in a special "class" he needs to graduate. He learns from another student, Kureha, that each person takes on their true form in this class. When each student reaches their personal goal, their most heart-felt dream will come true. Mashiro decides to use this class to become a true male.

But when another dreamer – a merciless knight – exposes his body's secret and Kureha's tragic past, Mashiro vows to protect the weaker dreamers.

Who is the real person behind the knight? While trying to identify the real people behind the facades, Mashiro is accosted by Sou, a male student he doesn't much like. Sou tells him "you're a girl" and then forces a kiss upon him. Wondering whether Sou could be another dreamer, maybe even the knight, Mashiro becomes obsessed with Sou.

In the midst of it all, his friend Shinbashi, who wishes for nothing but Kureha's happiness, sacrifices himself by graduating in Mashiro's place. Mashiro renews his vow to protect Kureha, and he rejects Sou...but for how long?

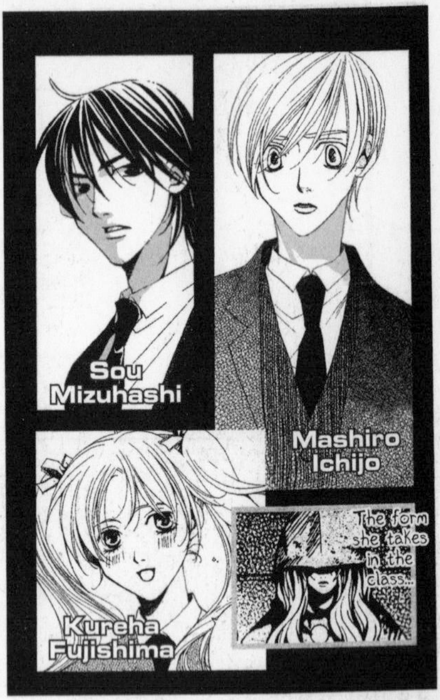
Mashiro Ichijo
Sou Mizuhashi
The form she takes in the class...
Kureha Fujishima

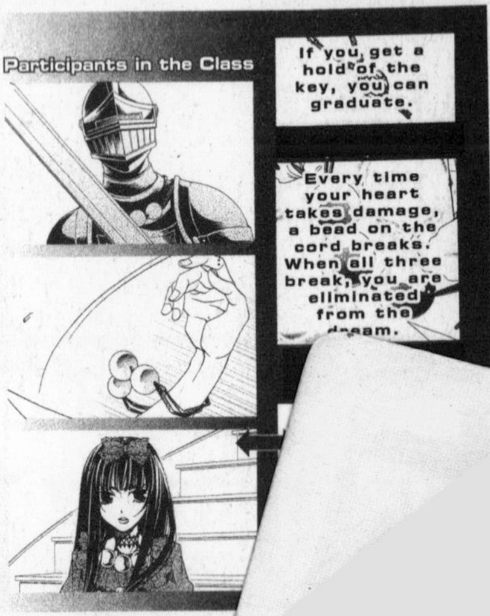
If you get a hold of the key, you can graduate.
Participants in the Class
Every time your heart takes damage, a bead on the cord breaks. When all three break, you are elliminated from the dream.

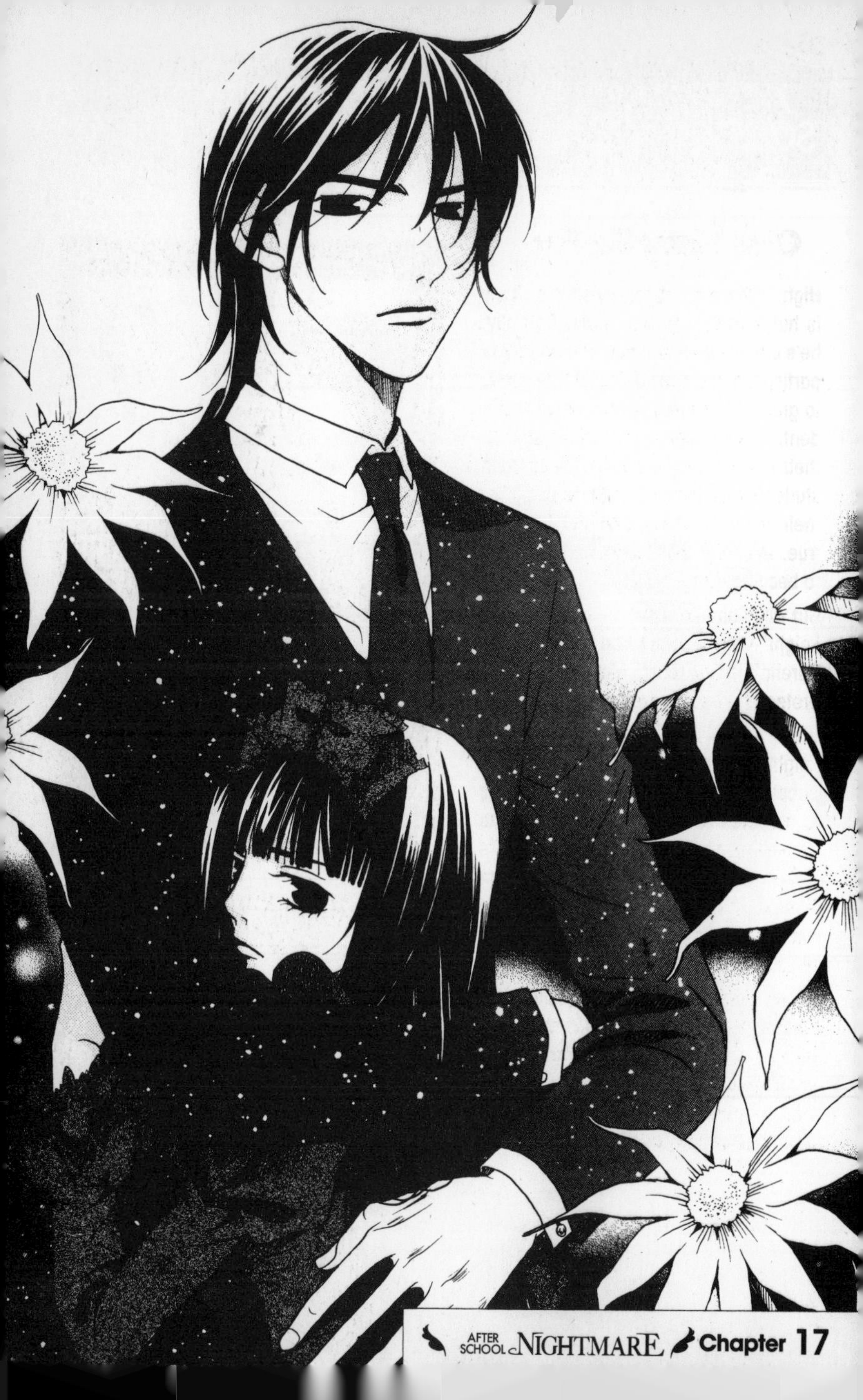
AFTER SCHOOL NIGHTMARE Chapter 17

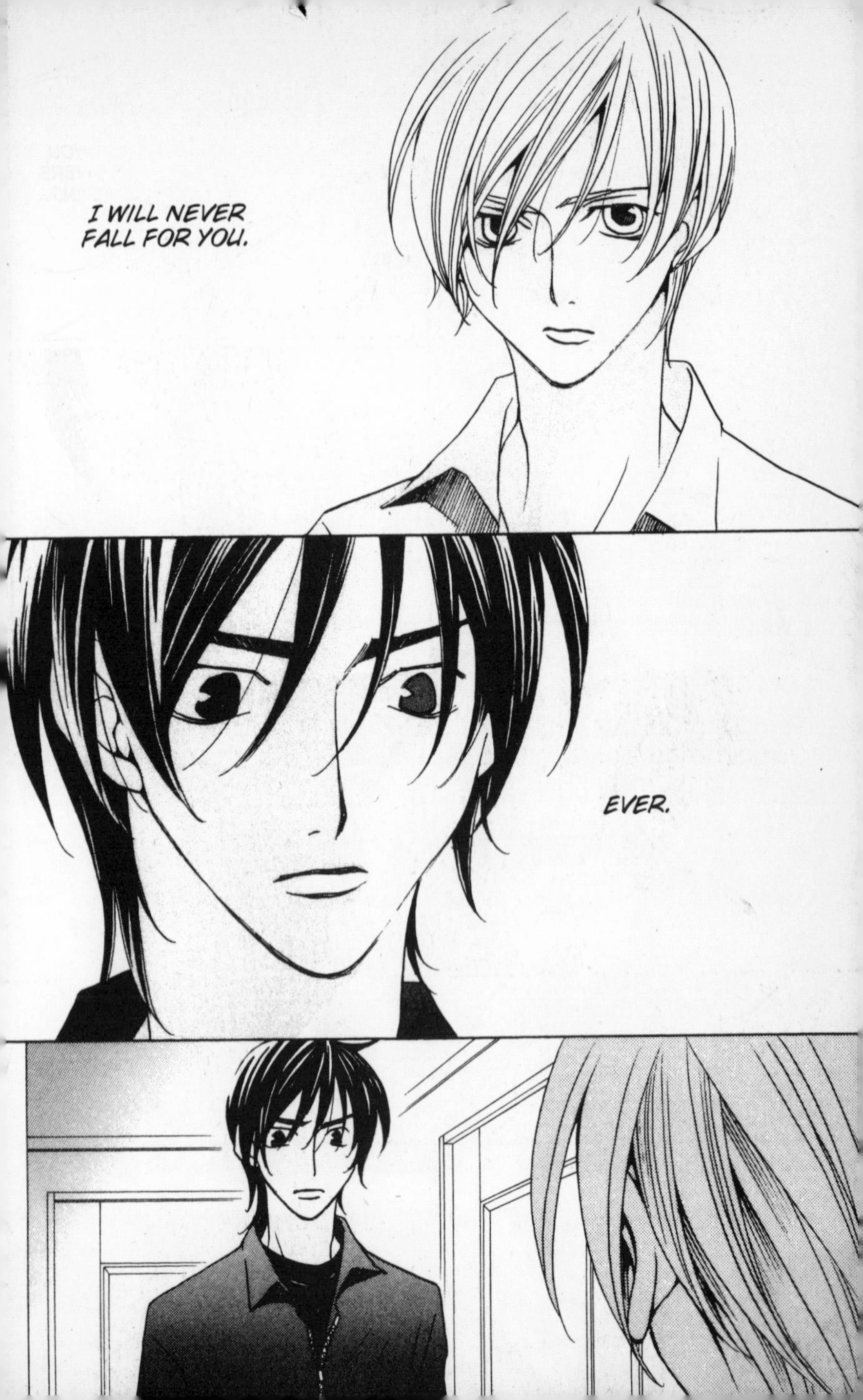
I WILL NEVER FALL FOR YOU.
EVER.

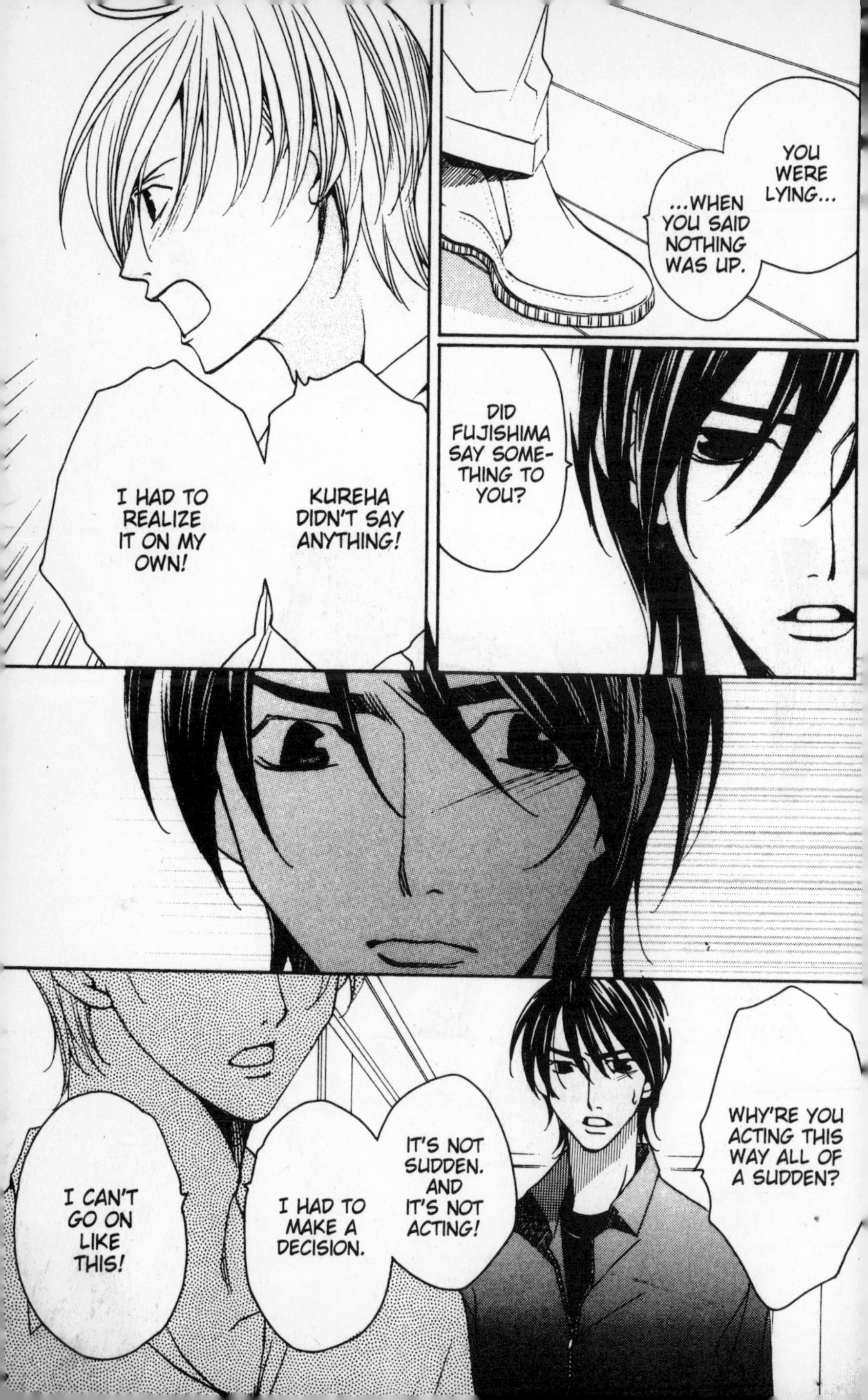
YOU WERE LYING...
...WHEN YOU SAID NOTHING WAS UP.
DID FUJISHIMA SAY SOME-THING TO YOU?
KUREHA DIDN'T SAY ANYTHING!
I HAD TO REALIZE IT ON MY OWN!
WHY'RE YOU ACTING THIS WAY ALL OF A SUDDEN?
IT'S NOT SUDDEN. AND IT'S NOT ACTING!
I HAD TO MAKE A DECISION.
I CAN'T GO ON LIKE THIS!

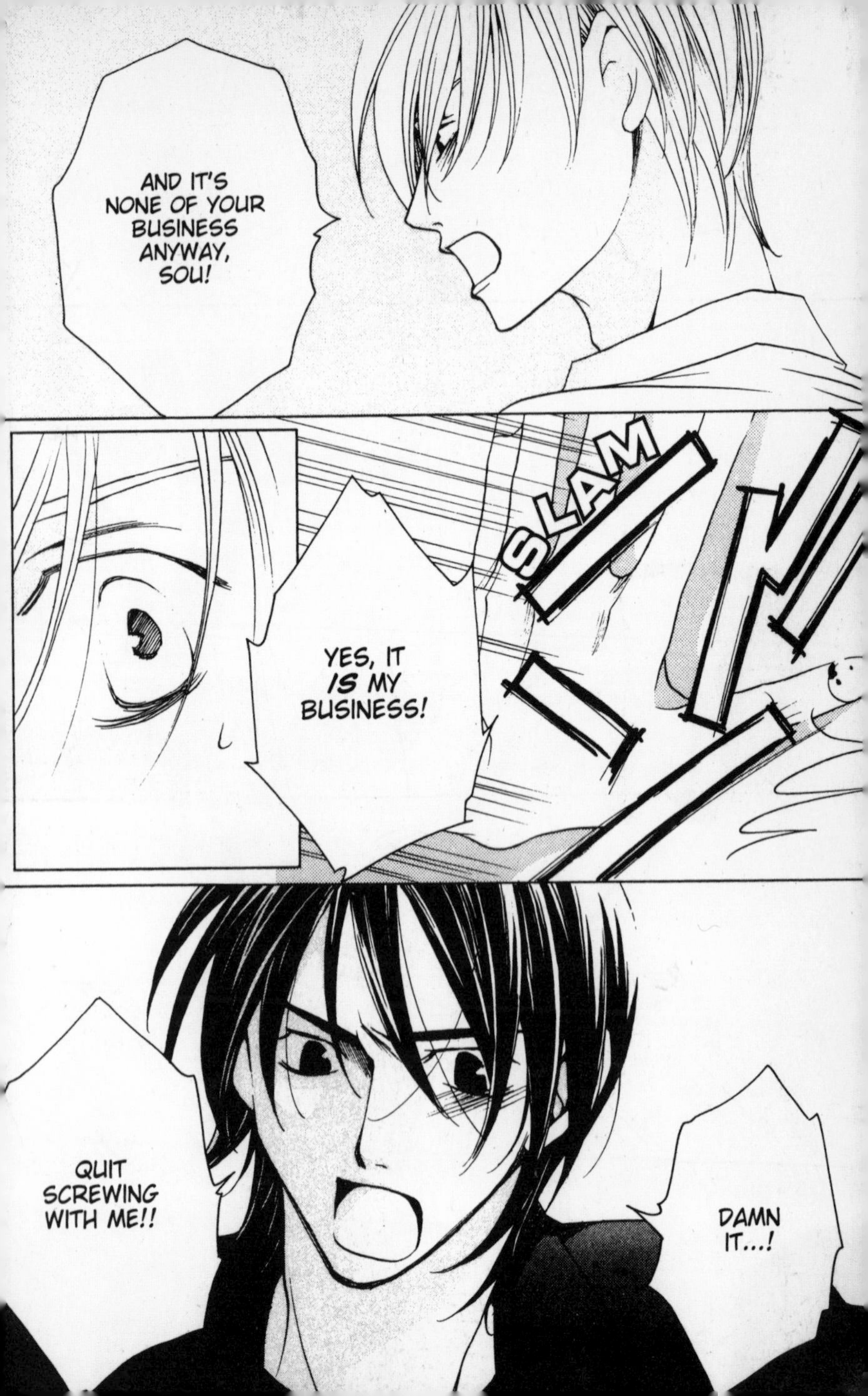
AND IT'S NONE OF YOUR BUSINESS ANYWAY, SOU!
SLAM
YES, IT *IS* MY BUSINESS!
DAMN IT...!
QUIT SCREWING WITH ME!!

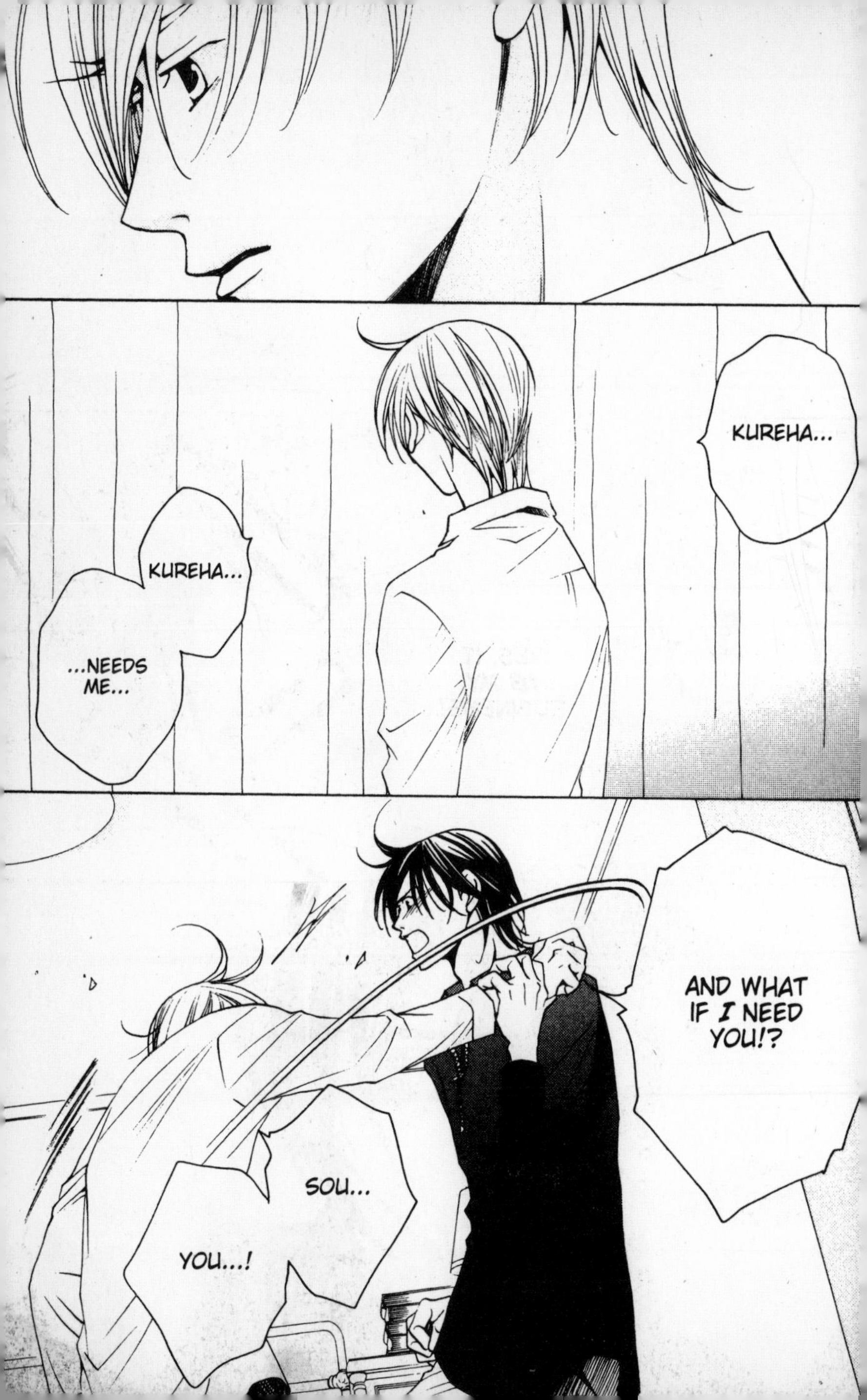
KUREHA...
KUREHA...
...NEEDS ME...
AND WHAT IF I NEED YOU!?
SOU...
YOU...!

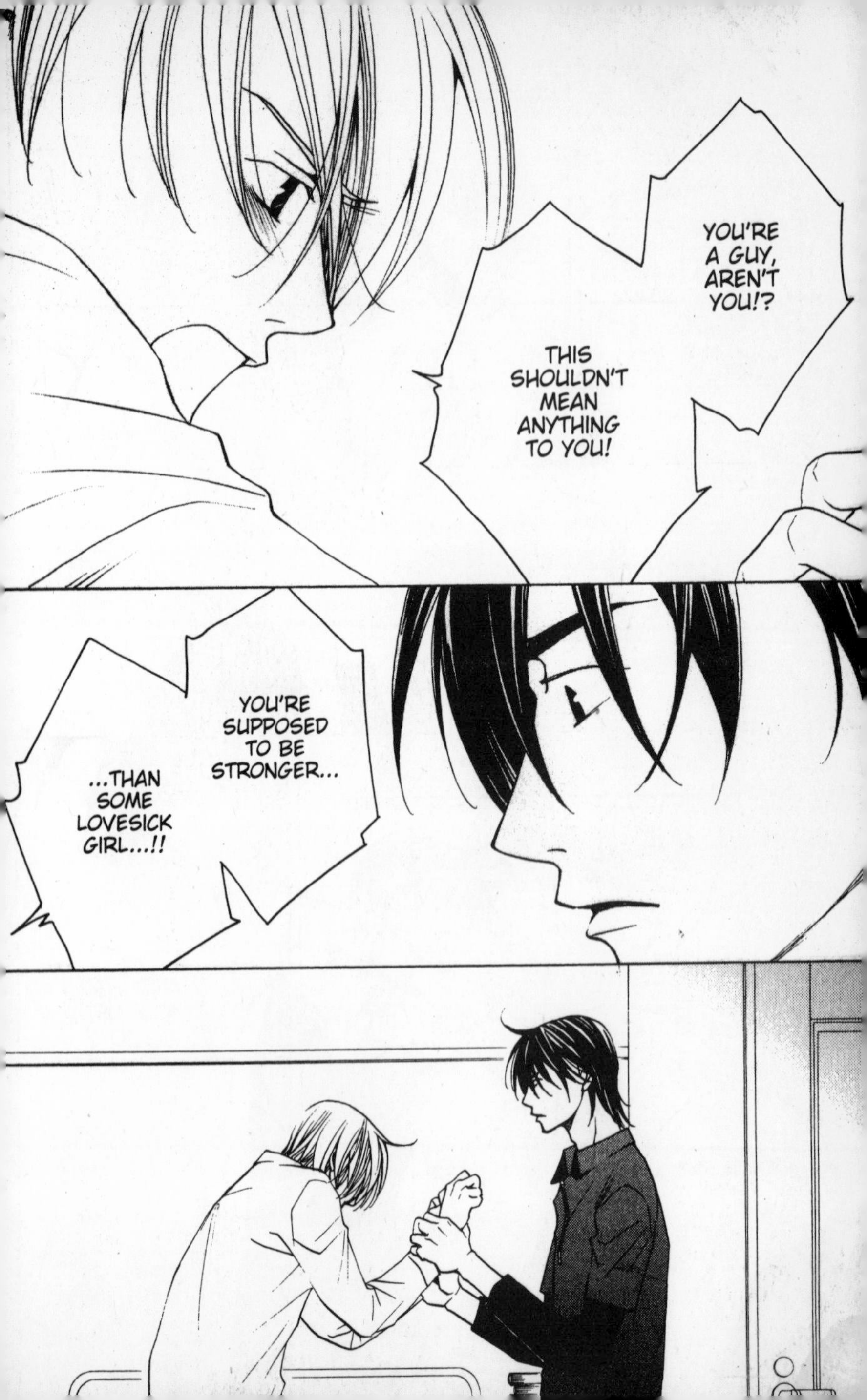
YOU'RE A GUY, AREN'T YOU!?
THIS SHOULDN'T MEAN ANYTHING TO YOU!
YOU'RE SUPPOSED TO BE STRONGER...
...THAN SOME LOVESICK GIRL...!!

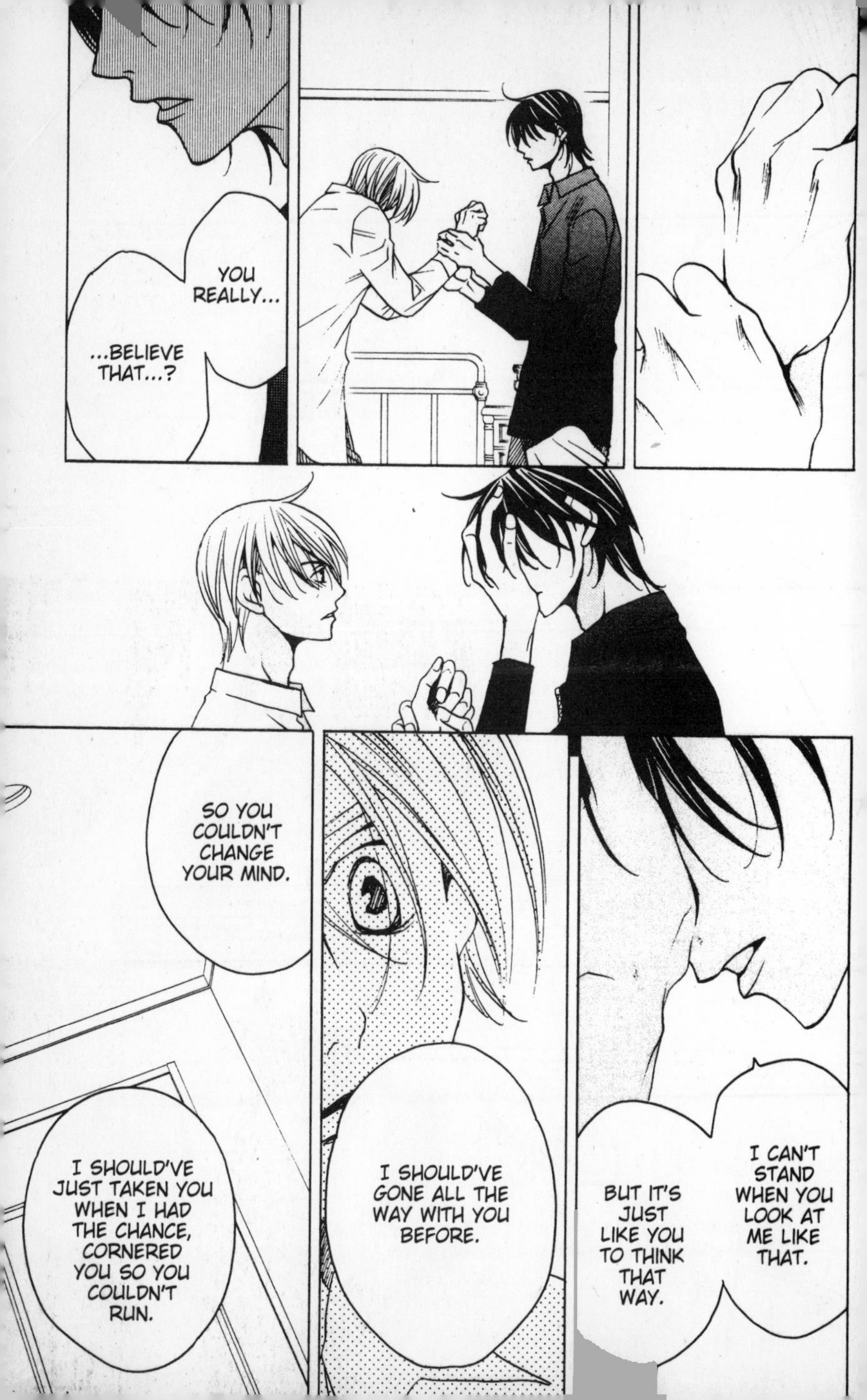
YOU REALLY...
...BELIEVE THAT...?
I CAN'T STAND WHEN YOU LOOK AT ME LIKE THAT.
BUT IT'S JUST LIKE YOU TO THINK THAT WAY.
I SHOULD'VE GONE ALL THE WAY WITH YOU BEFORE.
SO YOU COULDN'T CHANGE YOUR MIND.
I SHOULD'VE JUST TAKEN YOU WHEN I HAD THE CHANCE, CORNERED YOU SO YOU COULDN'T RUN.

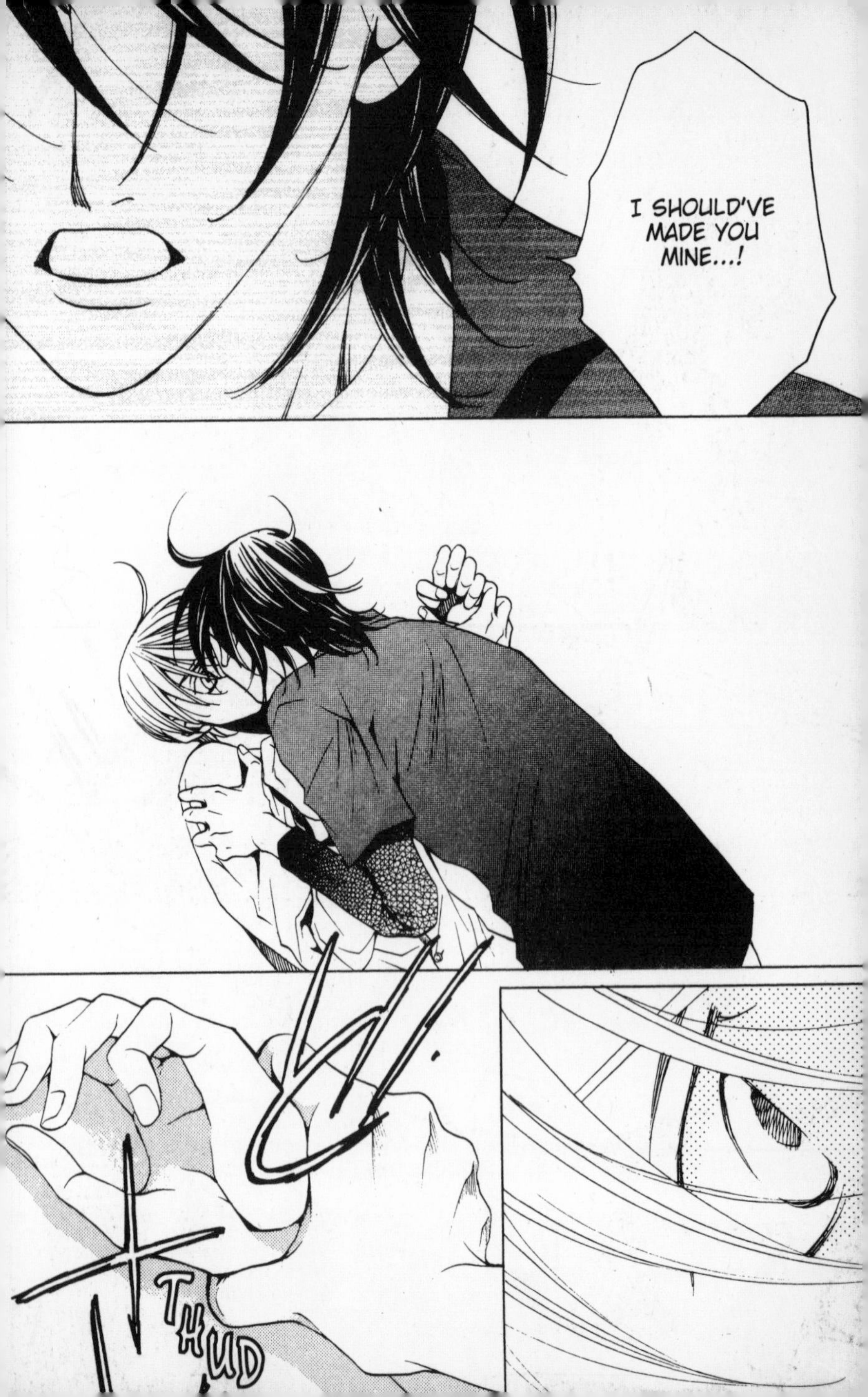
I SHOULD'VE MADE YOU MINE...!
THUD

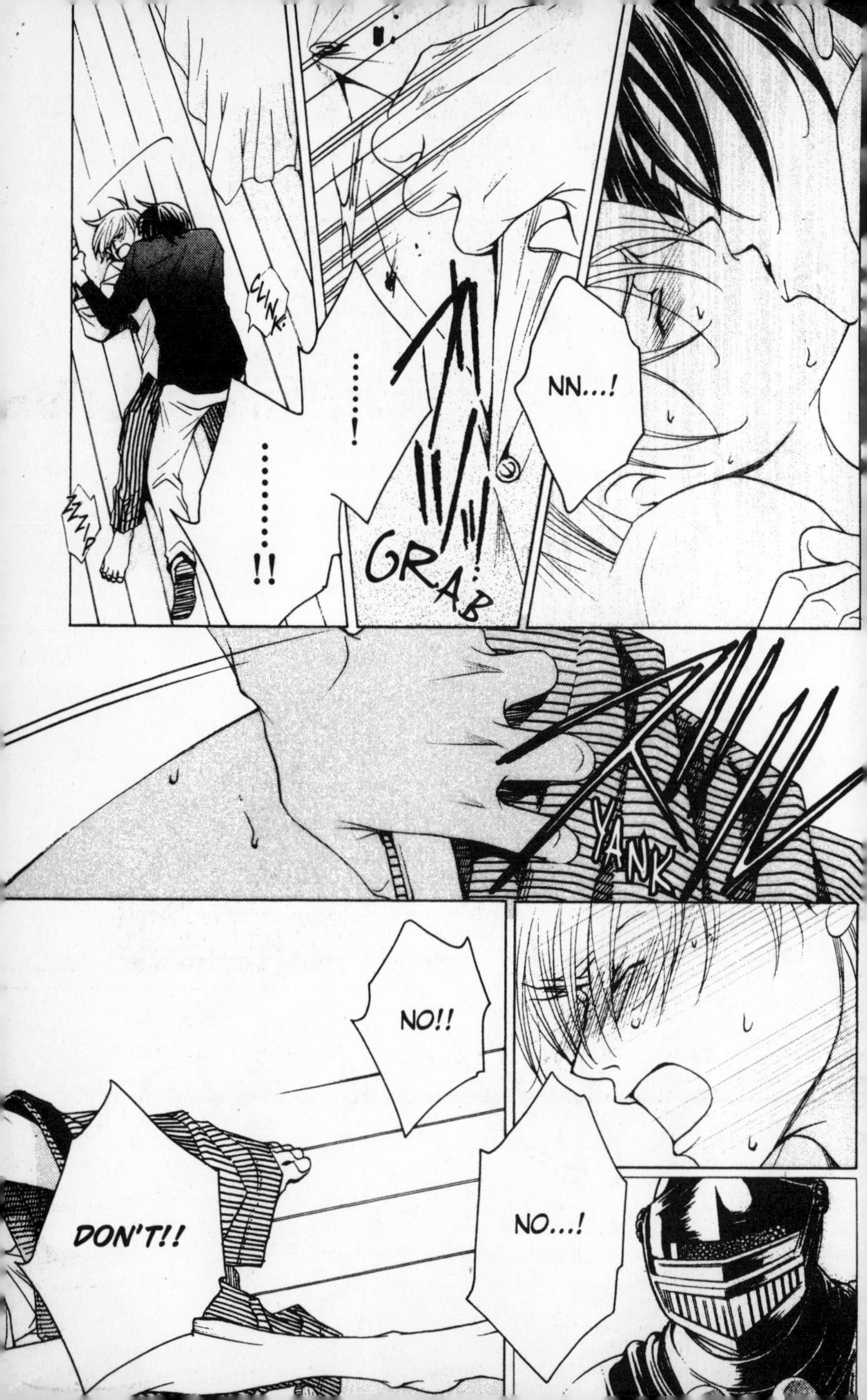
NN...!
GRAB
......!
......!!
CLINK
ZZZIP
YANK
NO!!
NO...!
DON'T!!

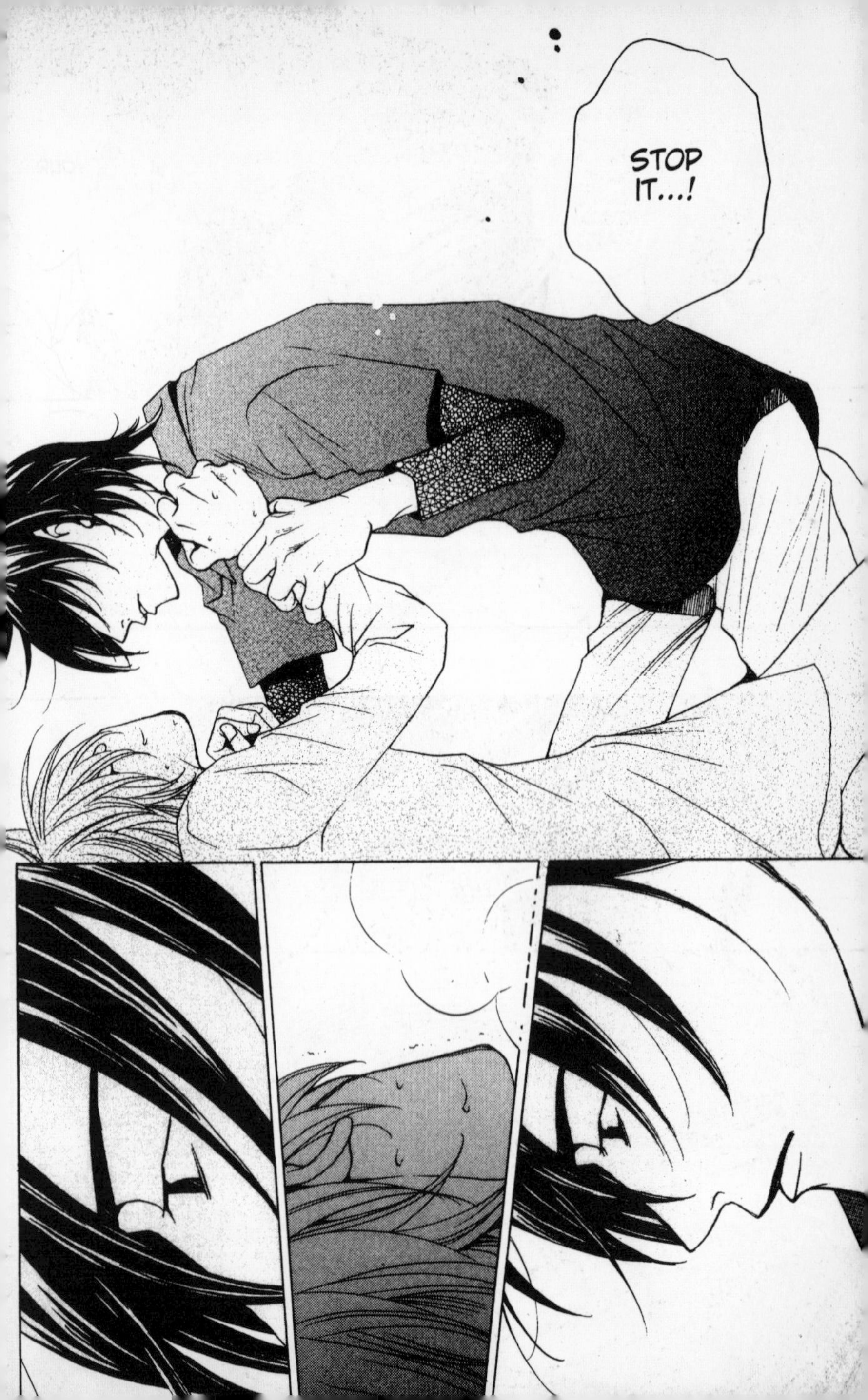
STOP IT...!

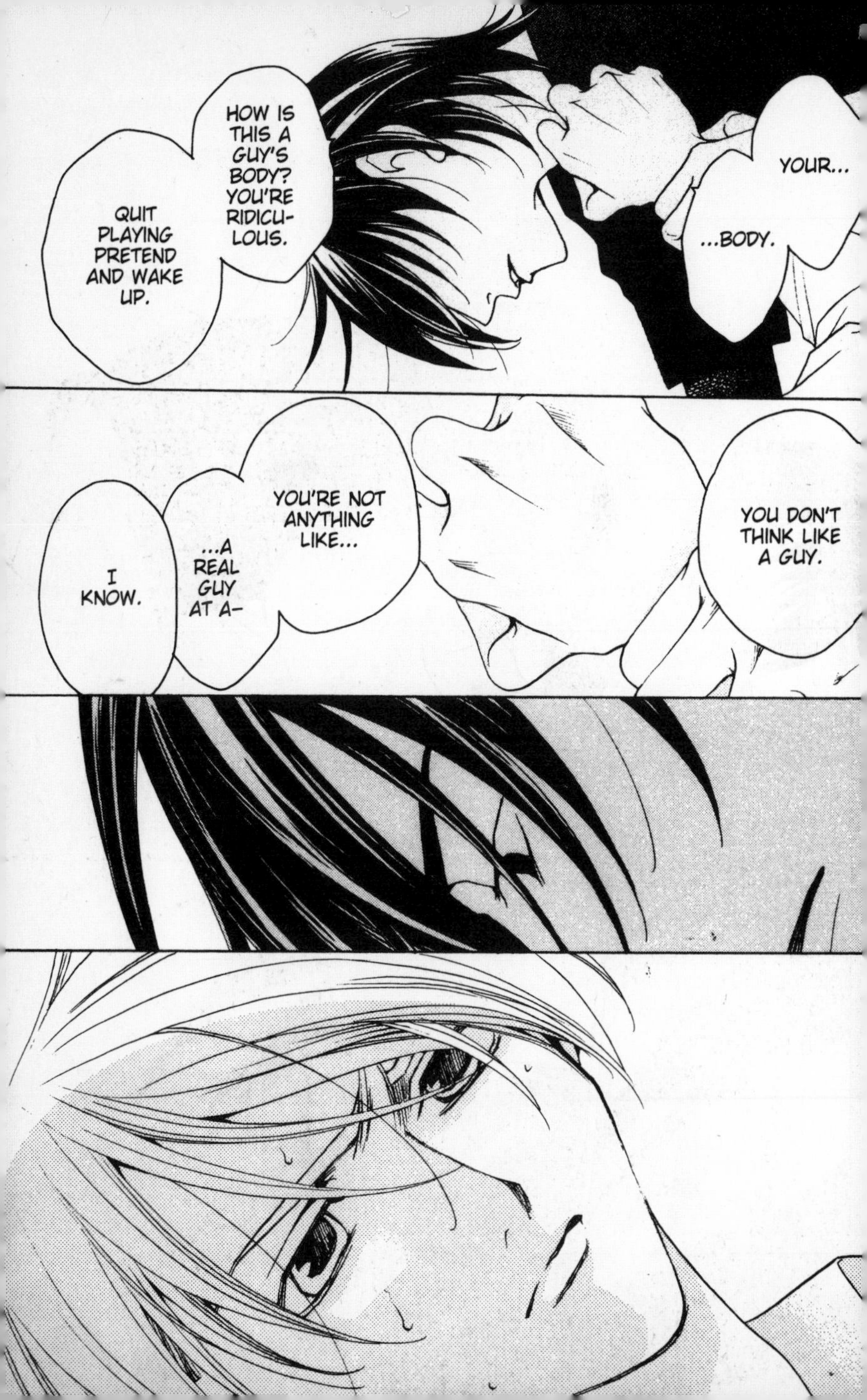
YOUR...
...BODY.
HOW IS THIS A GUY'S BODY? YOU'RE RIDICU-LOUS.
QUIT PLAYING PRETEND AND WAKE UP.
YOU DON'T THINK LIKE A GUY.
YOU'RE NOT ANYTHING LIKE...
...A REAL GUY AT A-
I KNOW.

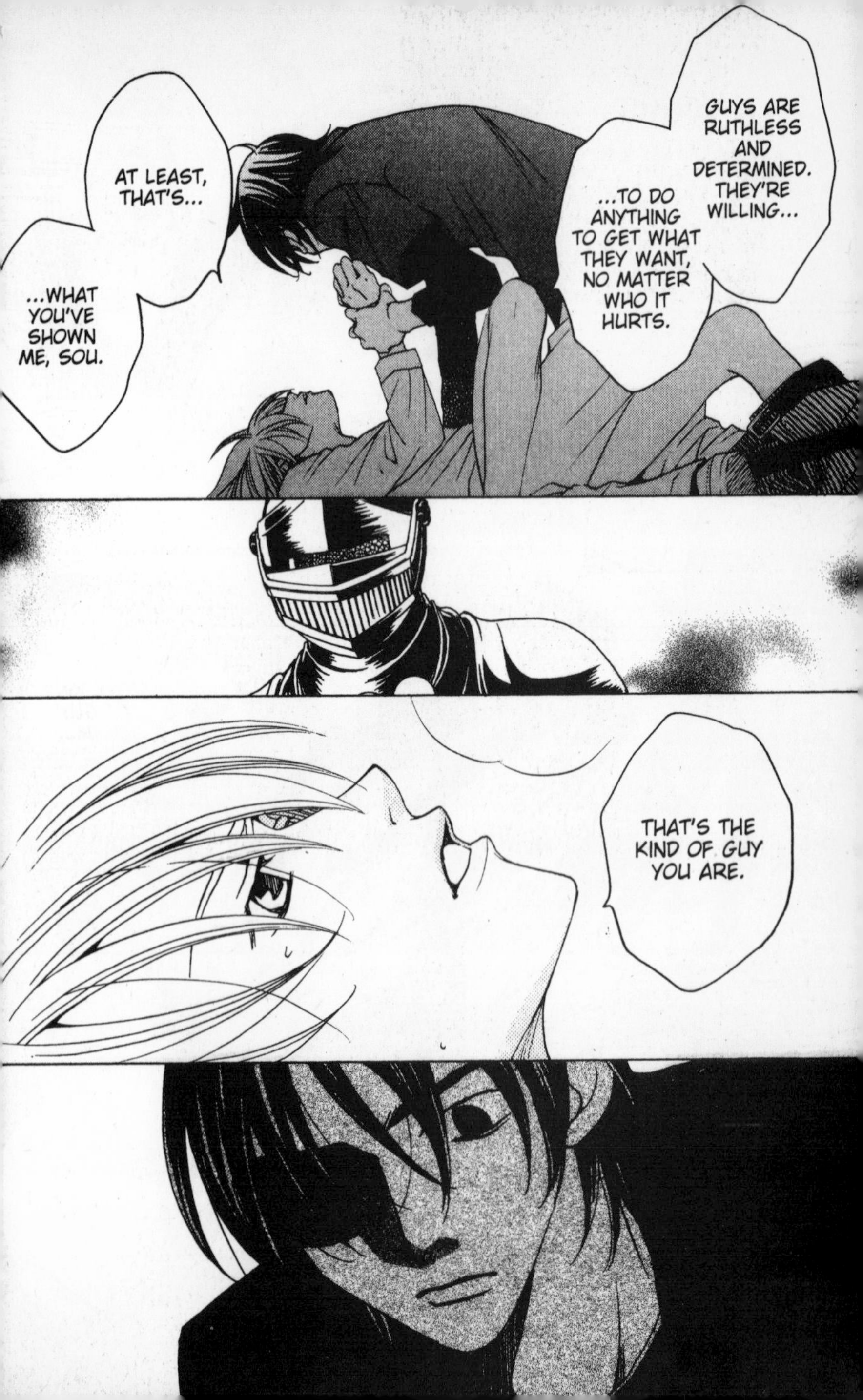
GUYS ARE RUTHLESS AND DETERMINED. THEY'RE WILLING...
...TO DO ANYTHING TO GET WHAT THEY WANT, NO MATTER WHO IT HURTS.
AT LEAST, THAT'S...
...WHAT YOU'VE SHOWN ME, SOU.
THAT'S THE KIND OF GUY YOU ARE.

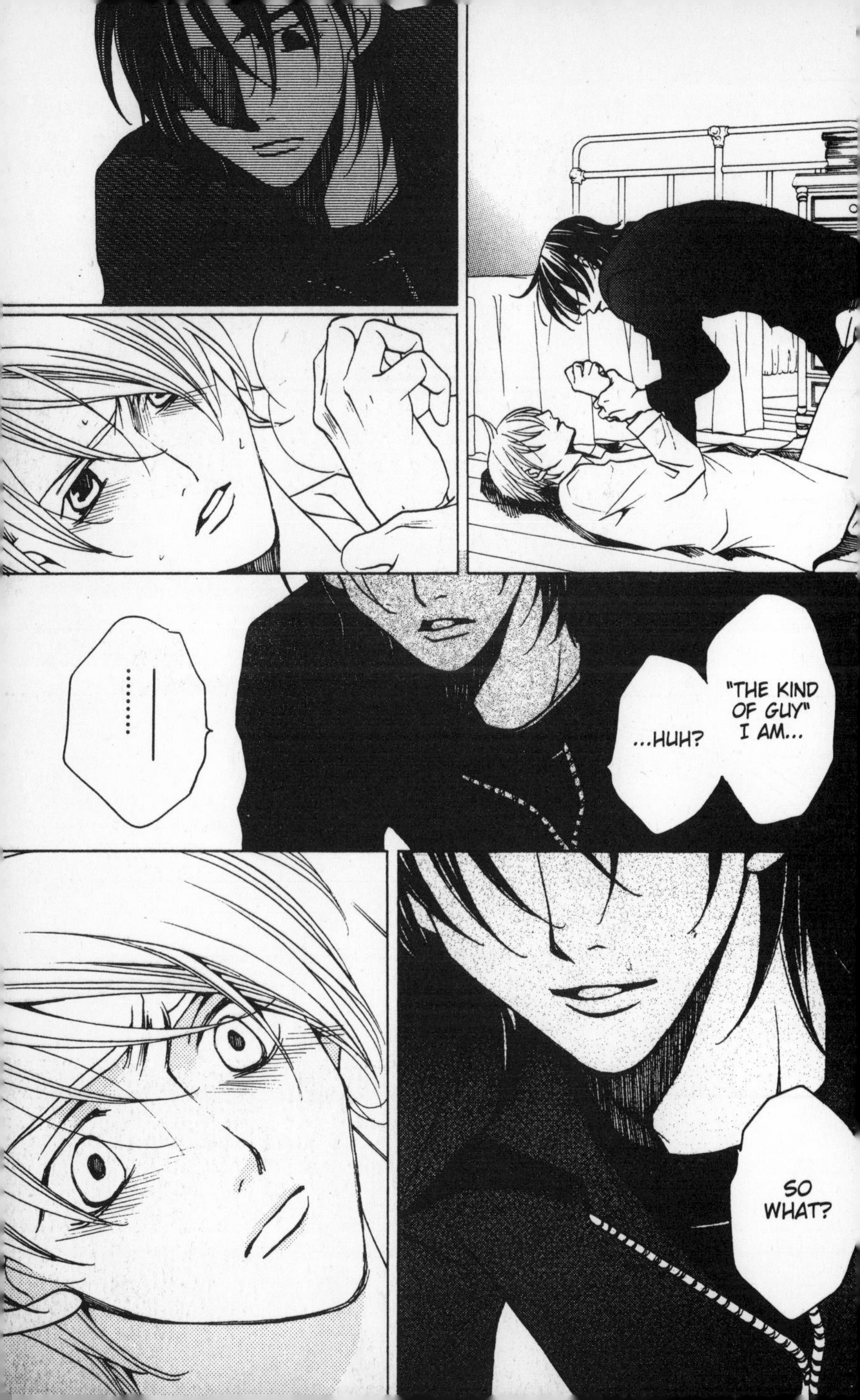

"THE KIND OF GUY" I AM...
...HUH?
......—
SO WHAT?

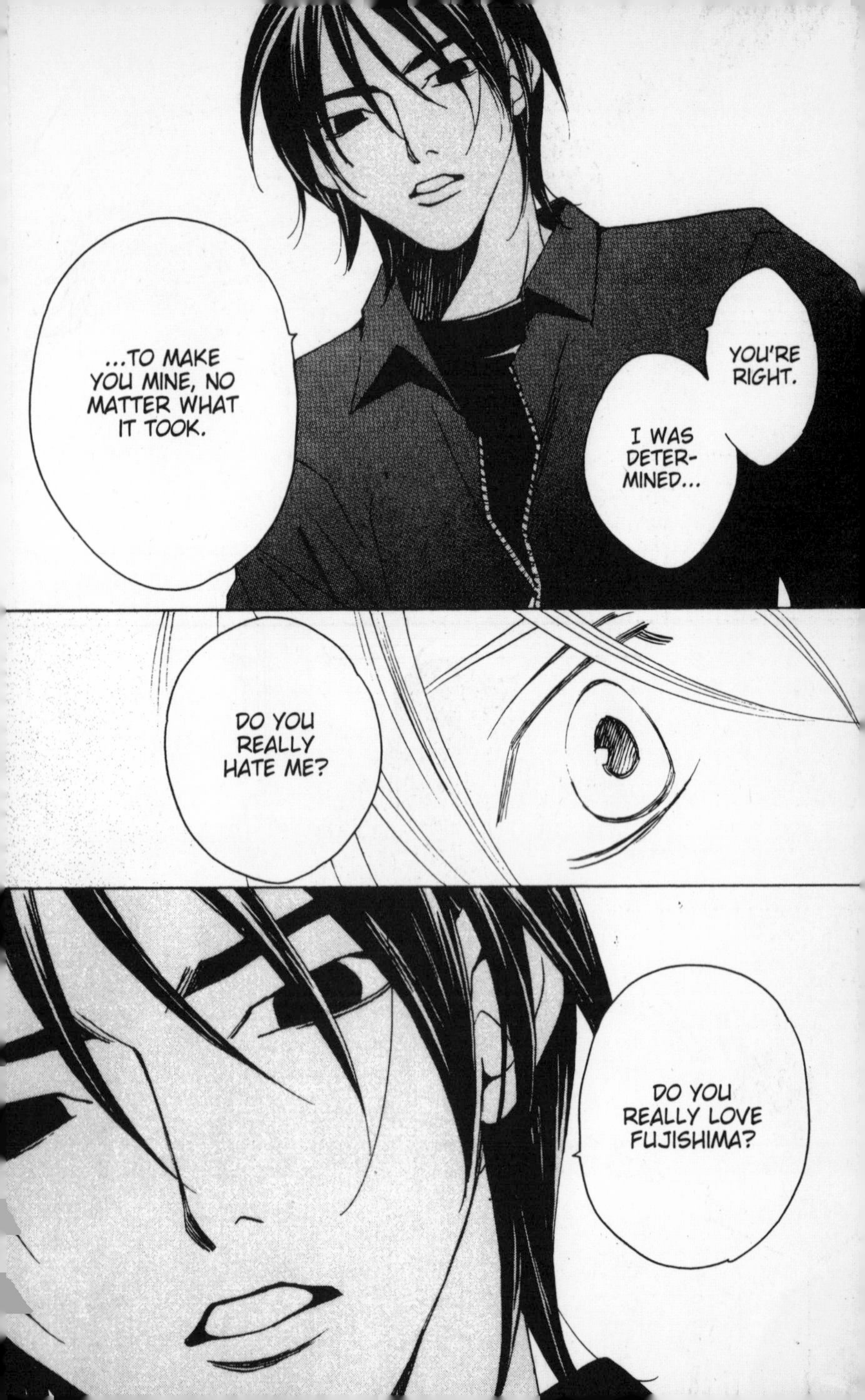
YOU'RE RIGHT. I WAS DETERMINED...
...TO MAKE YOU MINE, NO MATTER WHAT IT TOOK.
DO YOU REALLY HATE ME?
DO YOU REALLY LOVE FUJISHIMA?

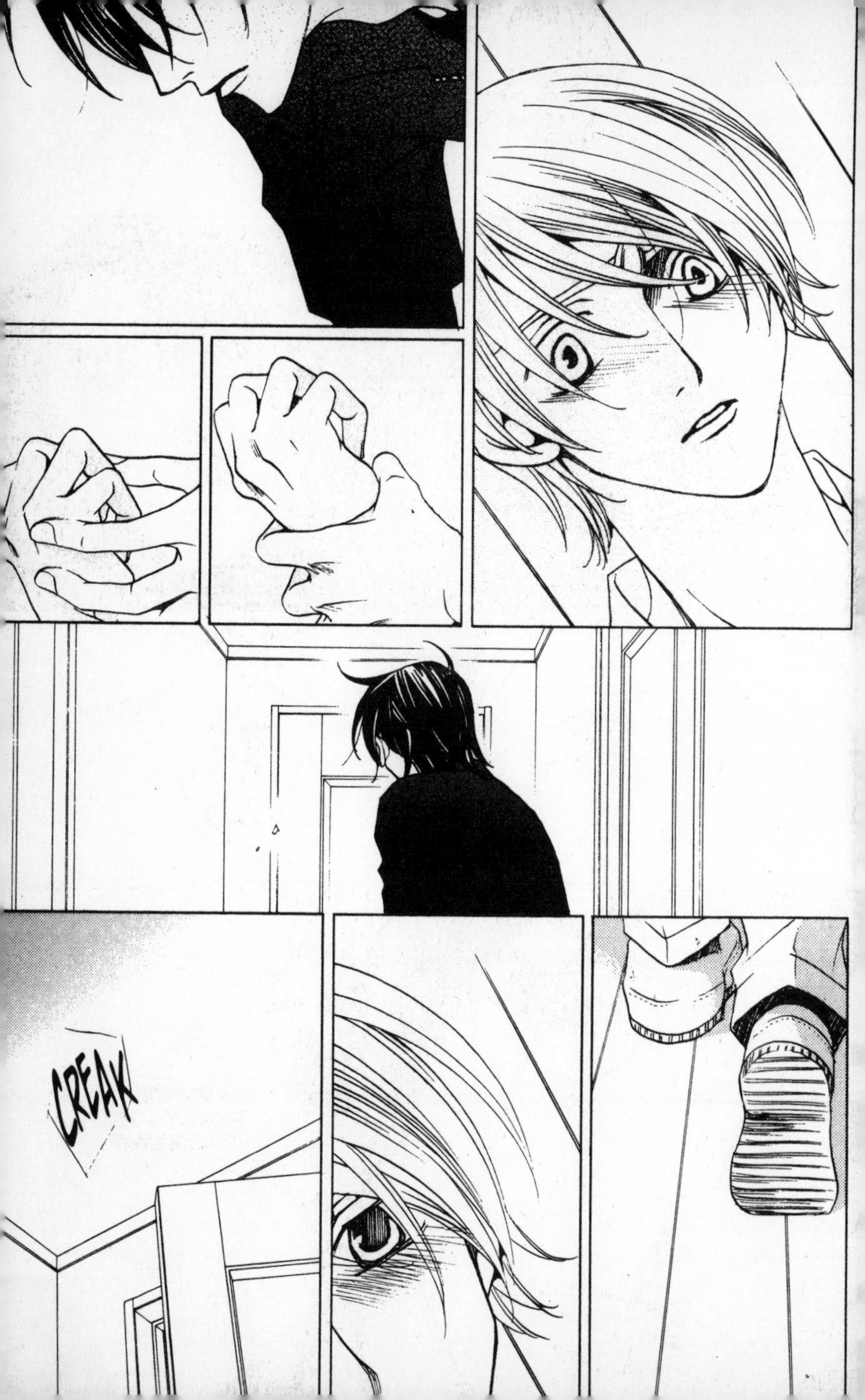
CREAK

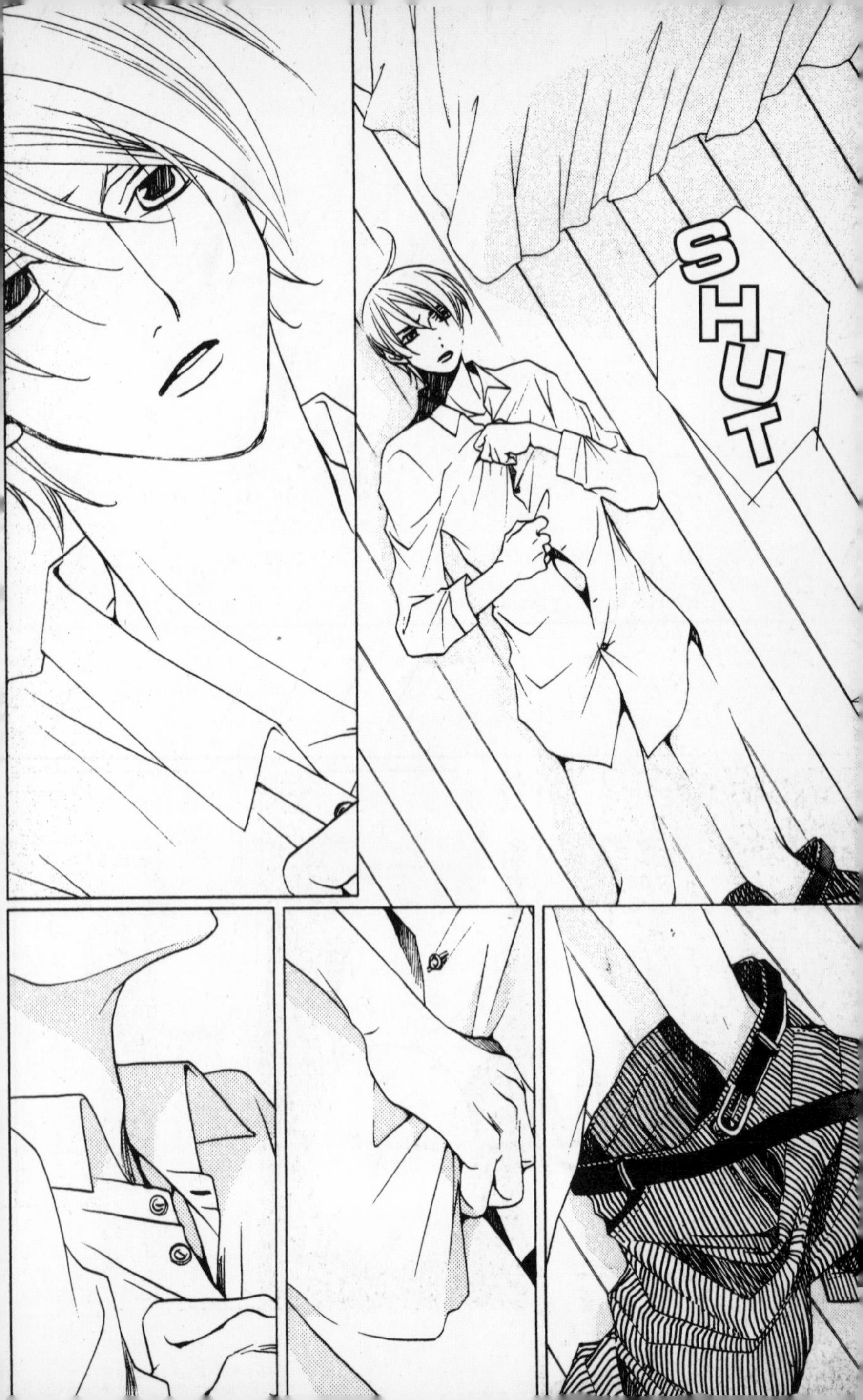
SHUT

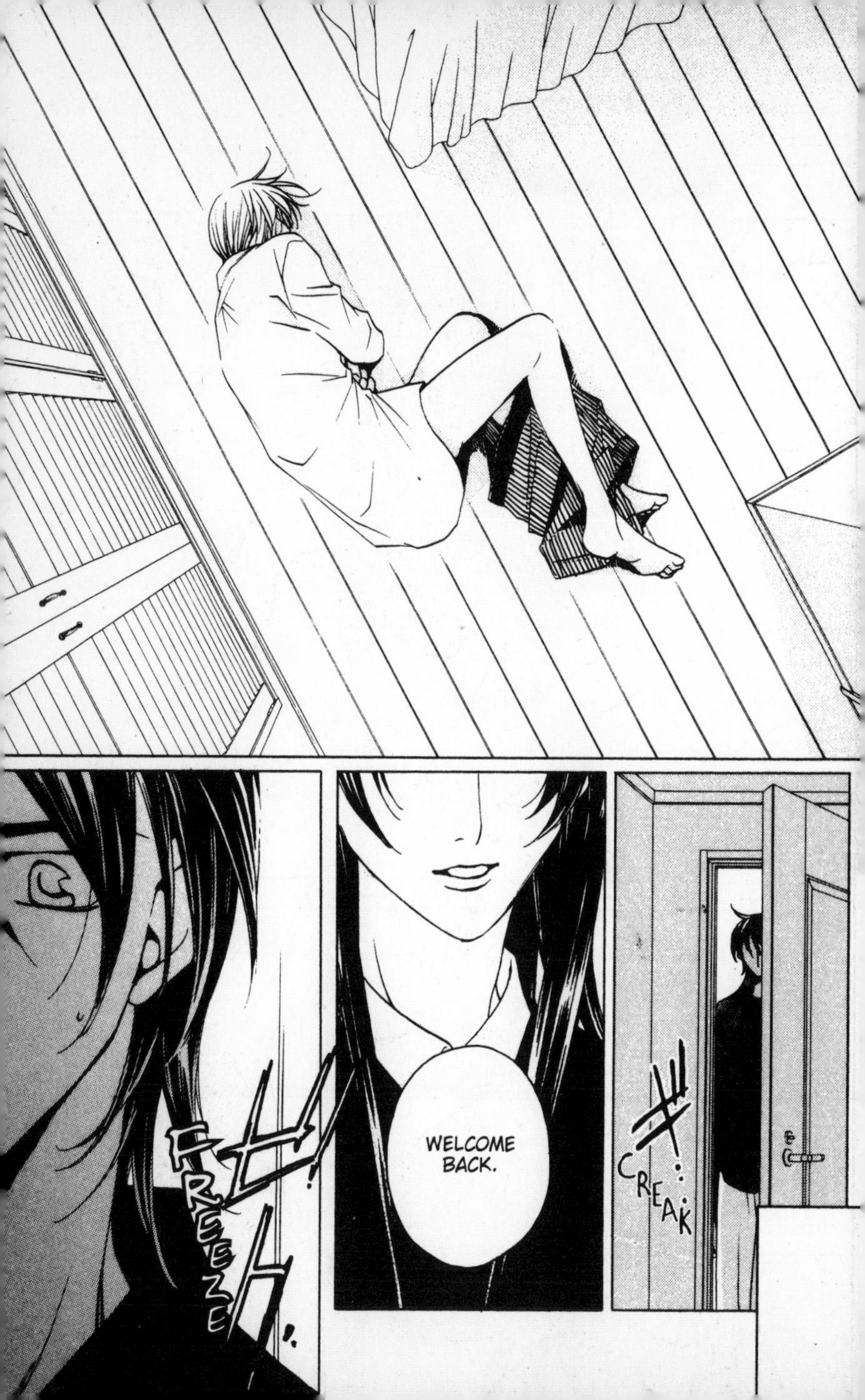
CREAK
WELCOME BACK.
FREEZE

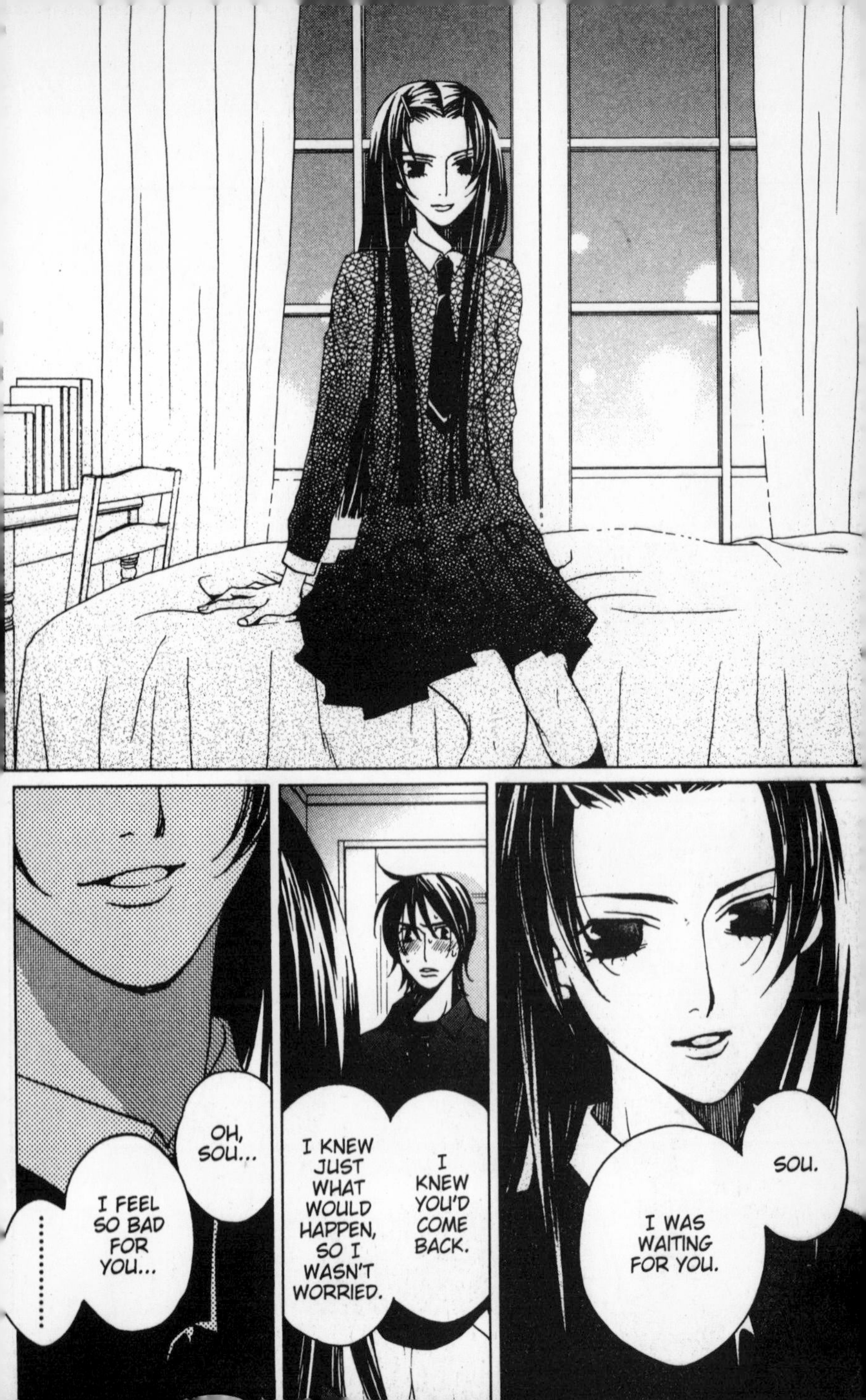
SOU.
I WAS WAITING FOR YOU.
I KNEW YOU'D COME BACK.
I KNEW JUST WHAT WOULD HAPPEN, SO I WASN'T WORRIED.
OH, SOU...
I FEEL SO BAD FOR YOU...
......

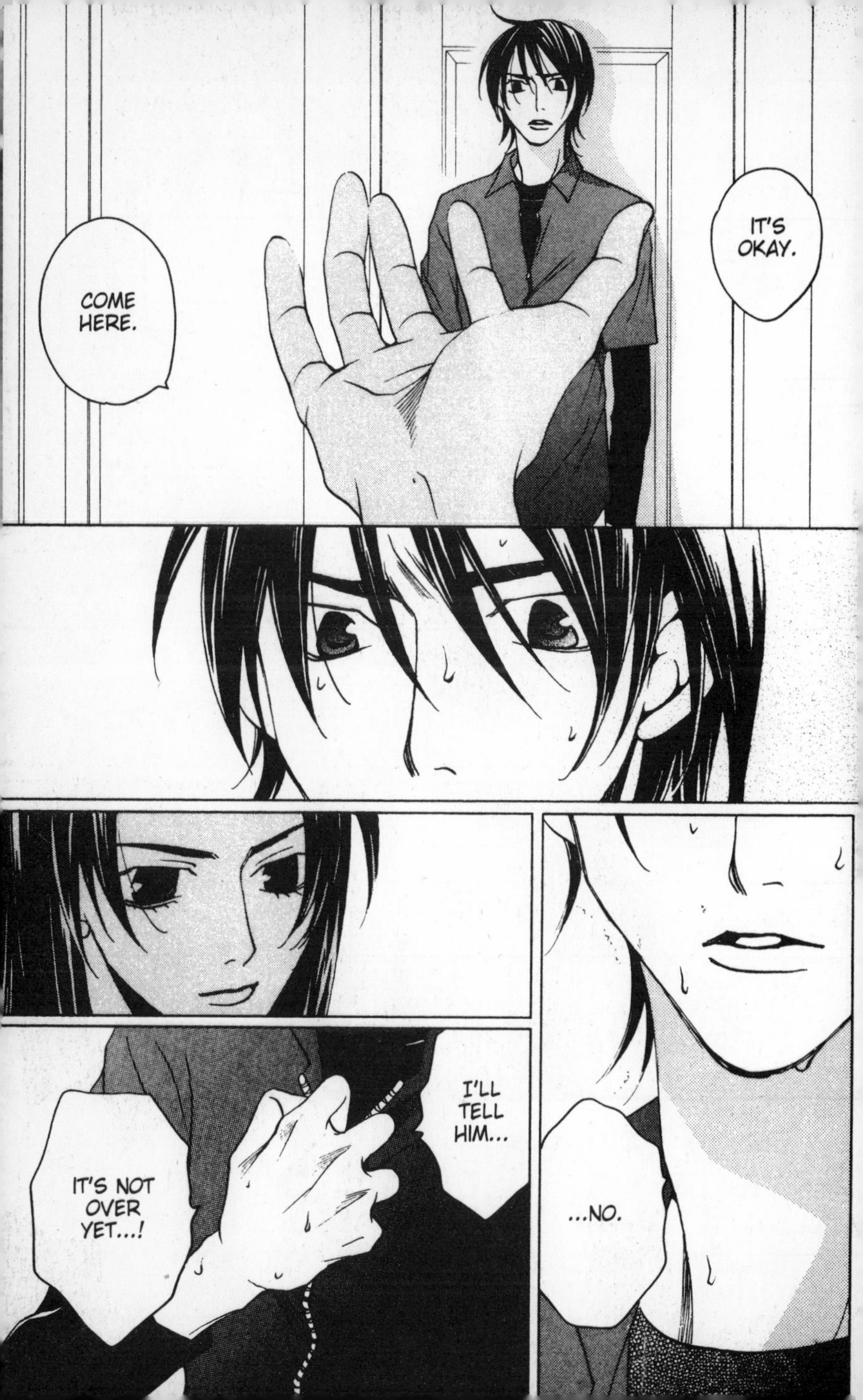
IT'S OKAY.
COME HERE.
...NO.
I'LL TELL HIM...
IT'S NOT OVER YET...!

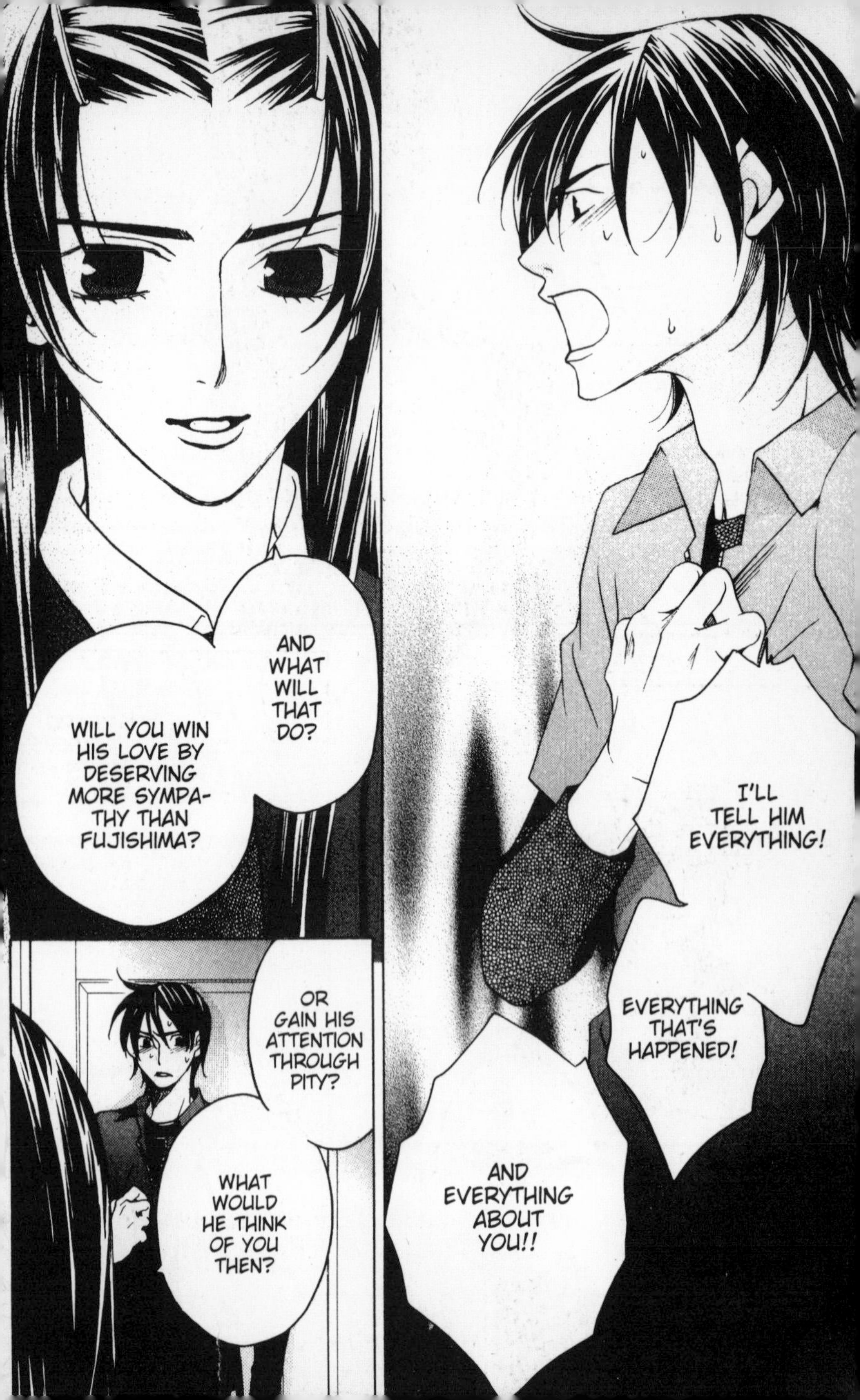
I'LL TELL HIM EVERYTHING!
EVERYTHING THAT'S HAPPENED!
AND EVERYTHING ABOUT YOU!!
AND WHAT WILL THAT DO?
WILL YOU WIN HIS LOVE BY DESERVING MORE SYMPA-THY THAN FUJISHIMA?
OR GAIN HIS ATTENTION THROUGH PITY?
WHAT WOULD HE THINK OF YOU THEN?

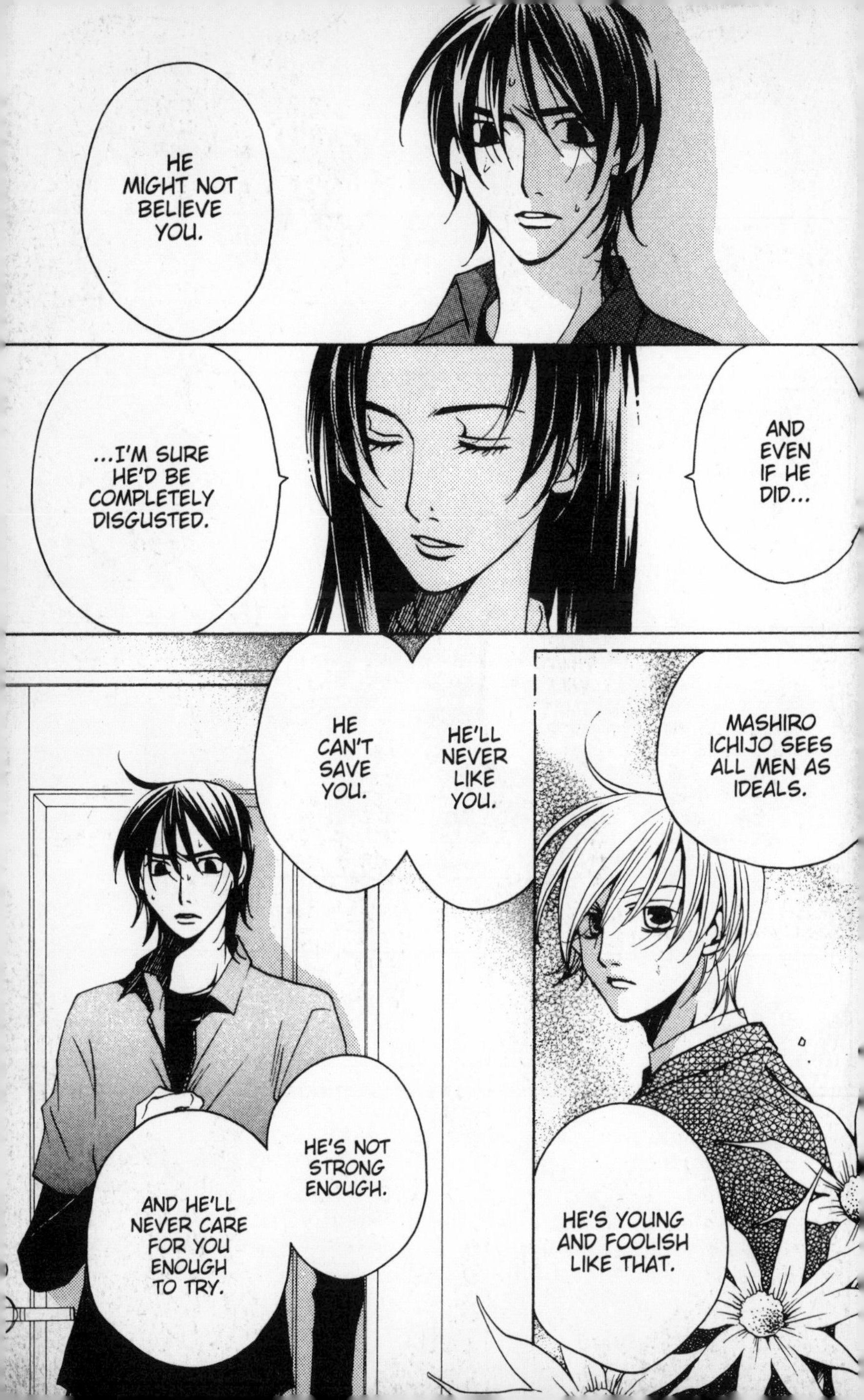
HE MIGHT NOT BELIEVE YOU.
AND EVEN IF HE DID...
...I'M SURE HE'D BE COMPLETELY DISGUSTED.
MASHIRO ICHIJO SEES ALL MEN AS IDEALS.
HE'S YOUNG AND FOOLISH LIKE THAT.
HE'LL NEVER LIKE YOU.
HE CAN'T SAVE YOU.
HE'S NOT STRONG ENOUGH.
AND HE'LL NEVER CARE FOR YOU ENOUGH TO TRY.

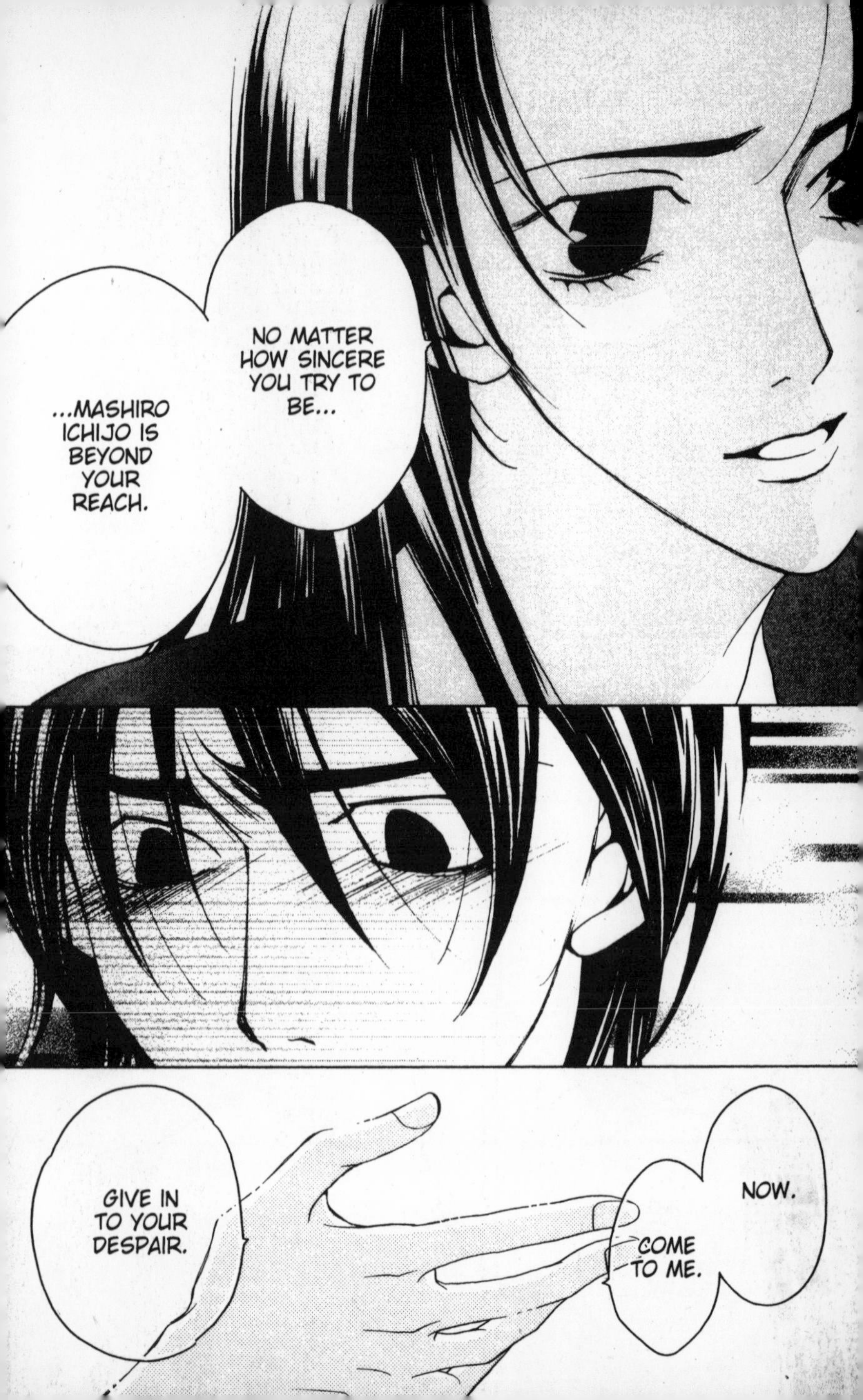
NO MATTER HOW SINCERE YOU TRY TO BE...
...MASHIRO ICHIJO IS BEYOND YOUR REACH.
NOW.
COME TO ME.
GIVE IN TO YOUR DESPAIR.

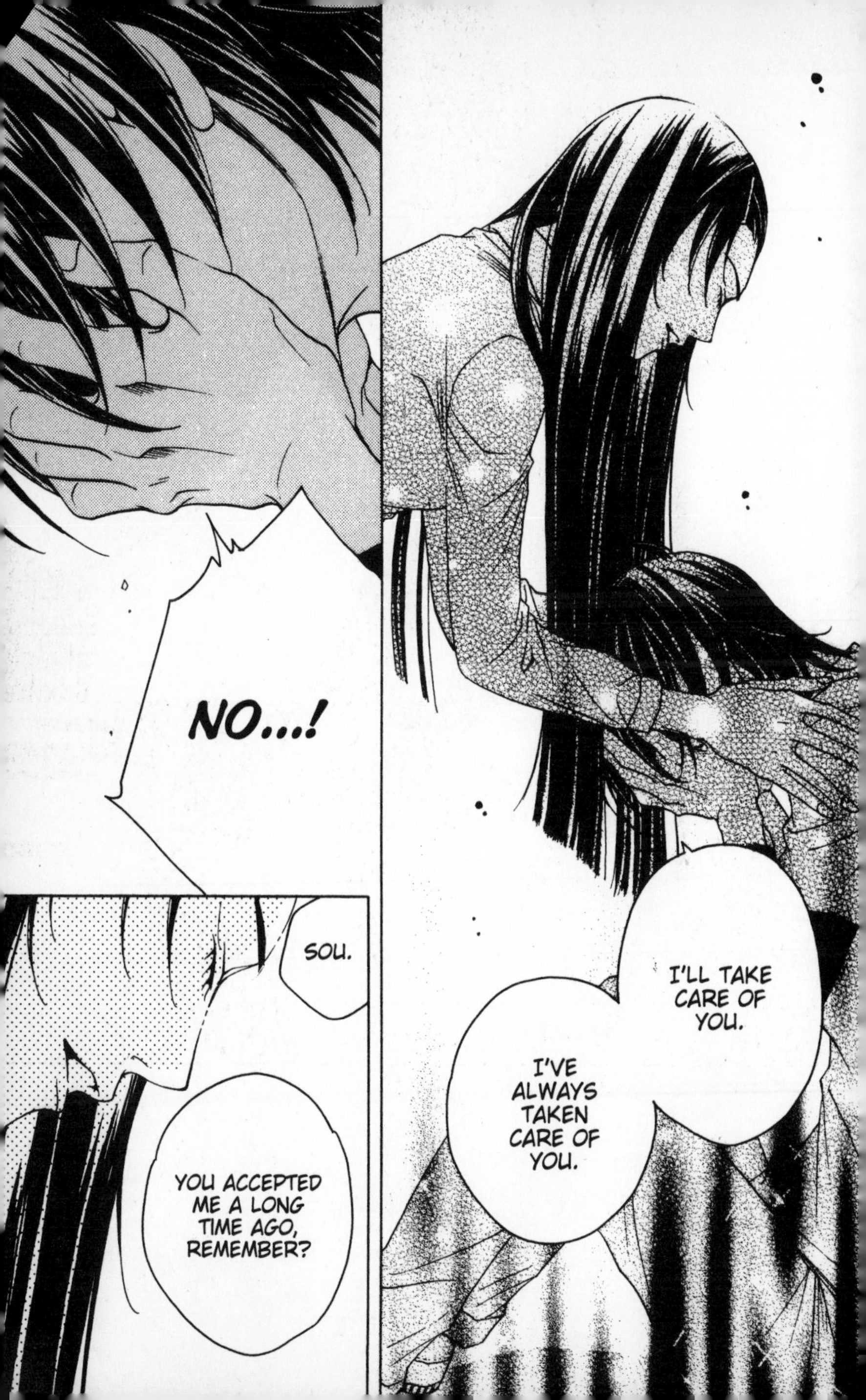
I'LL TAKE CARE OF YOU.
I'VE ALWAYS TAKEN CARE OF YOU.
NO...!
SOU.
YOU ACCEPTED ME A LONG TIME AGO, REMEMBER?

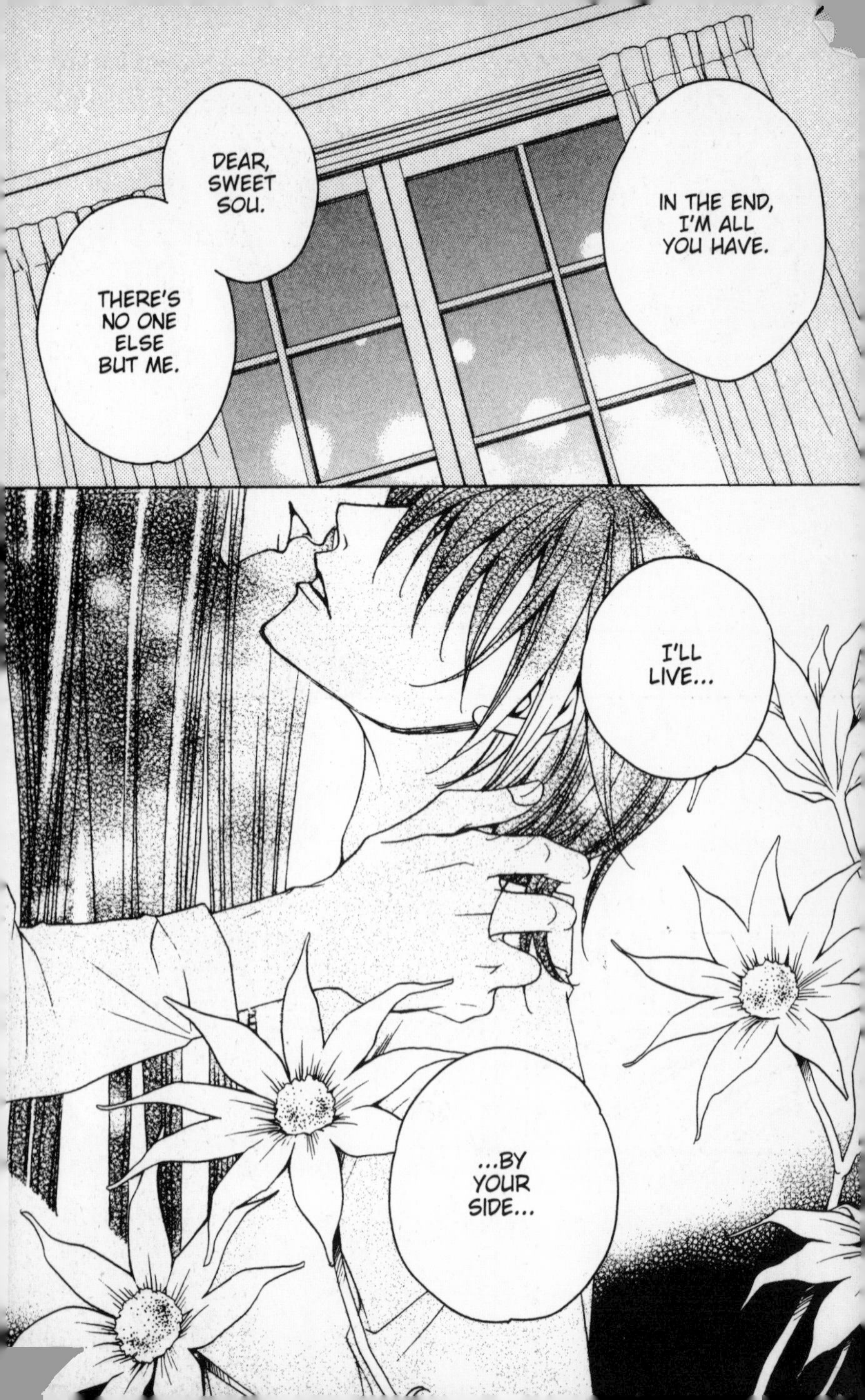
IN THE END, I'M ALL YOU HAVE.
DEAR, SWEET SOU.
THERE'S NO ONE ELSE BUT ME.
I'LL LIVE...
...BY YOUR SIDE...

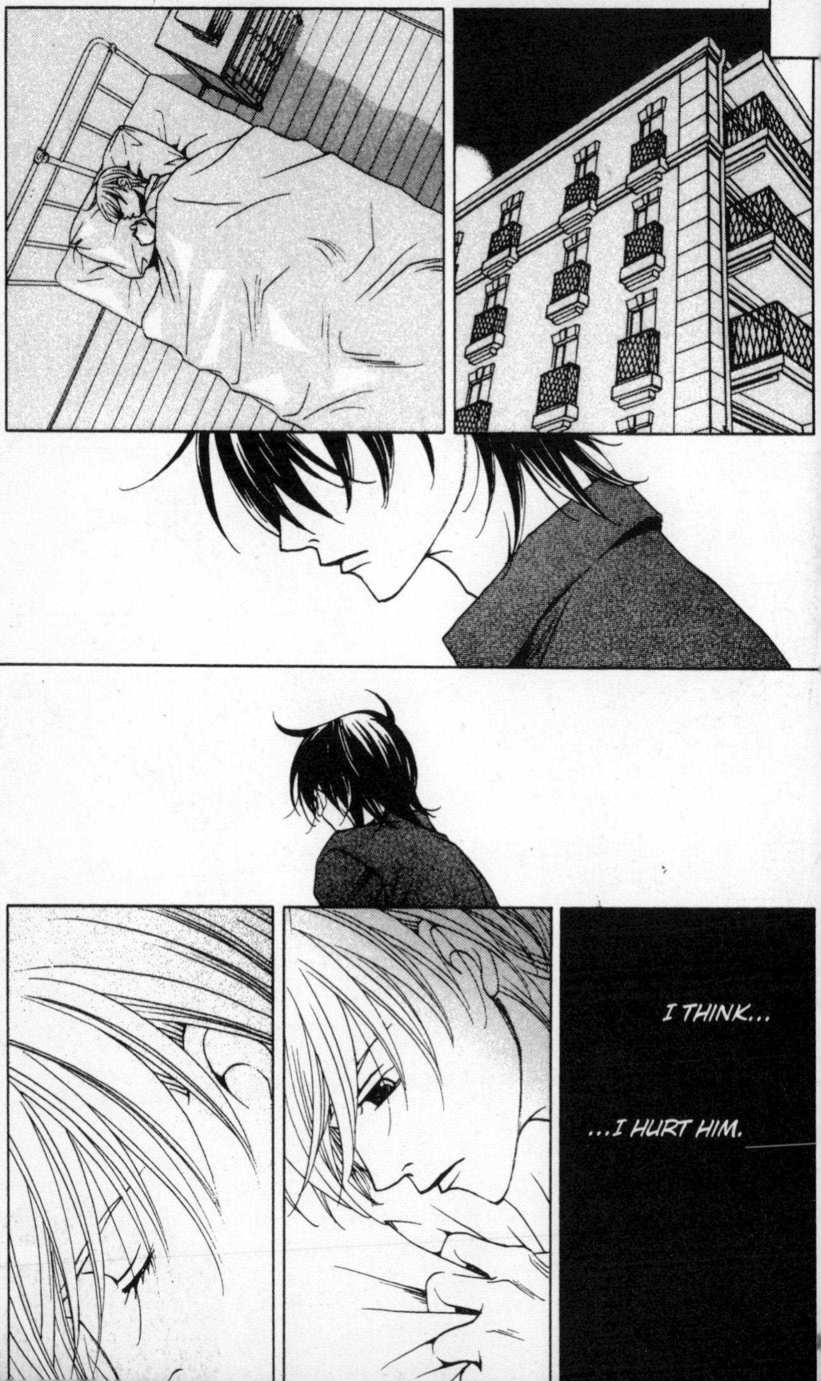
I THINK...
...I HURT HIM.

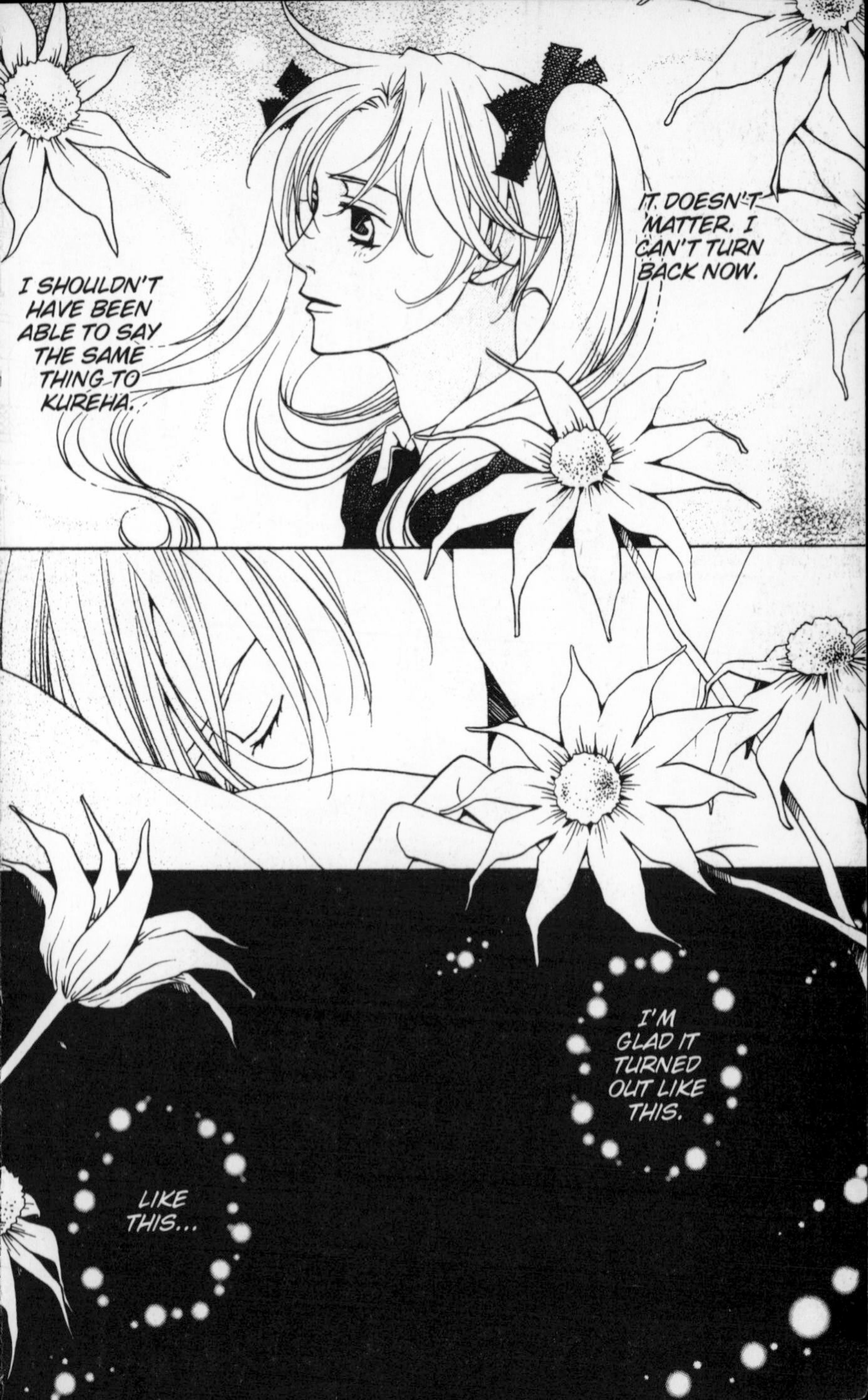
IT DOESN'T MATTER. I CAN'T TURN BACK NOW.
I SHOULDN'T HAVE BEEN ABLE TO SAY THE SAME THING TO KUREHA.
I'M GLAD IT TURNED OUT LIKE THIS.
LIKE THIS...

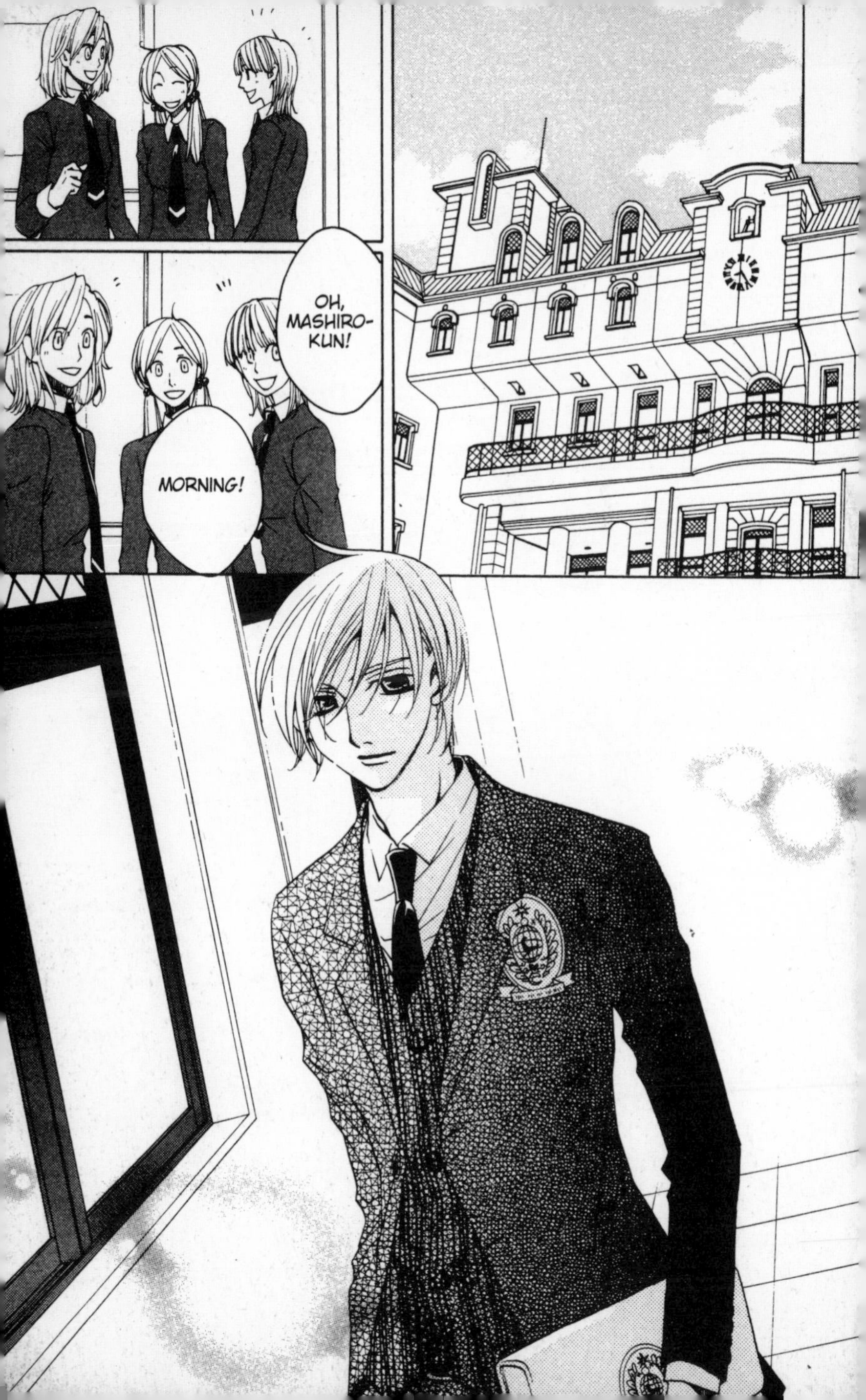
OH, MASHIRO-KUN!
MORNING!

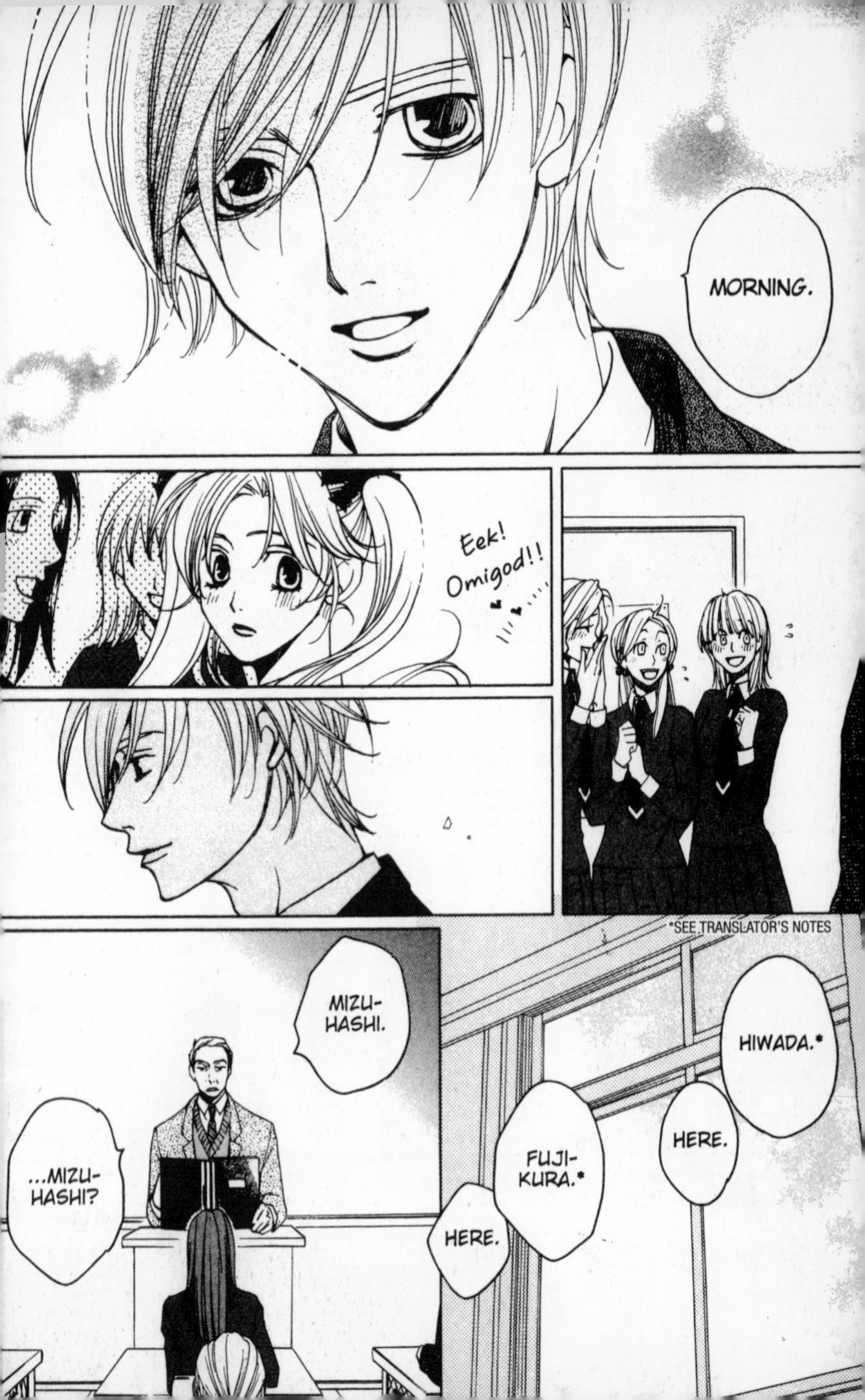
MORNING.
Eek! Omigod!!
HIWADA.*
HERE.
FUJI-KURA.*
HERE.
MIZU-HASHI.
...MIZU-HASHI?

*SEE TRANSLATOR'S NOTES

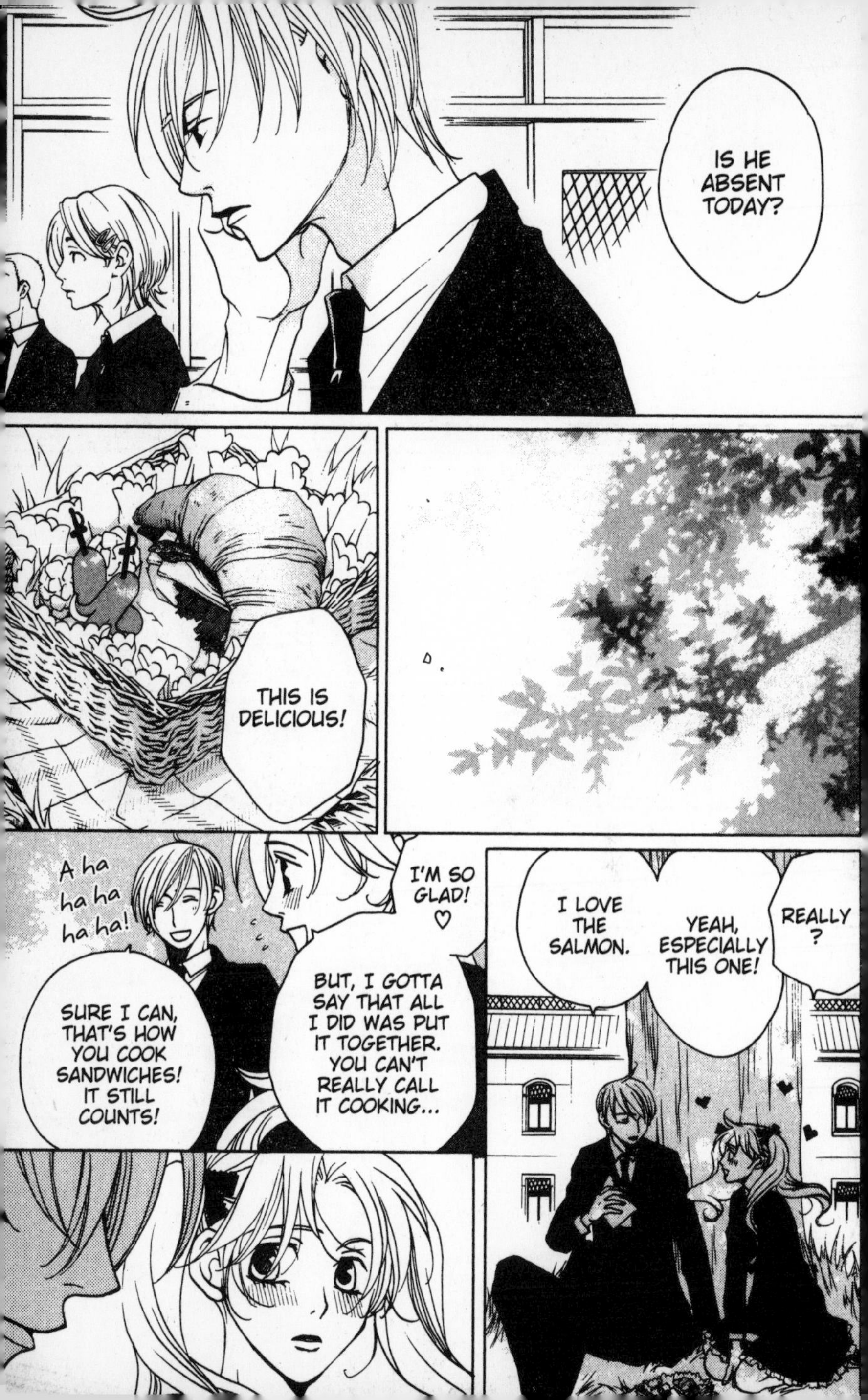
IS HE ABSENT TODAY?
THIS IS DELICIOUS!
REALLY?
YEAH, ESPECIALLY THIS ONE!
I LOVE THE SALMON.
I'M SO GLAD! ♡
BUT, I GOTTA SAY THAT ALL I DID WAS PUT IT TOGETHER. YOU CAN'T REALLY CALL IT COOKING...
A ha ha ha ha ha!
SURE I CAN, THAT'S HOW YOU COOK SANDWICHES! IT STILL COUNTS!

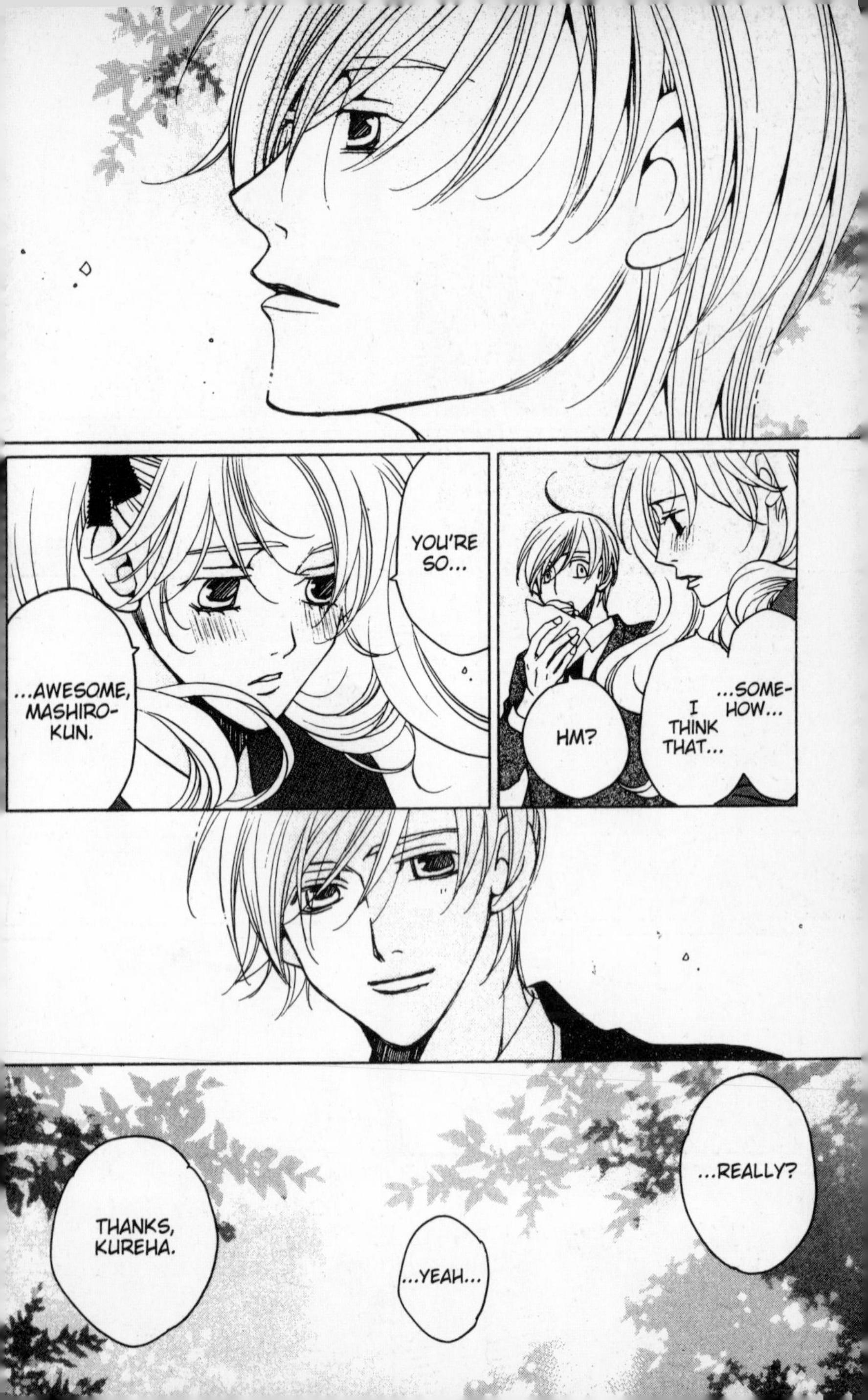
...SOME-HOW... I THINK THAT...
HM?
YOU'RE SO...
...AWESOME, MASHIRO-KUN.
...REALLY?
...YEAH...
THANKS, KUREHA.

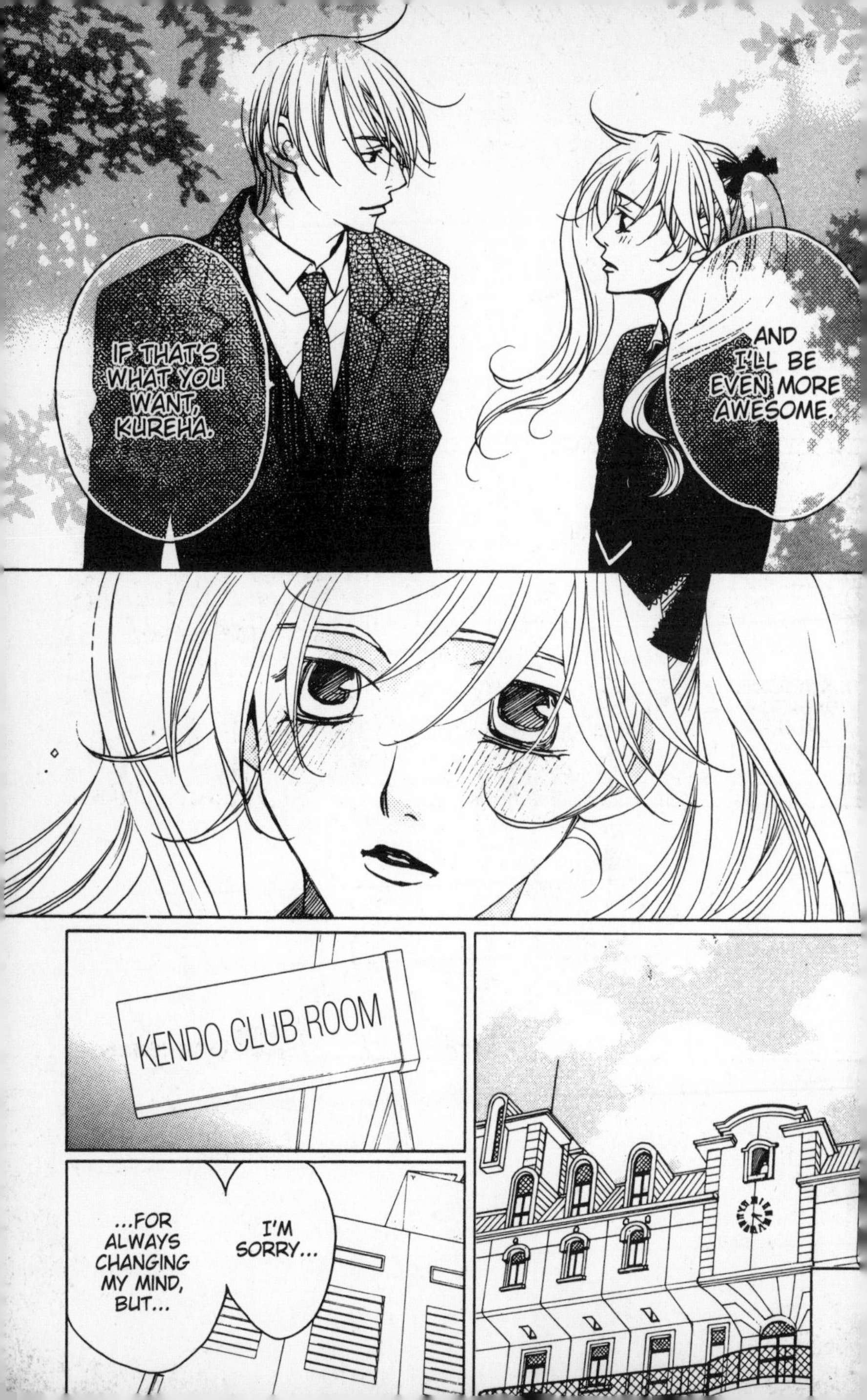
AND I'LL BE EVEN MORE AWESOME.
IF THAT'S WHAT YOU WANT, KUREHA.
KENDO CLUB ROOM
I'M SORRY...
...FOR ALWAYS CHANGING MY MIND, BUT...

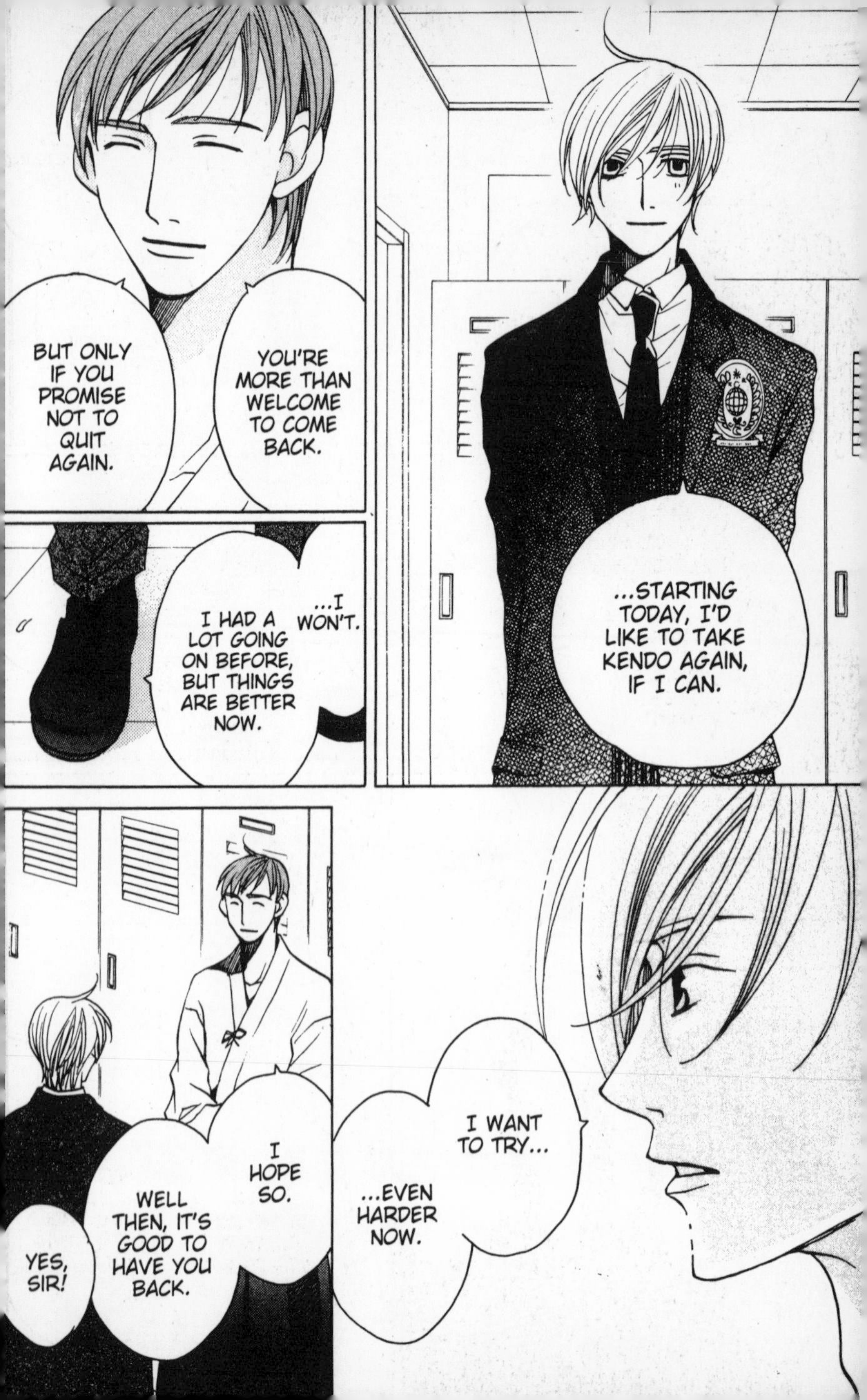
...STARTING TODAY, I'D LIKE TO TAKE KENDO AGAIN, IF I CAN.
YOU'RE MORE THAN WELCOME TO COME BACK.
BUT ONLY IF YOU PROMISE NOT TO QUIT AGAIN.
...I WON'T.
I HAD A LOT GOING ON BEFORE, BUT THINGS ARE BETTER NOW.
I WANT TO TRY...
...EVEN HARDER NOW.
I HOPE SO.
WELL THEN, IT'S GOOD TO HAVE YOU BACK.
YES, SIR!

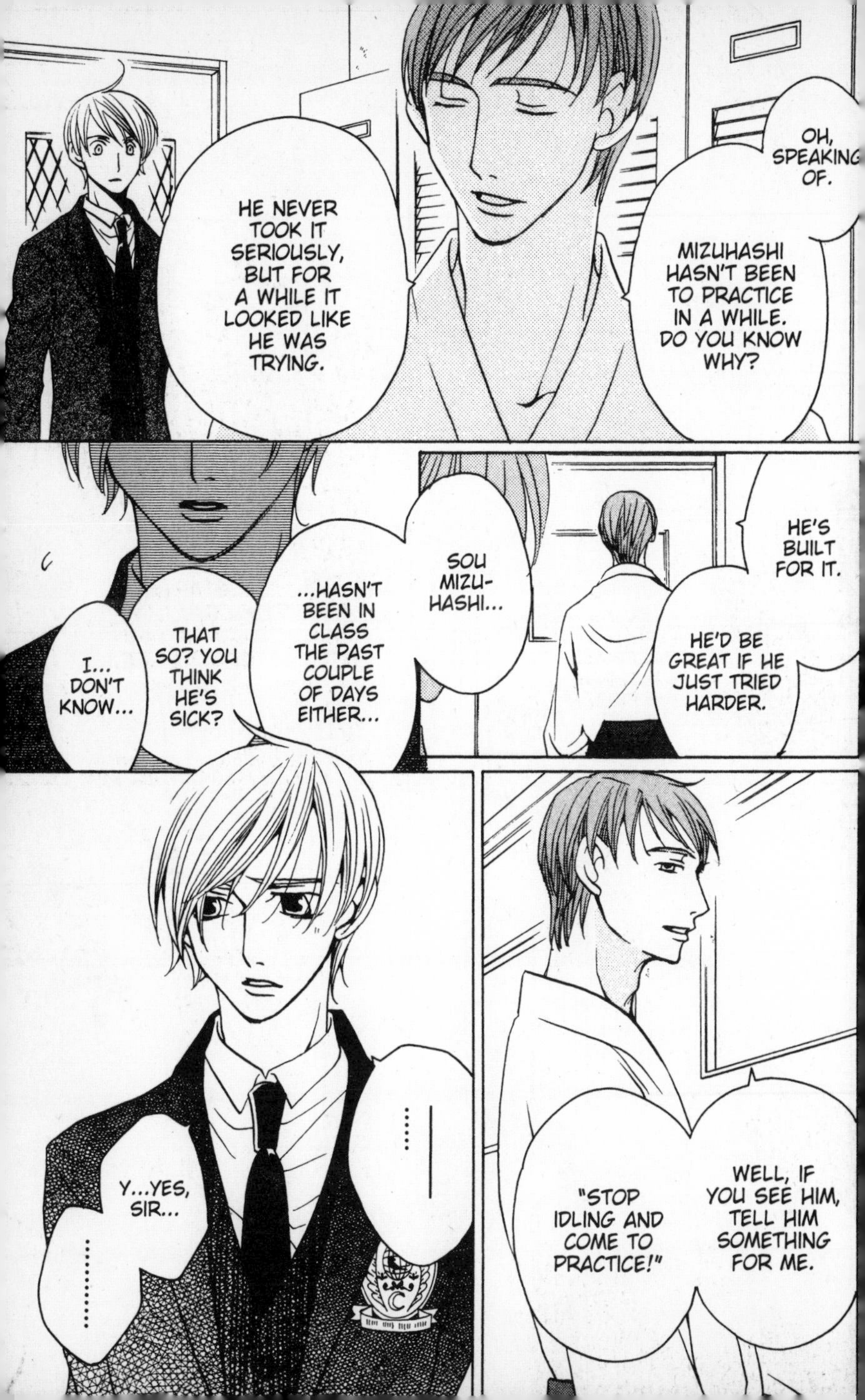
OH, SPEAKING OF.
MIZUHASHI HASN'T BEEN TO PRACTICE IN A WHILE. DO YOU KNOW WHY?
HE NEVER TOOK IT SERIOUSLY, BUT FOR A WHILE IT LOOKED LIKE HE WAS TRYING.
HE'S BUILT FOR IT.
HE'D BE GREAT IF HE JUST TRIED HARDER.
SOU MIZU-HASHI...
...HASN'T BEEN IN CLASS THE PAST COUPLE OF DAYS EITHER...
THAT SO? YOU THINK HE'S SICK?
I... DON'T KNOW...
WELL, IF YOU SEE HIM, TELL HIM SOMETHING FOR ME.
"STOP IDLING AND COME TO PRACTICE!"
......
Y...YES, SIR...
....

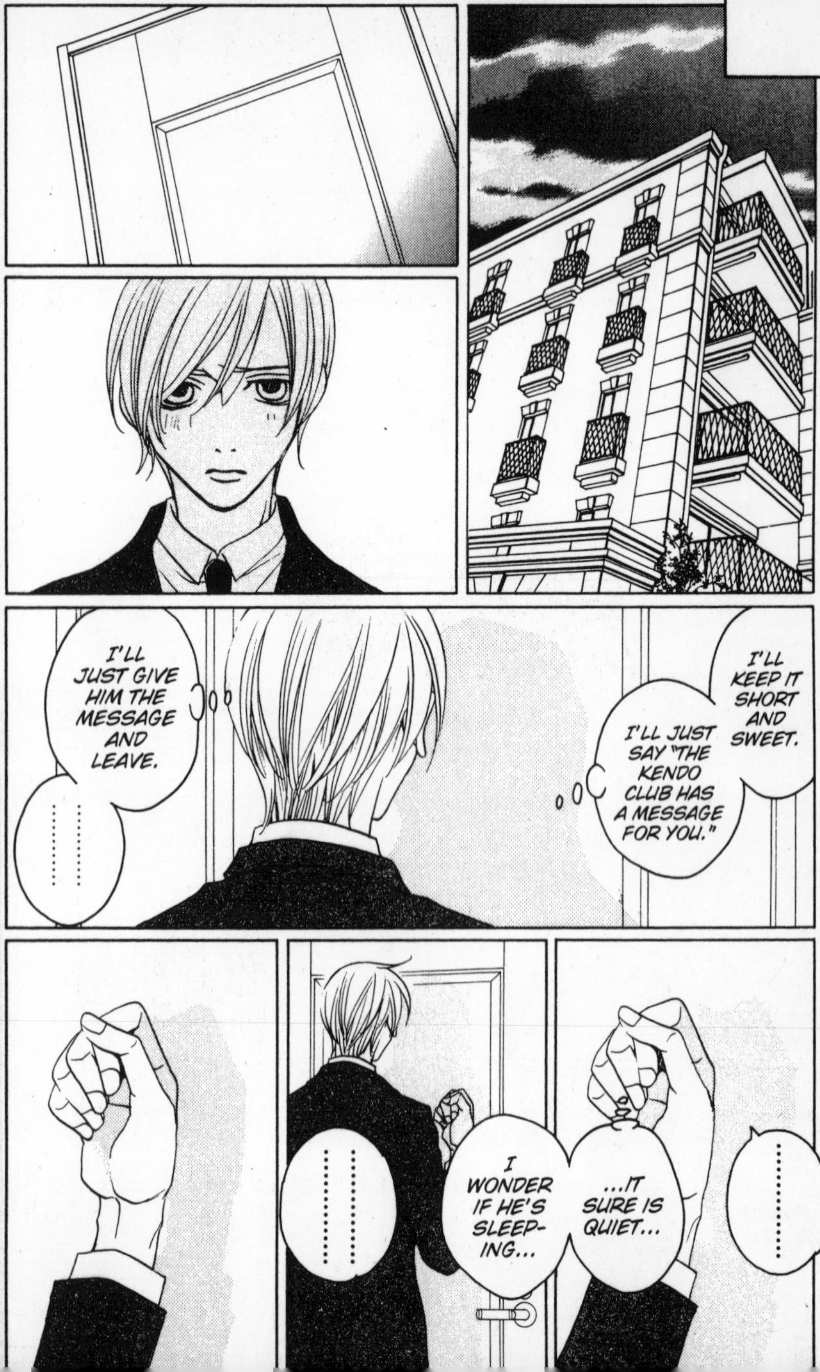
I'LL KEEP IT SHORT AND SWEET.
I'LL JUST SAY "THE KENDO CLUB HAS A MESSAGE FOR YOU."
I'LL JUST GIVE HIM THE MESSAGE AND LEAVE.
......
......
...IT SURE IS QUIET...
I WONDER IF HE'S SLEEP-ING...
......

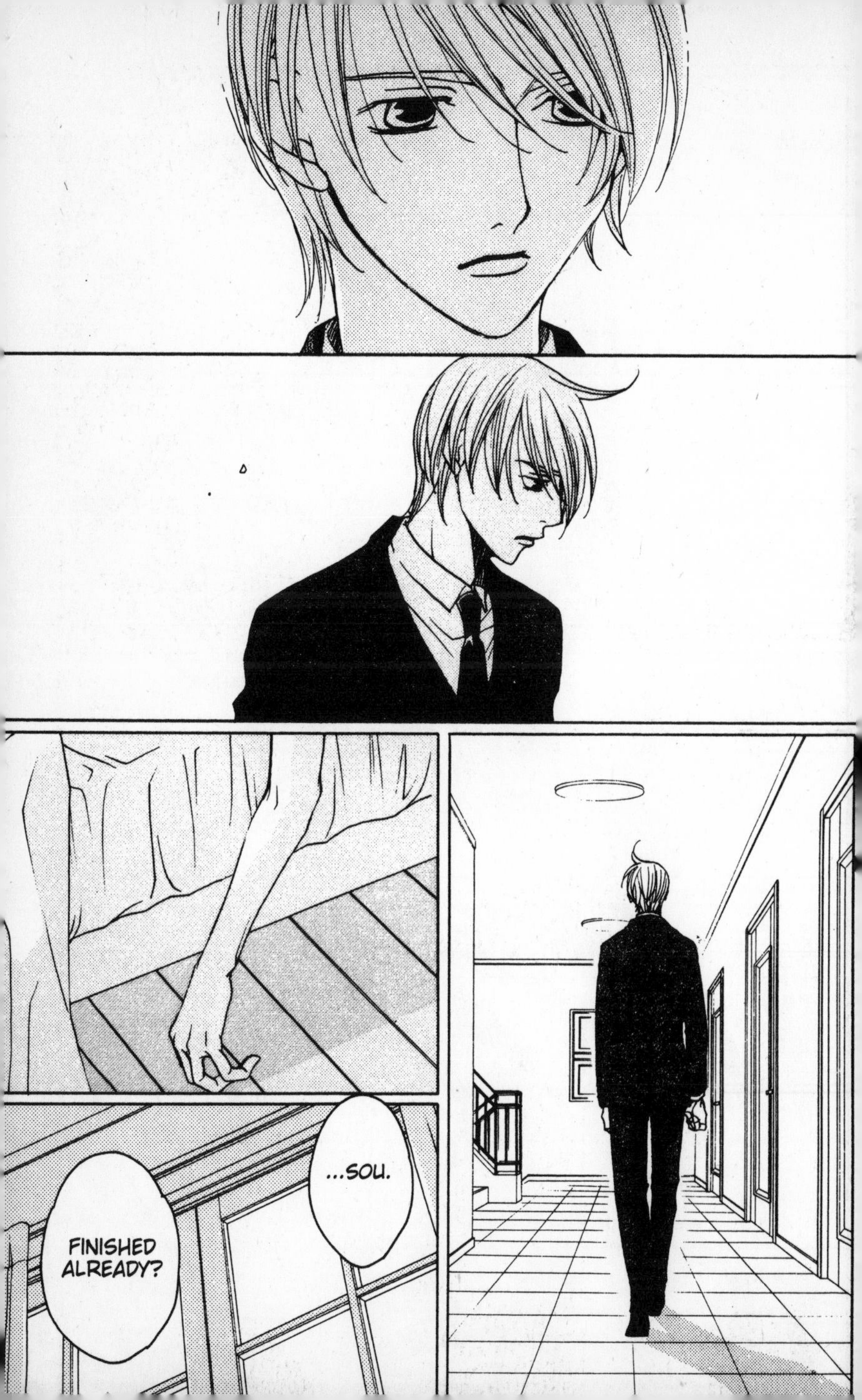
...SOU.
FINISHED ALREADY?

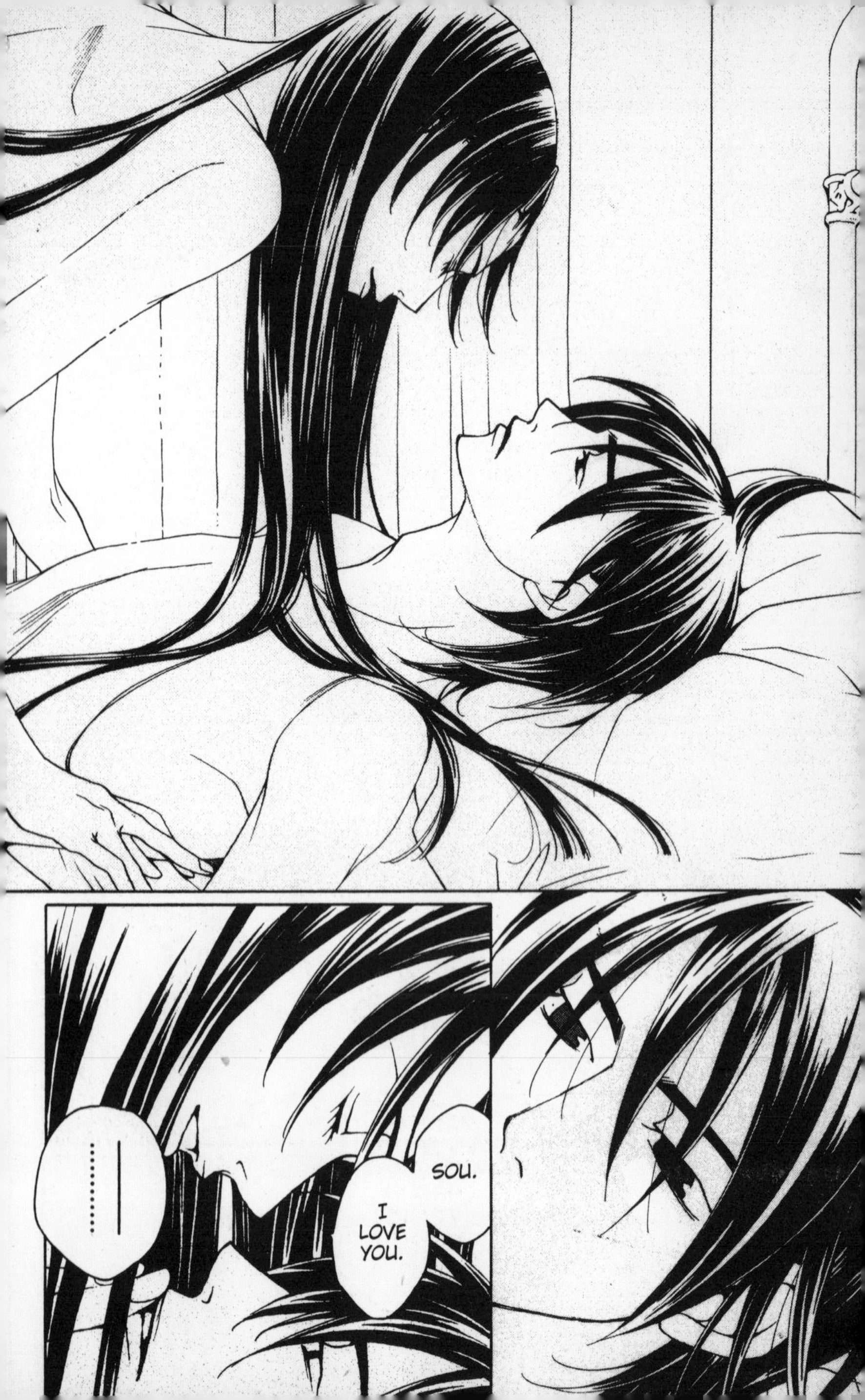
SOU. I LOVE YOU.
……—

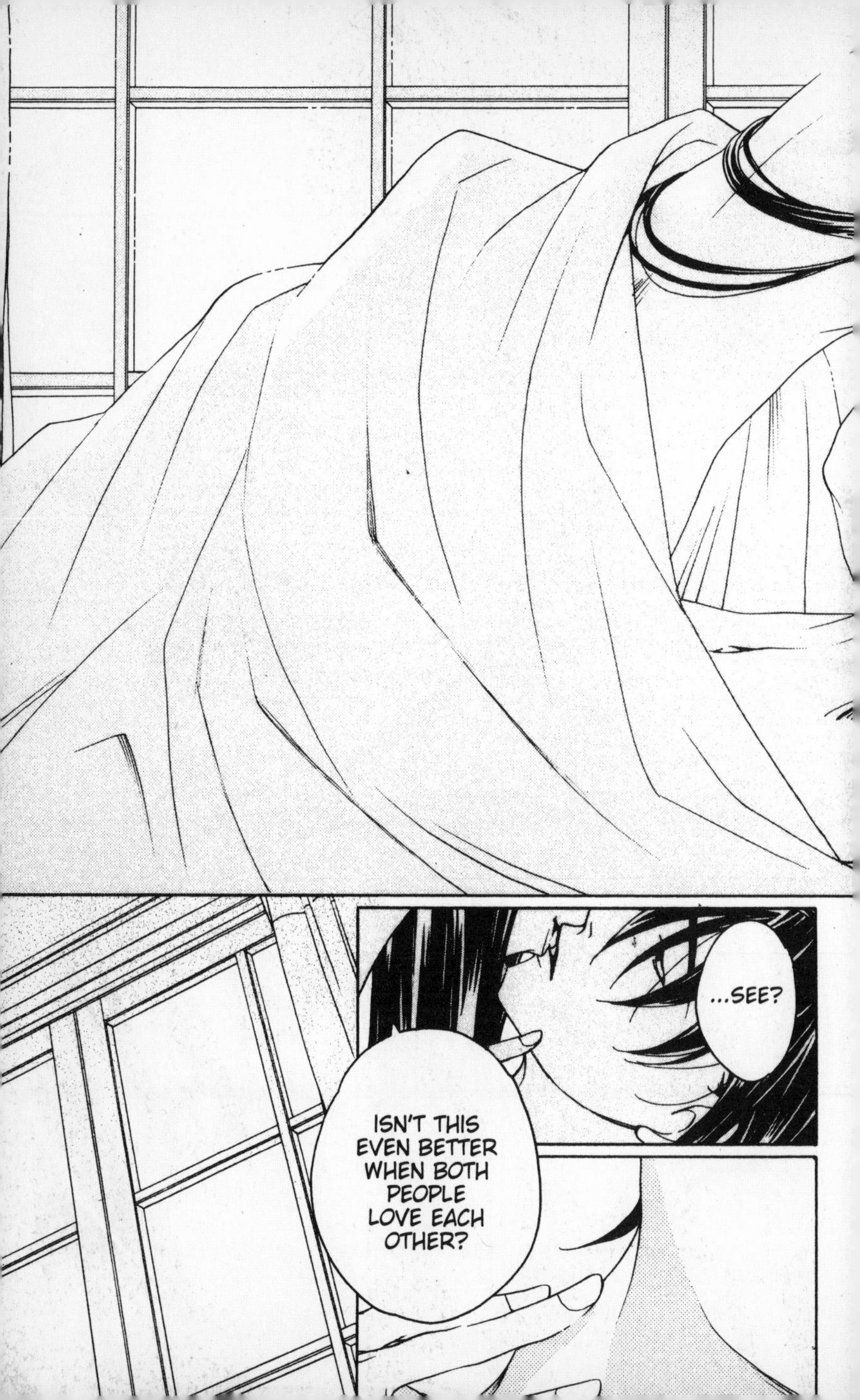
...SEE?
ISN'T THIS EVEN BETTER WHEN BOTH PEOPLE LOVE EACH OTHER?

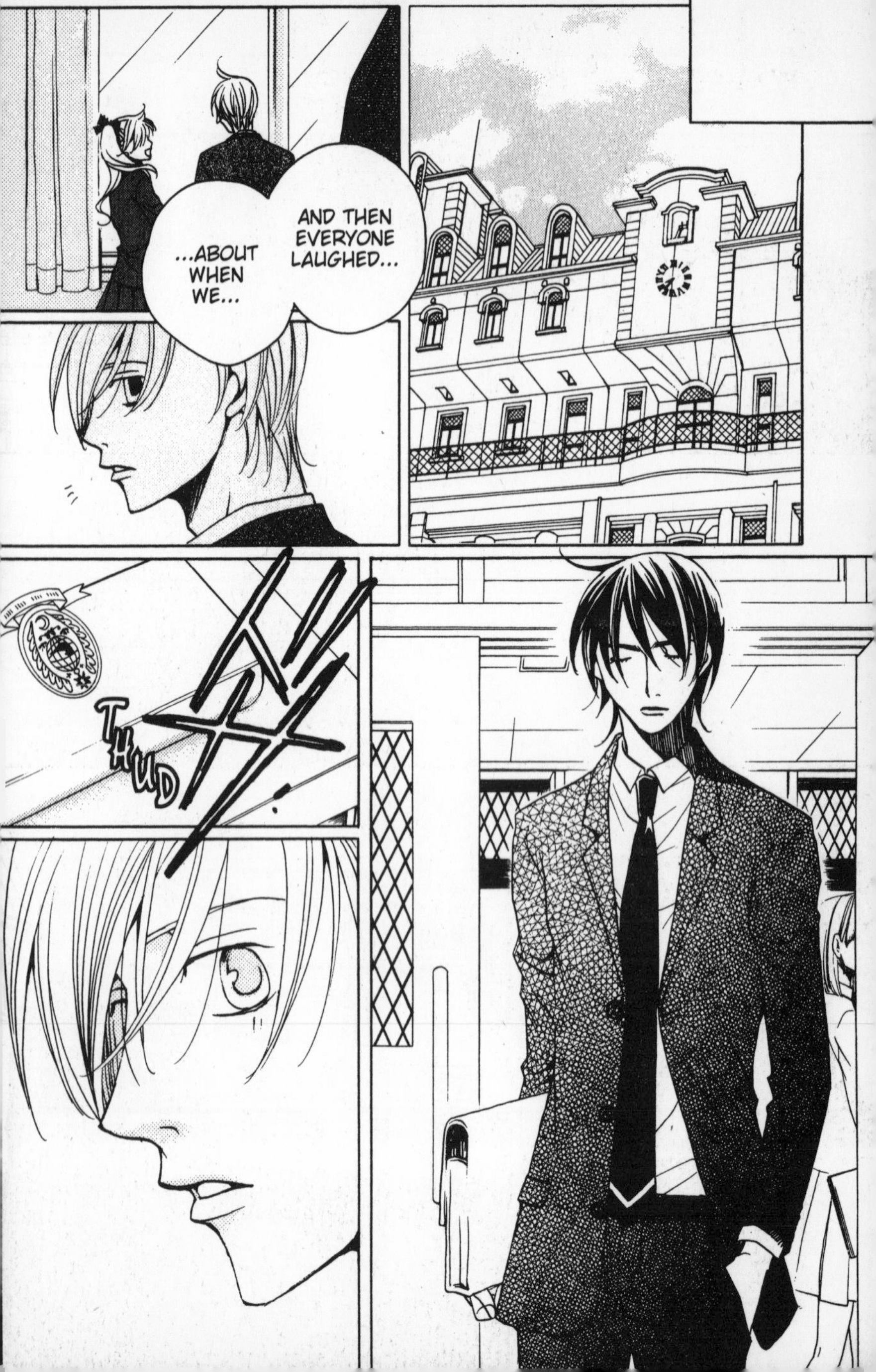
AND THEN EVERYONE LAUGHED...
...ABOUT WHEN WE...
THUD

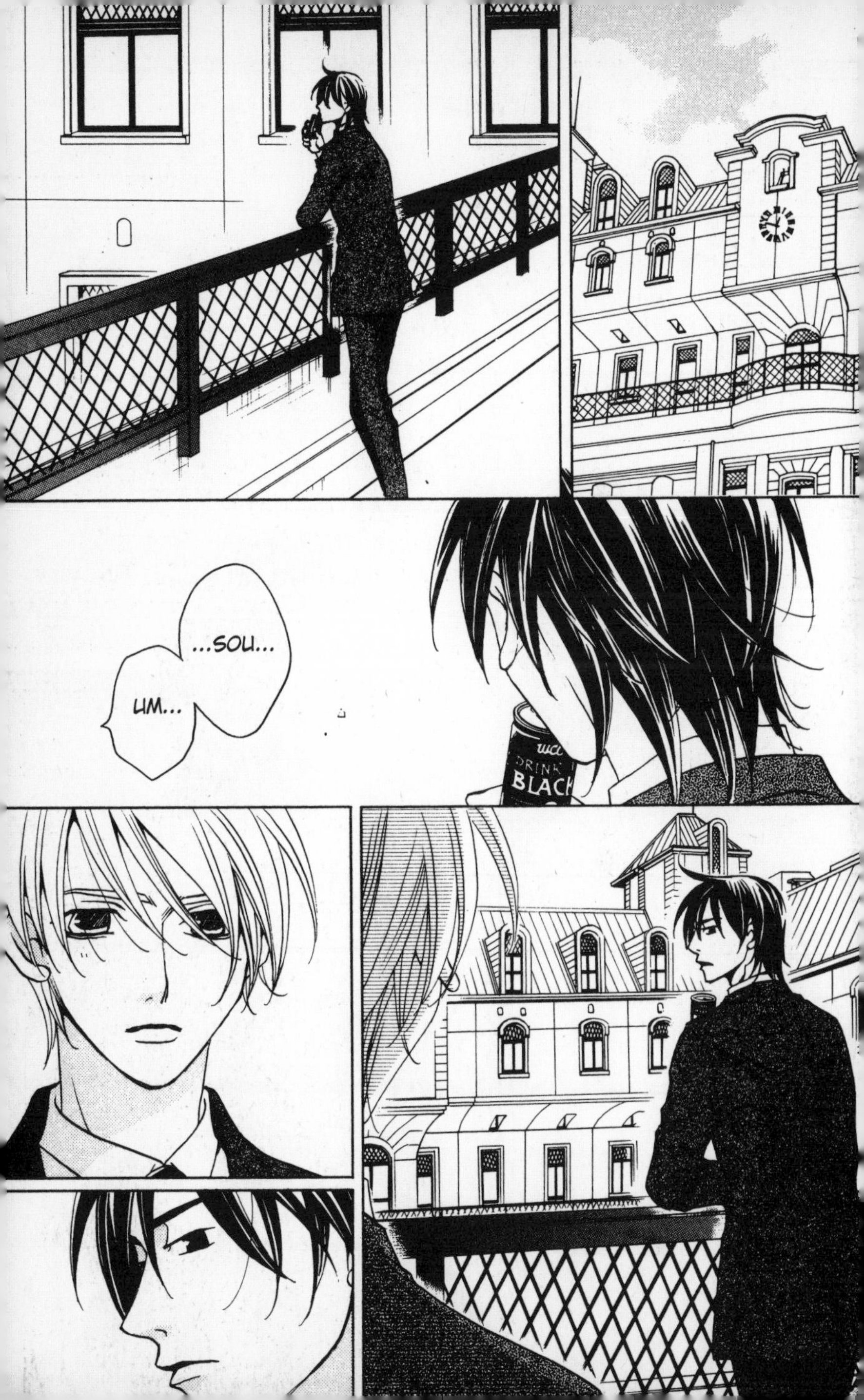
...SOU...
UM...
DRINK
BLACK

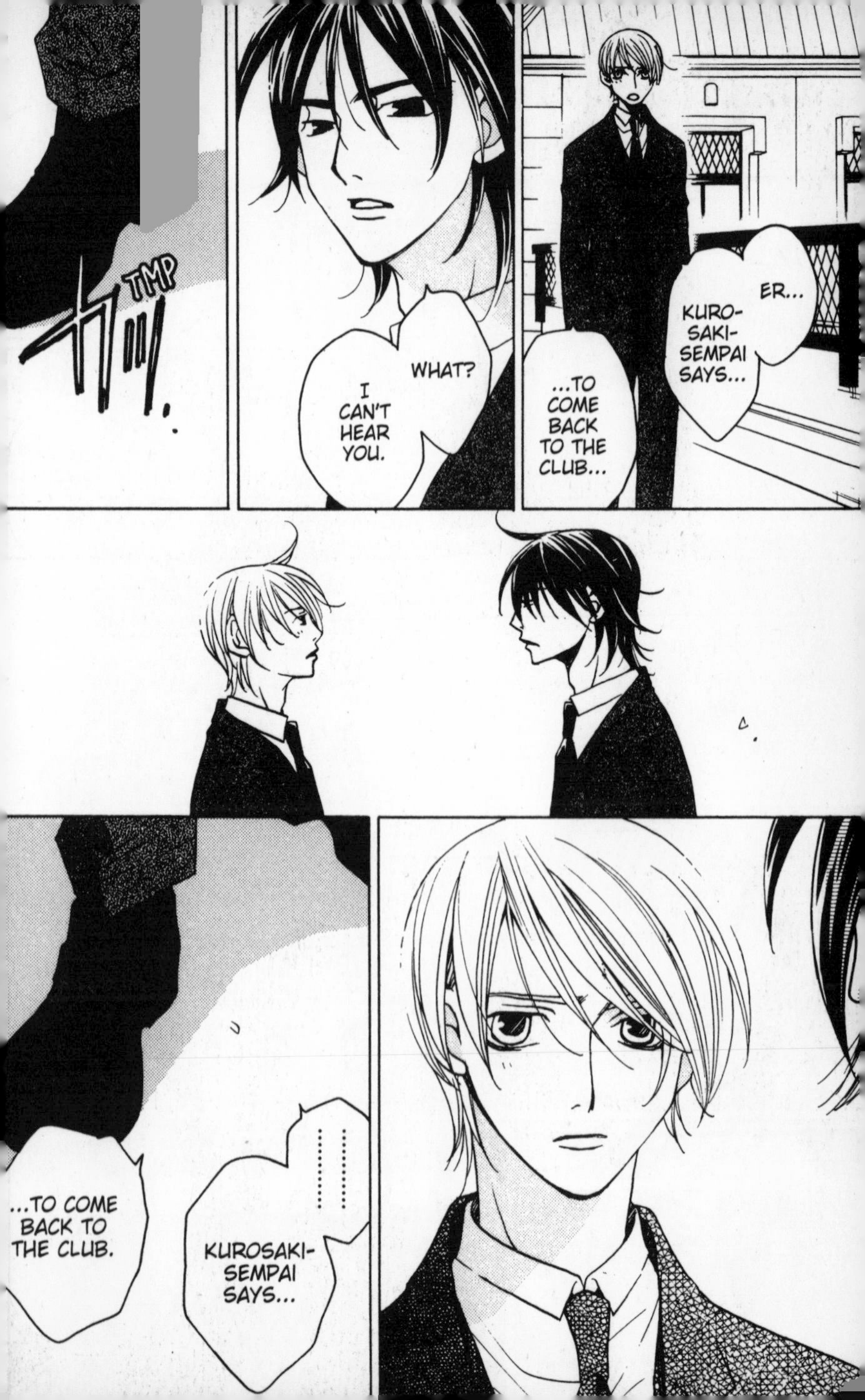
ER... KURO-SAKI-SEMPAI SAYS...
...TO COME BACK TO THE CLUB...
WHAT? I CAN'T HEAR YOU.
TMP
......
KUROSAKI-SEMPAI SAYS...
...TO COME BACK TO THE CLUB.

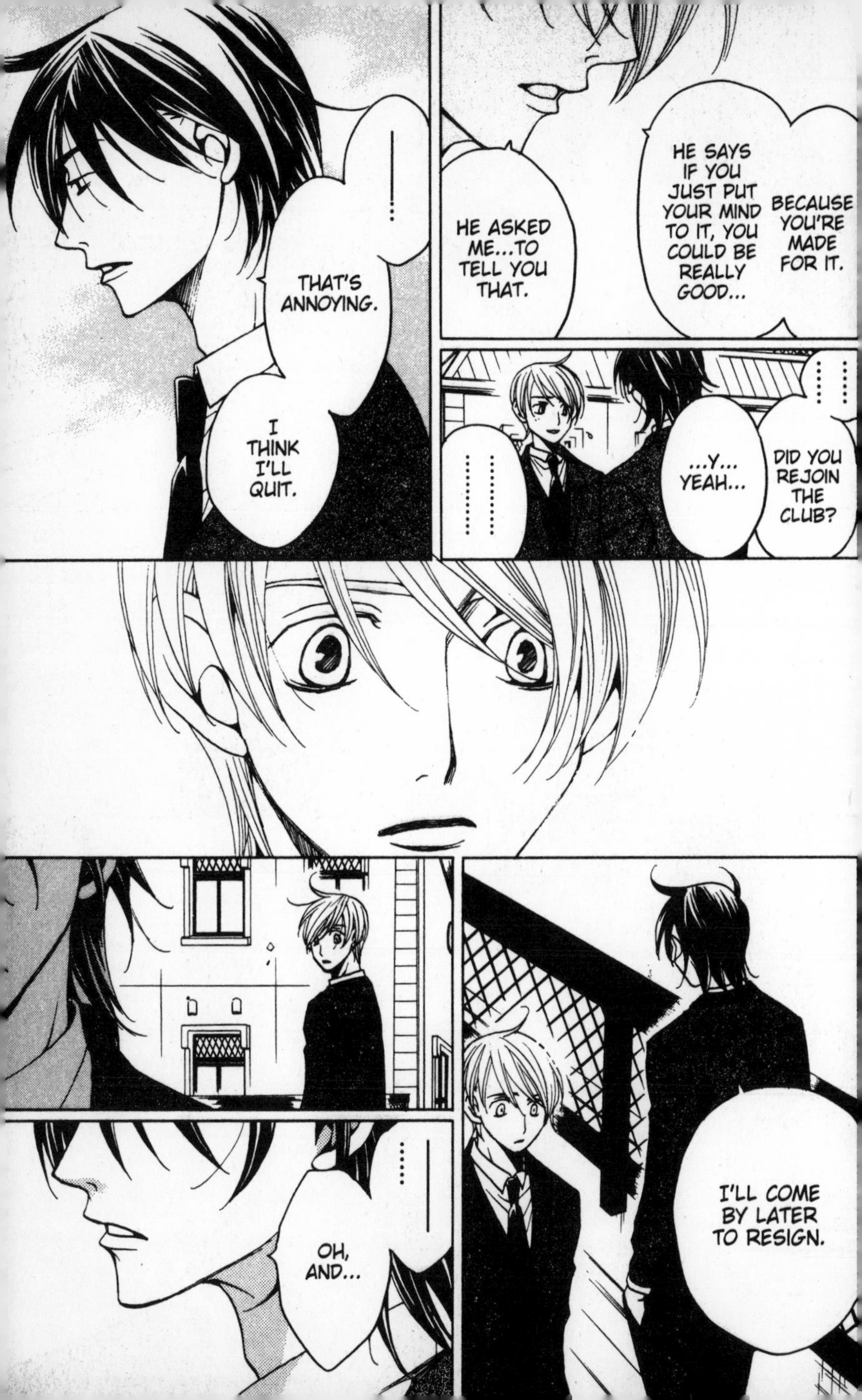
HE SAYS IF YOU JUST PUT YOUR MIND TO IT, YOU COULD BE REALLY GOOD... BECAUSE YOU'RE MADE FOR IT.
HE ASKED ME...TO TELL YOU THAT.
......
DID YOU REJOIN THE CLUB?
...Y... YEAH...
......
......
THAT'S ANNOYING.
I THINK I'LL QUIT.
I'LL COME BY LATER TO RESIGN.
......
OH, AND...

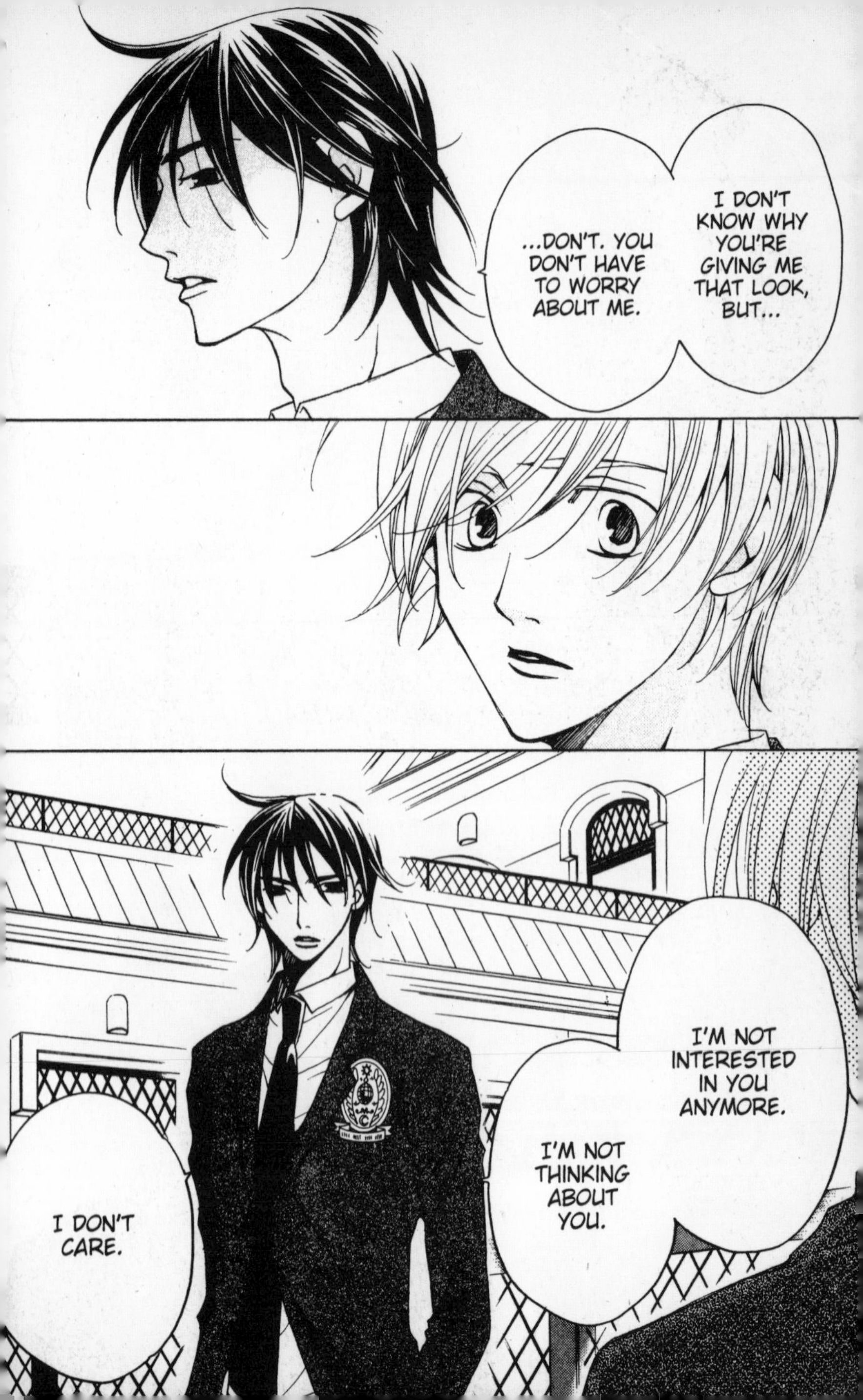
I DON'T KNOW WHY YOU'RE GIVING ME THAT LOOK, BUT...
...DON'T. YOU DON'T HAVE TO WORRY ABOUT ME.
I'M NOT INTERESTED IN YOU ANYMORE.
I'M NOT THINKING ABOUT YOU.
I DON'T CARE.

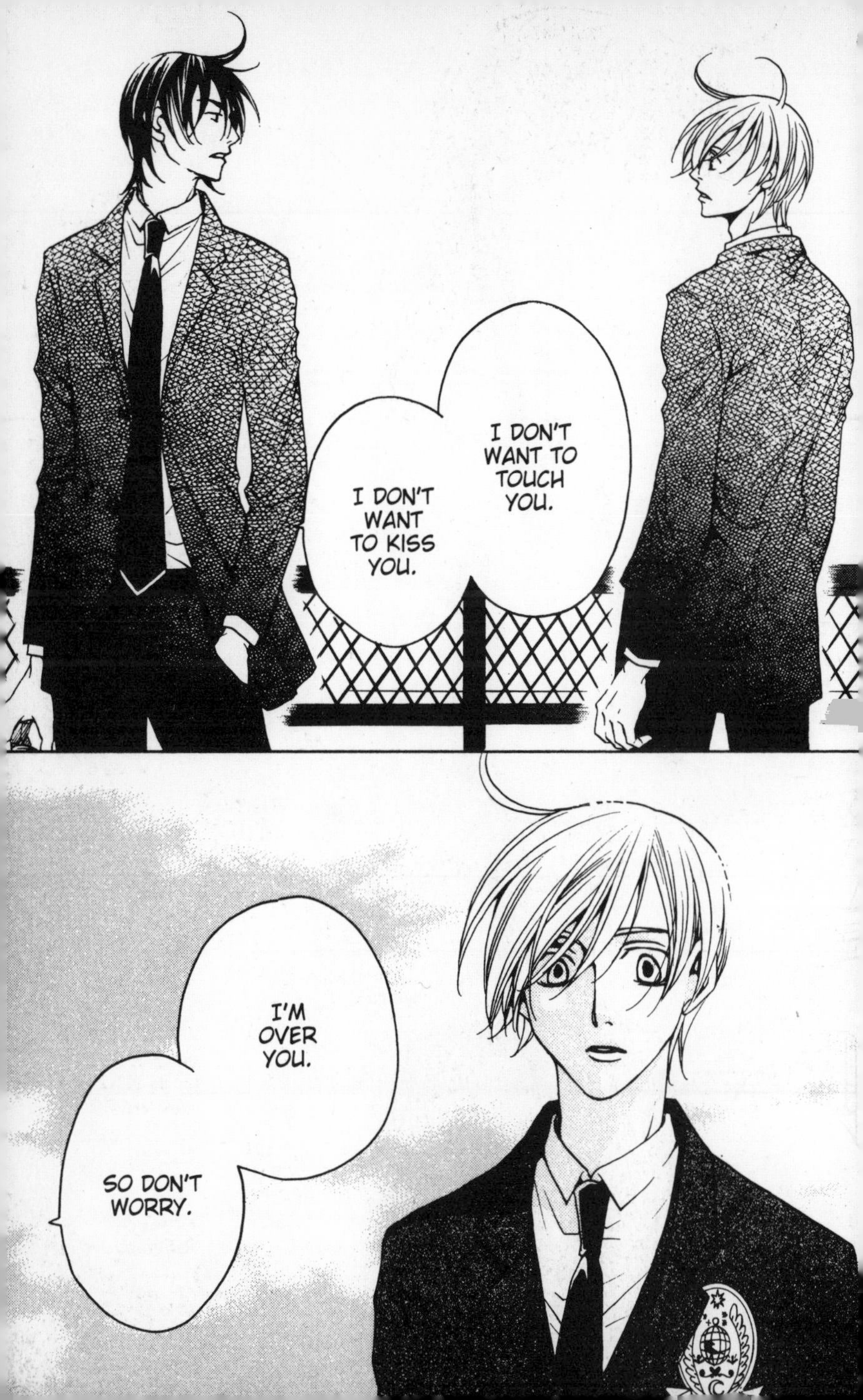
I DON'T WANT TO TOUCH YOU.
I DON'T WANT TO KISS YOU.
I'M OVER YOU.
SO DON'T WORRY.

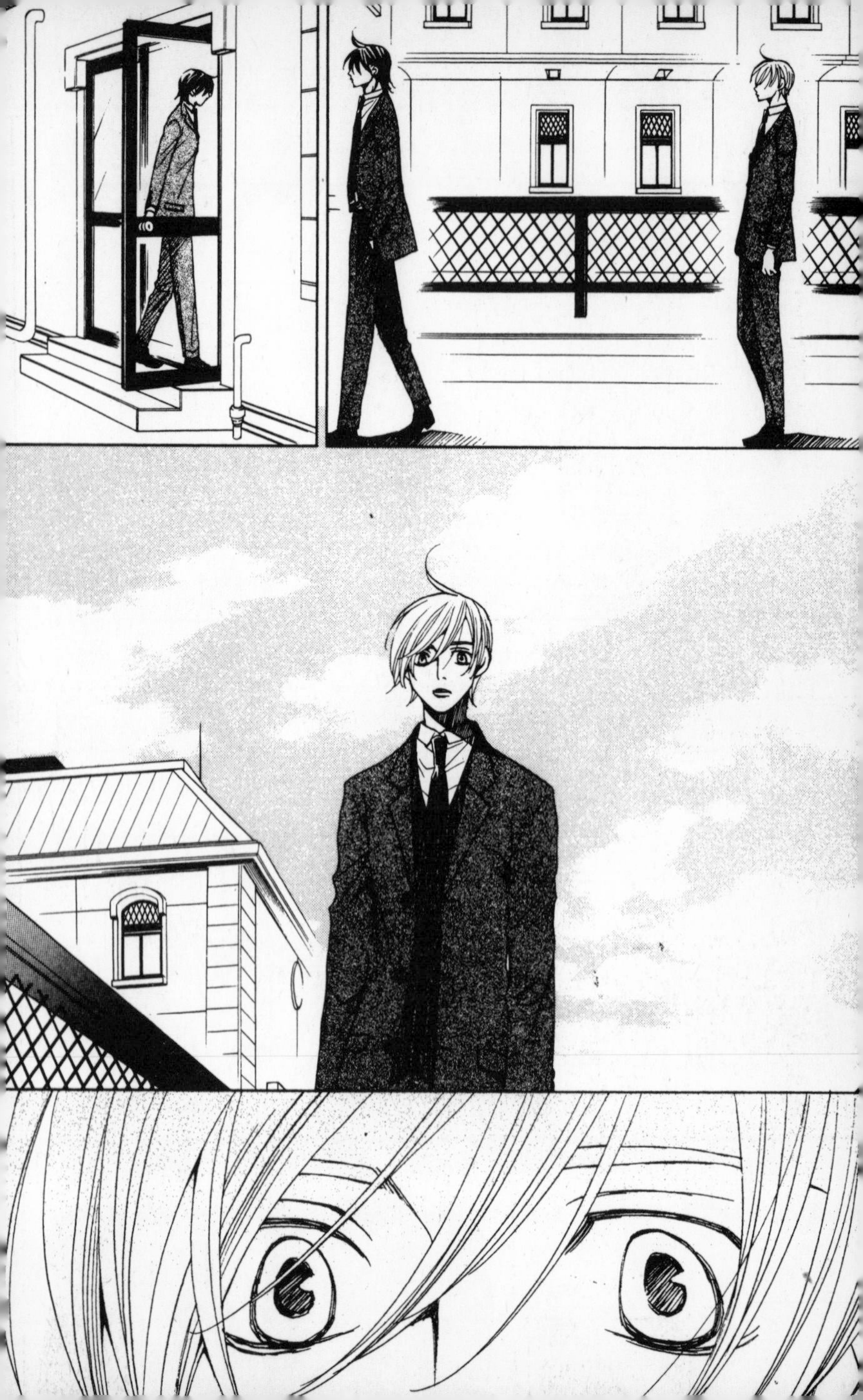

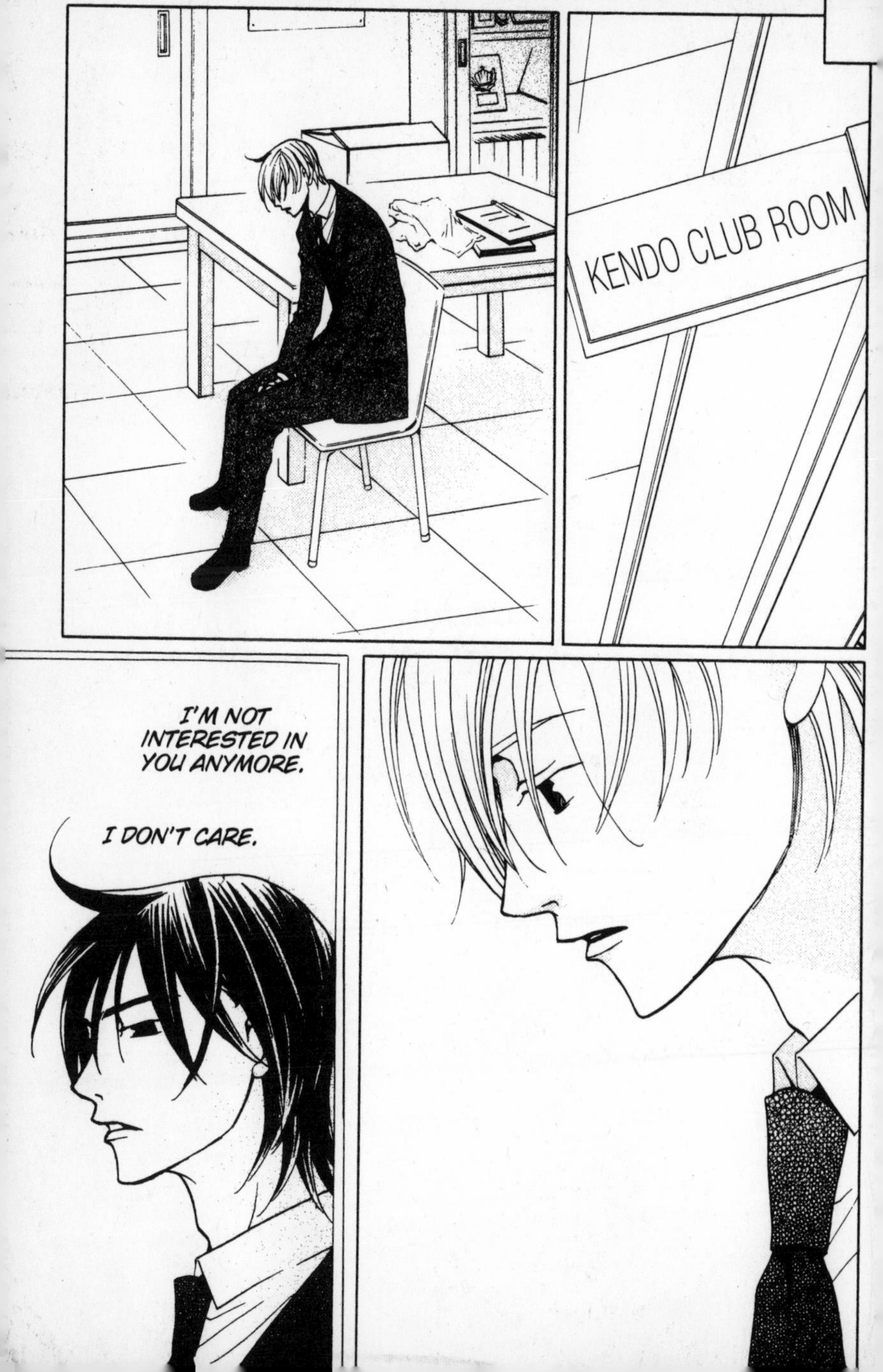
KENDO CLUB ROOM
I'M NOT INTERESTED IN YOU ANYMORE.
I DON'T CARE.

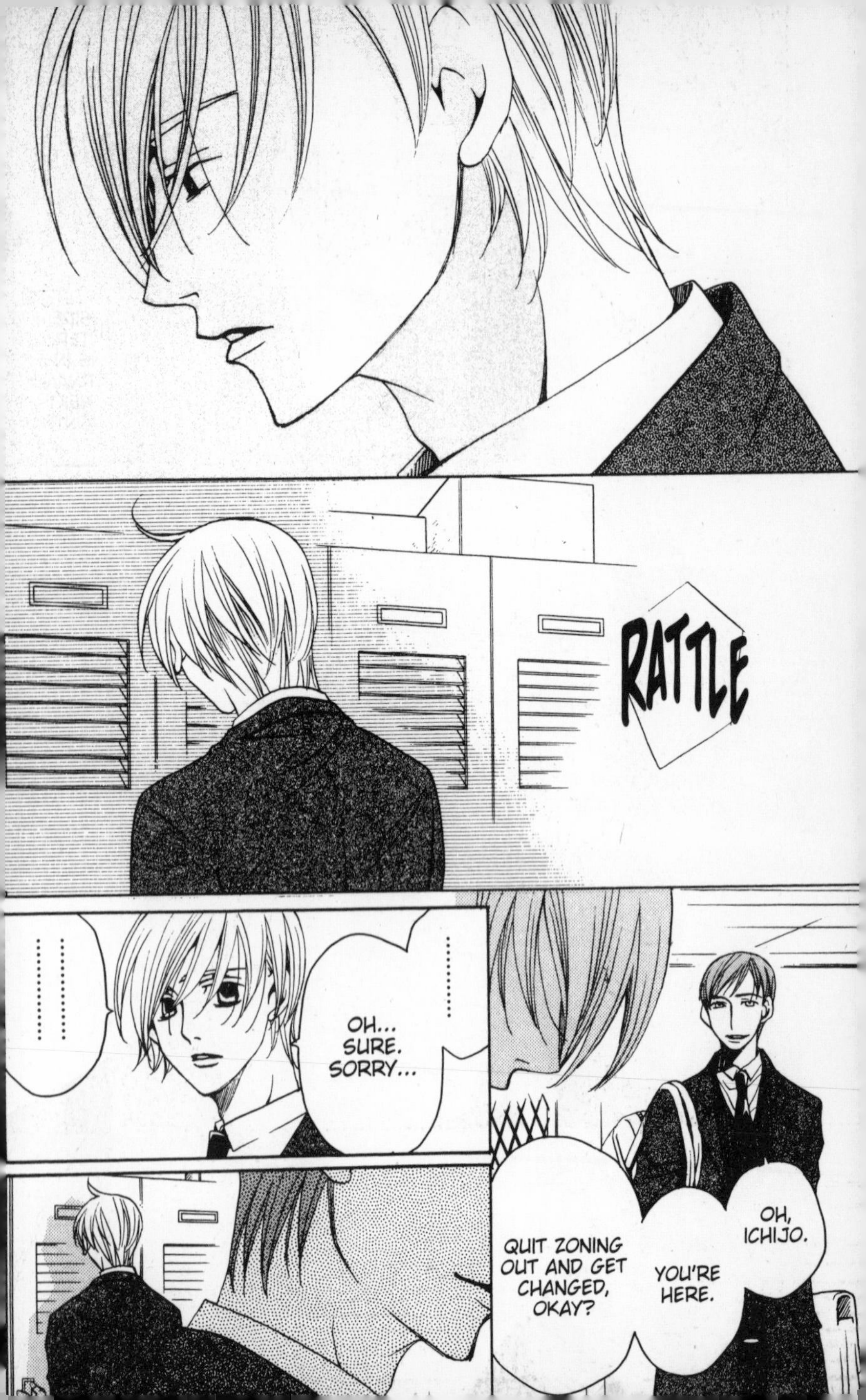
RATTLE
OH, ICHIJO.
YOU'RE HERE.
QUIT ZONING OUT AND GET CHANGED, OKAY?
......
OH... SURE. SORRY...
......

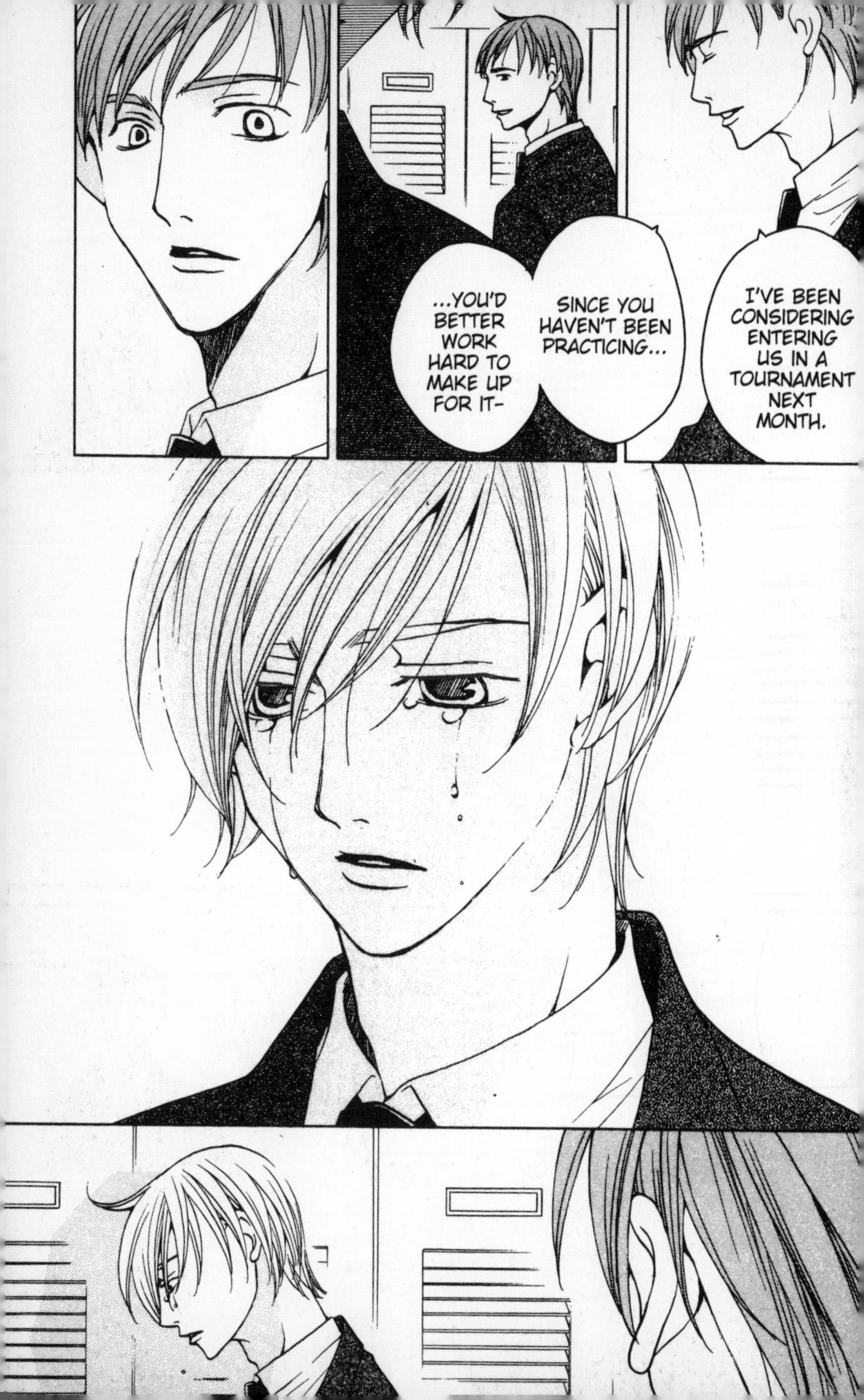
I'VE BEEN CONSIDERING ENTERING US IN A TOURNAMENT NEXT MONTH.
SINCE YOU HAVEN'T BEEN PRACTICING...
...YOU'D BETTER WORK HARD TO MAKE UP FOR IT-

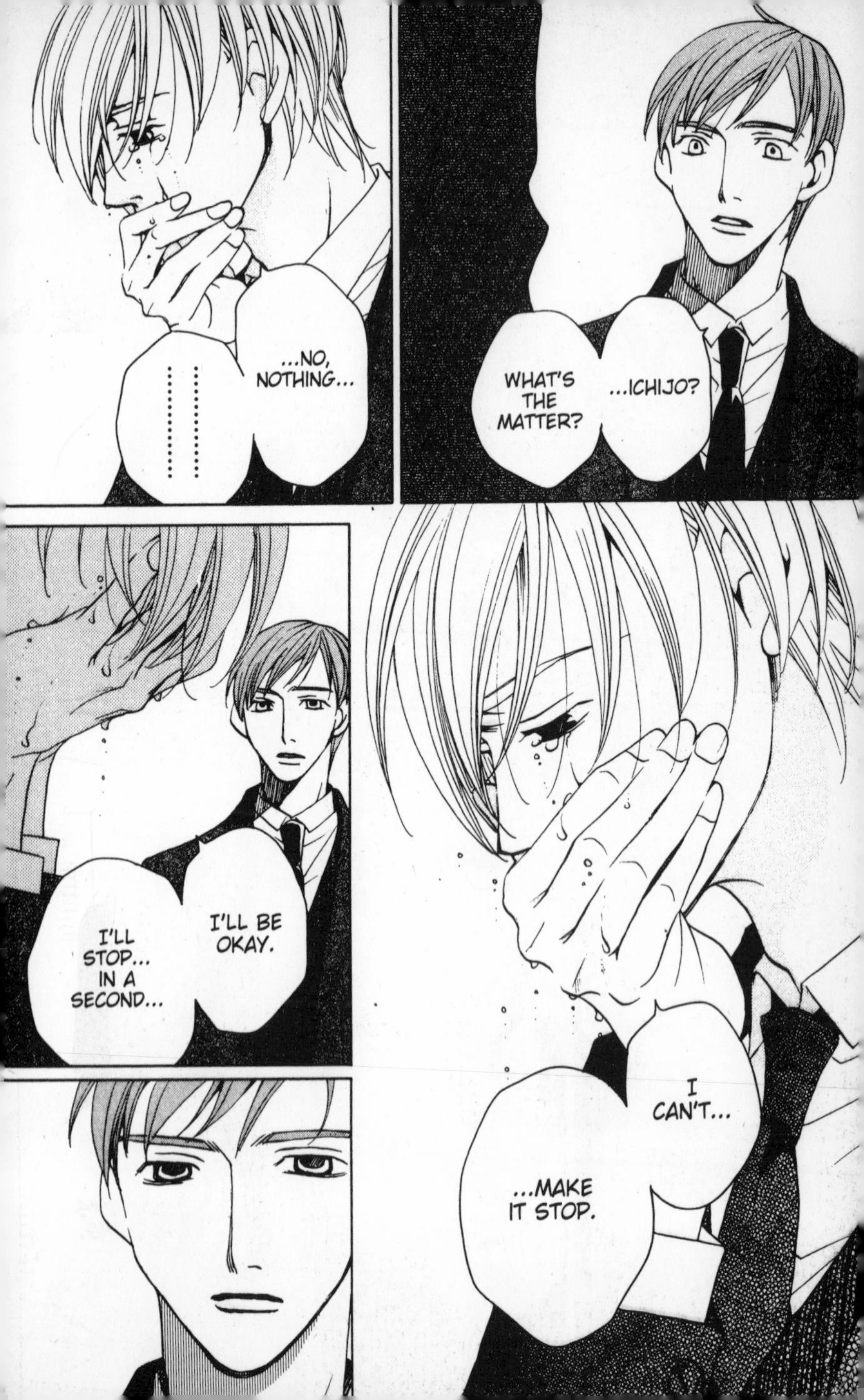
...ICHIJO?
WHAT'S THE MATTER?
...NO, NOTHING...
......
I CAN'T...
...MAKE IT STOP.
I'LL BE OKAY.
I'LL STOP... IN A SECOND...

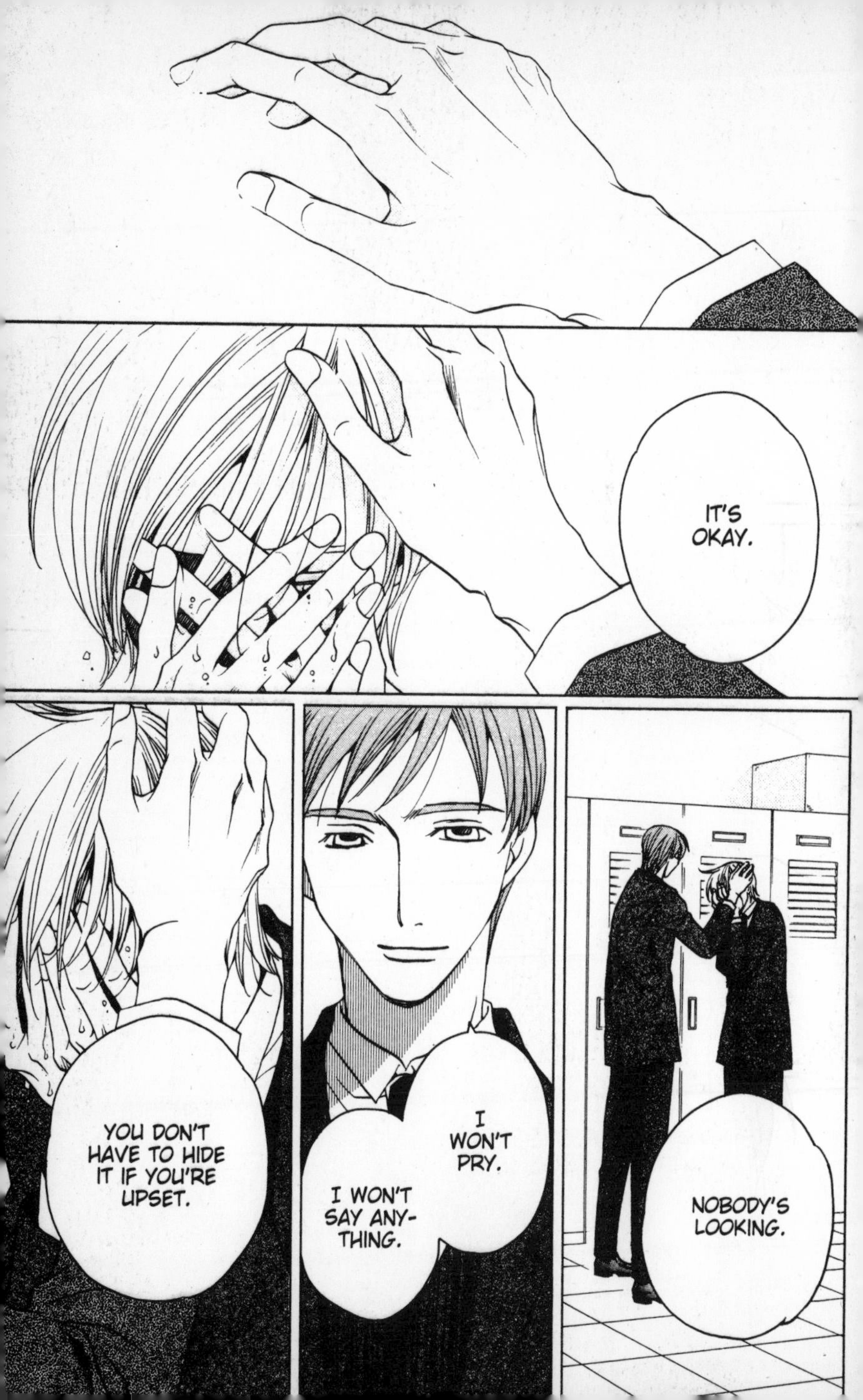
IT'S OKAY.
NOBODY'S LOOKING.
I WON'T PRY.
I WON'T SAY ANYTHING.
YOU DON'T HAVE TO HIDE IT IF YOU'RE UPSET.

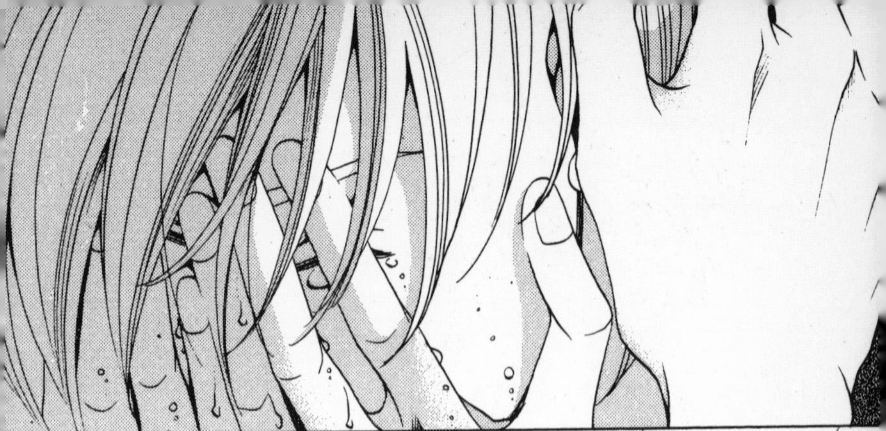

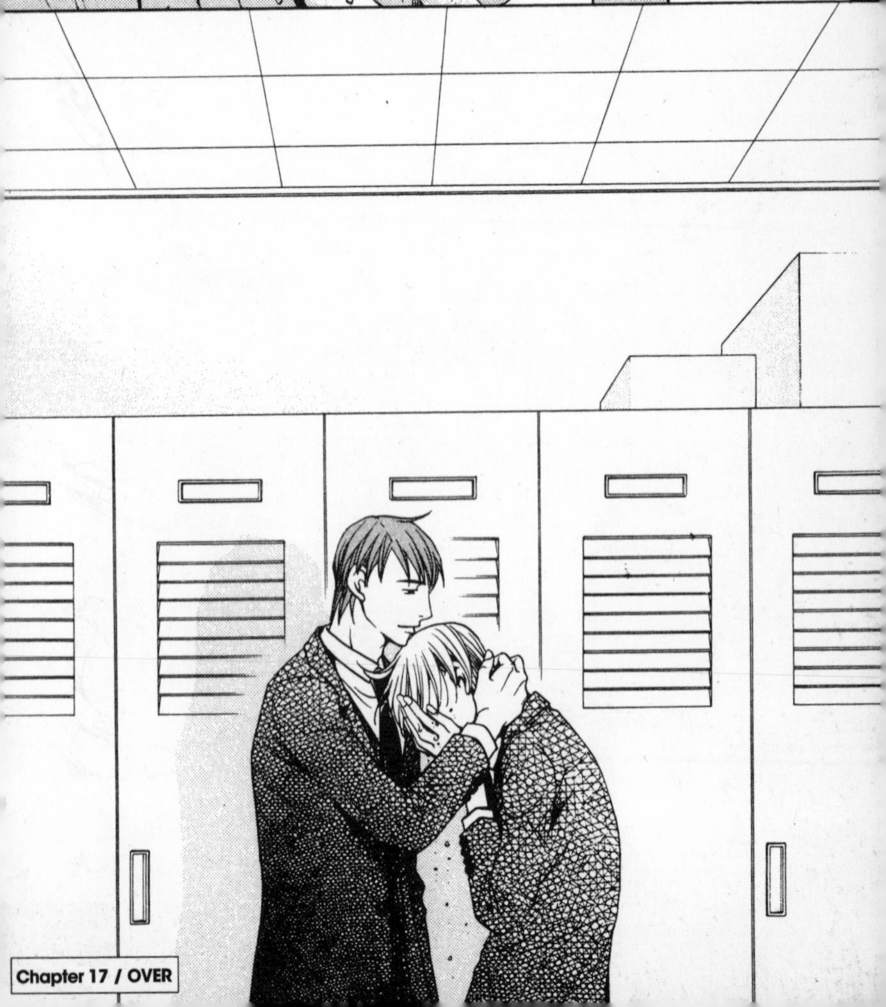
Chapter 17 / OVER

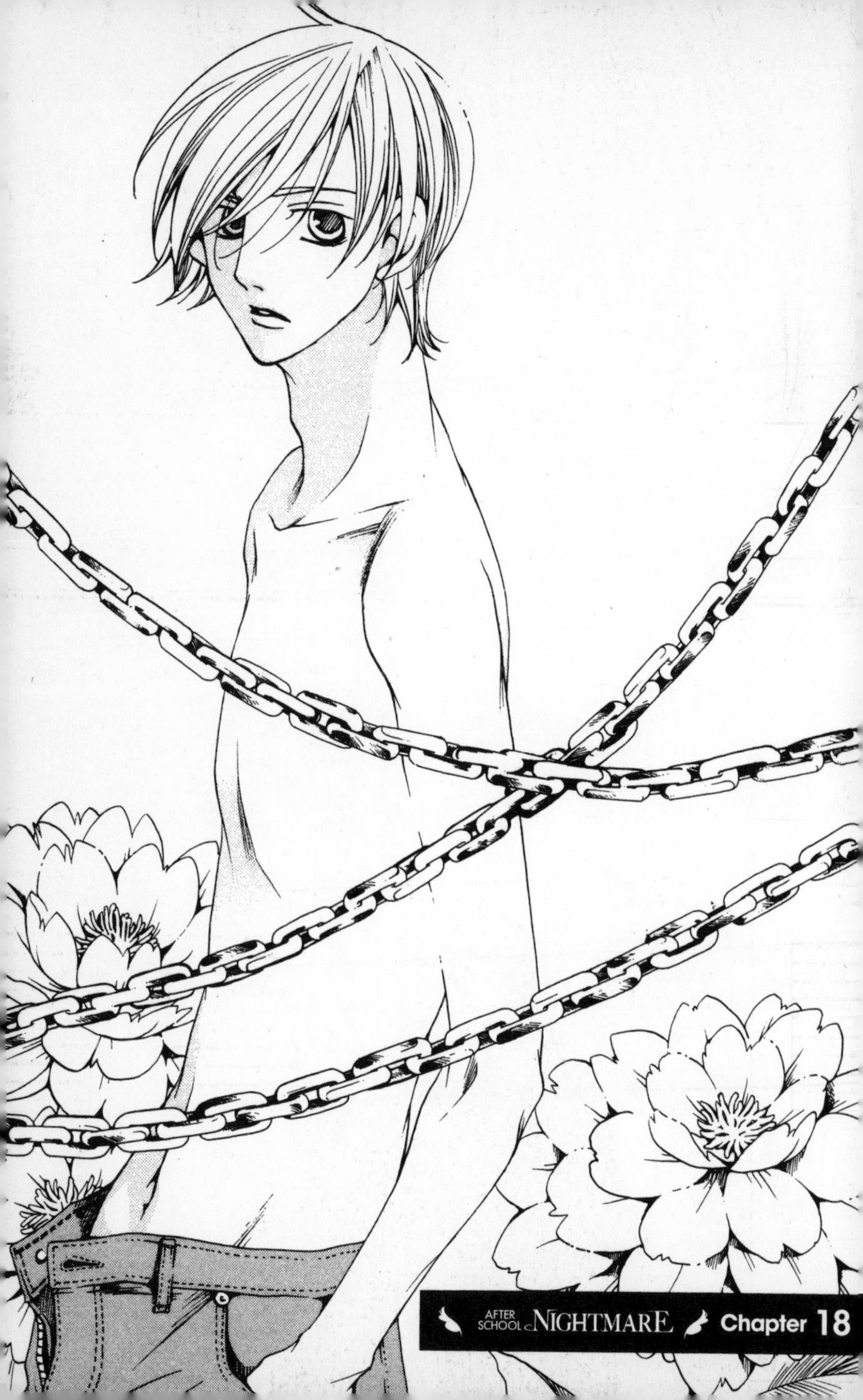
AFTER SCHOOL NIGHTMARE
Chapter 18

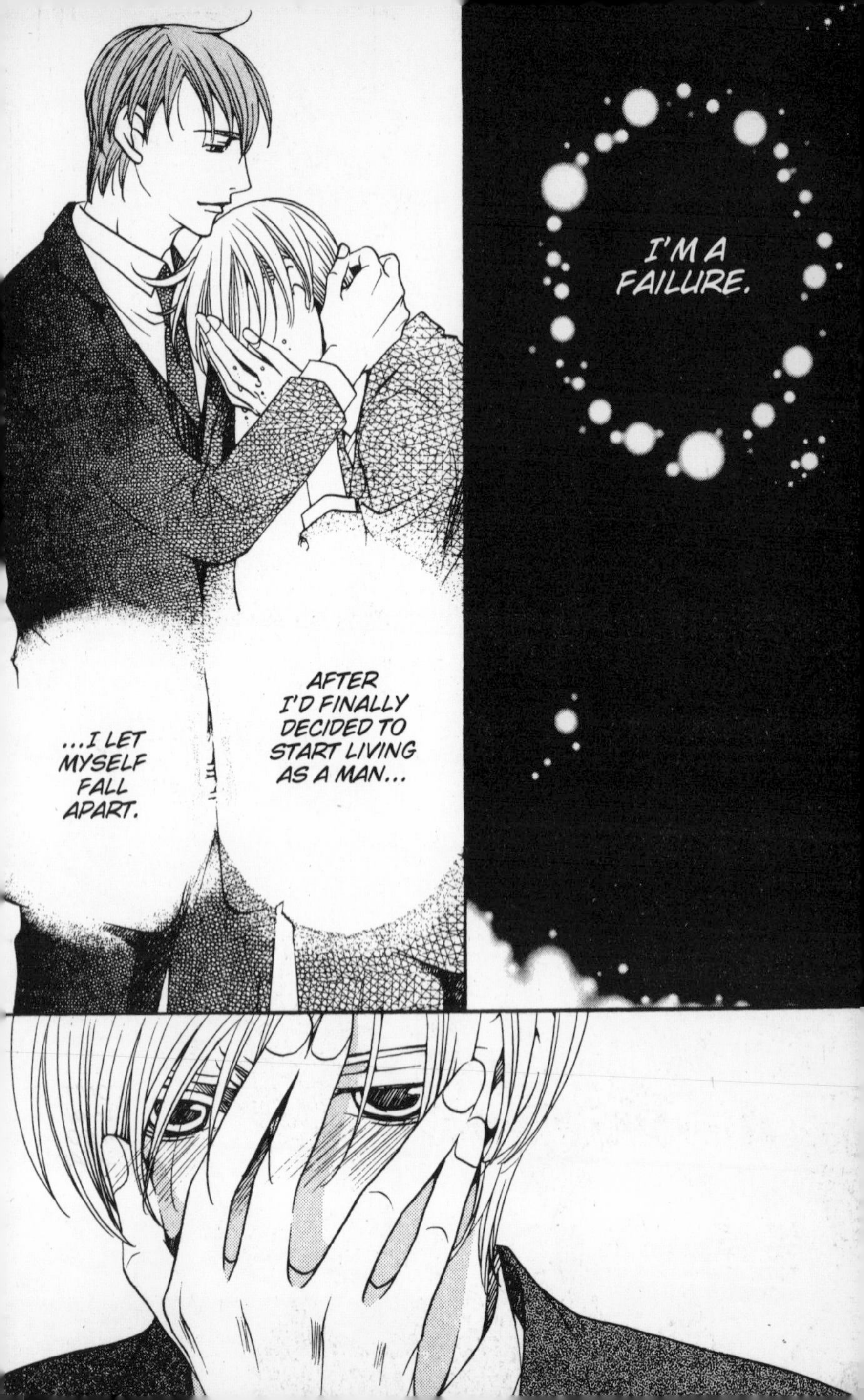
I'M A FAILURE.
AFTER I'D FINALLY DECIDED TO START LIVING AS A MAN...
...I LET MYSELF FALL APART.

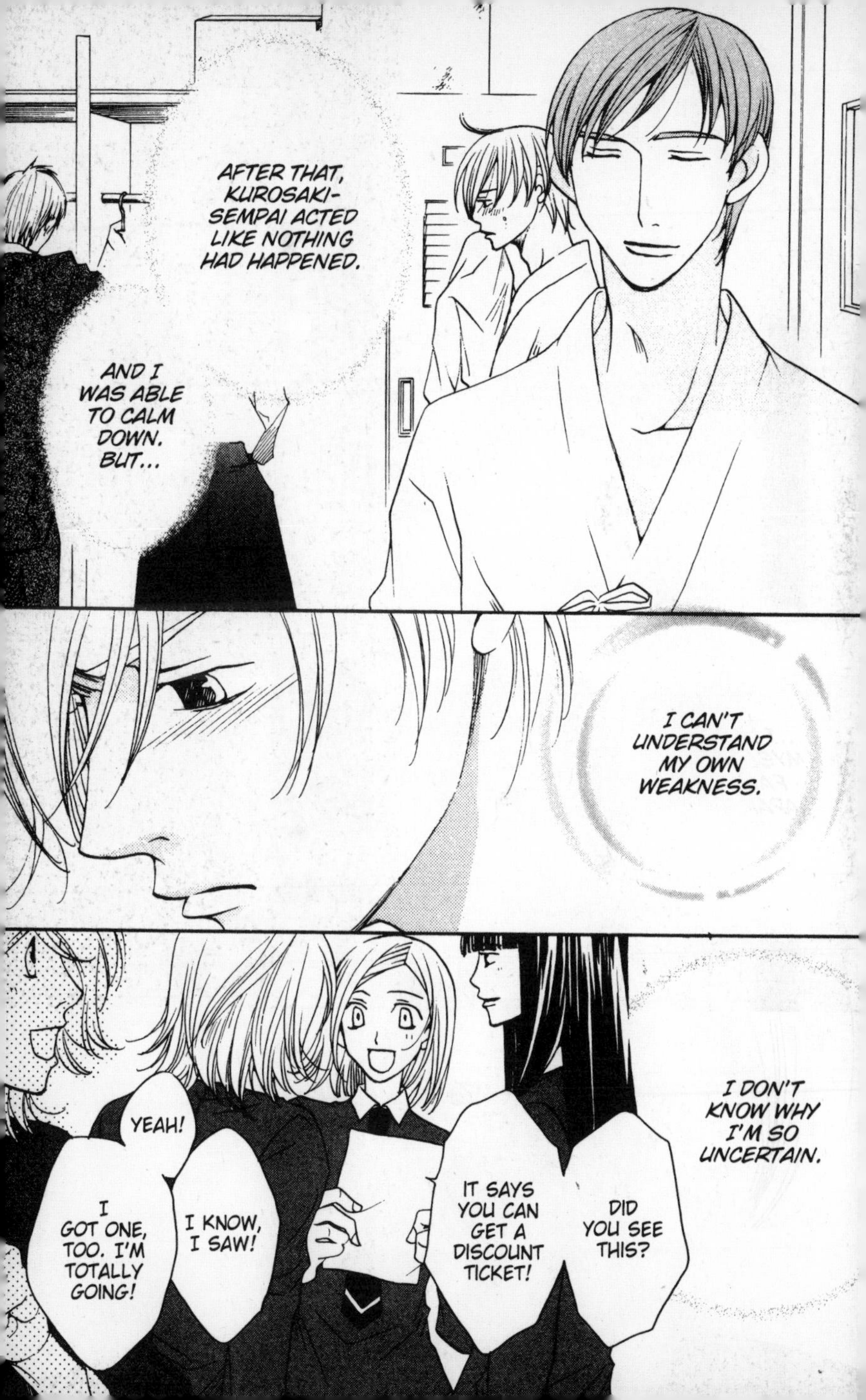
AFTER THAT, KUROSAKI-SEMPAI ACTED LIKE NOTHING HAD HAPPENED.
AND I WAS ABLE TO CALM DOWN. BUT...
I CAN'T UNDERSTAND MY OWN WEAKNESS.
I DON'T KNOW WHY I'M SO UNCERTAIN.
DID YOU SEE THIS?
IT SAYS YOU CAN GET A DISCOUNT TICKET!
YEAH!
I KNOW, I SAW!
I GOT ONE, TOO. I'M TOTALLY GOING!

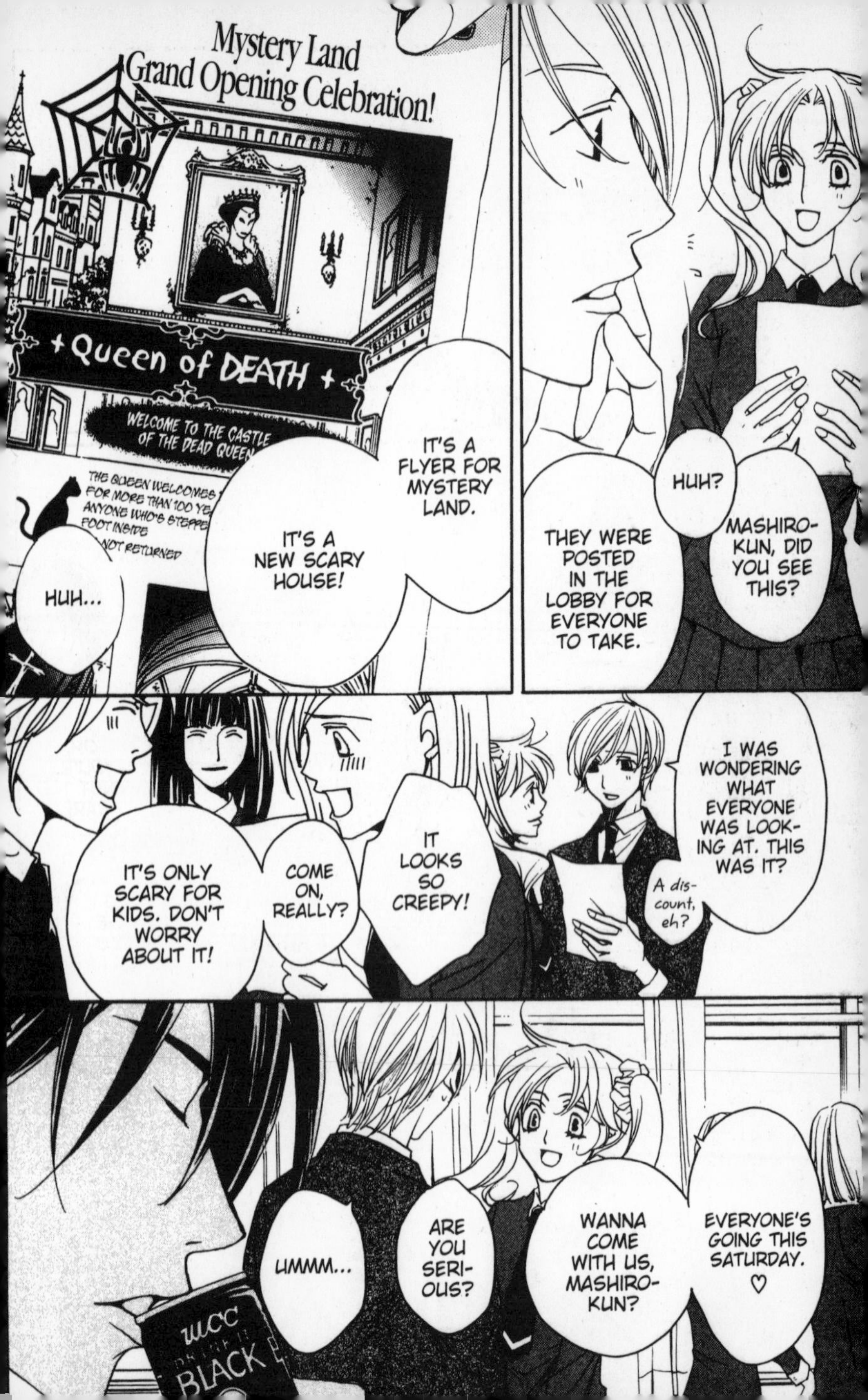
MASHIRO-KUN, DID YOU SEE THIS?
HUH?
THEY WERE POSTED IN THE LOBBY FOR EVERYONE TO TAKE.
Mystery Land Grand Opening Celebration!
Queen of DEATH
WELCOME TO THE CASTLE OF THE DEAD QUEEN
THE QUEEN WELCOMES
FOOT INSIDE
IT'S A FLYER FOR MYSTERY LAND.
IT'S A NEW SCARY HOUSE!
HUH...
I WAS WONDERING WHAT EVERYONE WAS LOOKING AT. THIS WAS IT?
A discount, eh?
IT LOOKS SO CREEPY!
COME ON, REALLY?
IT'S ONLY SCARY FOR KIDS. DON'T WORRY ABOUT IT!
EVERYONE'S GOING THIS SATURDAY. ♡
WANNA COME WITH US, MASHIRO-KUN?
ARE YOU SERIOUS?
UMMM...
BLACK

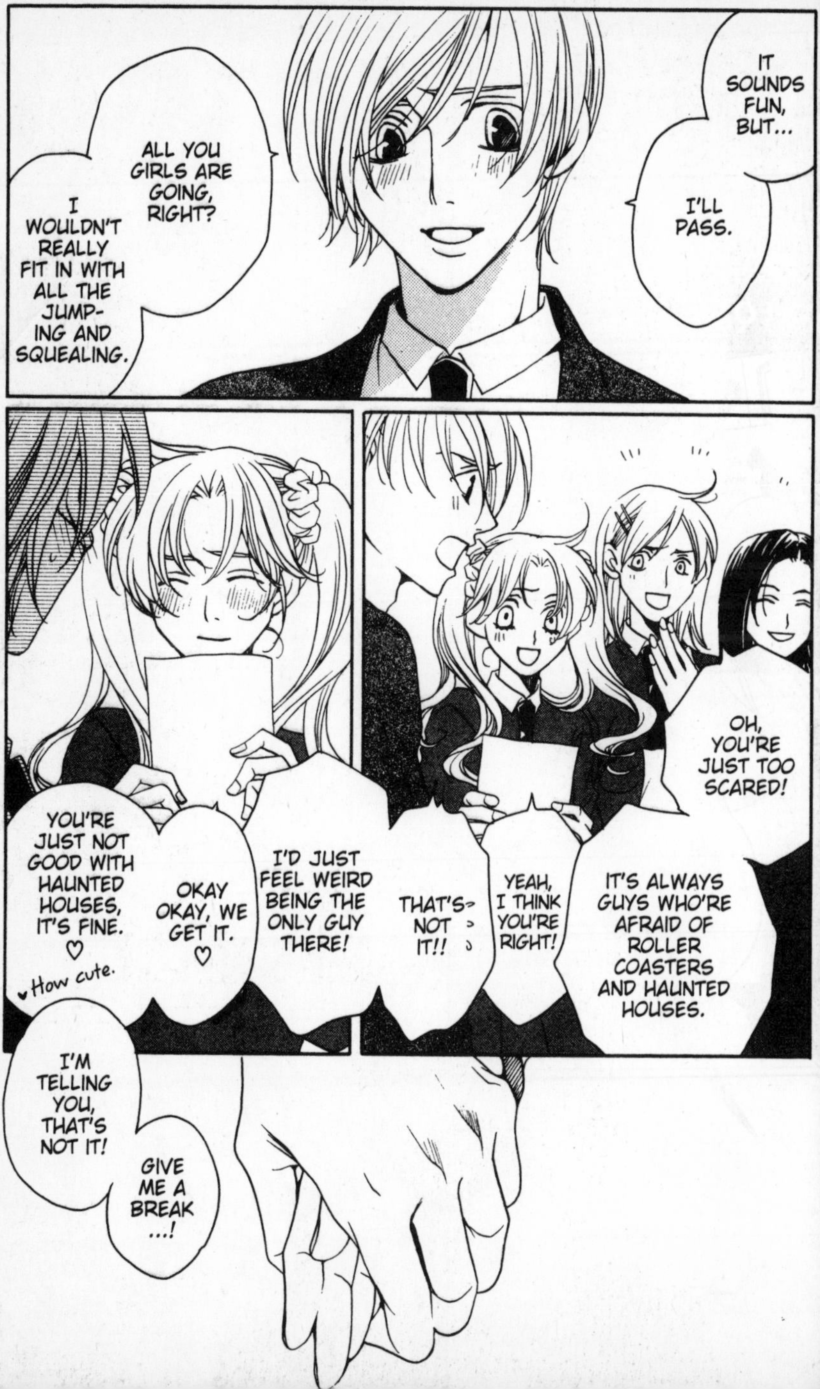
IT SOUNDS FUN, BUT...
I'LL PASS.
ALL YOU GIRLS ARE GOING, RIGHT?
I WOULDN'T REALLY FIT IN WITH ALL THE JUMPING AND SQUEALING.
OH, YOU'RE JUST TOO SCARED!
IT'S ALWAYS GUYS WHO'RE AFRAID OF ROLLER COASTERS AND HAUNTED HOUSES.
YEAH, I THINK YOU'RE RIGHT!
THAT'S NOT IT!!
I'D JUST FEEL WEIRD BEING THE ONLY GUY THERE!
OKAY OKAY, WE GET IT. ♡
YOU'RE JUST NOT GOOD WITH HAUNTED HOUSES, IT'S FINE. ♡
♥ How cute.
I'M TELLING YOU, THAT'S NOT IT!
GIVE ME A BREAK ...!

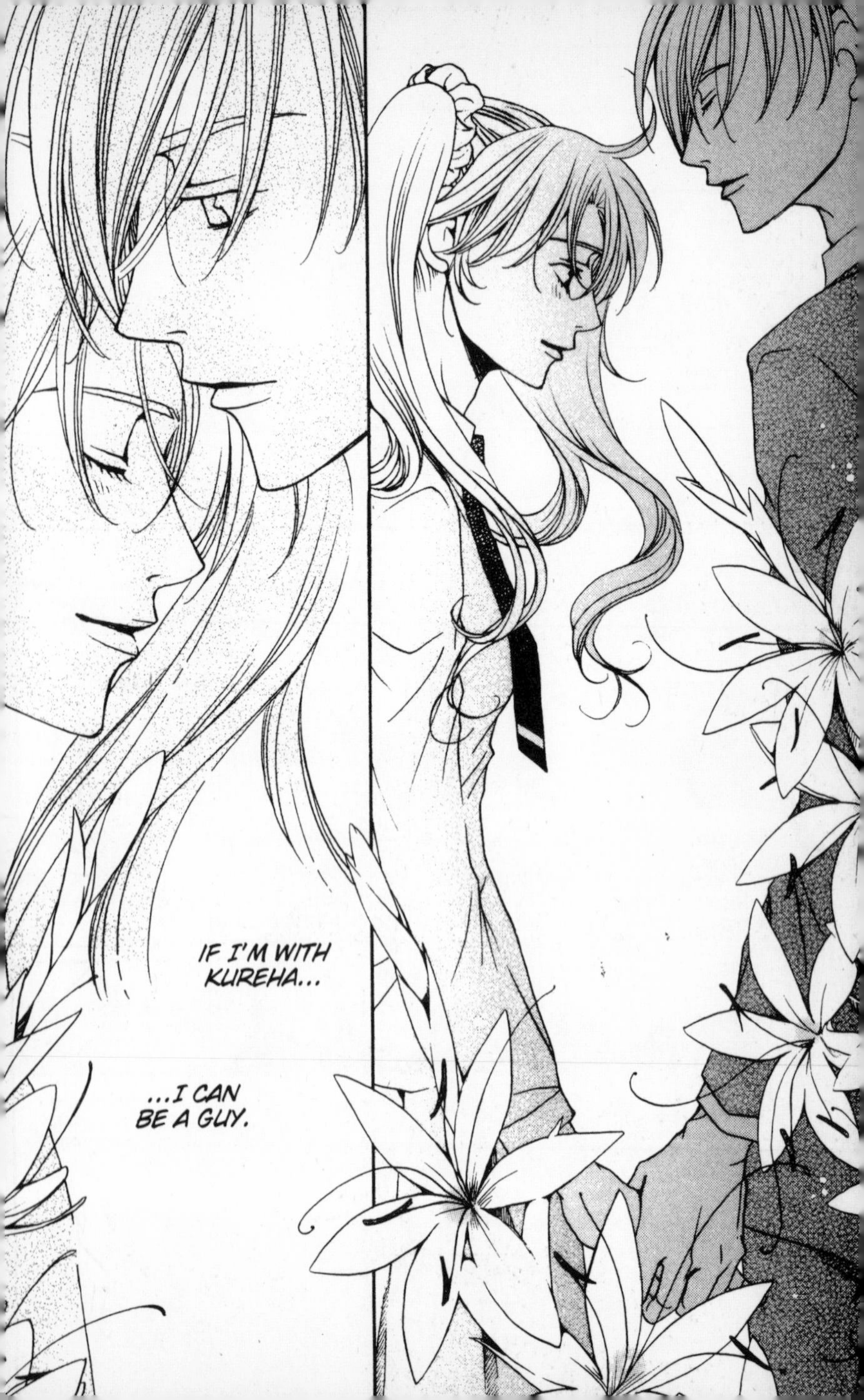
IF I'M WITH KUREHA...
...I CAN BE A GUY.

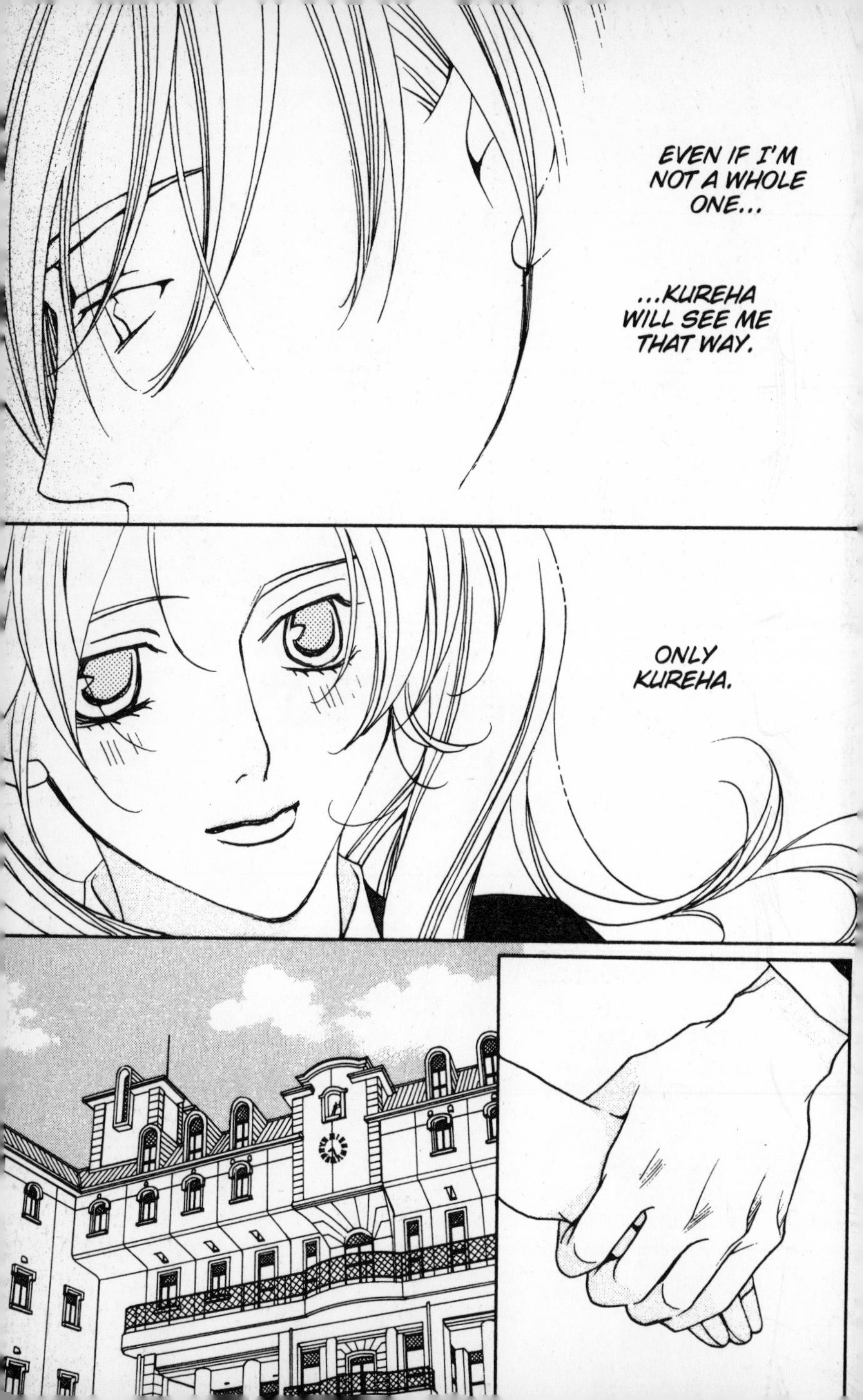
EVEN IF I'M NOT A WHOLE ONE...
...KUREHA WILL SEE ME THAT WAY.
ONLY KUREHA.

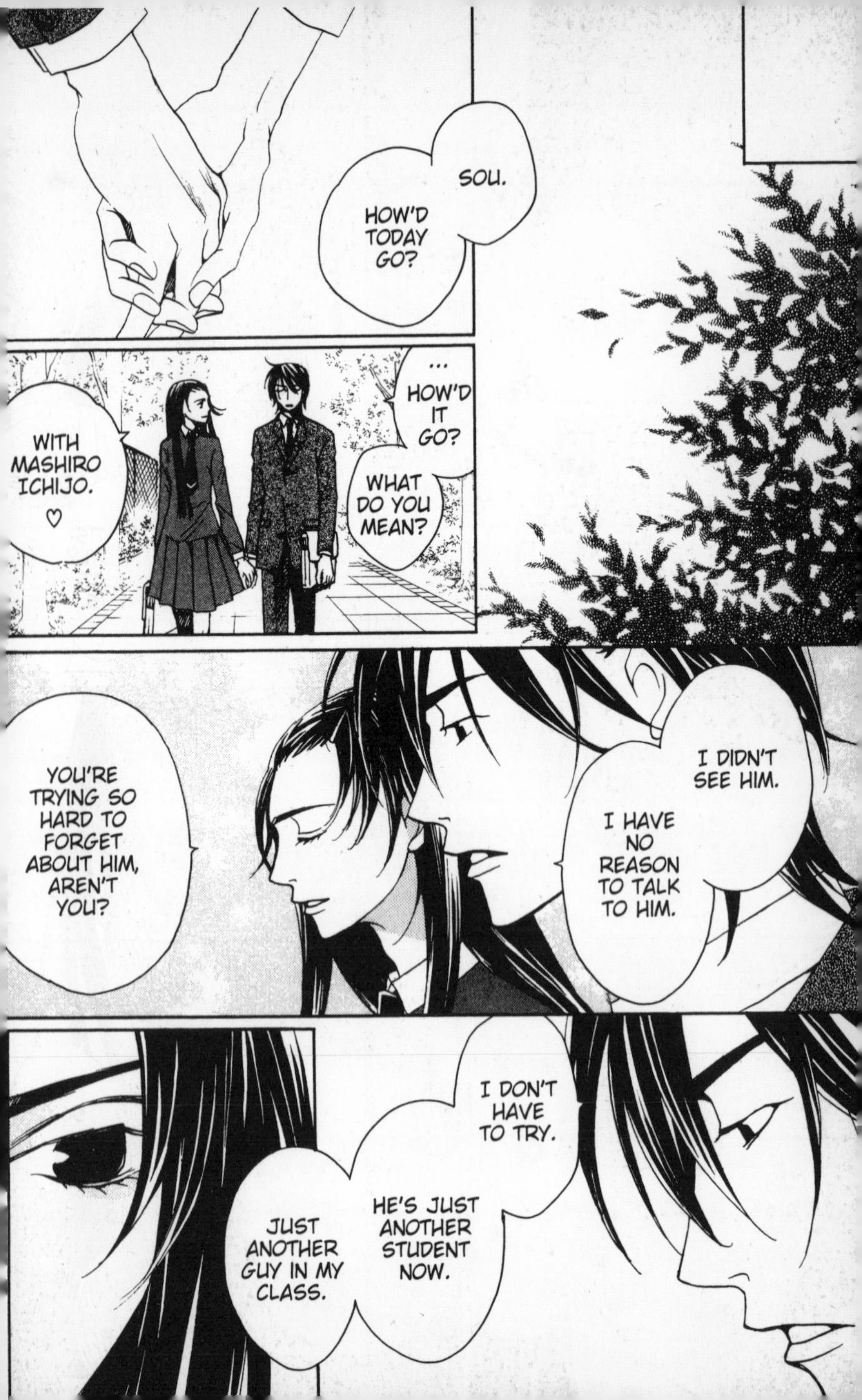
SOU.
HOW'D TODAY GO?
... HOW'D IT GO?
WHAT DO YOU MEAN?
WITH MASHIRO ICHIJO. ♡
I DIDN'T SEE HIM.
I HAVE NO REASON TO TALK TO HIM.
YOU'RE TRYING SO HARD TO FORGET ABOUT HIM, AREN'T YOU?
I DON'T HAVE TO TRY.
HE'S JUST ANOTHER STUDENT NOW.
JUST ANOTHER GUY IN MY CLASS.

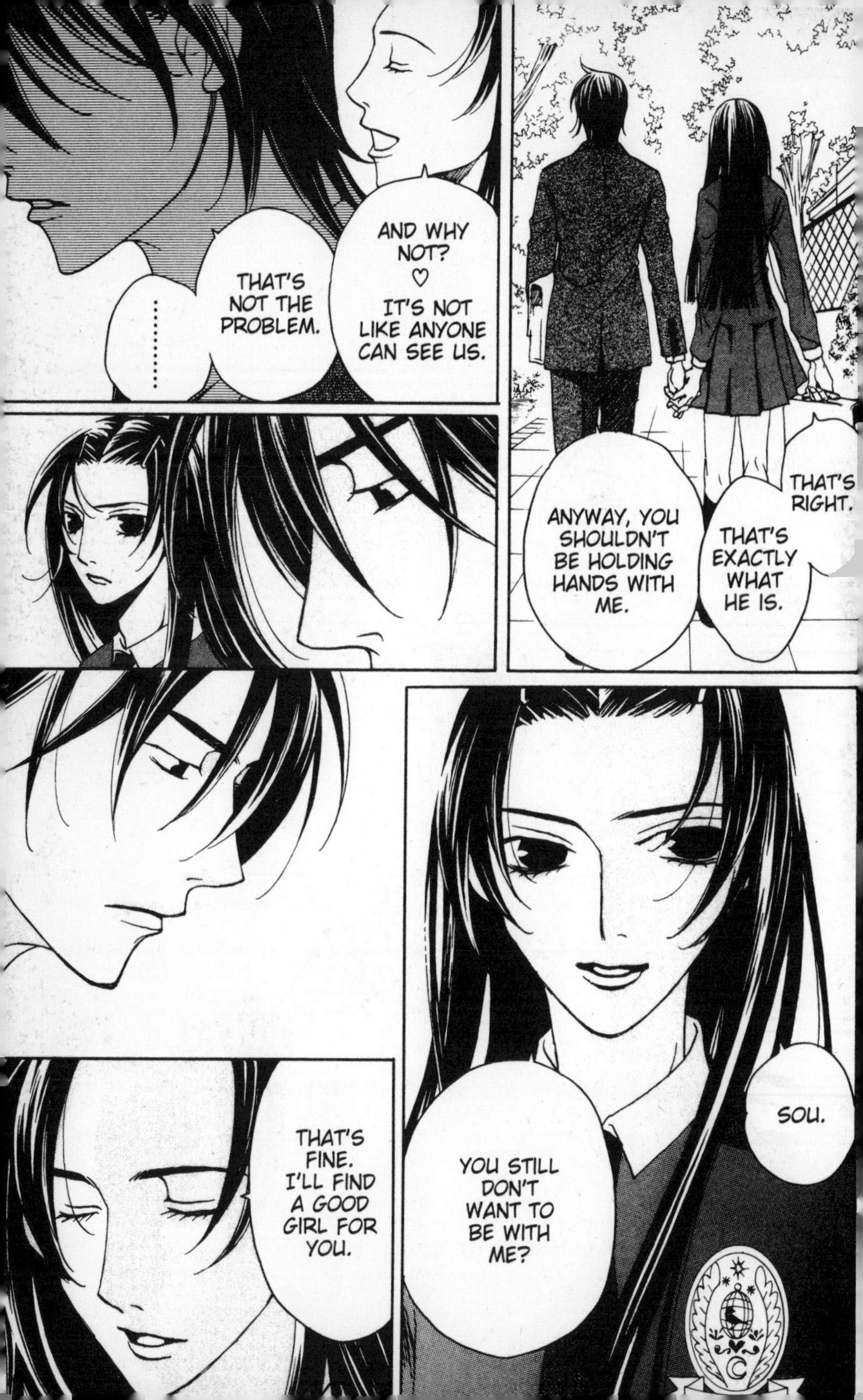
THAT'S RIGHT.
THAT'S EXACTLY WHAT HE IS.
ANYWAY, YOU SHOULDN'T BE HOLDING HANDS WITH ME.
AND WHY NOT? ♡ IT'S NOT LIKE ANYONE CAN SEE US.
THAT'S NOT THE PROBLEM.
......
SOU.
YOU STILL DON'T WANT TO BE WITH ME?
THAT'S FINE. I'LL FIND A GOOD GIRL FOR YOU.

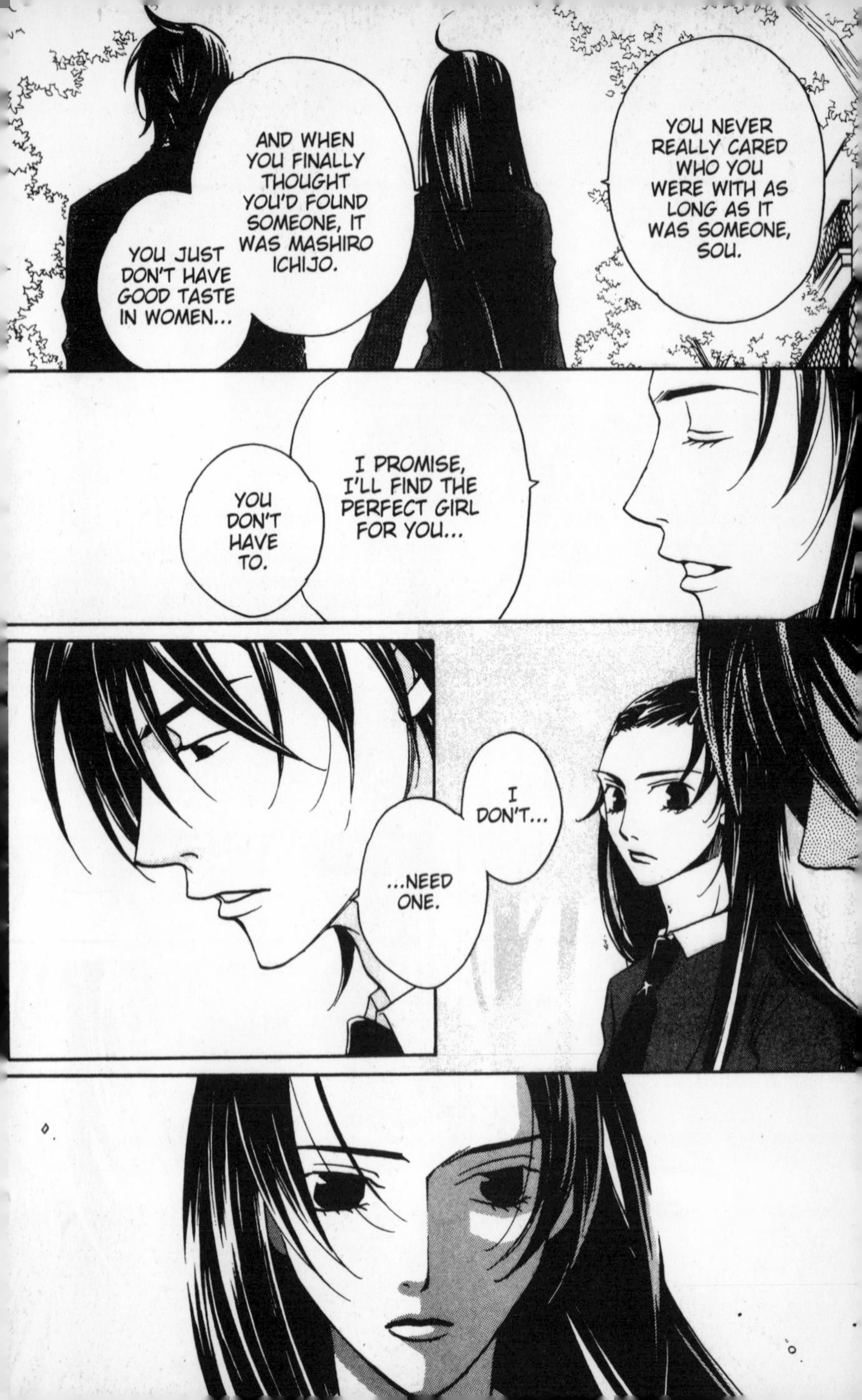
YOU NEVER REALLY CARED WHO YOU WERE WITH AS LONG AS IT WAS SOMEONE, SOU.
AND WHEN YOU FINALLY THOUGHT YOU'D FOUND SOMEONE, IT WAS MASHIRO ICHIJO.
YOU JUST DON'T HAVE GOOD TASTE IN WOMEN...
I PROMISE, I'LL FIND THE PERFECT GIRL FOR YOU...
YOU DON'T HAVE TO.
I DON'T...
...NEED ONE.

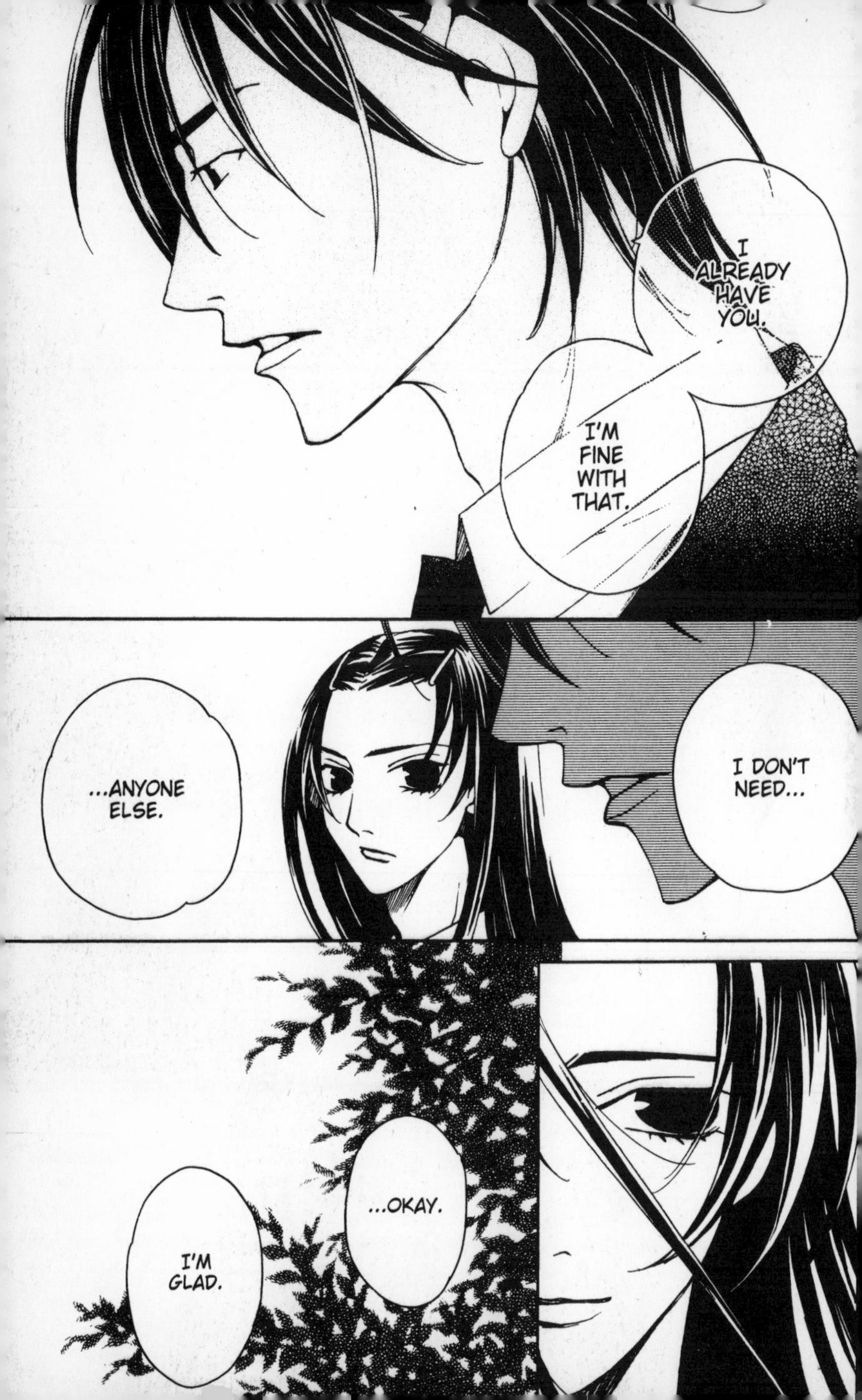
I ALREADY HAVE YOU.
I'M FINE WITH THAT.
I DON'T NEED...
...ANYONE ELSE.
...OKAY.
I'M GLAD.

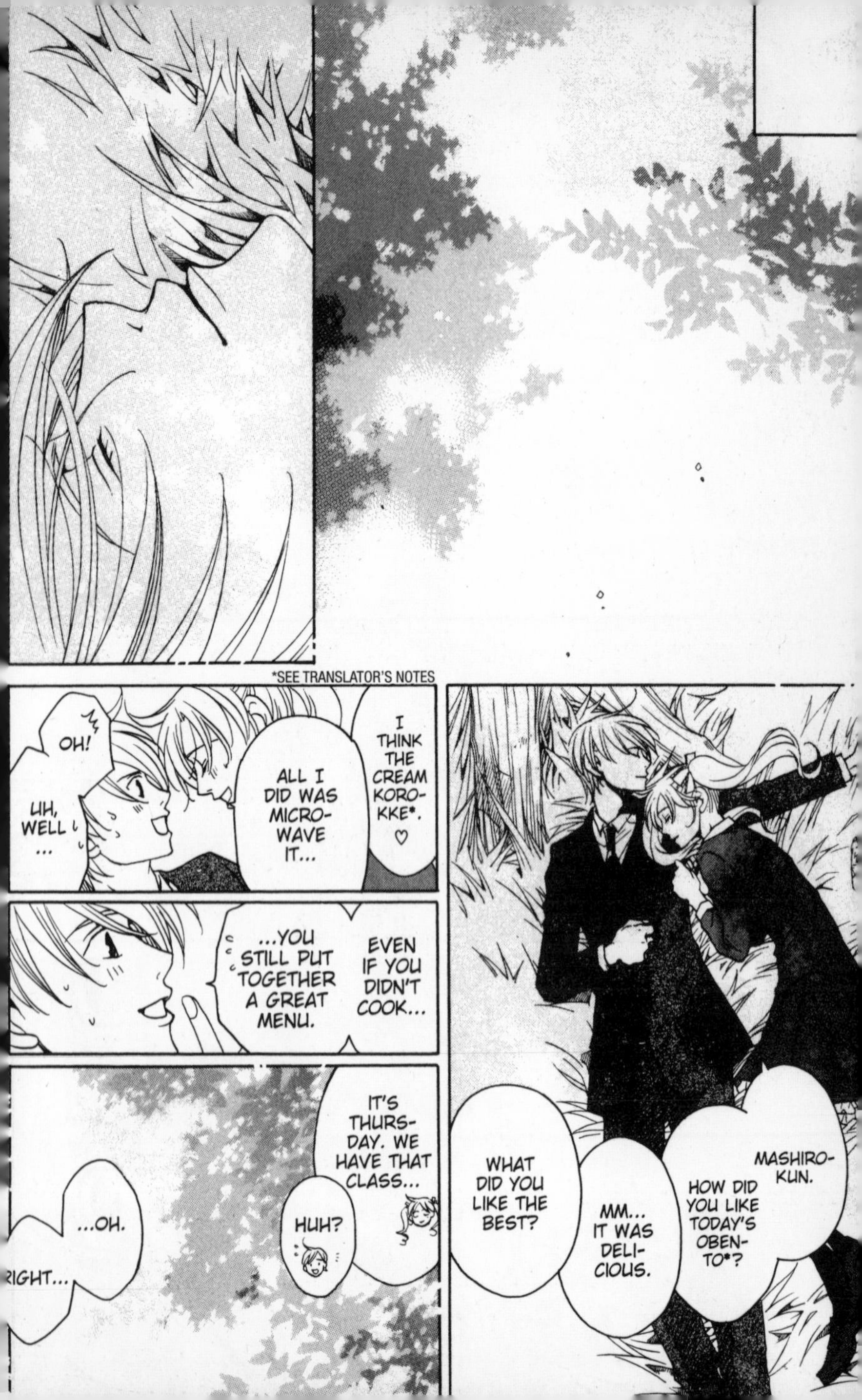
MASHIRO-KUN.
HOW DID YOU LIKE TODAY'S OBENTO*?
MM... IT WAS DELICIOUS.
WHAT DID YOU LIKE THE BEST?
I THINK THE CREAM KOROKKE*. ♡
ALL I DID WAS MICROWAVE IT...
OH!
UH, WELL...
EVEN IF YOU DIDN'T COOK...
...YOU STILL PUT TOGETHER A GREAT MENU.
IT'S THURSDAY. WE HAVE THAT CLASS...
HUH?
...OH.
RIGHT...
*SEE TRANSLATOR'S NOTES

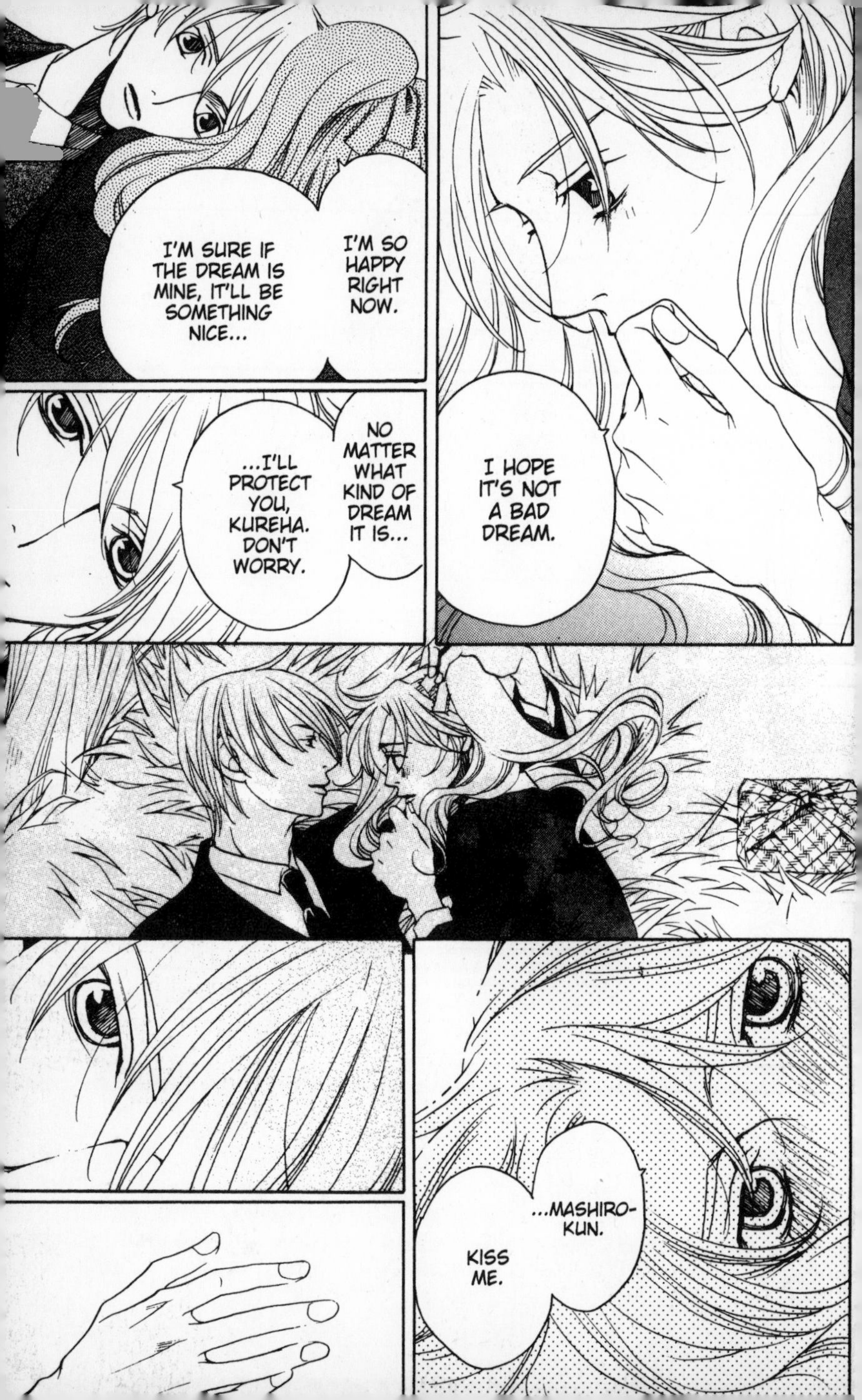
I HOPE IT'S NOT A BAD DREAM.
I'M SO HAPPY RIGHT NOW.
I'M SURE IF THE DREAM IS MINE, IT'LL BE SOMETHING NICE...
NO MATTER WHAT KIND OF DREAM IT IS...
...I'LL PROTECT YOU, KUREHA. DON'T WORRY.
...MASHIRO-KUN.
KISS ME.

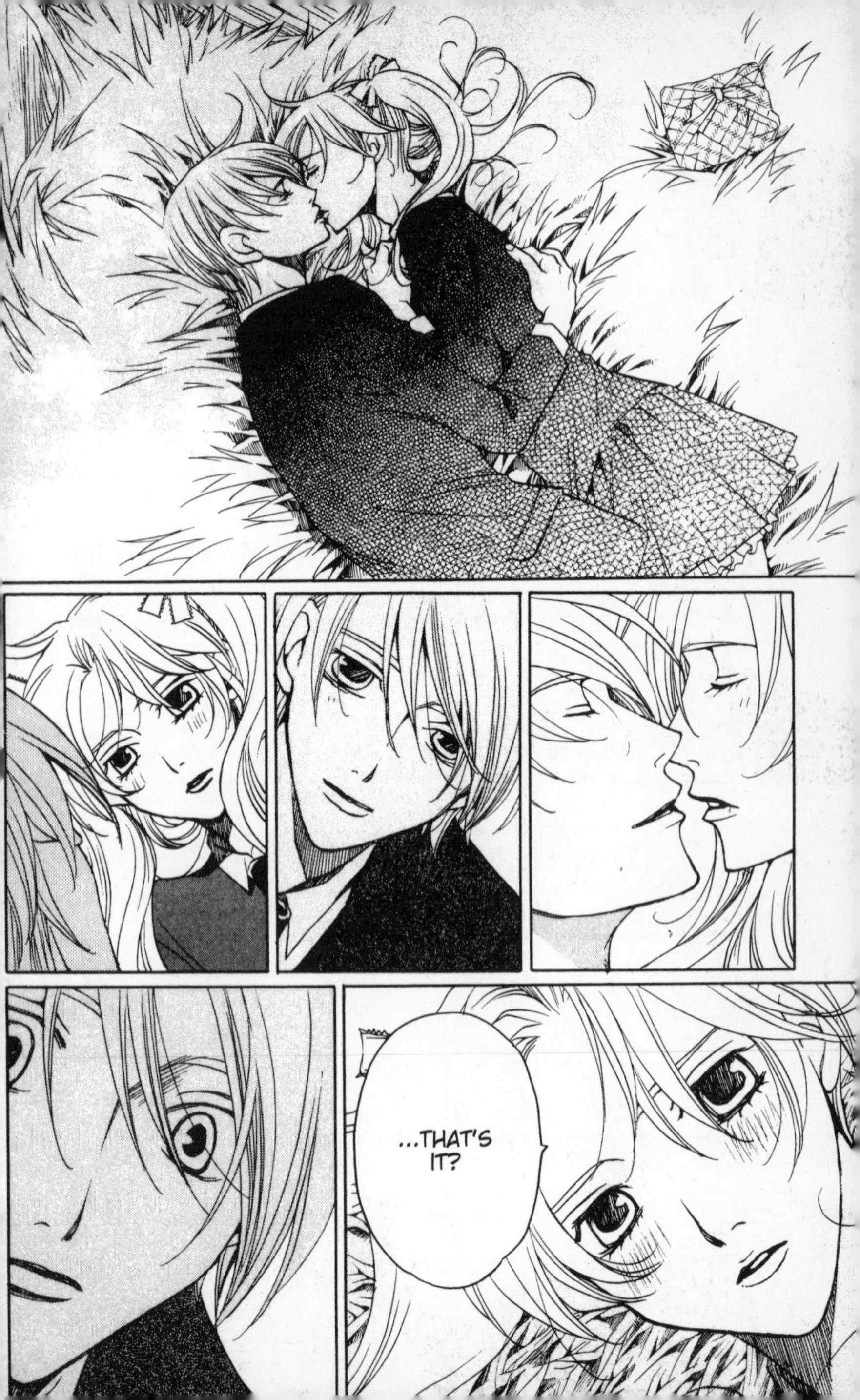
...THAT'S IT?

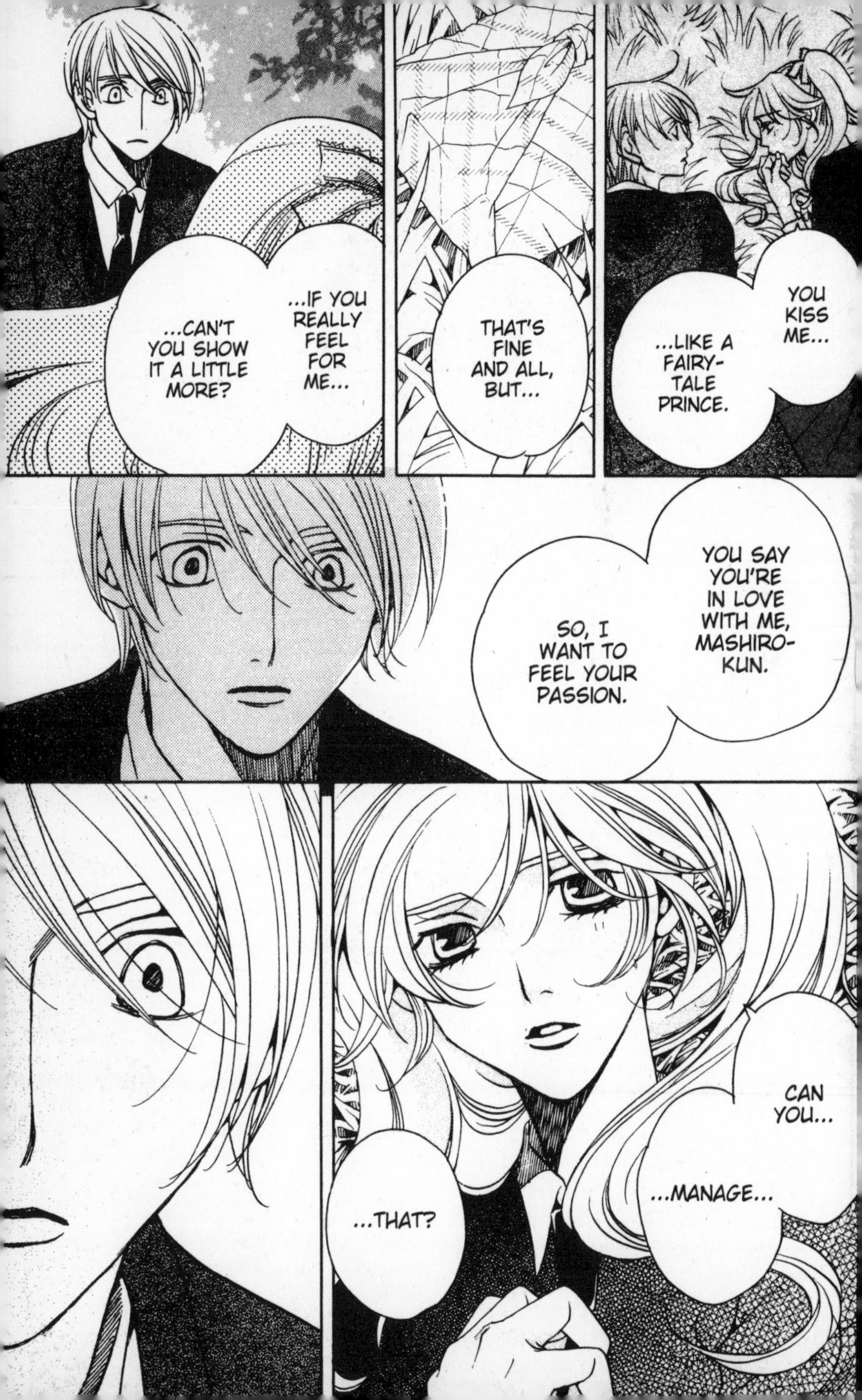
YOU KISS ME...
...LIKE A FAIRY-TALE PRINCE.
THAT'S FINE AND ALL, BUT...
...IF YOU REALLY FEEL FOR ME...
...CAN'T YOU SHOW IT A LITTLE MORE?
YOU SAY YOU'RE IN LOVE WITH ME, MASHIRO-KUN.
SO, I WANT TO FEEL YOUR PASSION.
CAN YOU...
...MANAGE...
...THAT?

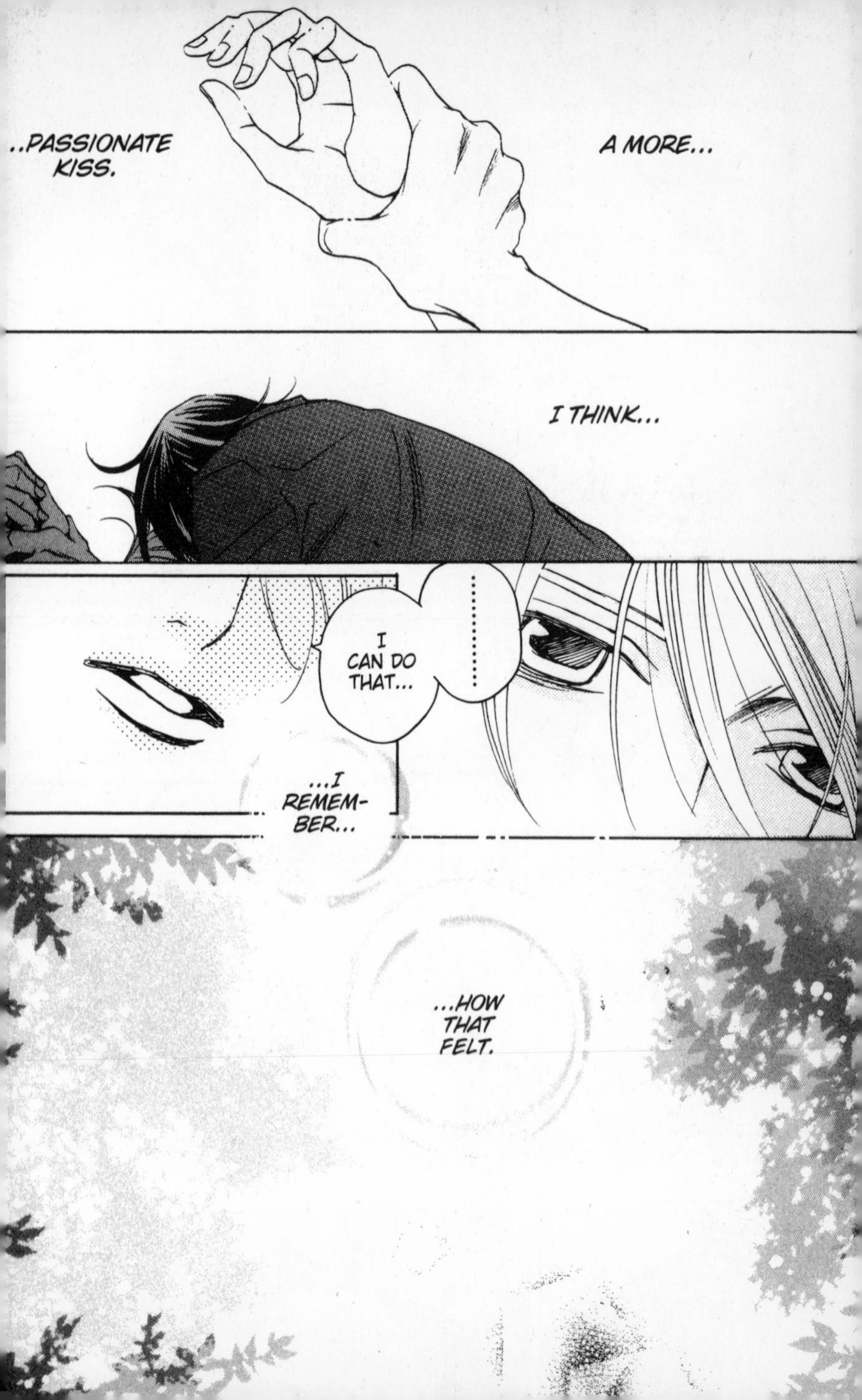

A MORE...
..PASSIONATE KISS.
I THINK...
......
I CAN DO THAT...
...I REMEMBER...
...HOW THAT FELT.

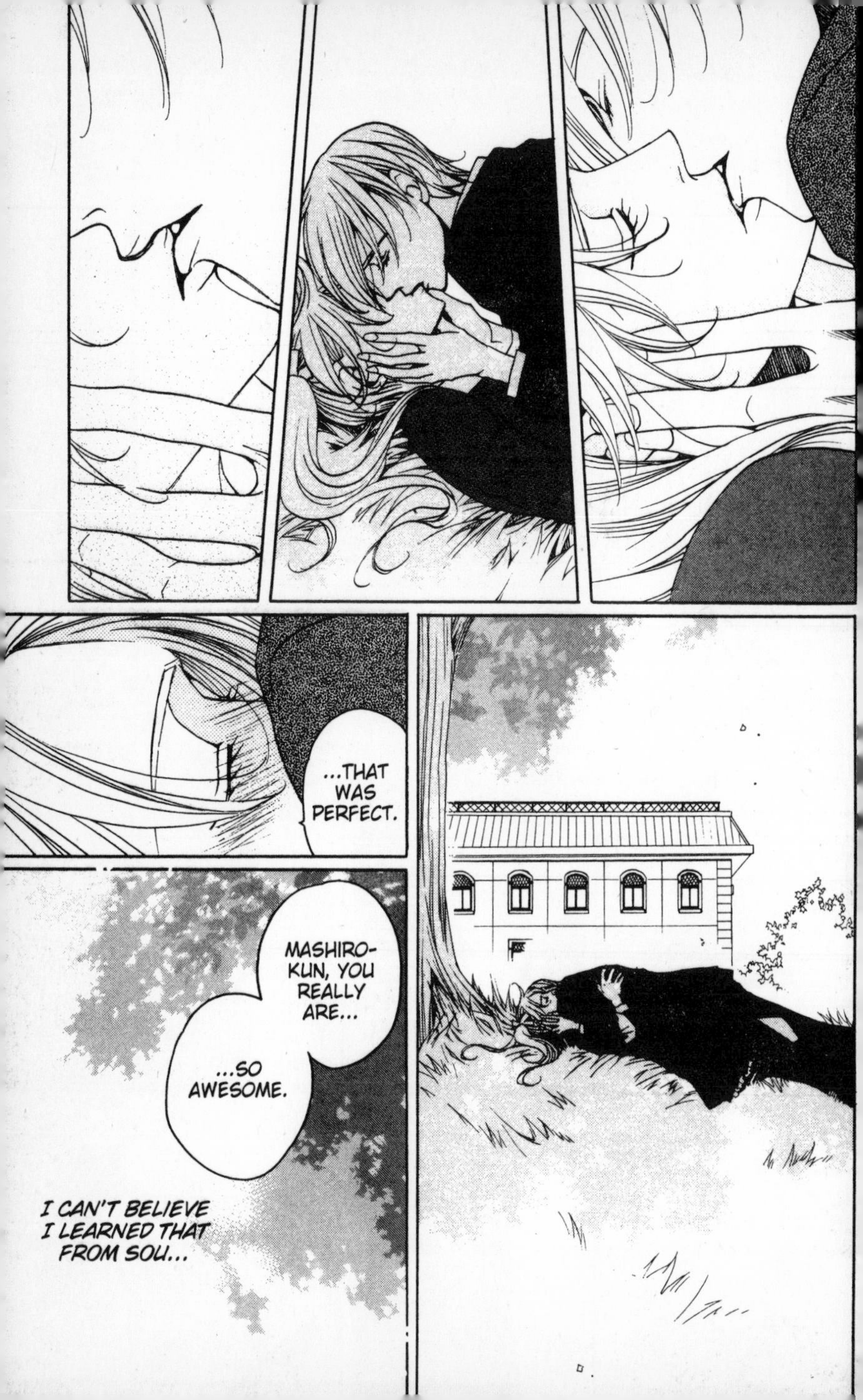
...THAT WAS PERFECT.
MASHIRO-KUN, YOU REALLY ARE...
...SO AWESOME.
I CAN'T BELIEVE I LEARNED THAT FROM SOU...

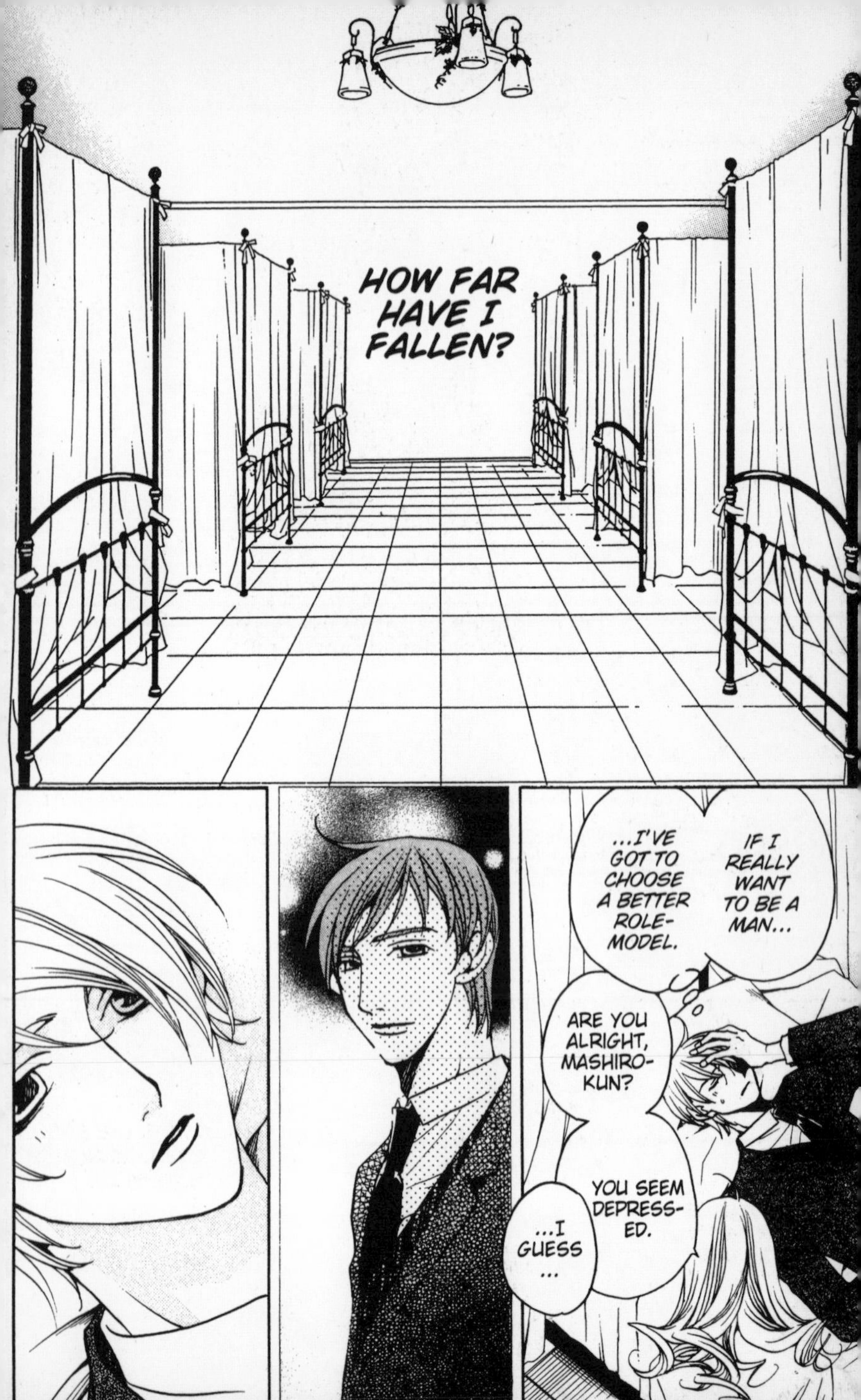
HOW FAR HAVE I FALLEN?
IF I REALLY WANT TO BE A MAN...
...I'VE GOT TO CHOOSE A BETTER ROLE-MODEL.
ARE YOU ALRIGHT, MASHIRO-KUN?
YOU SEEM DEPRESS-ED.
...I GUESS...

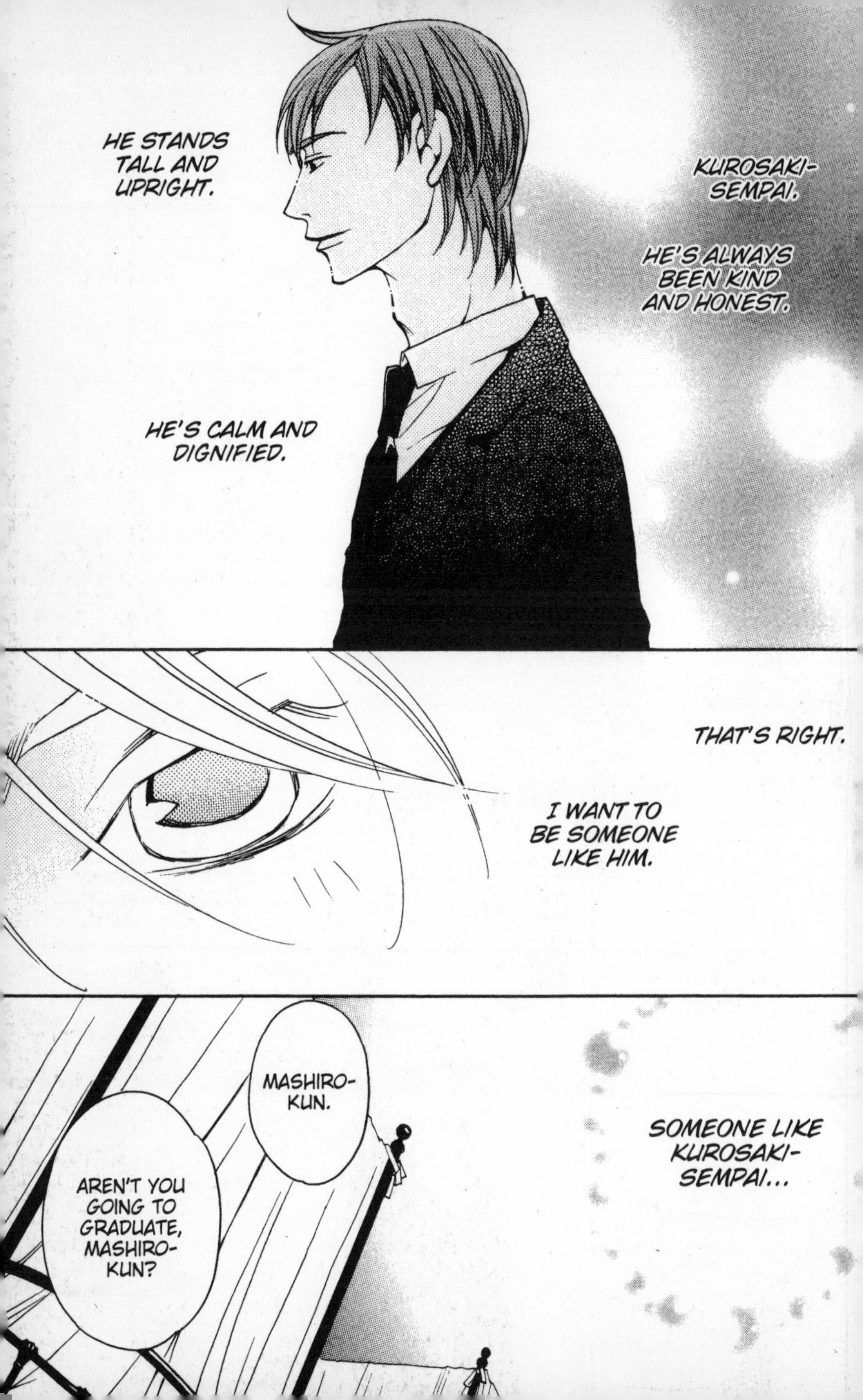
KUROSAKI-SEMPAI.
HE'S ALWAYS BEEN KIND AND HONEST.
HE STANDS TALL AND UPRIGHT.
HE'S CALM AND DIGNIFIED.
THAT'S RIGHT.
I WANT TO BE SOMEONE LIKE HIM.
SOMEONE LIKE KUROSAKI-SEMPAI...
MASHIRO-KUN.
AREN'T YOU GOING TO GRADUATE, MASHIRO-KUN?

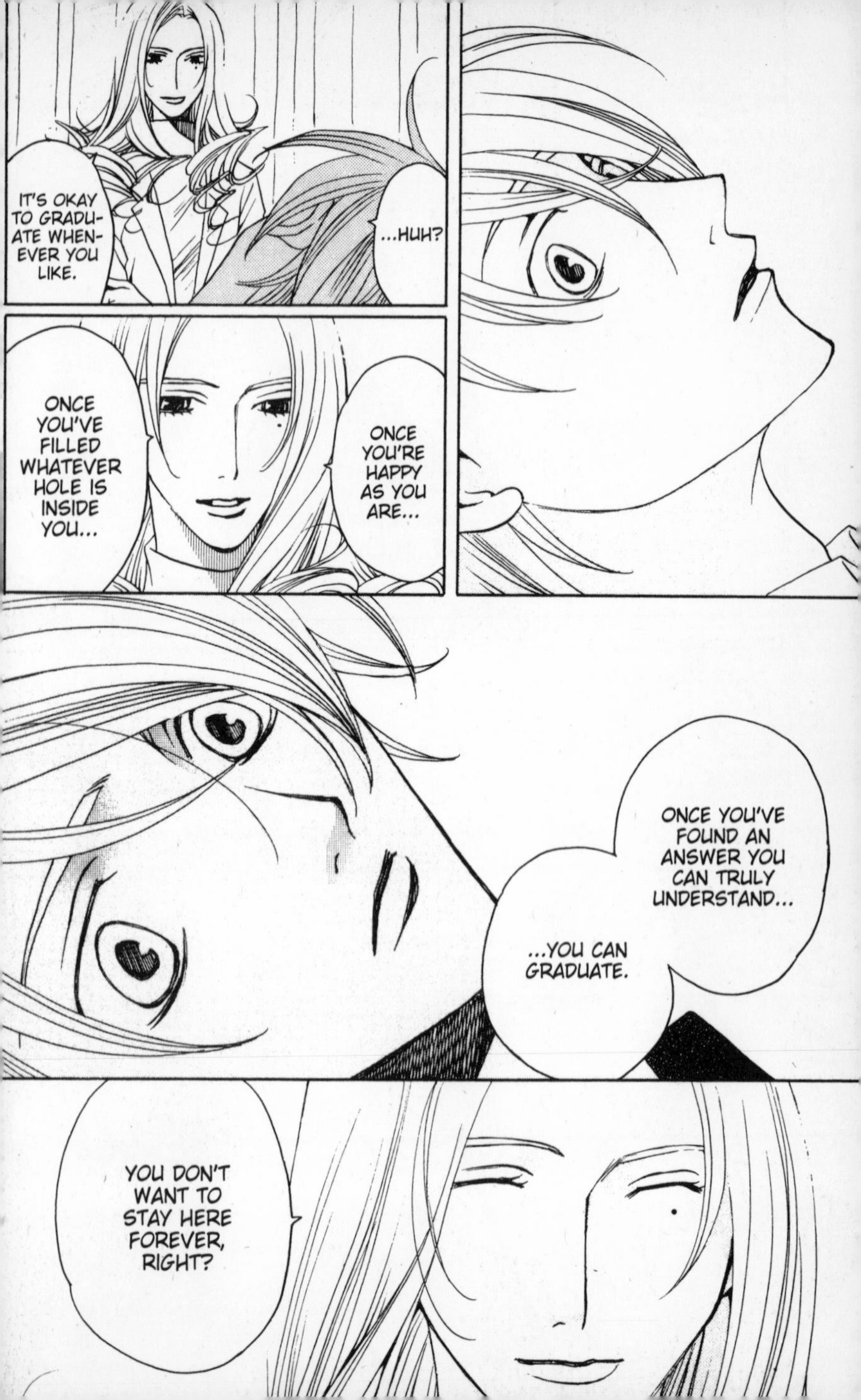
IT'S OKAY TO GRADU-ATE WHEN-EVER YOU LIKE.
...HUH?
ONCE YOU'RE HAPPY AS YOU ARE...
ONCE YOU'VE FILLED WHATEVER HOLE IS INSIDE YOU...
ONCE YOU'VE FOUND AN ANSWER YOU CAN TRULY UNDERSTAND...
...YOU CAN GRADUATE.
YOU DON'T WANT TO STAY HERE FOREVER, RIGHT?

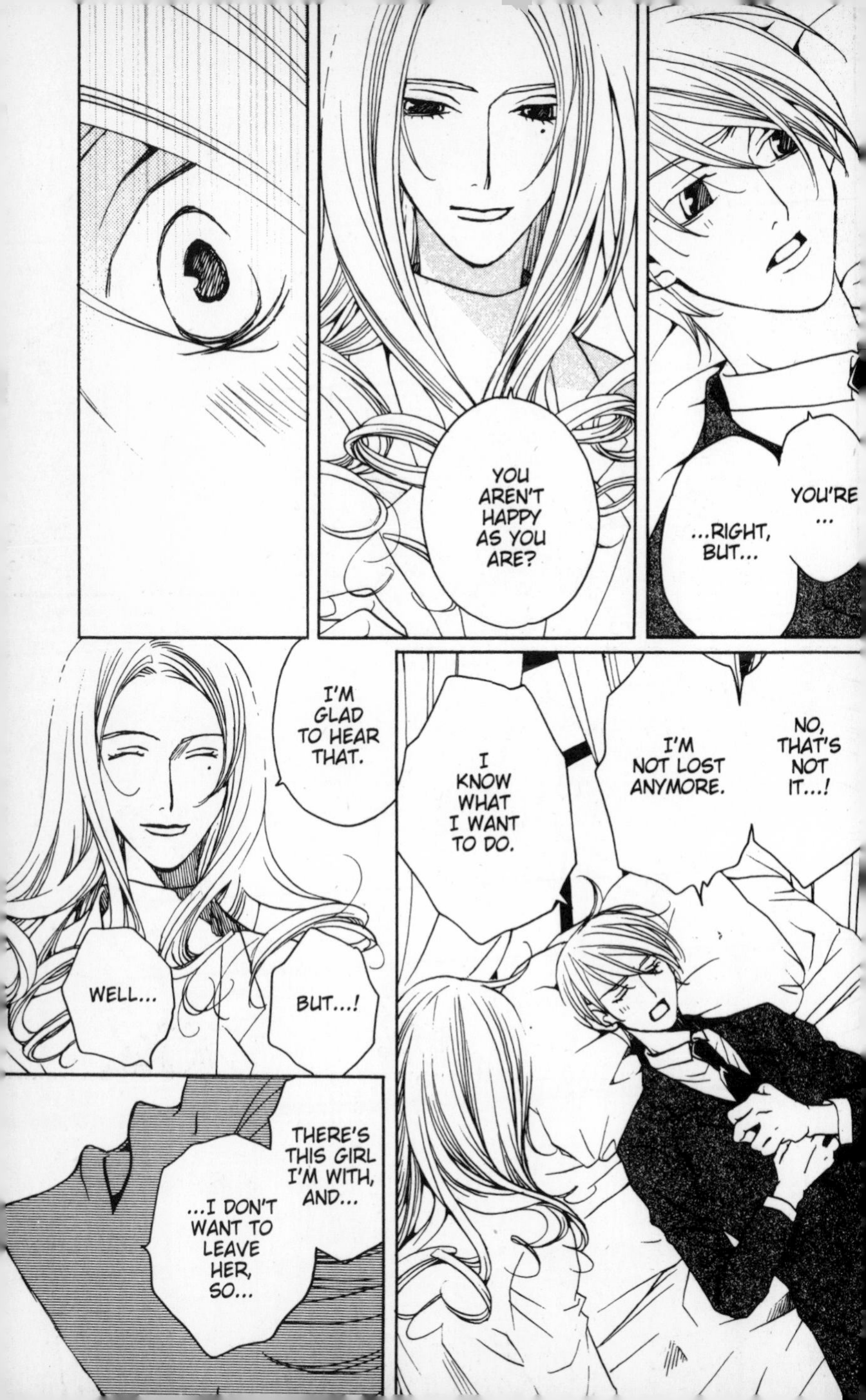
YOU'RE ...
...RIGHT, BUT...
YOU AREN'T HAPPY AS YOU ARE?
NO, THAT'S NOT IT...!
I'M NOT LOST ANYMORE.
I KNOW WHAT I WANT TO DO.
I'M GLAD TO HEAR THAT.
BUT...!
WELL...
THERE'S THIS GIRL I'M WITH, AND...
...I DON'T WANT TO LEAVE HER, SO...

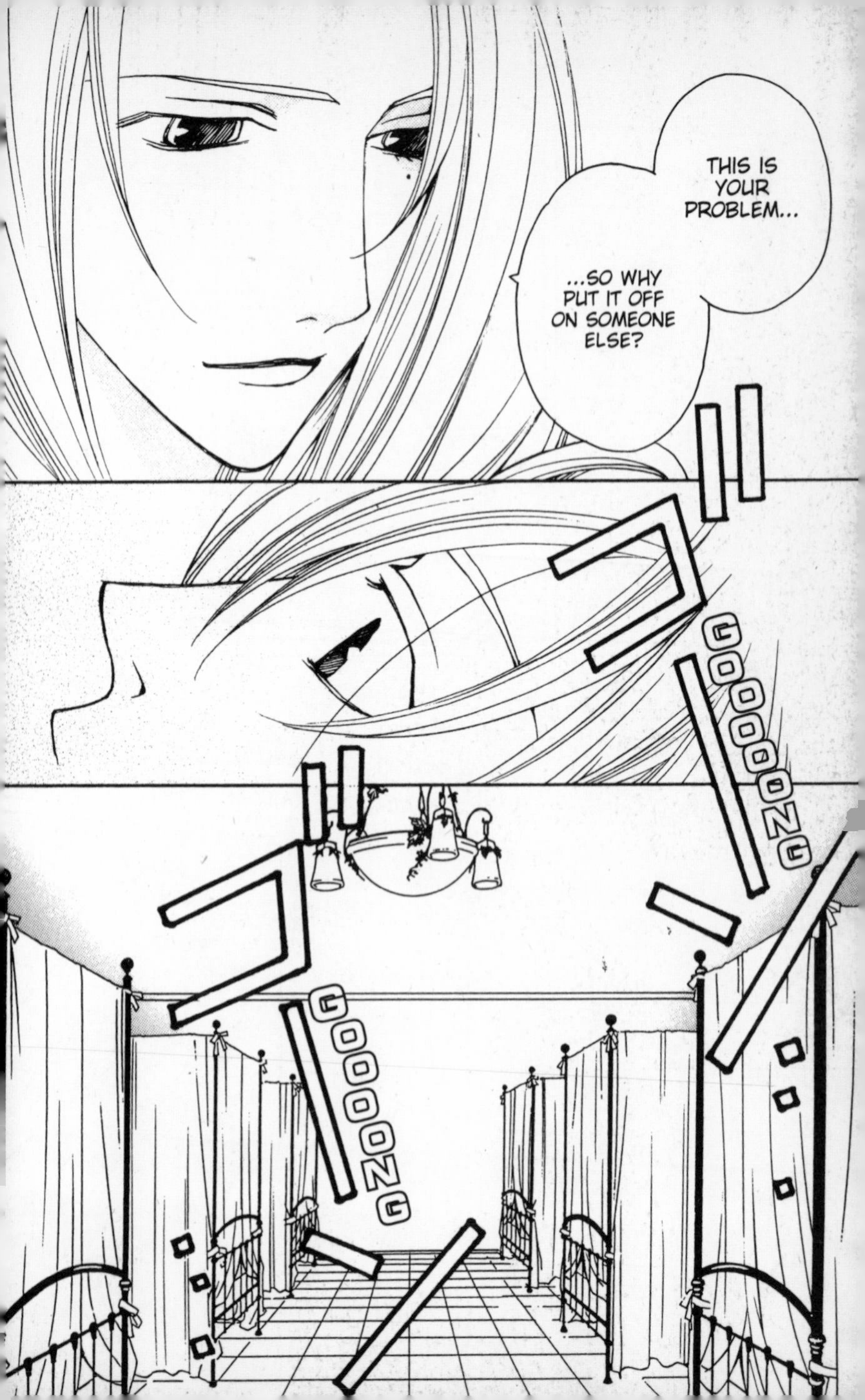
THIS IS YOUR PROBLEM...
...SO WHY PUT IT OFF ON SOMEONE ELSE?
GOOOOONG
GOOOOONG

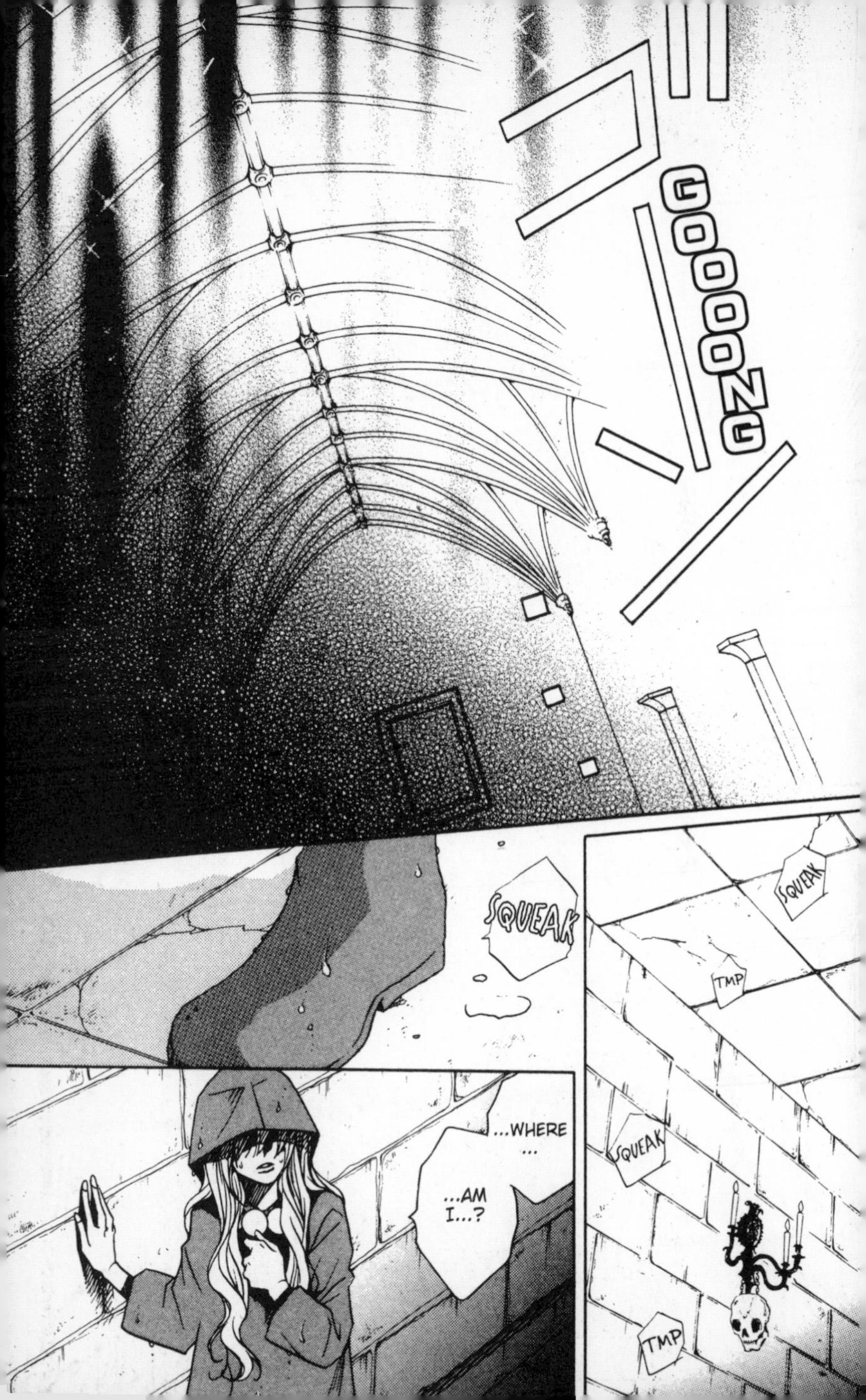
GOOOONG
SQUEAK
TMP
SQUEAK
TMP
SQUEAK
...WHERE
...
...AM
I...?

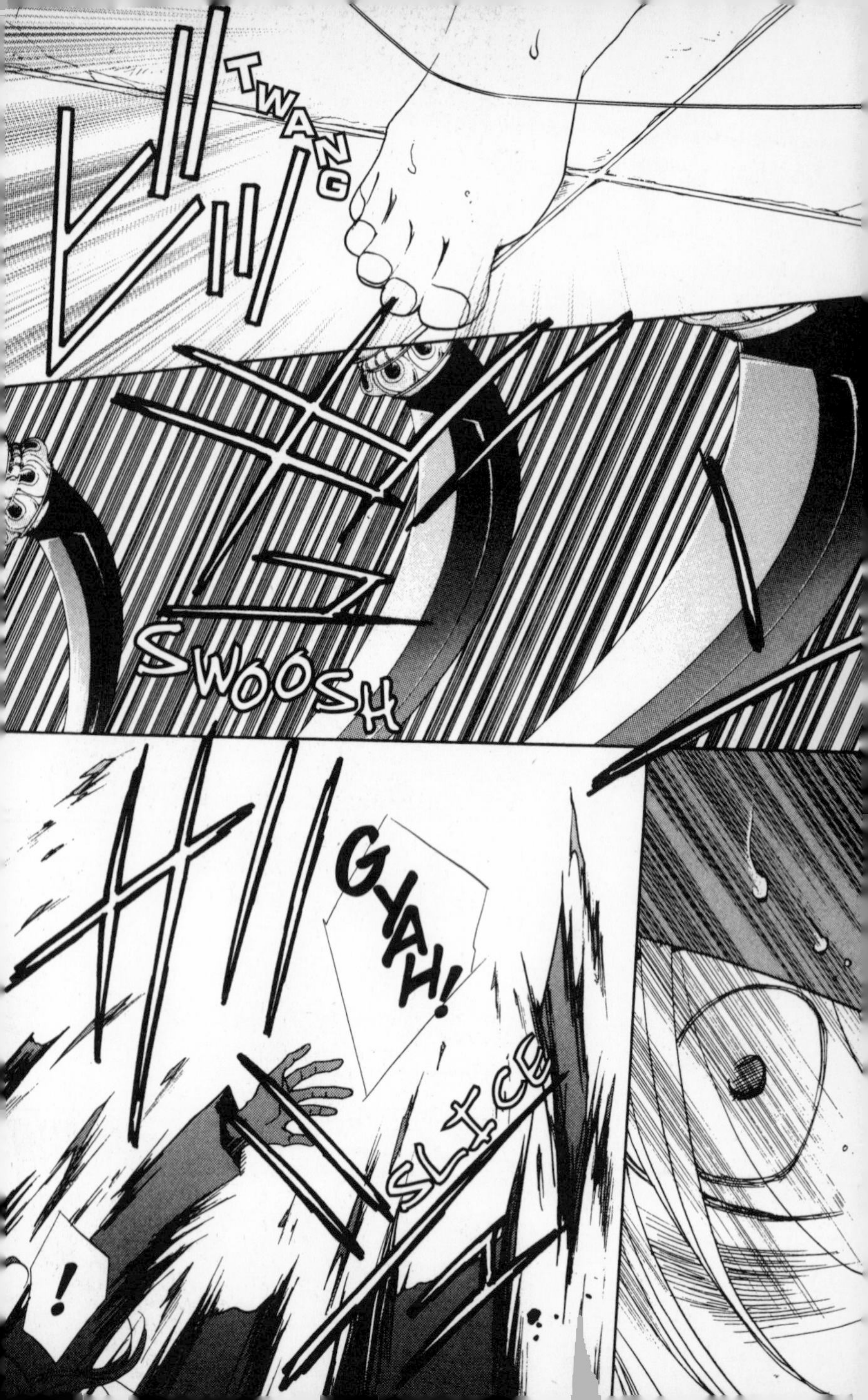
TWANG
SWOOSH
GAAH!
SLICE
!

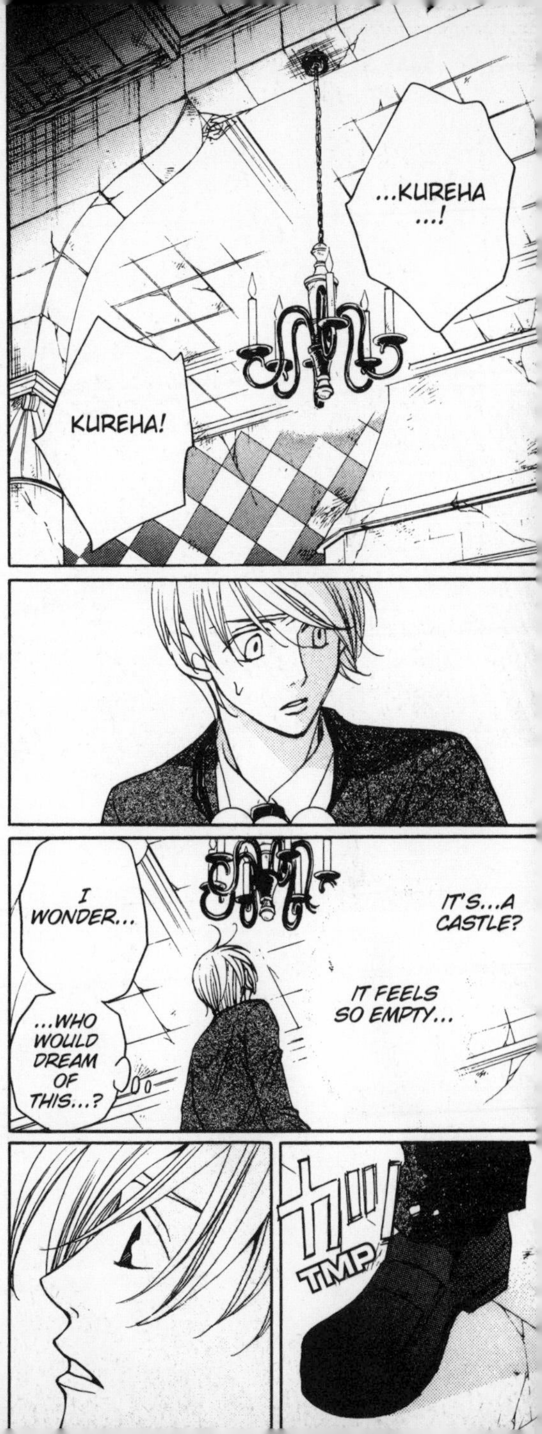
...KUREHA ...!
KUREHA!
IT'S...A CASTLE?
IT FEELS SO EMPTY...
I WONDER...
...WHO WOULD DREAM OF THIS...?
TMP

This is the blazer version of the girls' uniform I'd first planned.

I think it looks really good on Mashiro, but after thinking, "In his torso shots, it's hard to distinguish from the guys' uniform" and "Hmm, maybe it could fit the dark fantasy feeling more?" I changed the design.

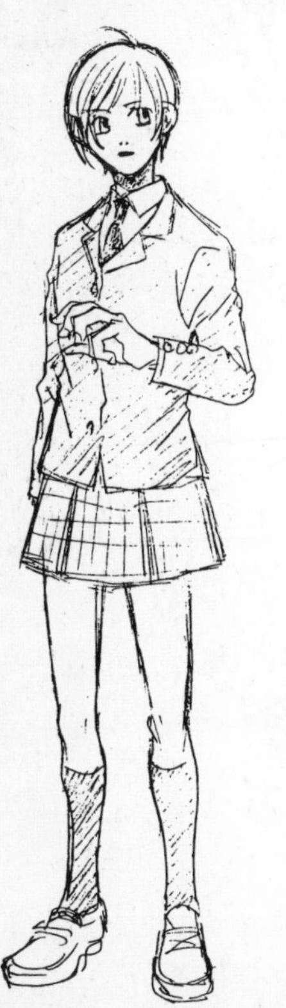

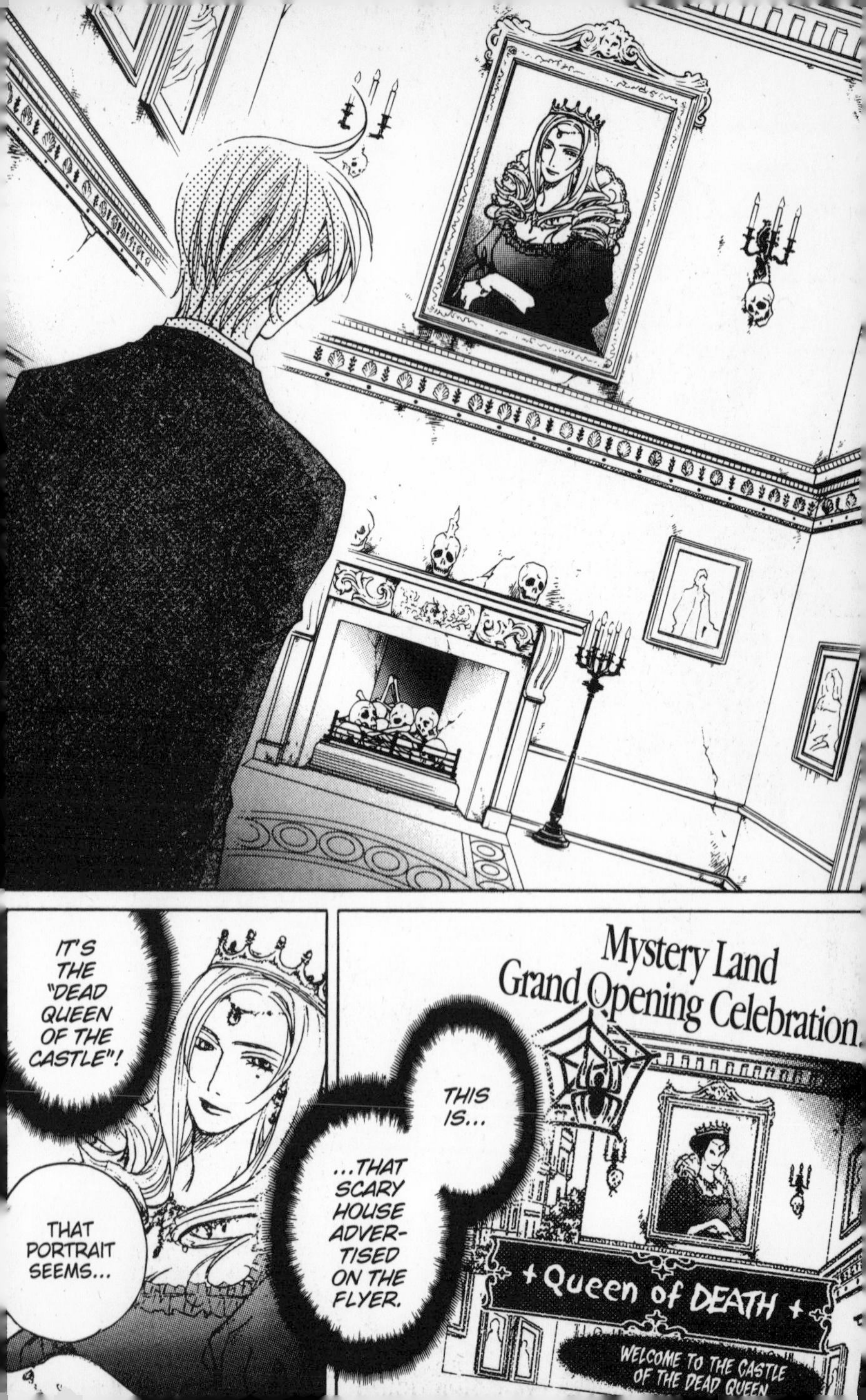
Mystery Land
Grand Opening Celebration
+ Queen of DEATH +
WELCOME TO THE CASTLE OF THE DEAD QUEEN
THIS IS...
...THAT SCARY HOUSE ADVER-TISED ON THE FLYER.
IT'S THE "DEAD QUEEN OF THE CASTLE"!
THAT PORTRAIT SEEMS...

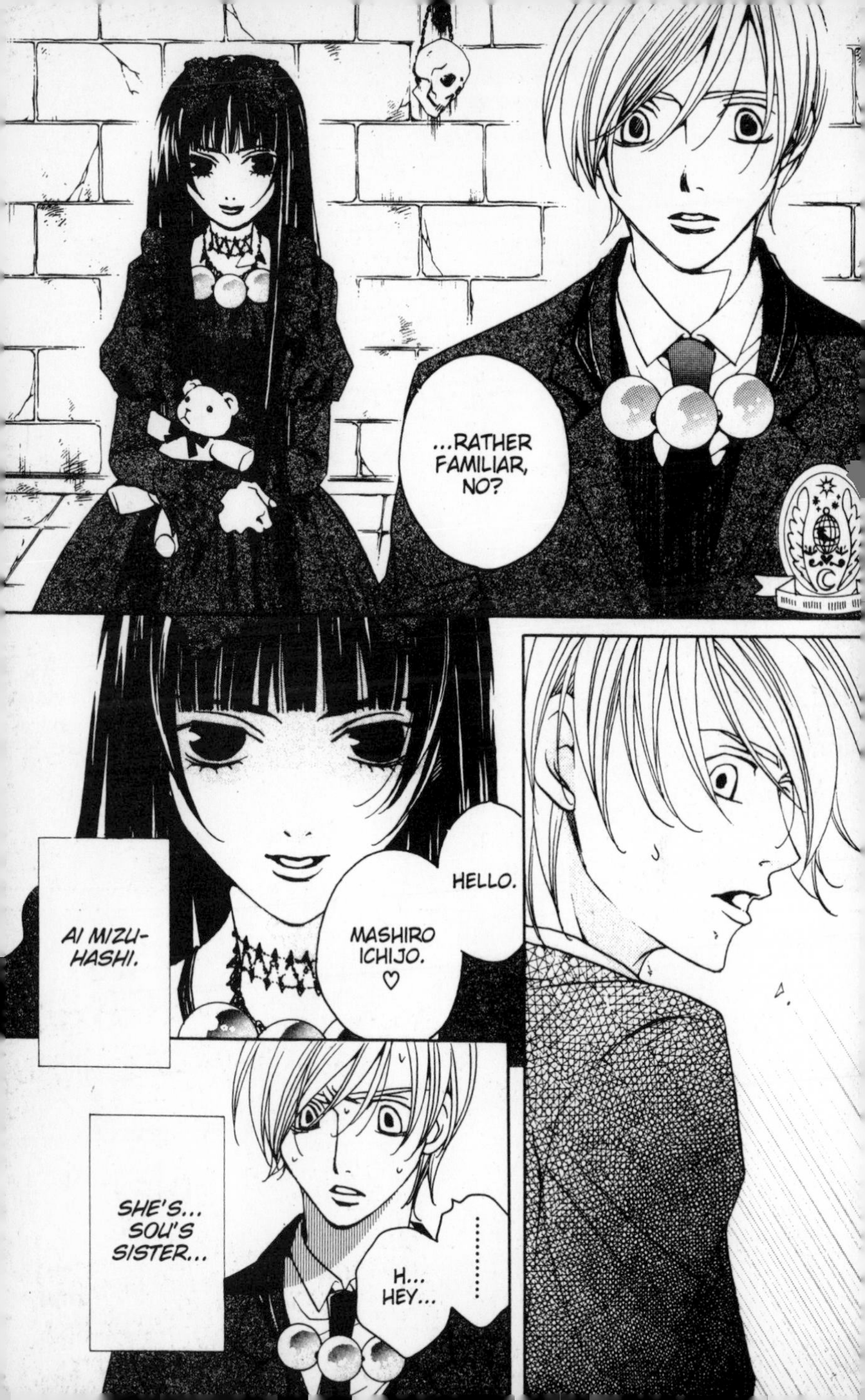

...RATHER FAMILIAR, NO?
HELLO.
MASHIRO ICHIJO. ♡
AI MIZU-HASHI.
......
H... HEY...
SHE'S... SOU'S SISTER...

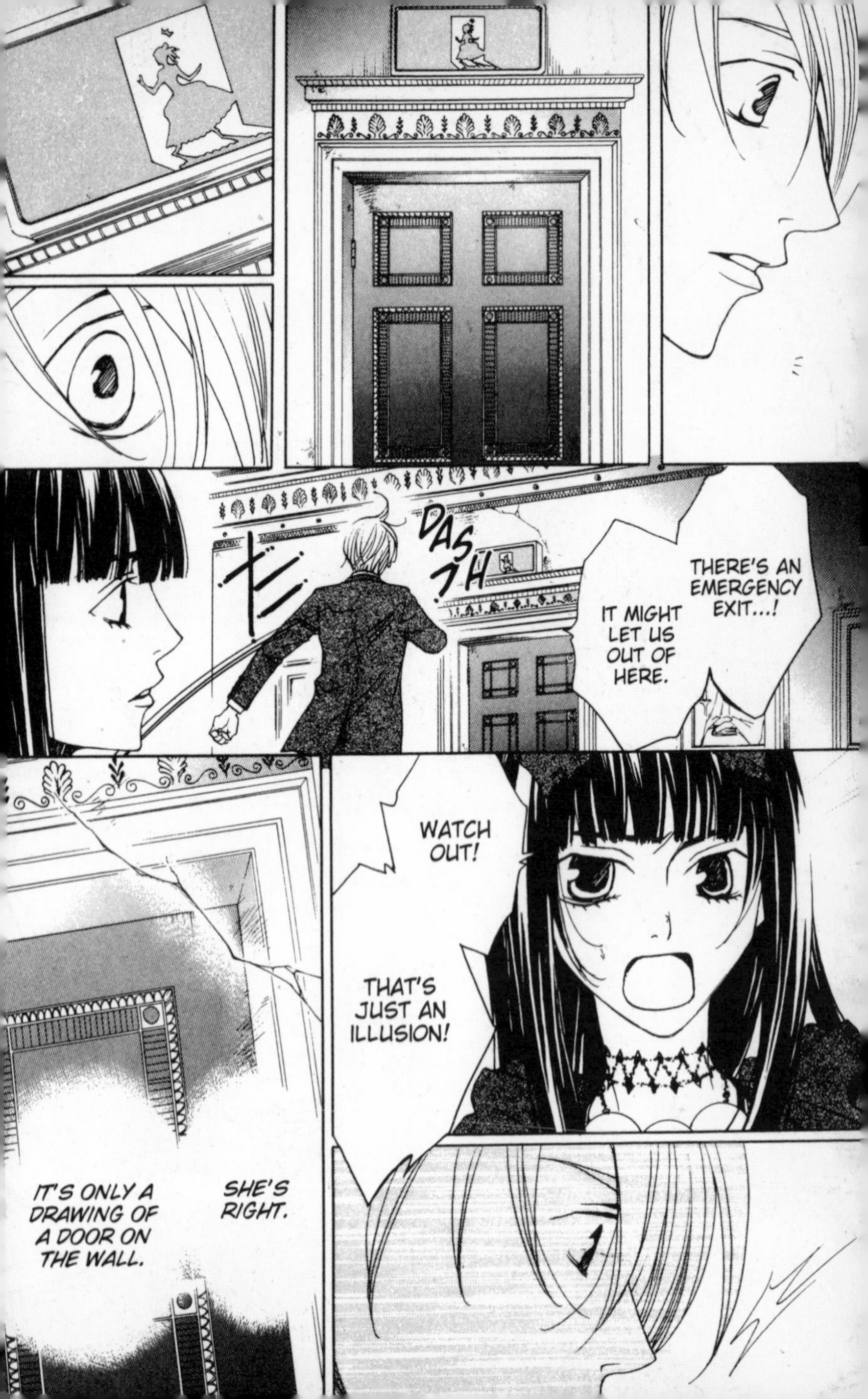
THERE'S AN EMERGENCY EXIT...!
IT MIGHT LET US OUT OF HERE.
DASH
WATCH OUT!
THAT'S JUST AN ILLUSION!
SHE'S RIGHT.
IT'S ONLY A DRAWING OF A DOOR ON THE WALL.

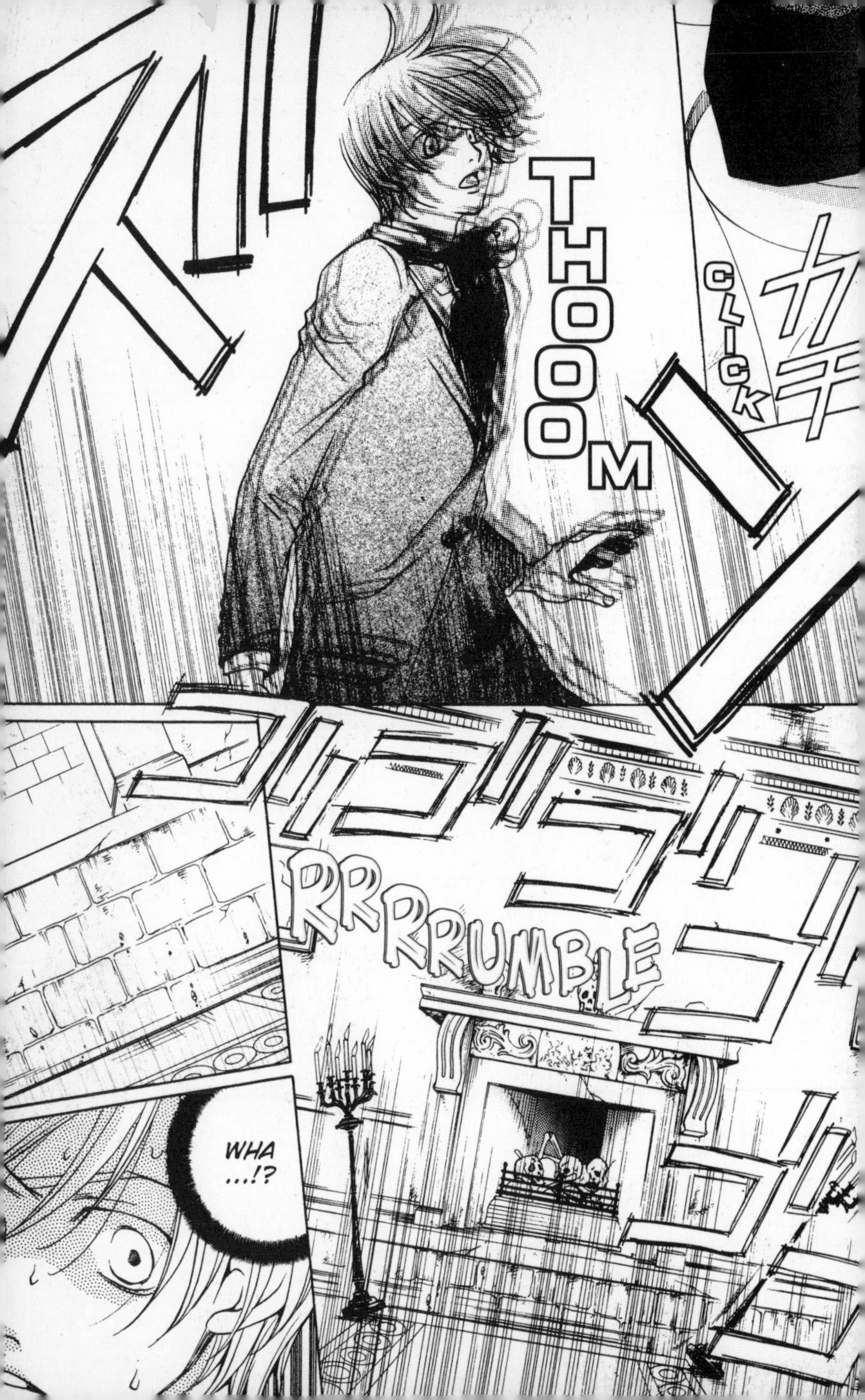
カチ
CLICK
THOOOM
RRRRUMBLE
WHA ...!?

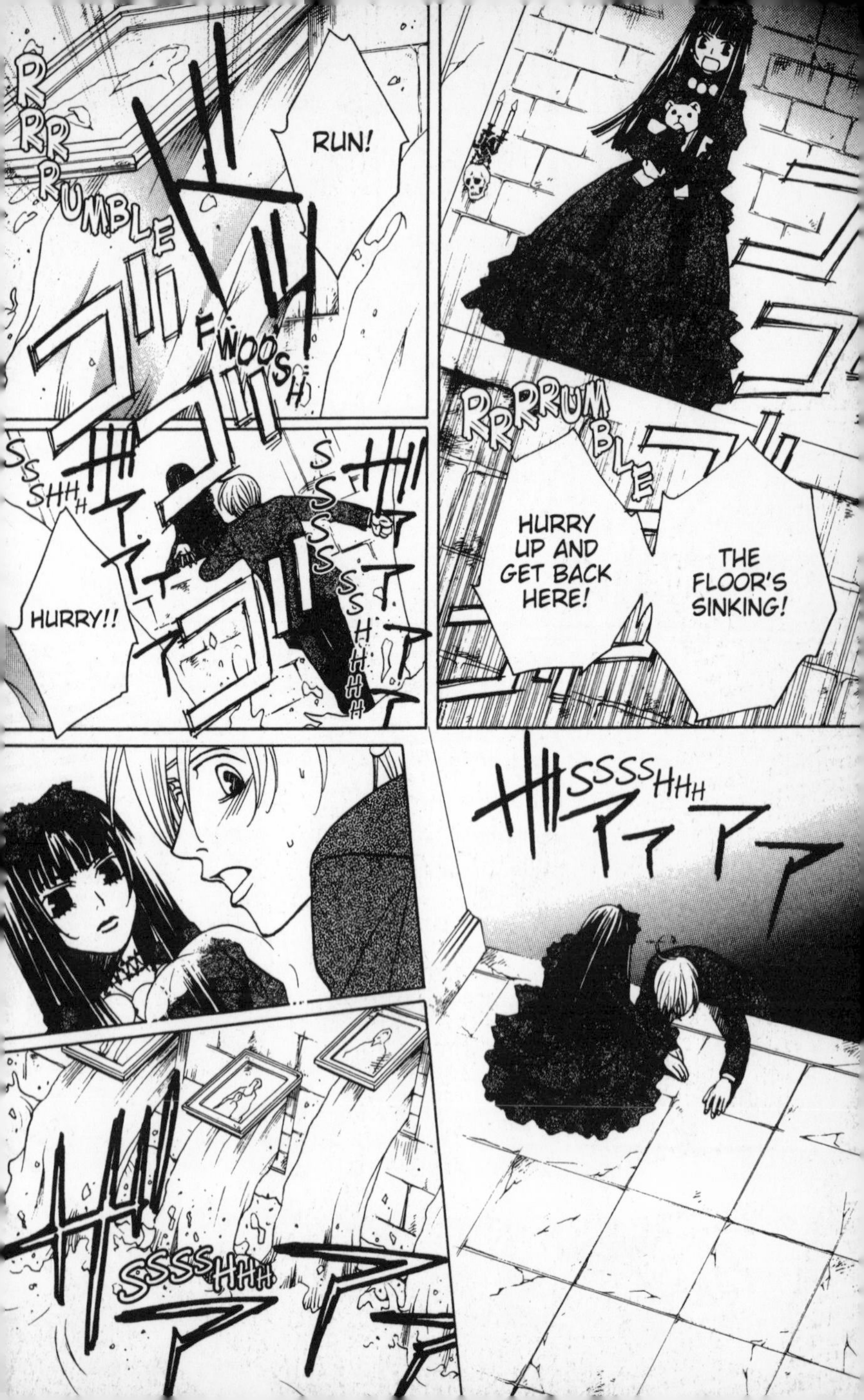
RRRRRUMBLE
THE FLOOR'S SINKING!
HURRY UP AND GET BACK HERE!
RUN!
RRRRUMBLE
FWOOSH
SSSSSSHHHHH
SSSHHH
HURRY!!
SSSSHHH
SSSSHHH

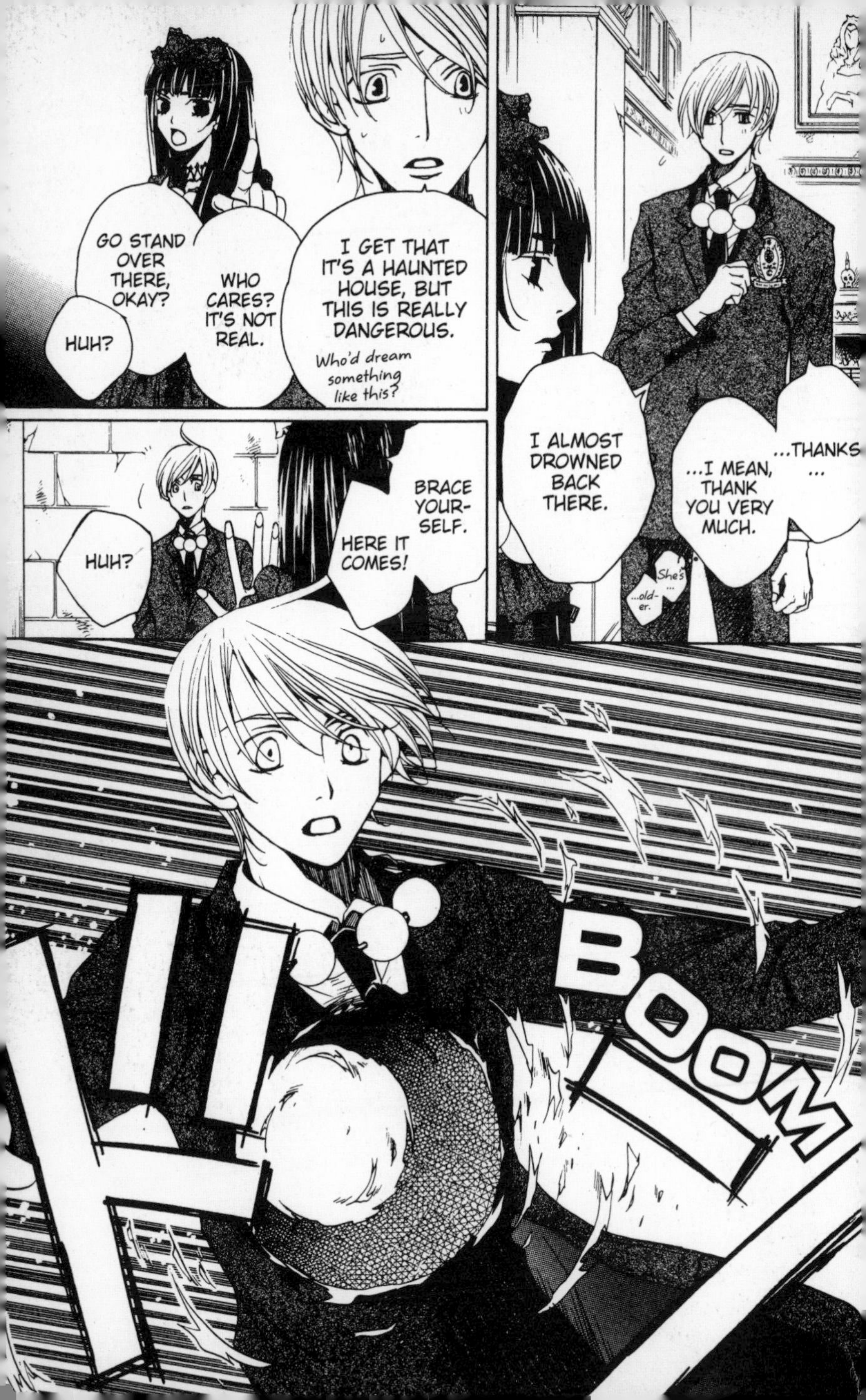
...THANKS...
...I MEAN, THANK YOU VERY MUCH.
I ALMOST DROWNED BACK THERE.
She's... ...older.
I GET THAT IT'S A HAUNTED HOUSE, BUT THIS IS REALLY DANGEROUS.
Who'd dream something like this?
WHO CARES? IT'S NOT REAL.
GO STAND OVER THERE, OKAY?
HUH?
BRACE YOURSELF.
HERE IT COMES!
HUH?
BOOM

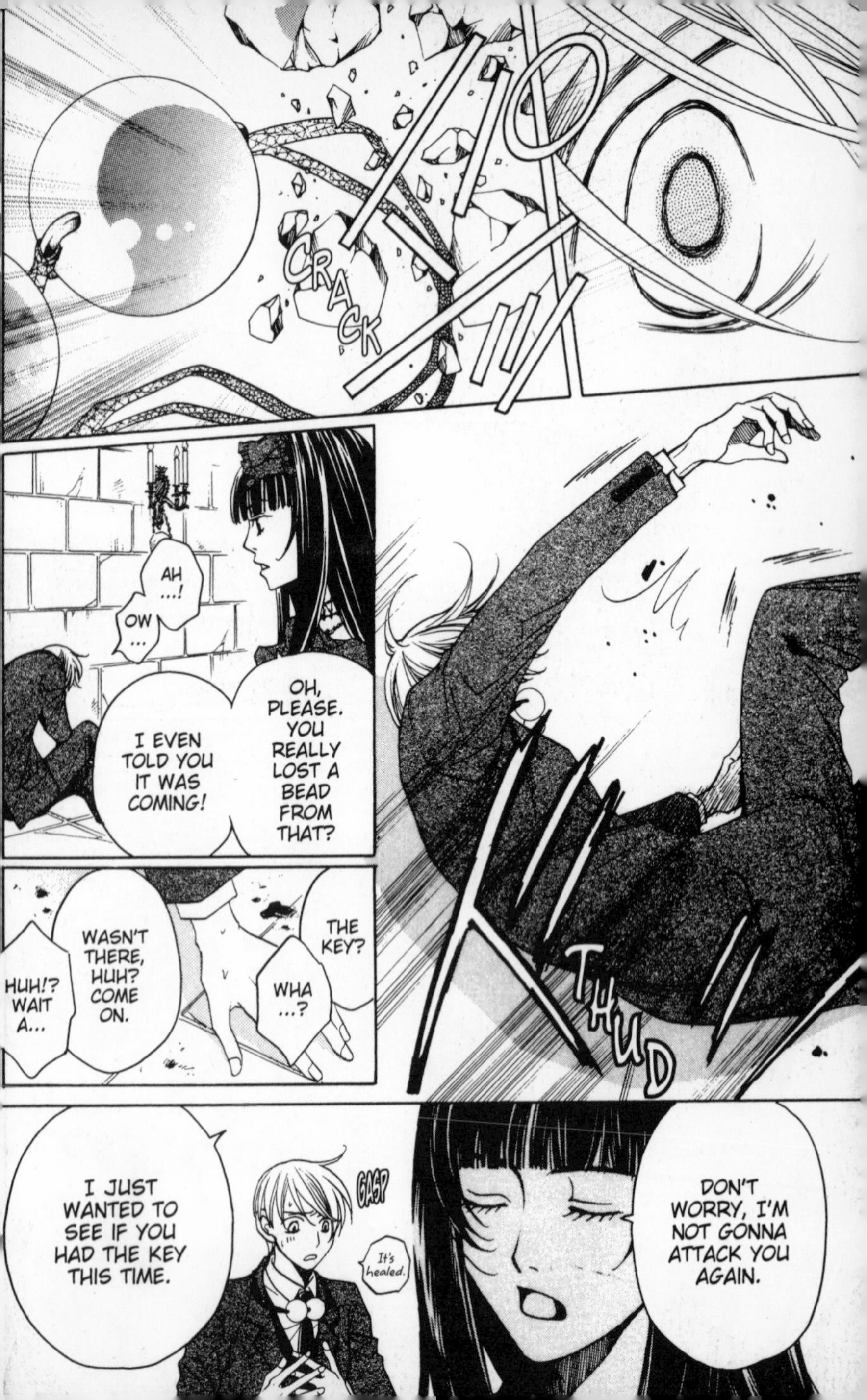
CRACK
THUD
AH ...!
OW ...
OH, PLEASE. YOU REALLY LOST A BEAD FROM THAT?
I EVEN TOLD YOU IT WAS COMING!
THE KEY?
WHA ...?
WASN'T THERE, HUH? COME ON.
HUH!? WAIT A...
DON'T WORRY, I'M NOT GONNA ATTACK YOU AGAIN.
GASP
It's healed.
I JUST WANTED TO SEE IF YOU HAD THE KEY THIS TIME.

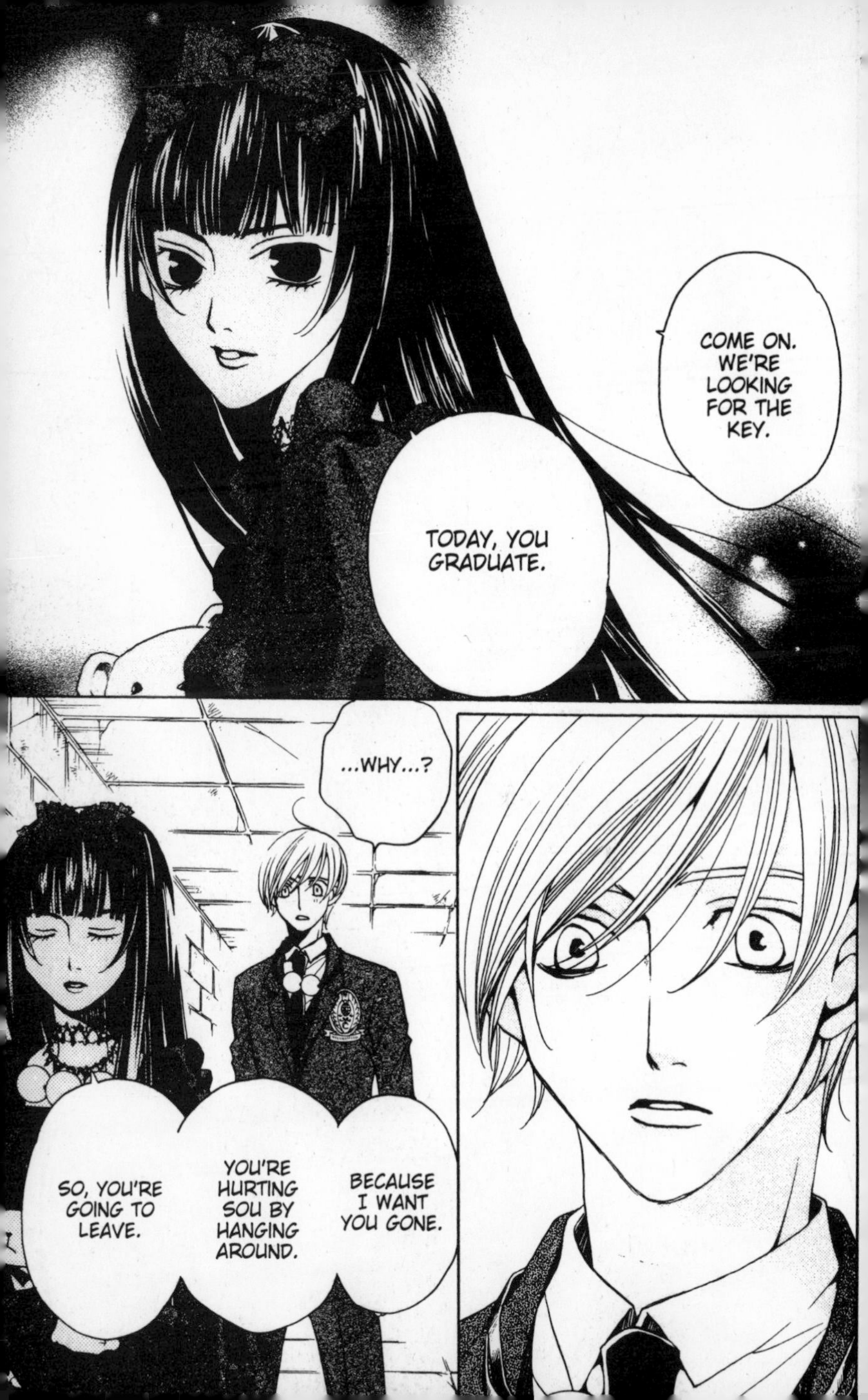
COME ON. WE'RE LOOKING FOR THE KEY.
TODAY, YOU GRADUATE.
...WHY...?
BECAUSE I WANT YOU GONE.
YOU'RE HURTING SOU BY HANGING AROUND.
SO, YOU'RE GOING TO LEAVE.

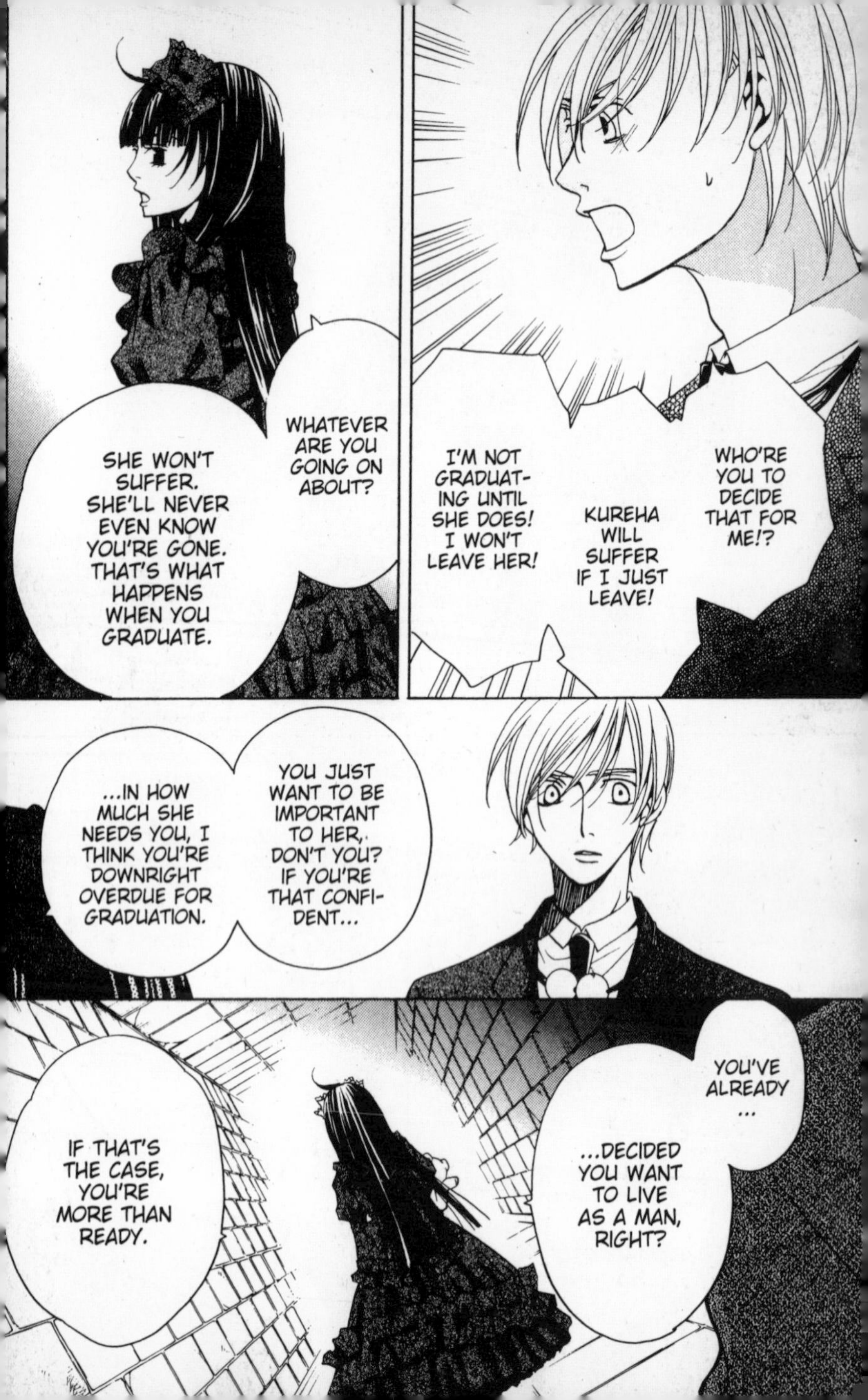
WHO'RE YOU TO DECIDE THAT FOR ME!?
KUREHA WILL SUFFER IF I JUST LEAVE!
I'M NOT GRADUAT-ING UNTIL SHE DOES! I WON'T LEAVE HER!
WHATEVER ARE YOU GOING ON ABOUT?
SHE WON'T SUFFER. SHE'LL NEVER EVEN KNOW YOU'RE GONE. THAT'S WHAT HAPPENS WHEN YOU GRADUATE.
YOU JUST WANT TO BE IMPORTANT TO HER, DON'T YOU? IF YOU'RE THAT CONFI-DENT...
...IN HOW MUCH SHE NEEDS YOU, I THINK YOU'RE DOWNRIGHT OVERDUE FOR GRADUATION.
YOU'VE ALREADY ...
...DECIDED YOU WANT TO LIVE AS A MAN, RIGHT?
IF THAT'S THE CASE, YOU'RE MORE THAN READY.

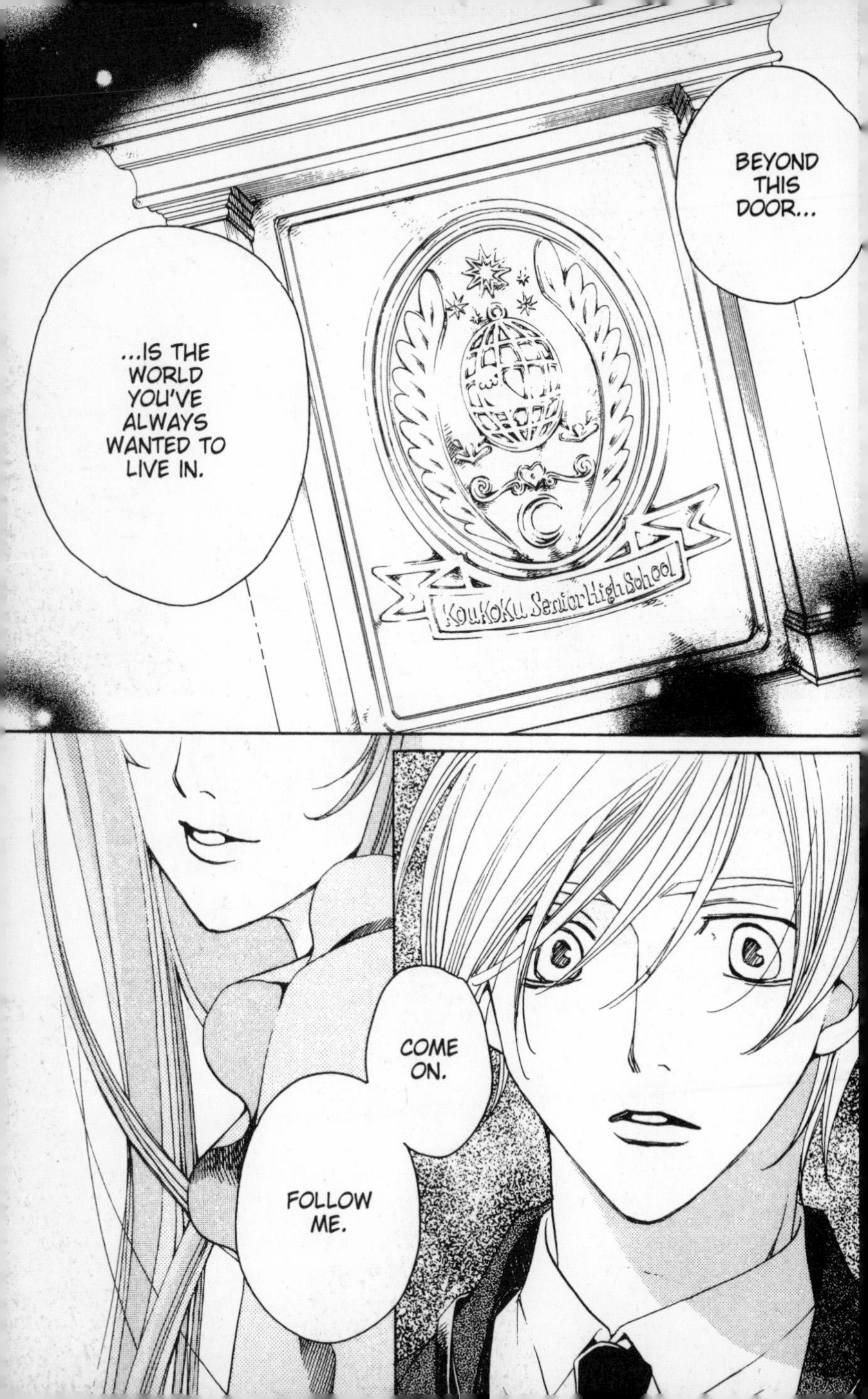
BEYOND THIS DOOR...
...IS THE WORLD YOU'VE ALWAYS WANTED TO LIVE IN.
KouKoKu Senior High School
COME ON.
FOLLOW ME.

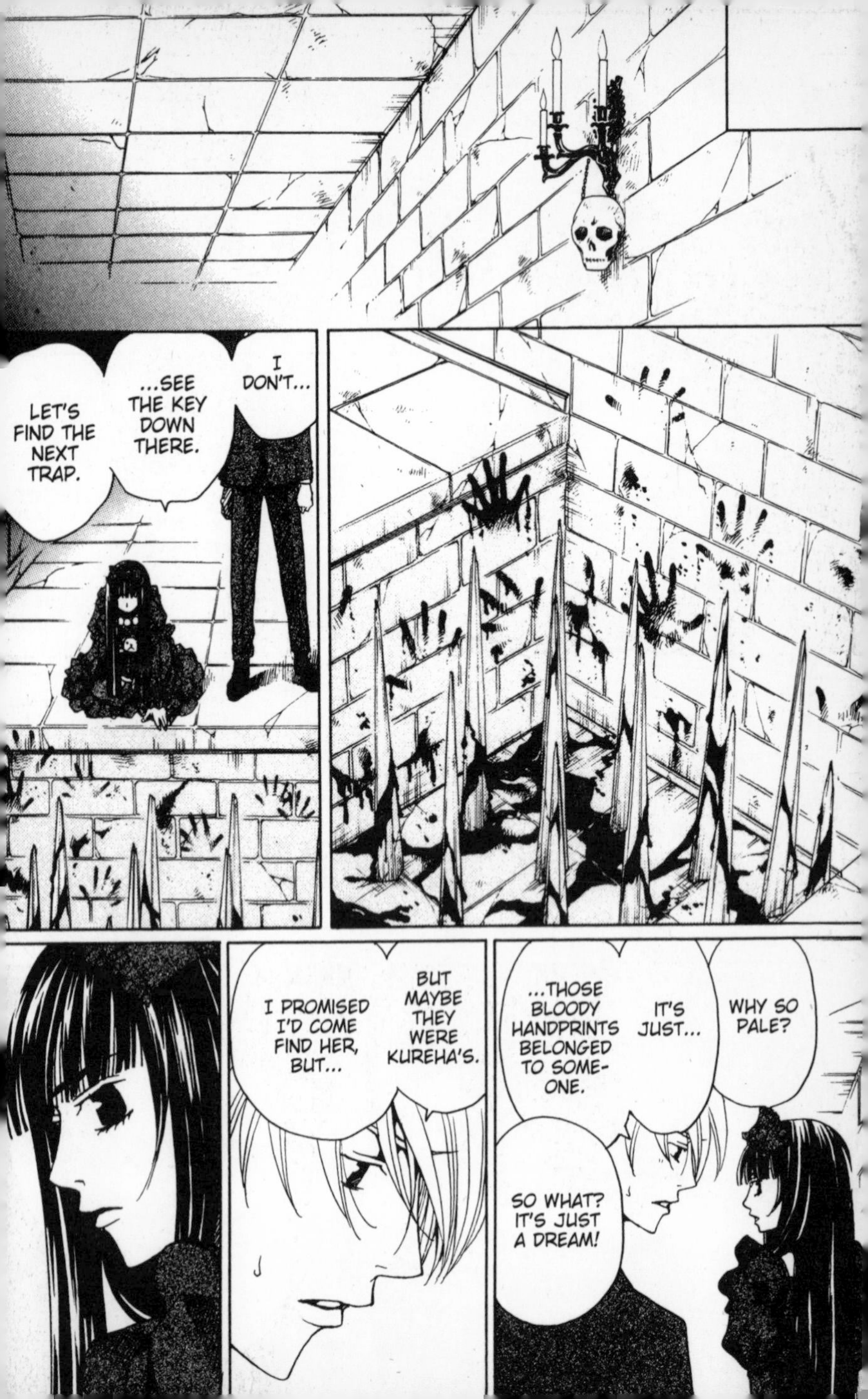
I DON'T...
...SEE THE KEY DOWN THERE.
LET'S FIND THE NEXT TRAP.
WHY SO PALE?
IT'S JUST...
...THOSE BLOODY HANDPRINTS BELONGED TO SOME-ONE.
SO WHAT? IT'S JUST A DREAM!
BUT MAYBE THEY WERE KUREHA'S.
I PROMISED I'D COME FIND HER, BUT...

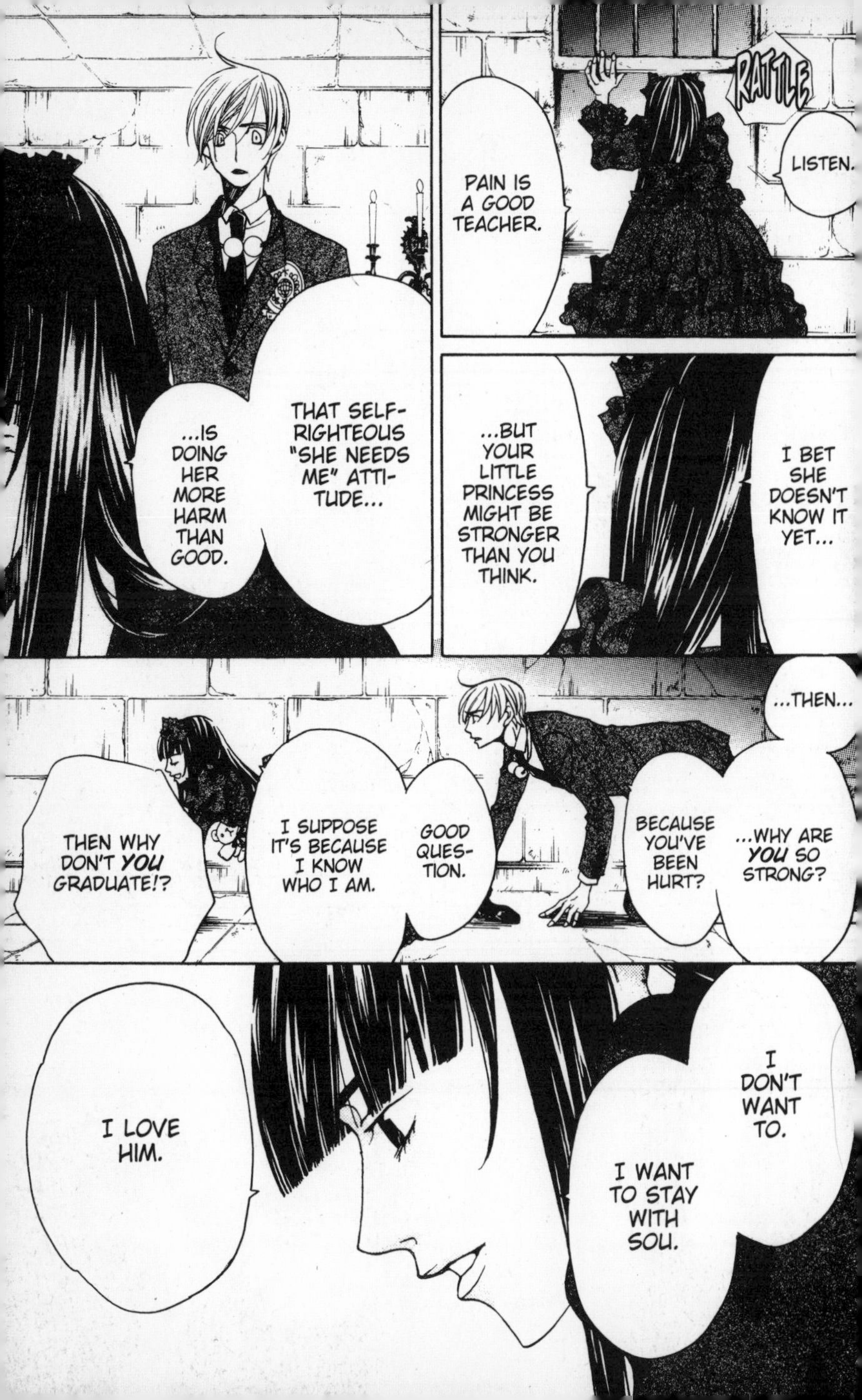
RATTLE
LISTEN.
PAIN IS A GOOD TEACHER.
I BET SHE DOESN'T KNOW IT YET...
...BUT YOUR LITTLE PRINCESS MIGHT BE STRONGER THAN YOU THINK.
THAT SELF-RIGHTEOUS "SHE NEEDS ME" ATTITUDE...
...IS DOING HER MORE HARM THAN GOOD.
...THEN...
...WHY ARE *YOU* SO STRONG?
BECAUSE YOU'VE BEEN HURT?
GOOD QUESTION.
I SUPPOSE IT'S BECAUSE I KNOW WHO I AM.
THEN WHY DON'T *YOU* GRADUATE!?
I DON'T WANT TO.
I WANT TO STAY WITH SOU.
I LOVE HIM.

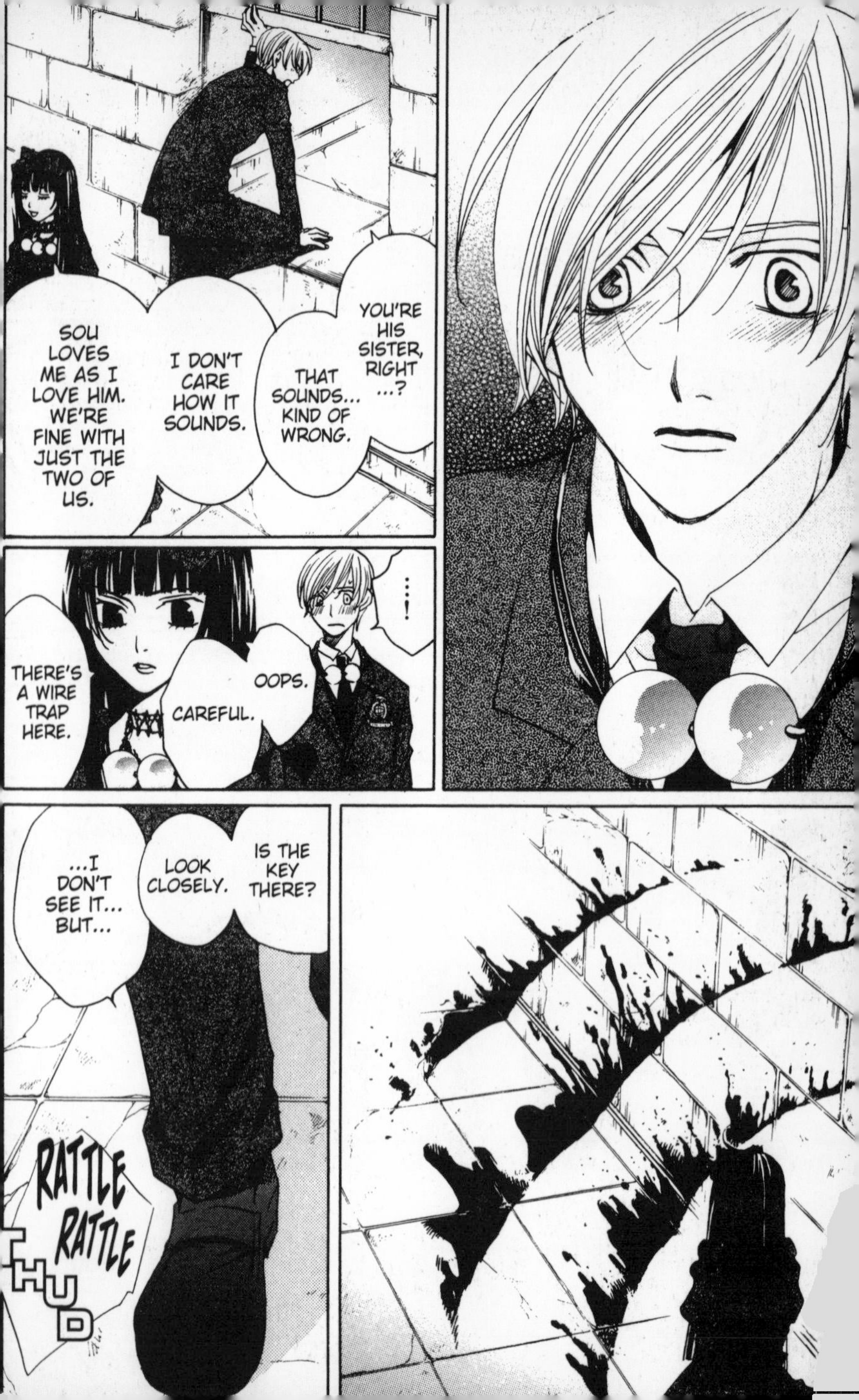
YOU'RE HIS SISTER, RIGHT ...?
THAT SOUNDS... KIND OF WRONG.
I DON'T CARE HOW IT SOUNDS.
SOU LOVES ME AS I LOVE HIM. WE'RE FINE WITH JUST THE TWO OF US.
...!
OOPS.
CAREFUL.
THERE'S A WIRE TRAP HERE.
IS THE KEY THERE?
LOOK CLOSELY.
...I DON'T SEE IT... BUT...
RATTLE RATTLE
THUD

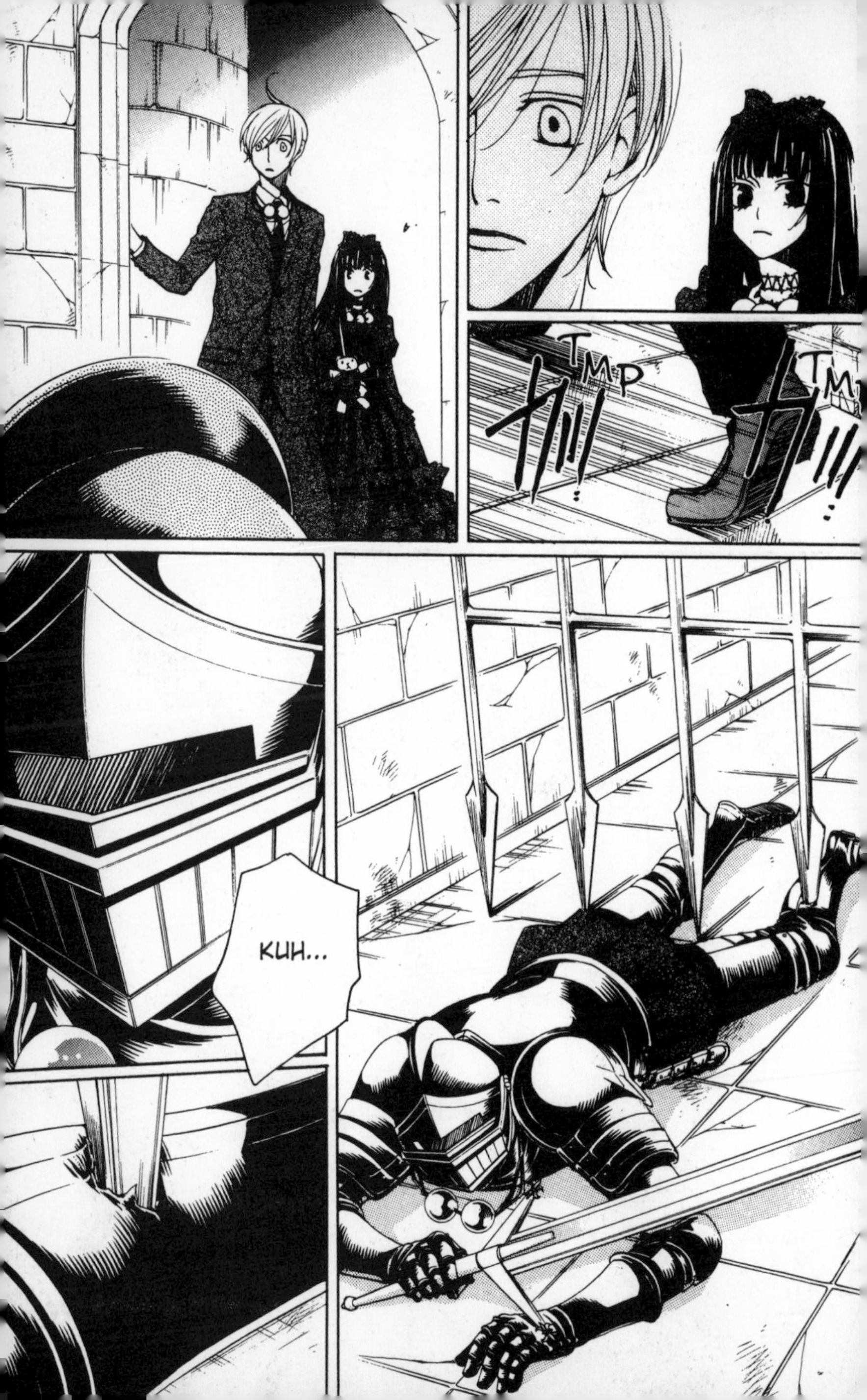
TMP
TMP
KUH...

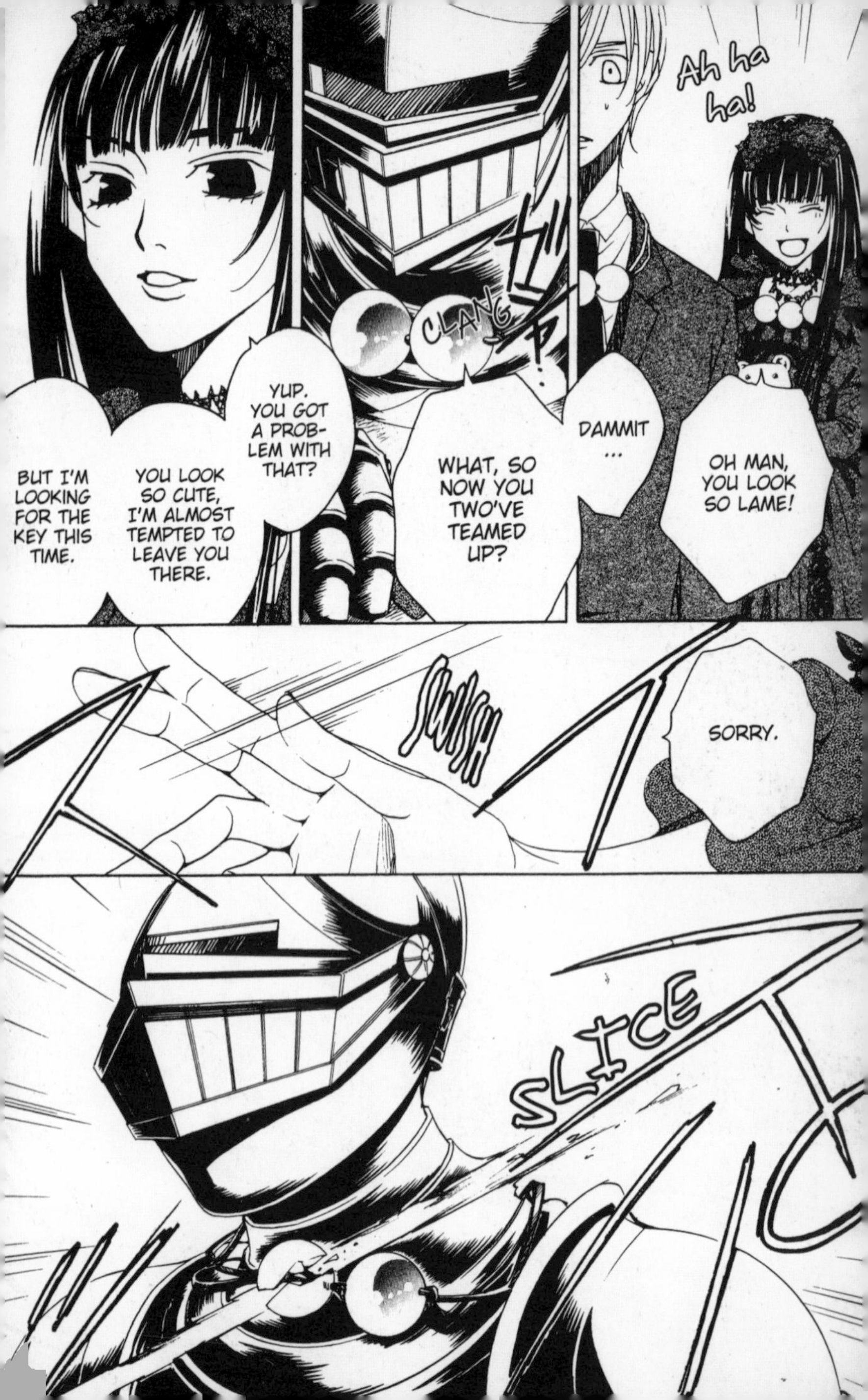
Ah ha ha!
OH MAN, YOU LOOK SO LAME!
DAMMIT ...
CLANG
WHAT, SO NOW YOU TWO'VE TEAMED UP?
YUP. YOU GOT A PROB-LEM WITH THAT?
YOU LOOK SO CUTE, I'M ALMOST TEMPTED TO LEAVE YOU THERE.
BUT I'M LOOKING FOR THE KEY THIS TIME.
SORRY.
SWISH
SLICE

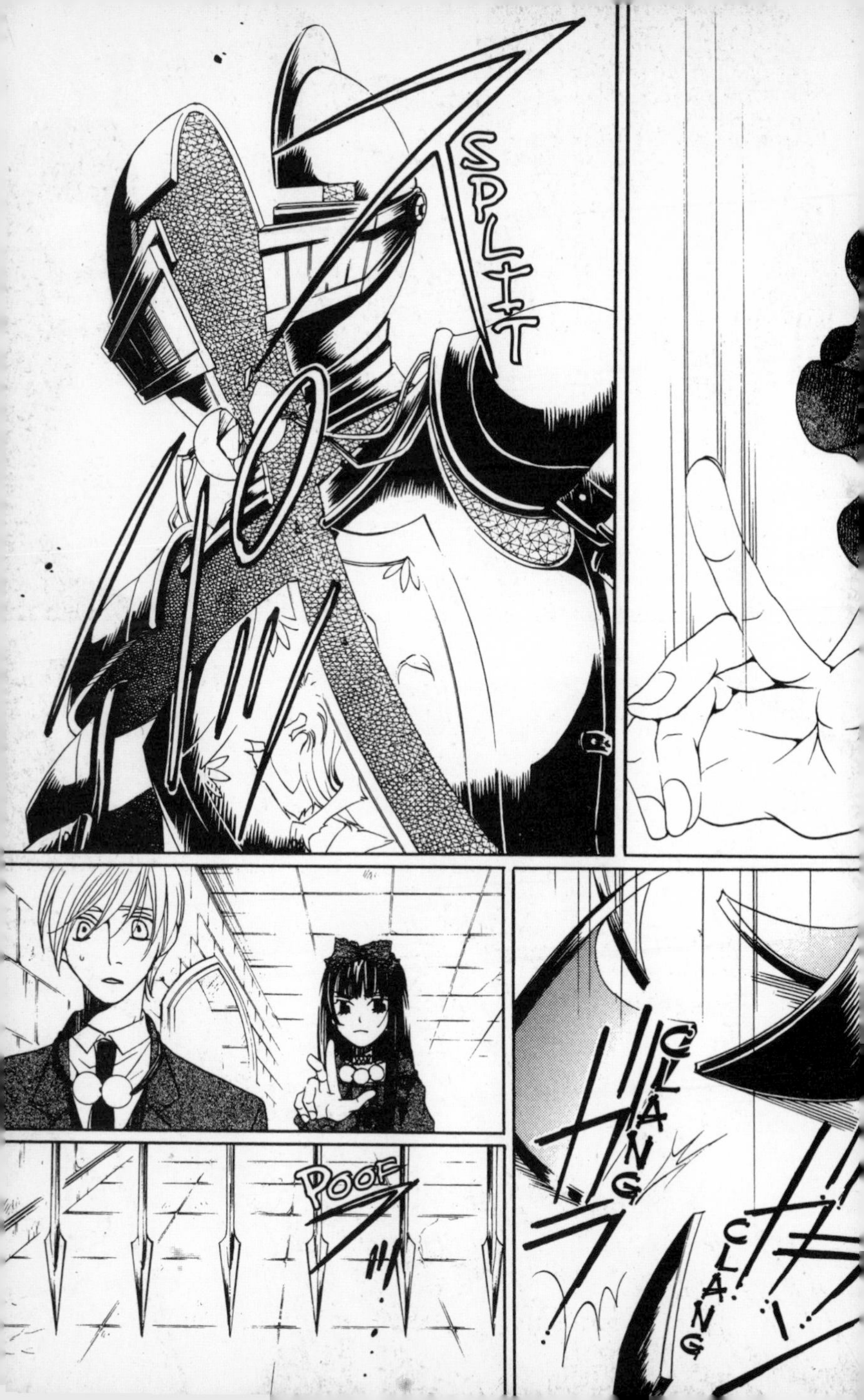
SPLIT
CLANG
CLANG
POOF

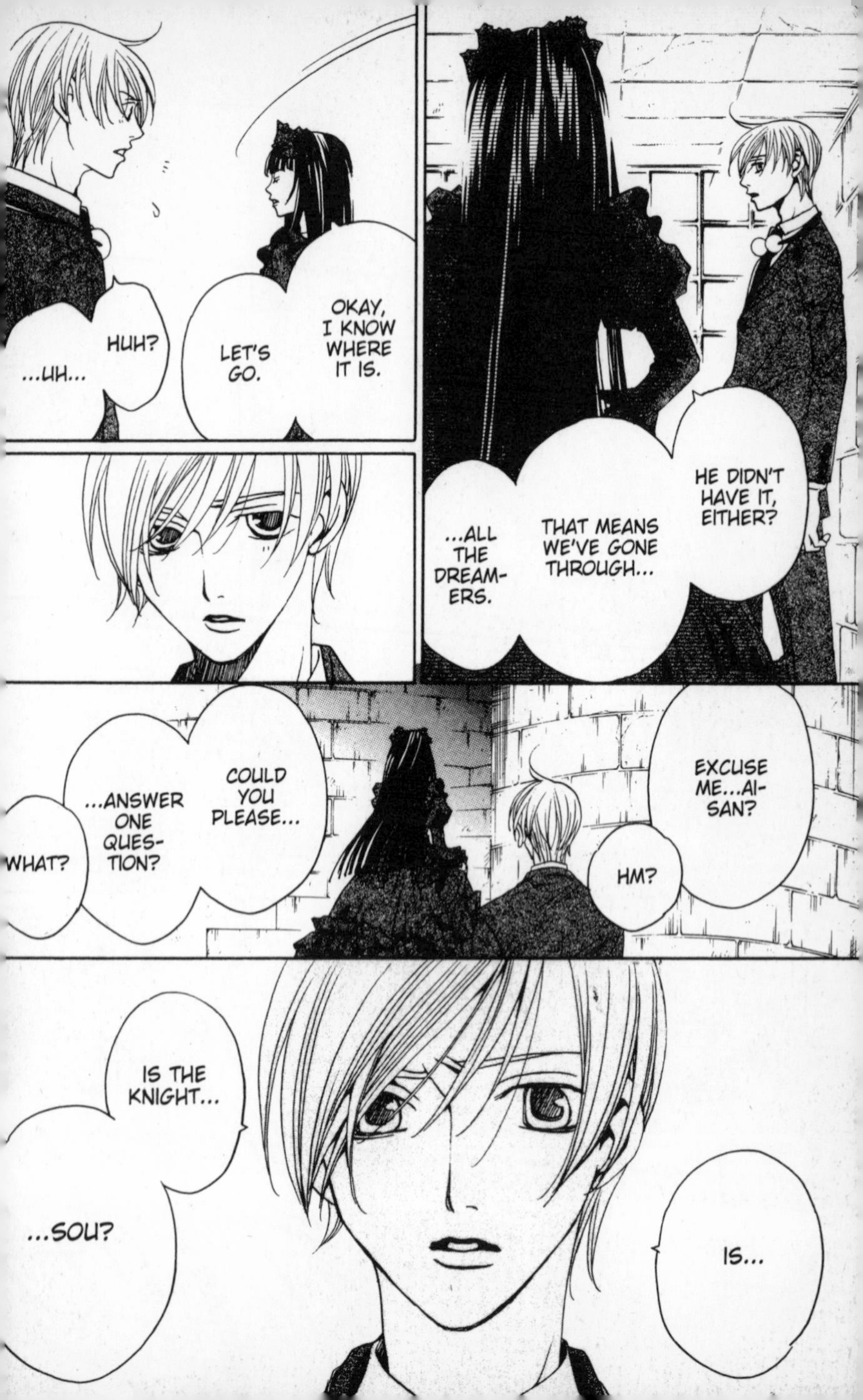
HE DIDN'T HAVE IT, EITHER?
THAT MEANS WE'VE GONE THROUGH...
...ALL THE DREAM-ERS.
OKAY, I KNOW WHERE IT IS.
LET'S GO.
HUH?
...UH...
EXCUSE ME...AI-SAN?
HM?
COULD YOU PLEASE...
...ANSWER ONE QUES-TION?
WHAT?
IS...
IS THE KNIGHT...
...SOU?

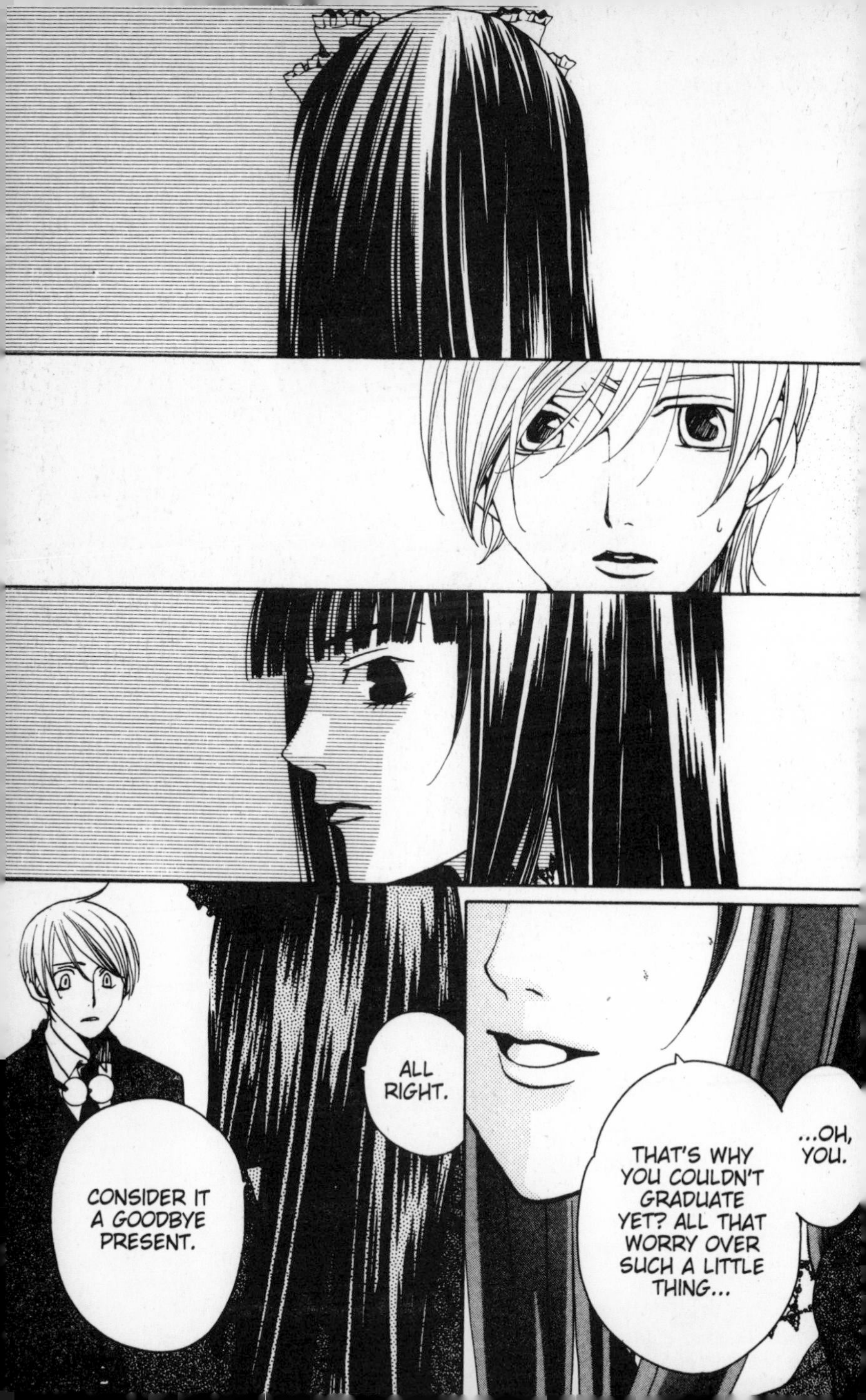
...OH, YOU.
THAT'S WHY YOU COULDN'T GRADUATE YET? ALL THAT WORRY OVER SUCH A LITTLE THING...
ALL RIGHT.
CONSIDER IT A GOODBYE PRESENT.

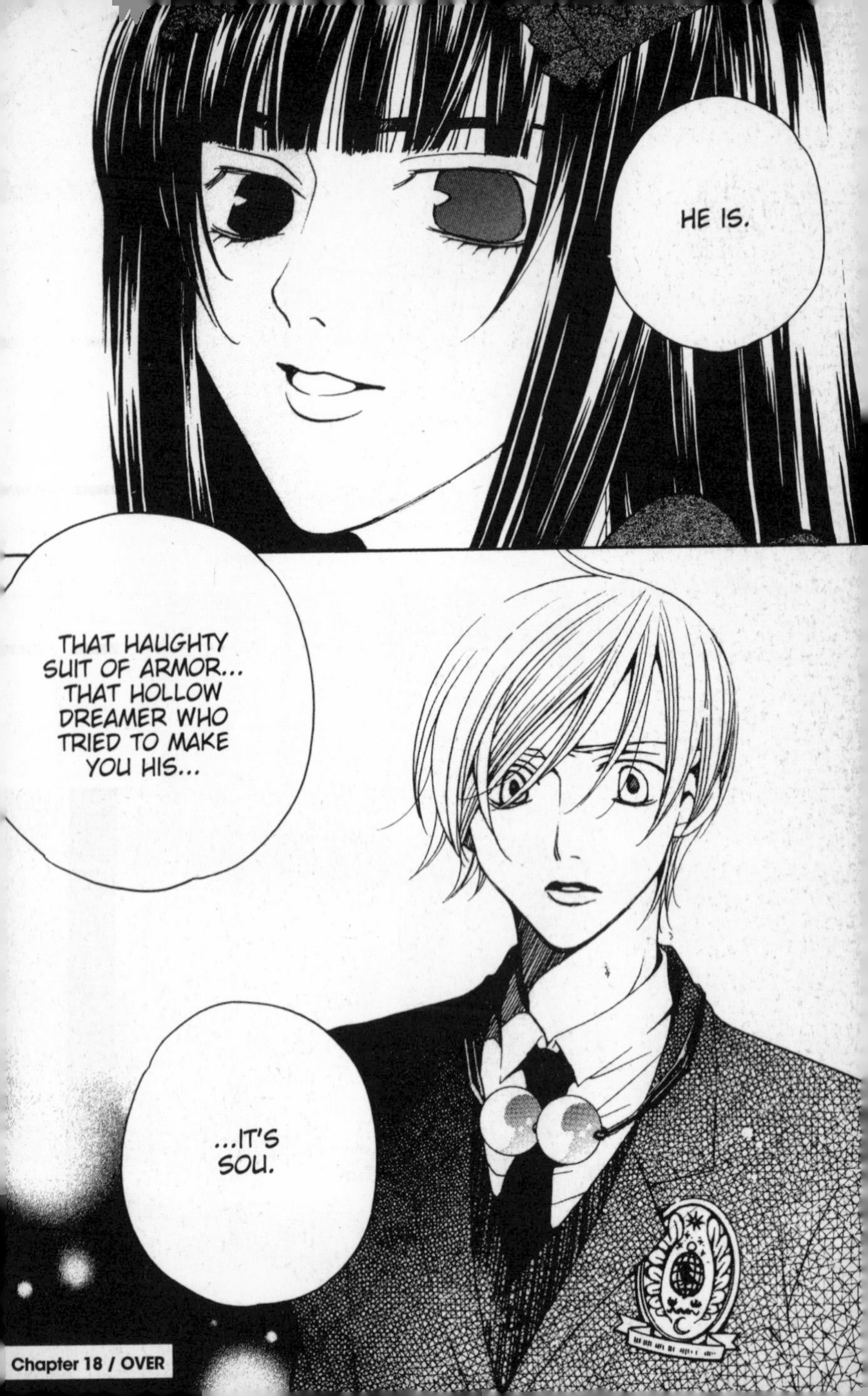
HE IS.
THAT HAUGHTY SUIT OF ARMOR... THAT HOLLOW DREAMER WHO TRIED TO MAKE YOU HIS...
...IT'S SOU.
Chapter 18 / OVER

AFTER SCHOOL NIGHTMARE Chapter 19

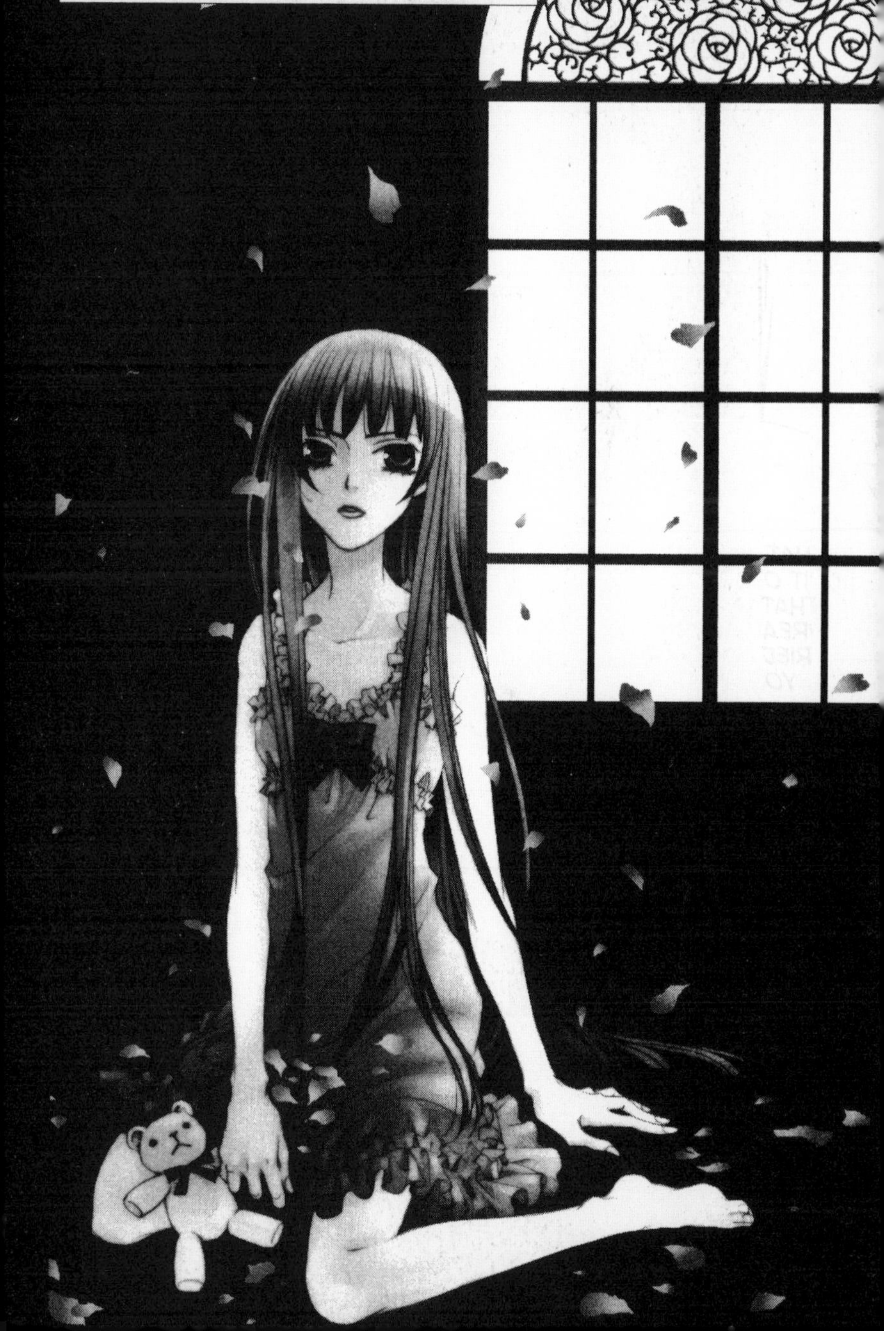

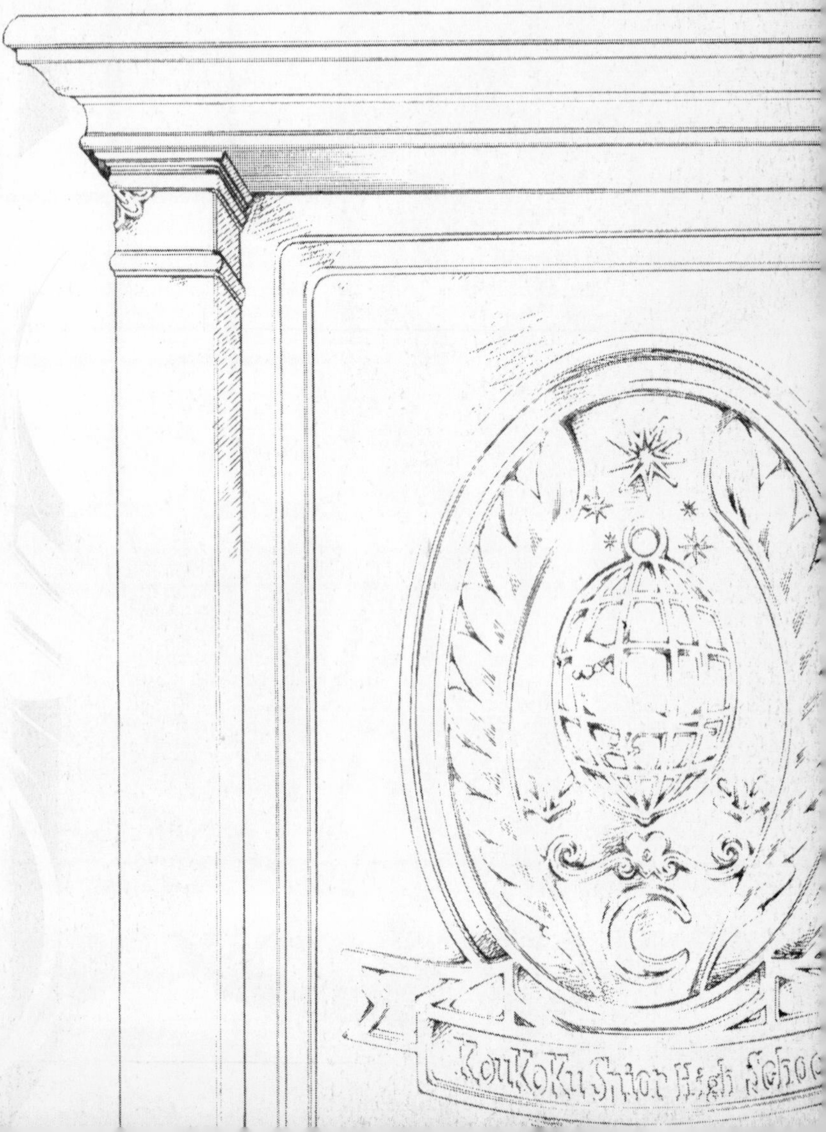
KouKoKu Snior High Schoo

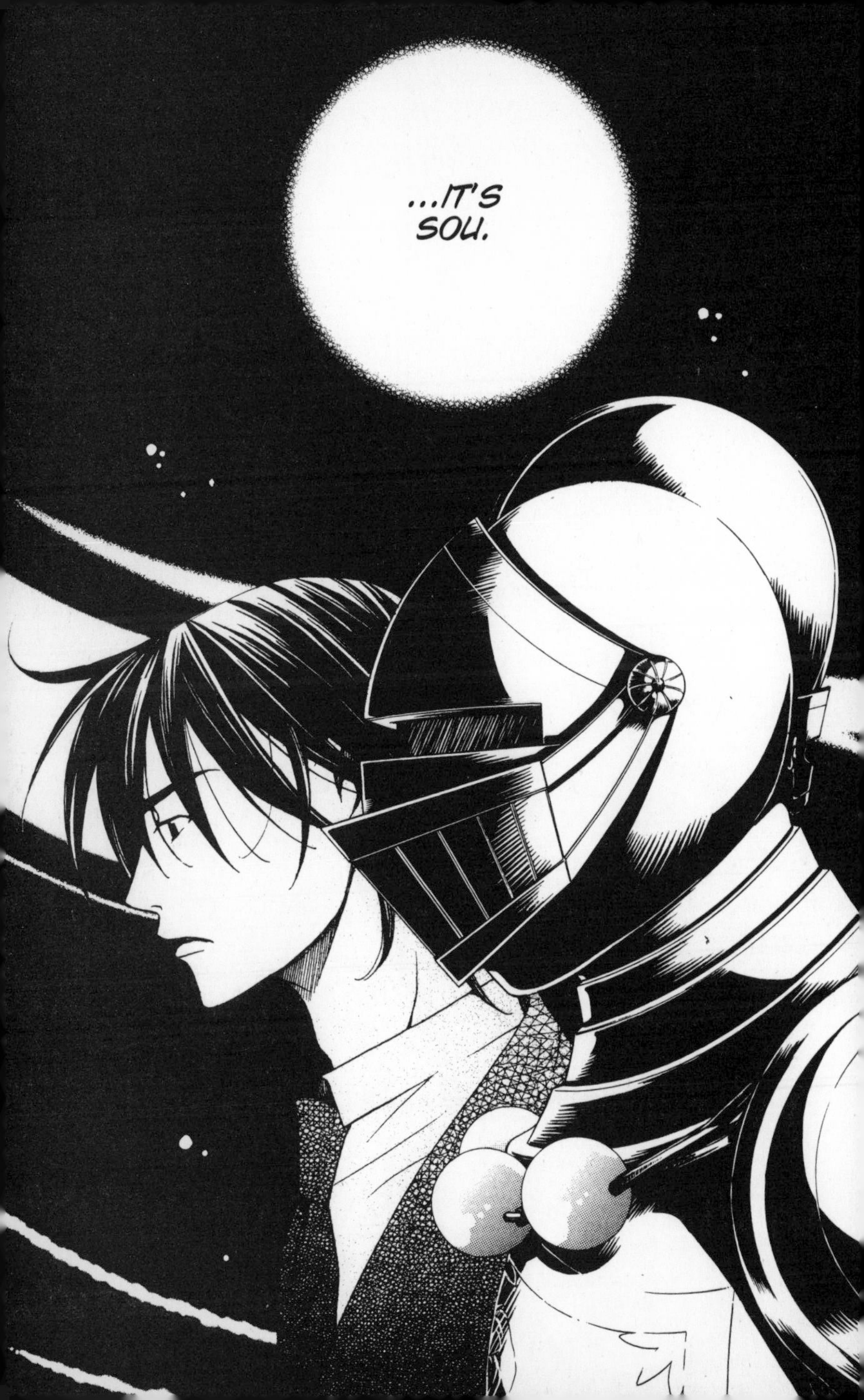
...IT'S SOU.

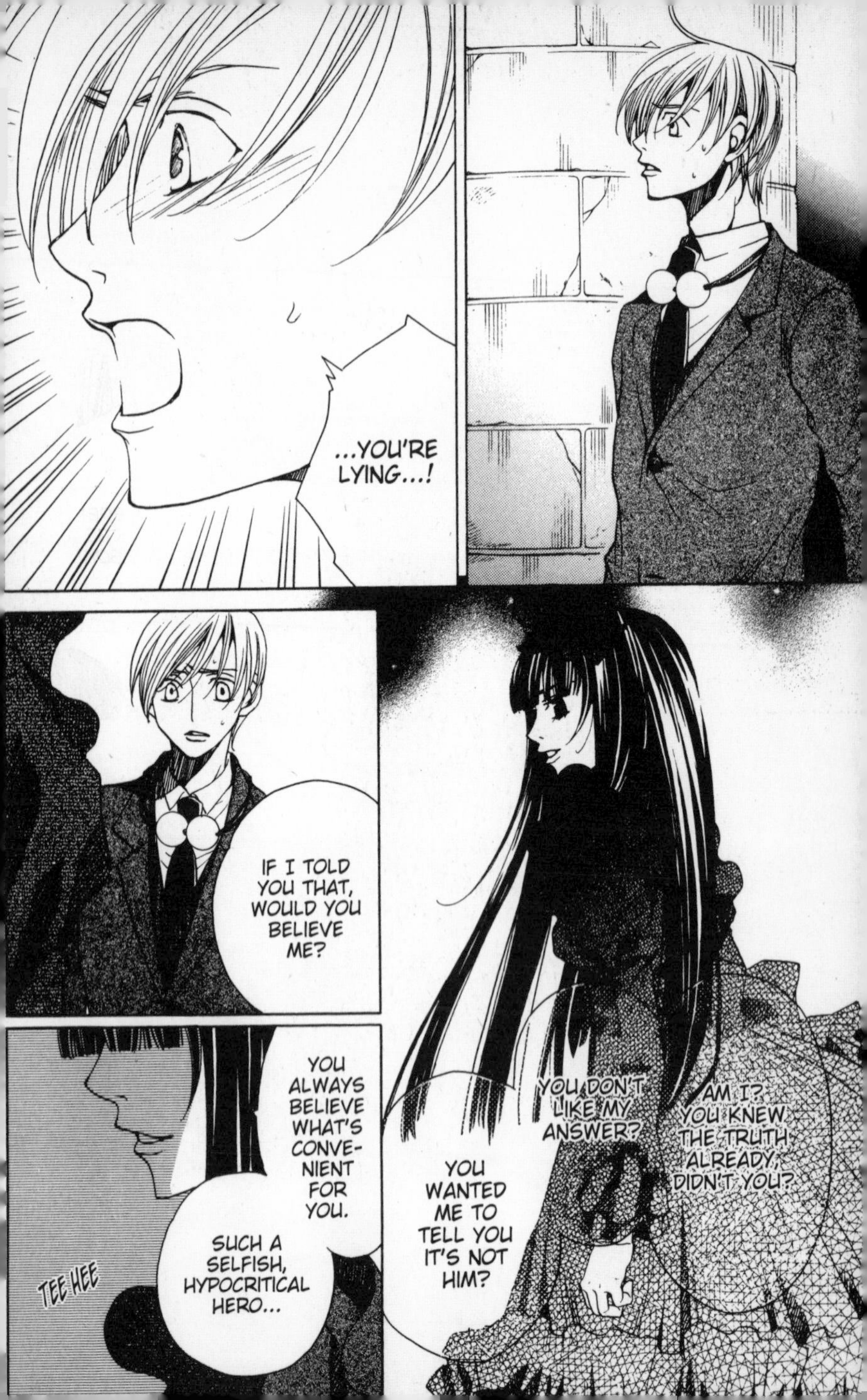
...YOU'RE LYING...!
AM I? YOU KNEW THE TRUTH ALREADY, DIDN'T YOU?
YOU DON'T LIKE MY ANSWER?
YOU WANTED ME TO TELL YOU IT'S NOT HIM?
IF I TOLD YOU THAT, WOULD YOU BELIEVE ME?
YOU ALWAYS BELIEVE WHAT'S CONVE-NIENT FOR YOU.
SUCH A SELFISH, HYPOCRITICAL HERO...
TEE HEE

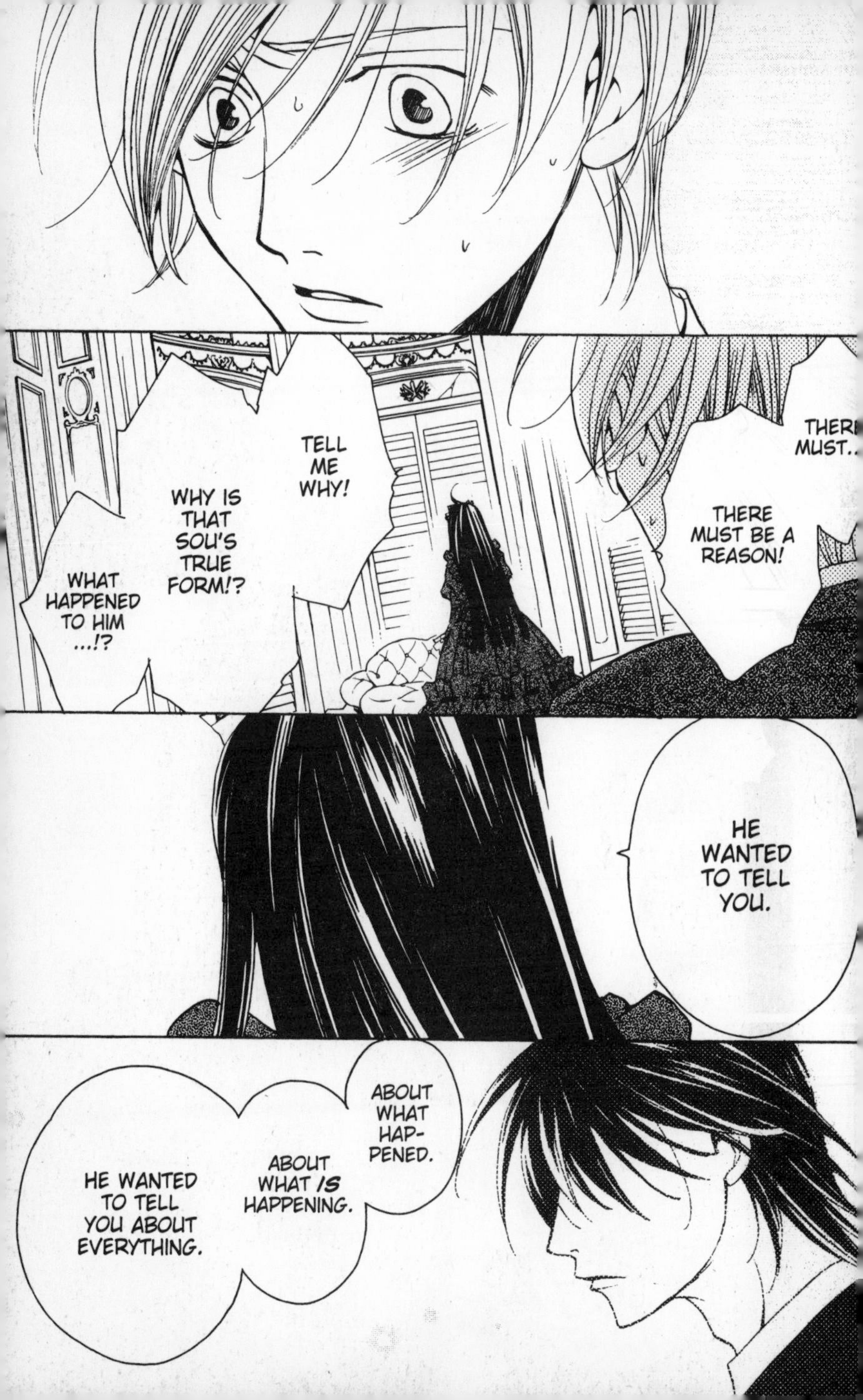
THERE MUST..
THERE MUST BE A REASON!
TELL ME WHY!
WHY IS THAT SOU'S TRUE FORM!?
WHAT HAPPENED TO HIM ...!?
HE WANTED TO TELL YOU.
ABOUT WHAT HAP-PENED.
ABOUT WHAT *IS* HAPPENING.
HE WANTED TO TELL YOU ABOUT EVERYTHING.

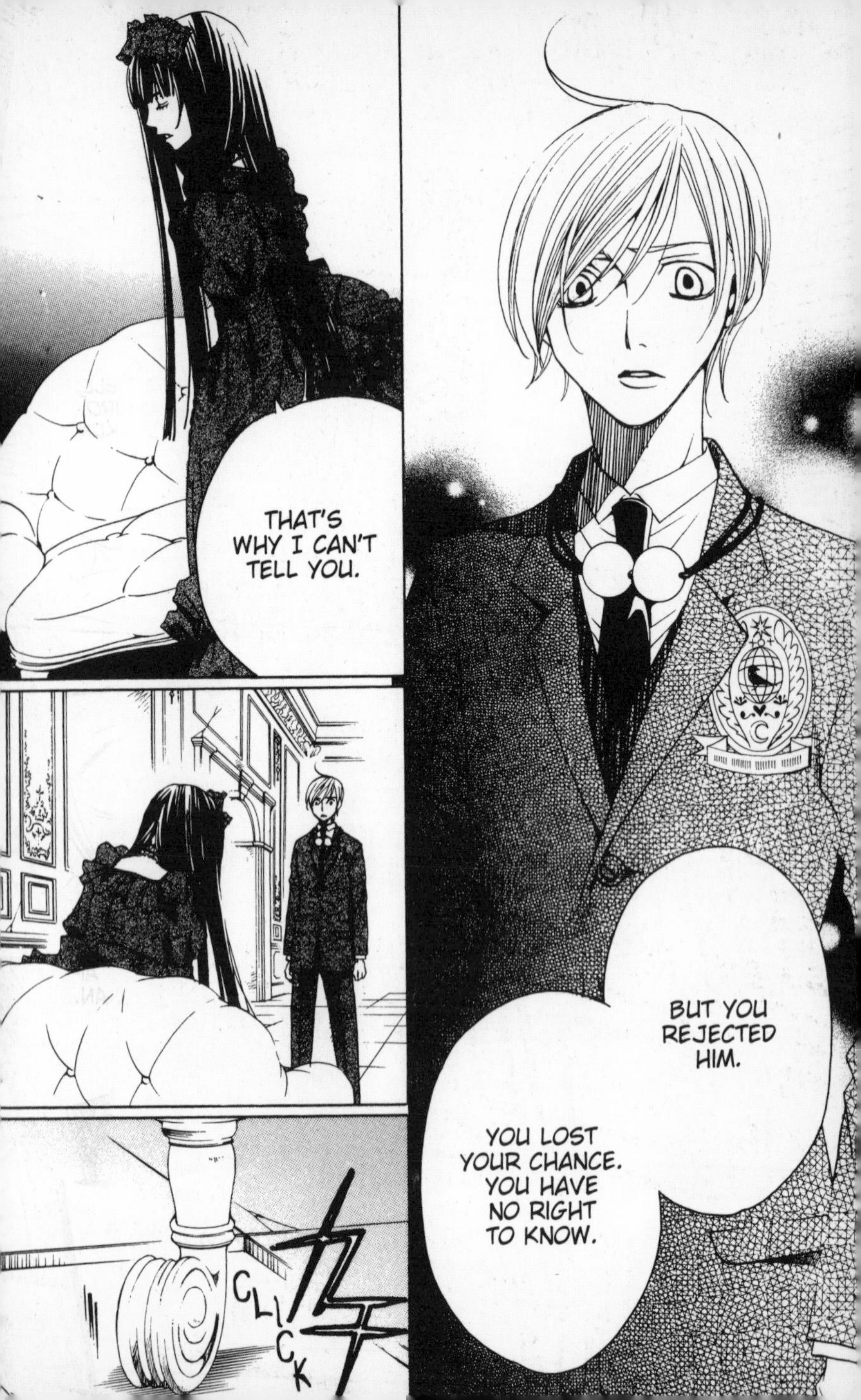
BUT YOU REJECTED HIM.
YOU LOST YOUR CHANCE. YOU HAVE NO RIGHT TO KNOW.
THAT'S WHY I CAN'T TELL YOU.
CLICK

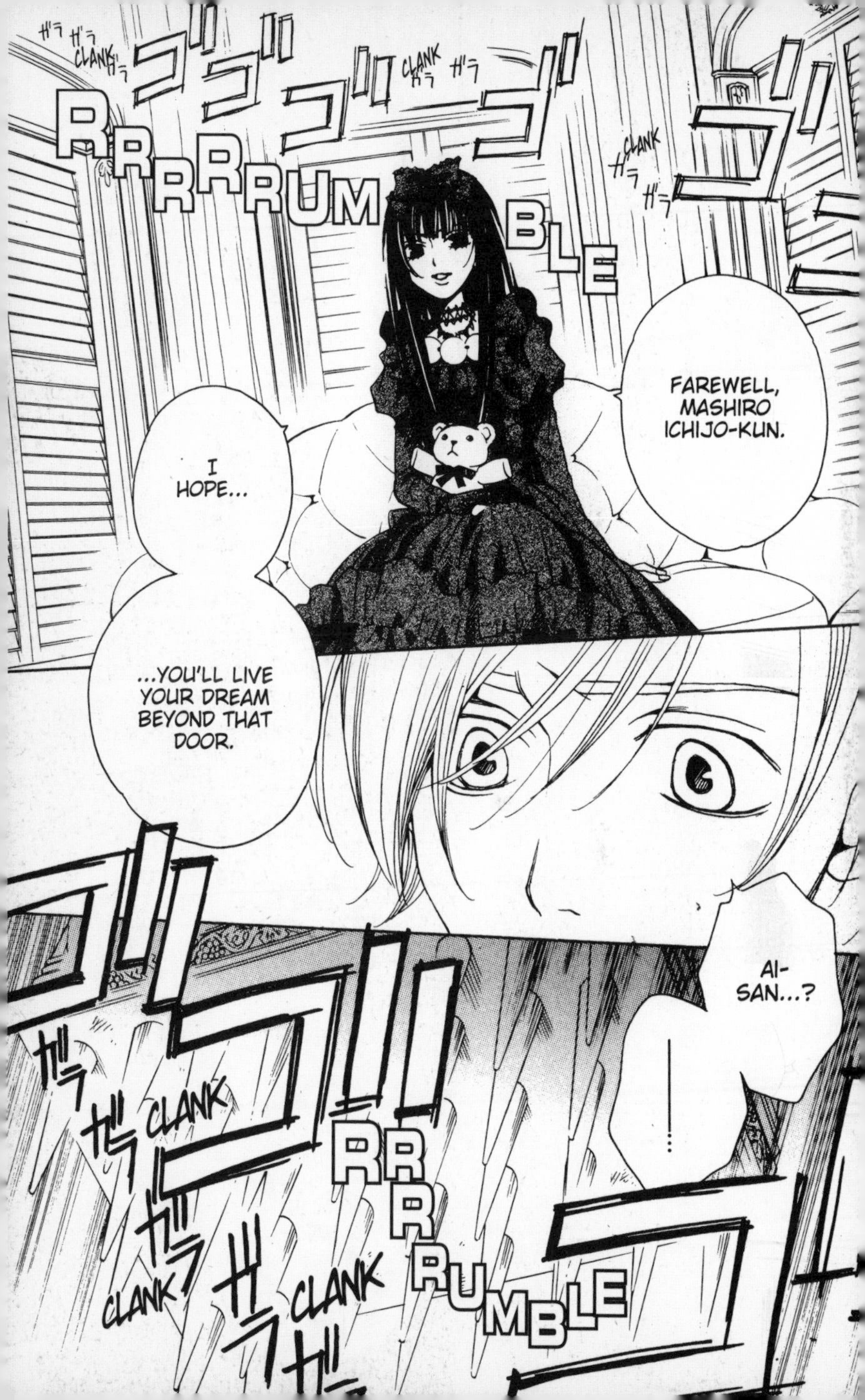
CLANK CLANK CLANK
RRRRRUMBLE
FAREWELL, MASHIRO ICHIJO-KUN.
I HOPE...
...YOU'LL LIVE YOUR DREAM BEYOND THAT DOOR.
AI-SAN...?
......
CLANK CLANK CLANK
RRRRUMBLE

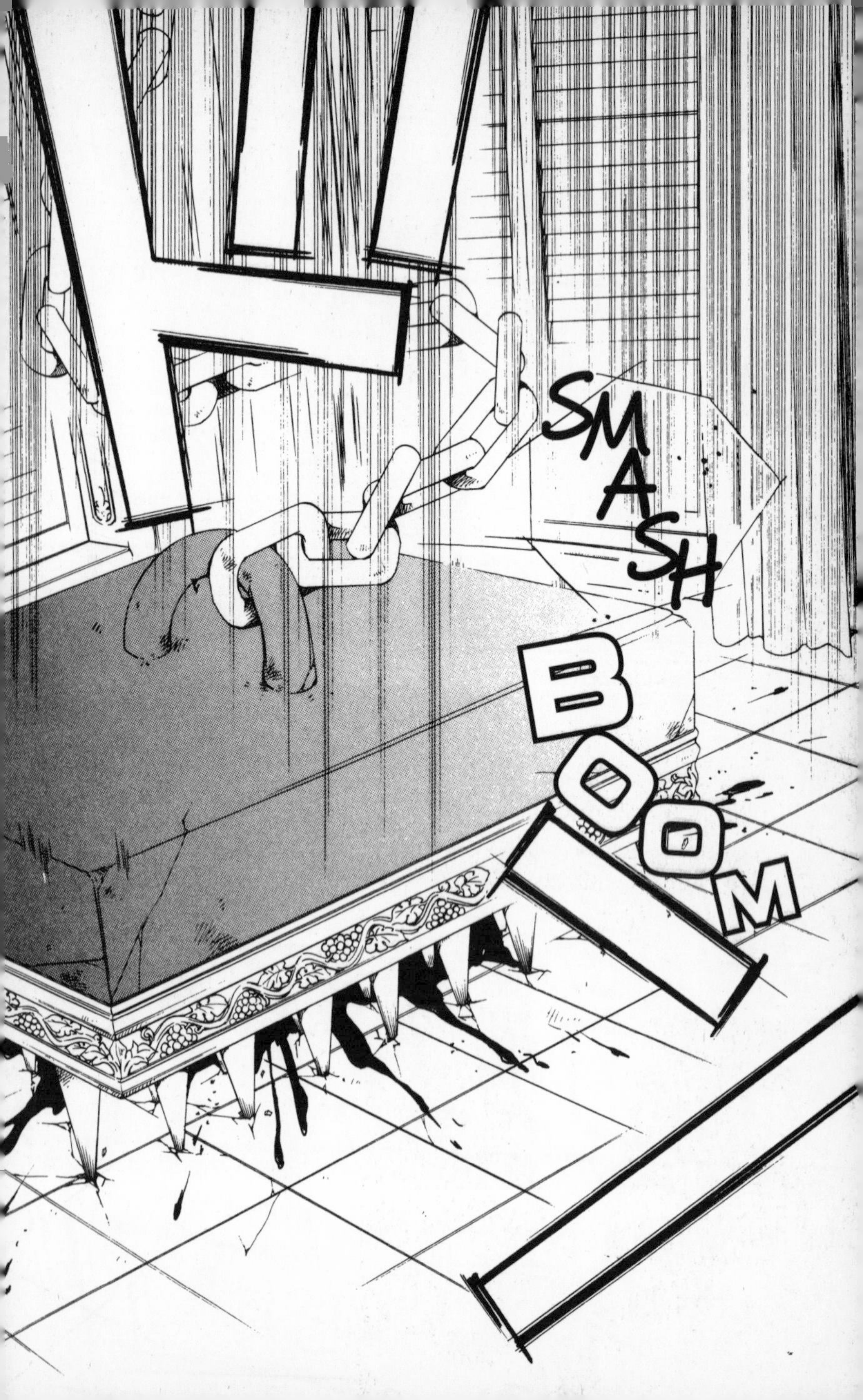
SMASH
BOOM

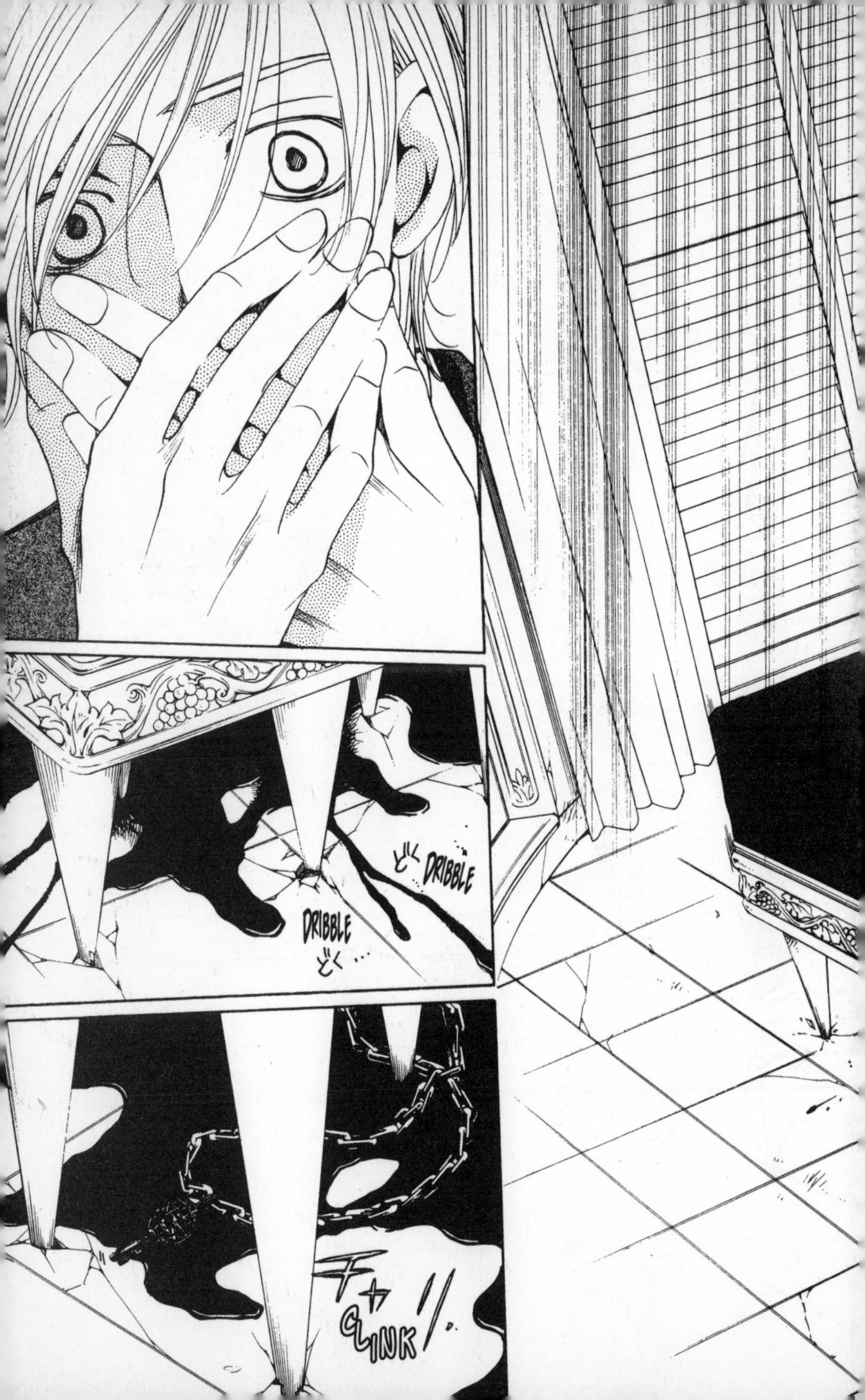
どく DRIBBLE
DRIBBLE
どく…
チャ
CLINK!!

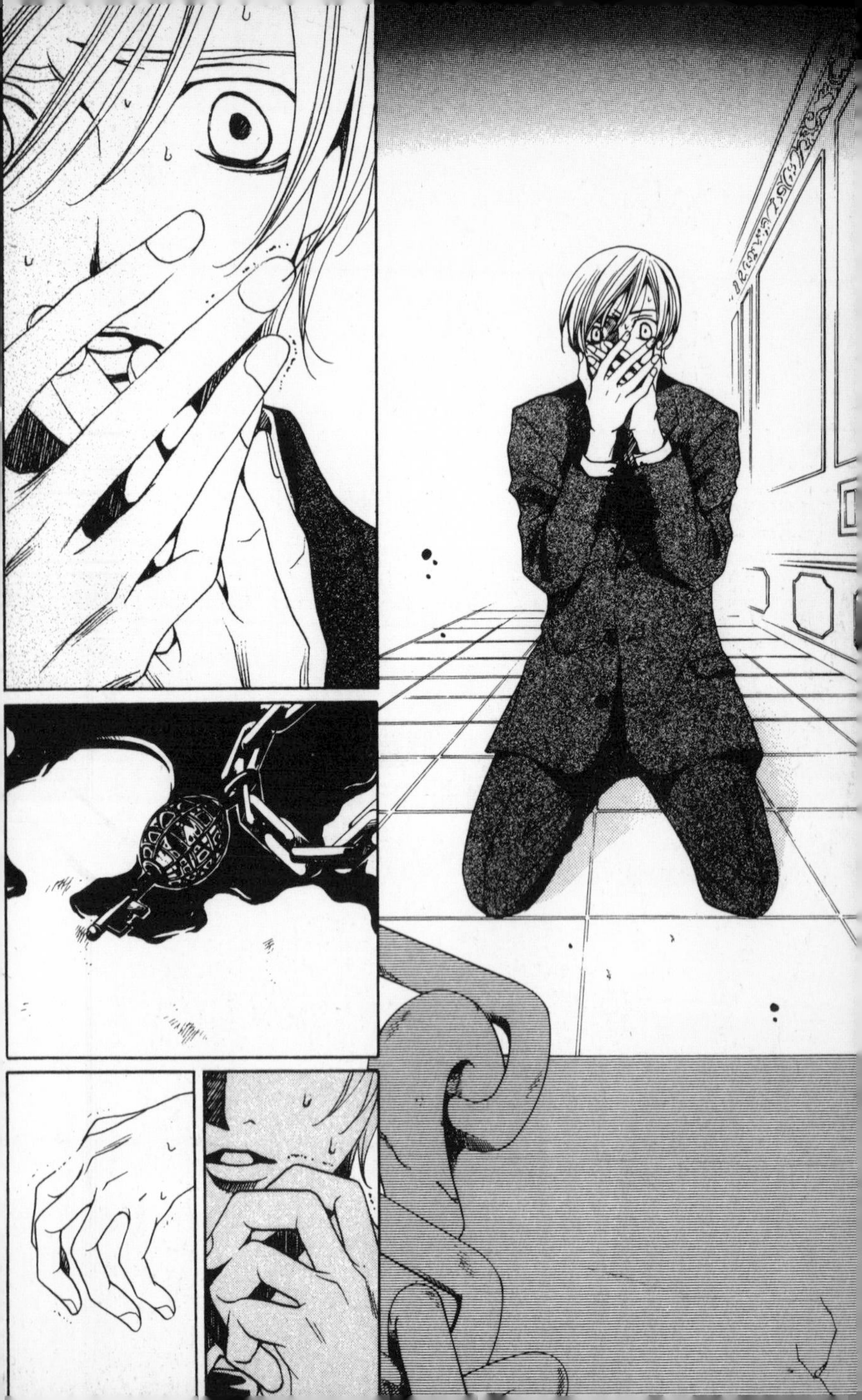

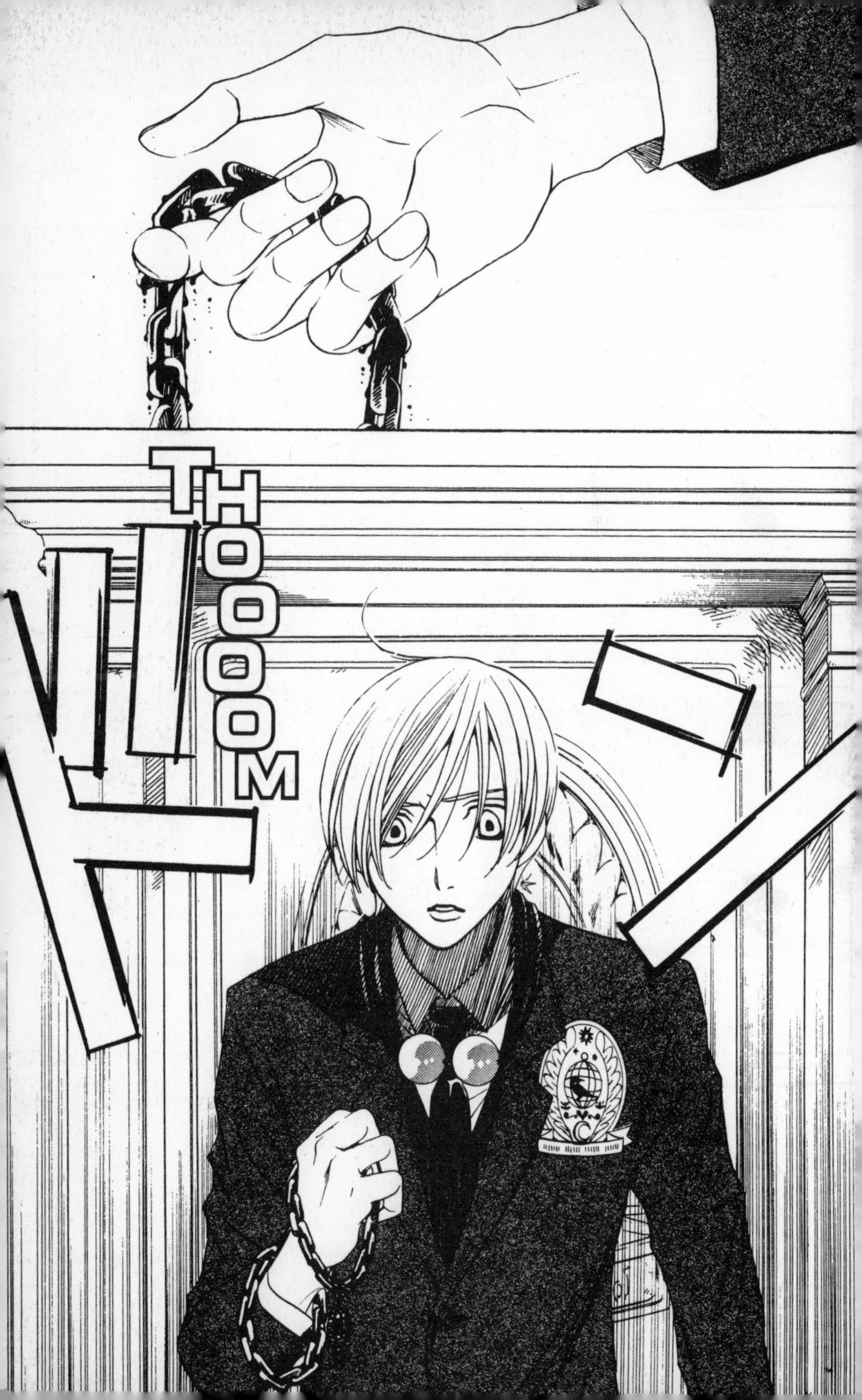
THOOOOM

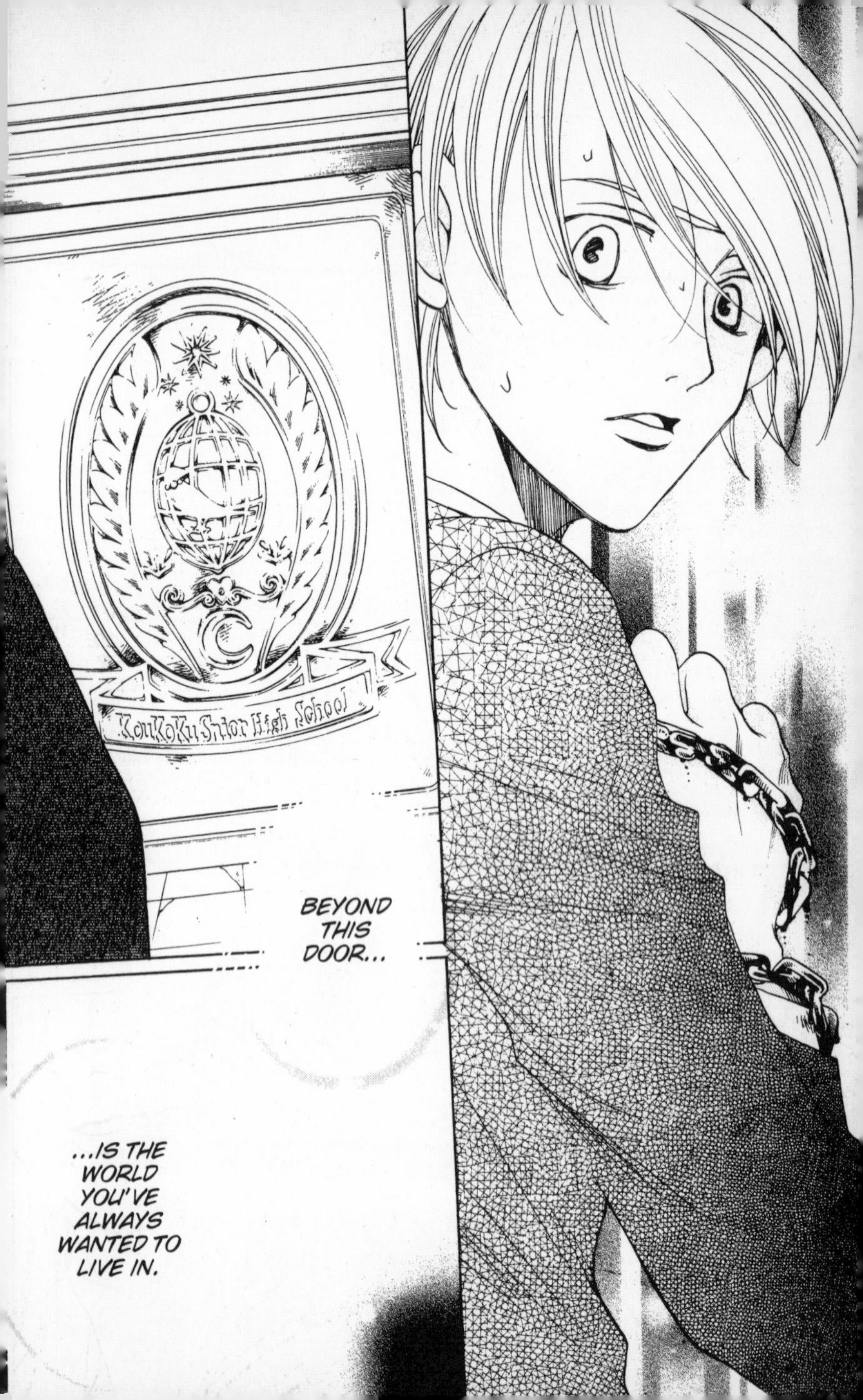
KouKoKu Snior High School
BEYOND THIS DOOR...
...IS THE WORLD YOU'VE ALWAYS WANTED TO LIVE IN.

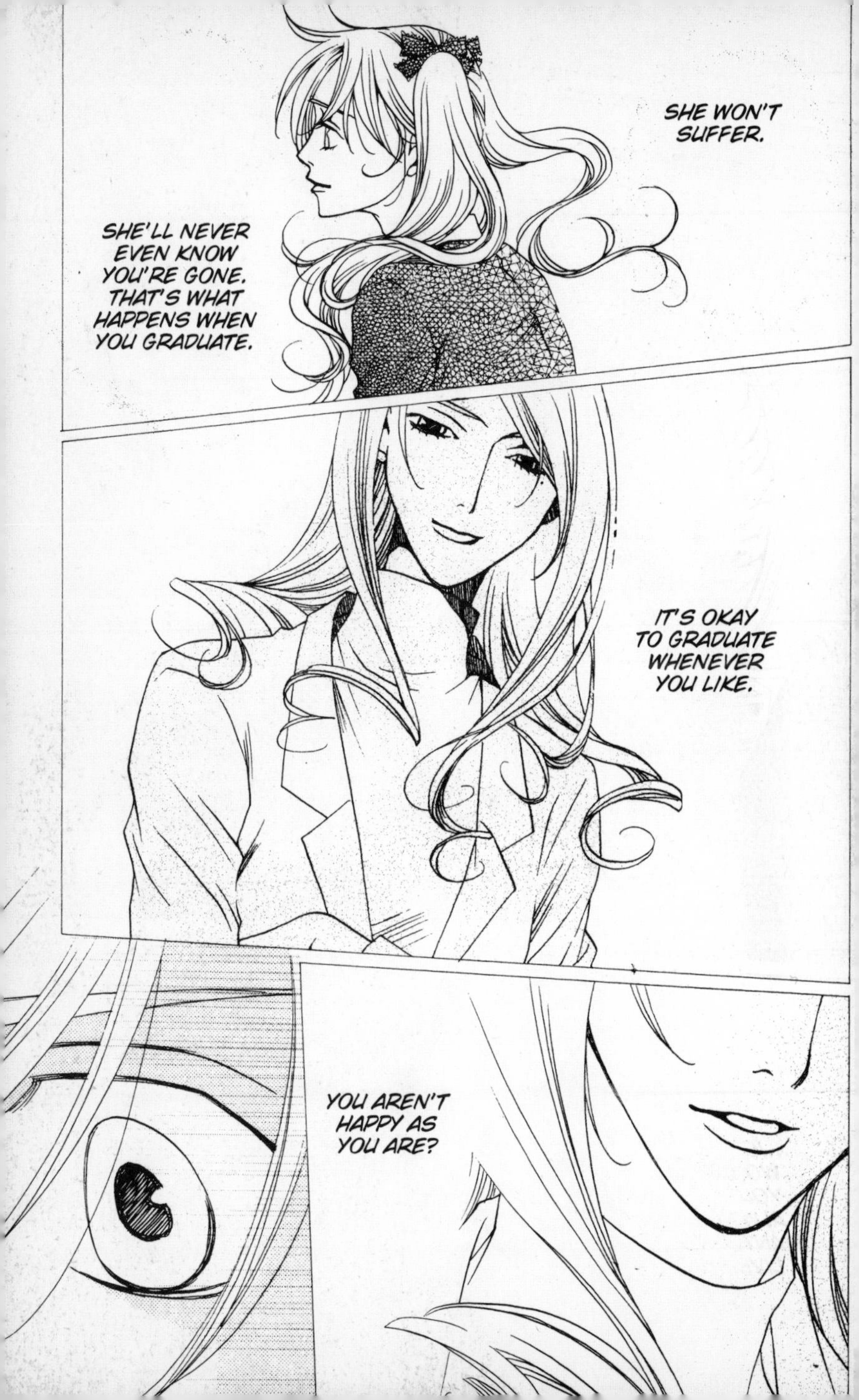
SHE WON'T SUFFER.
SHE'LL NEVER EVEN KNOW YOU'RE GONE. THAT'S WHAT HAPPENS WHEN YOU GRADUATE.
IT'S OKAY TO GRADUATE WHENEVER YOU LIKE.
YOU AREN'T HAPPY AS YOU ARE?

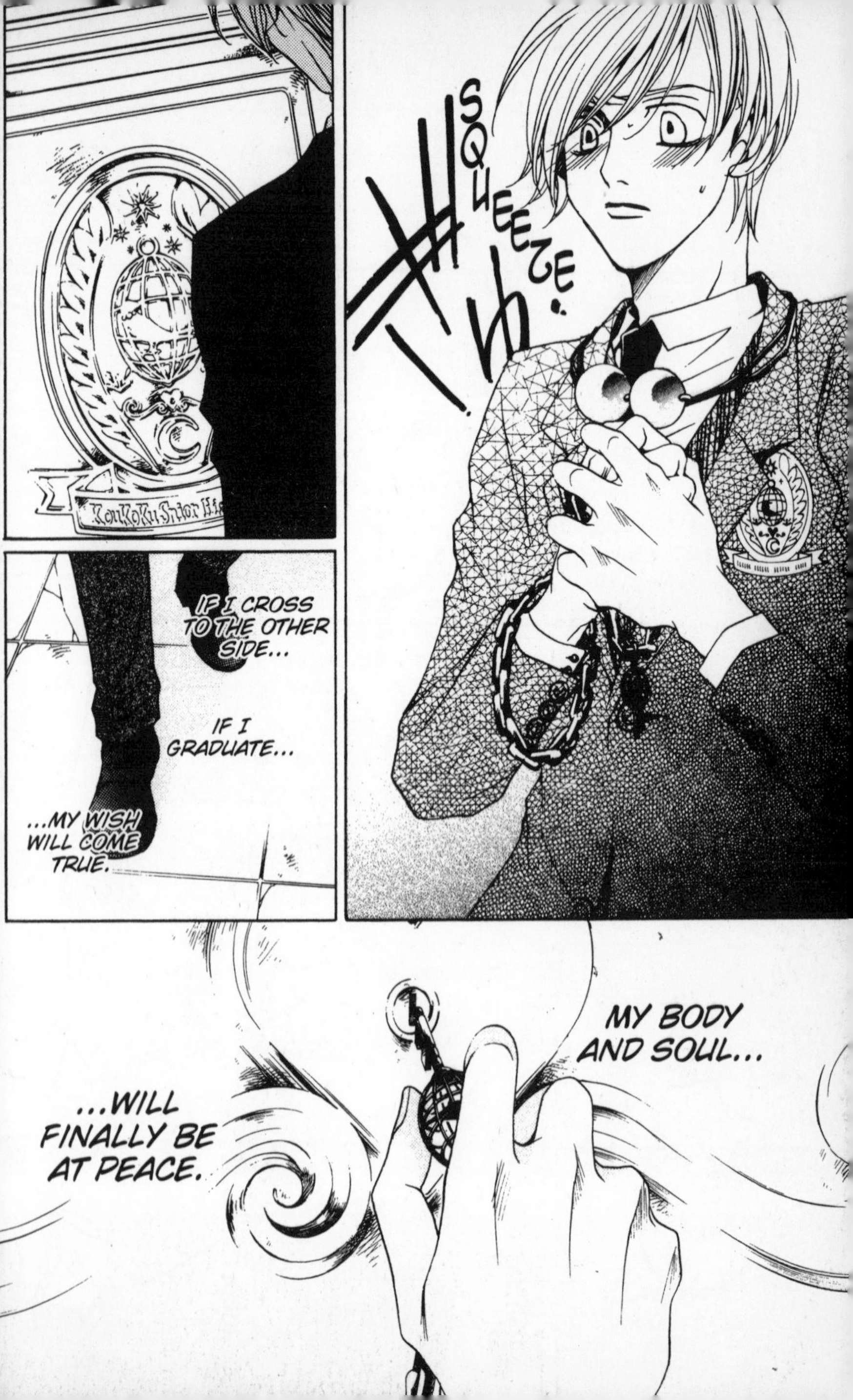
SQUEEZE
IF I CROSS TO THE OTHER SIDE...
IF I GRADUATE...
...MY WISH WILL COME TRUE.
MY BODY AND SOUL...
...WILL FINALLY BE AT PEACE.

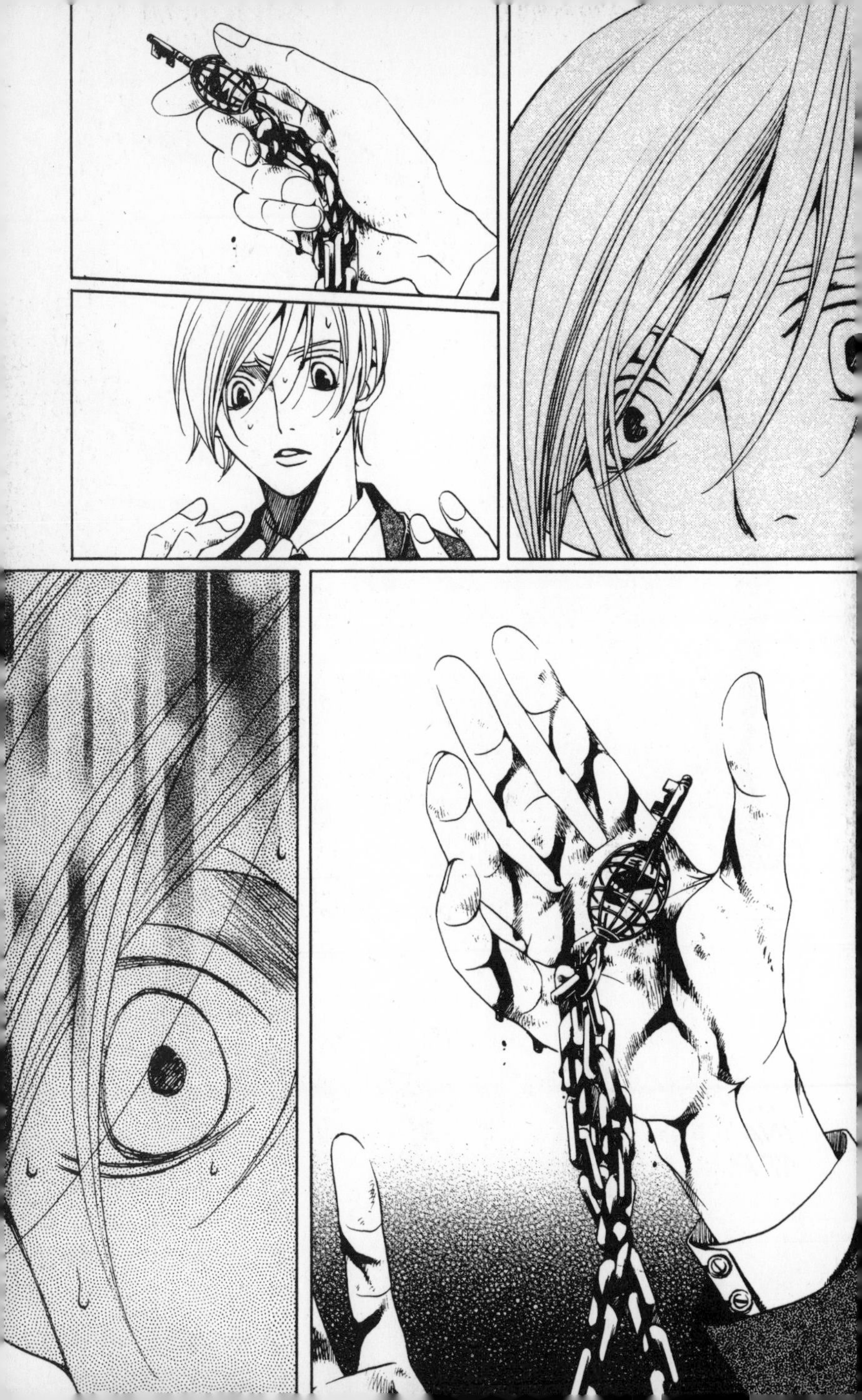

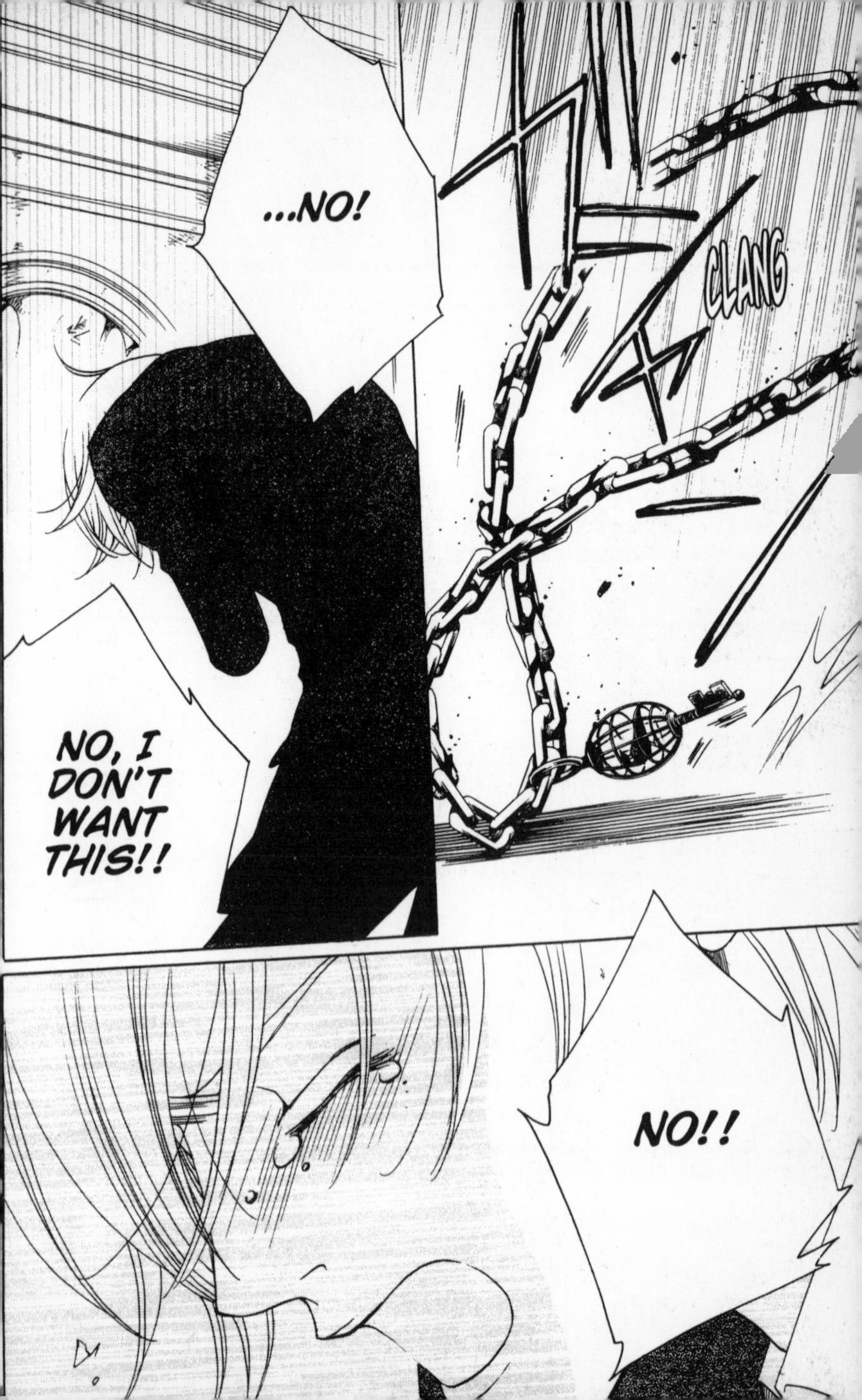
CLANG
...NO!
NO, I DON'T WANT THIS!!
NO!!

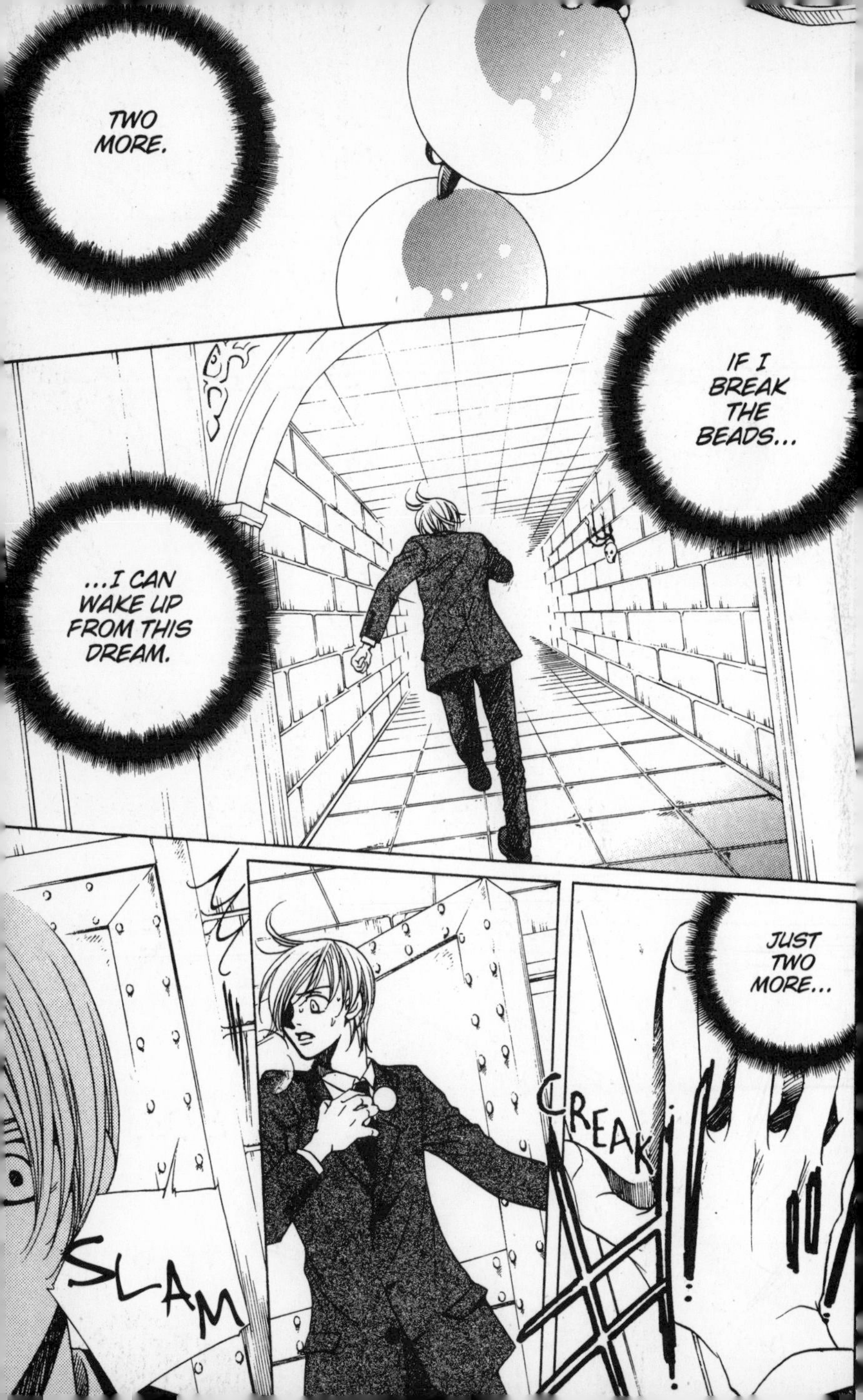
TWO MORE.
IF I BREAK THE BEADS...
...I CAN WAKE UP FROM THIS DREAM.
JUST TWO MORE...
CREAK
SLAM

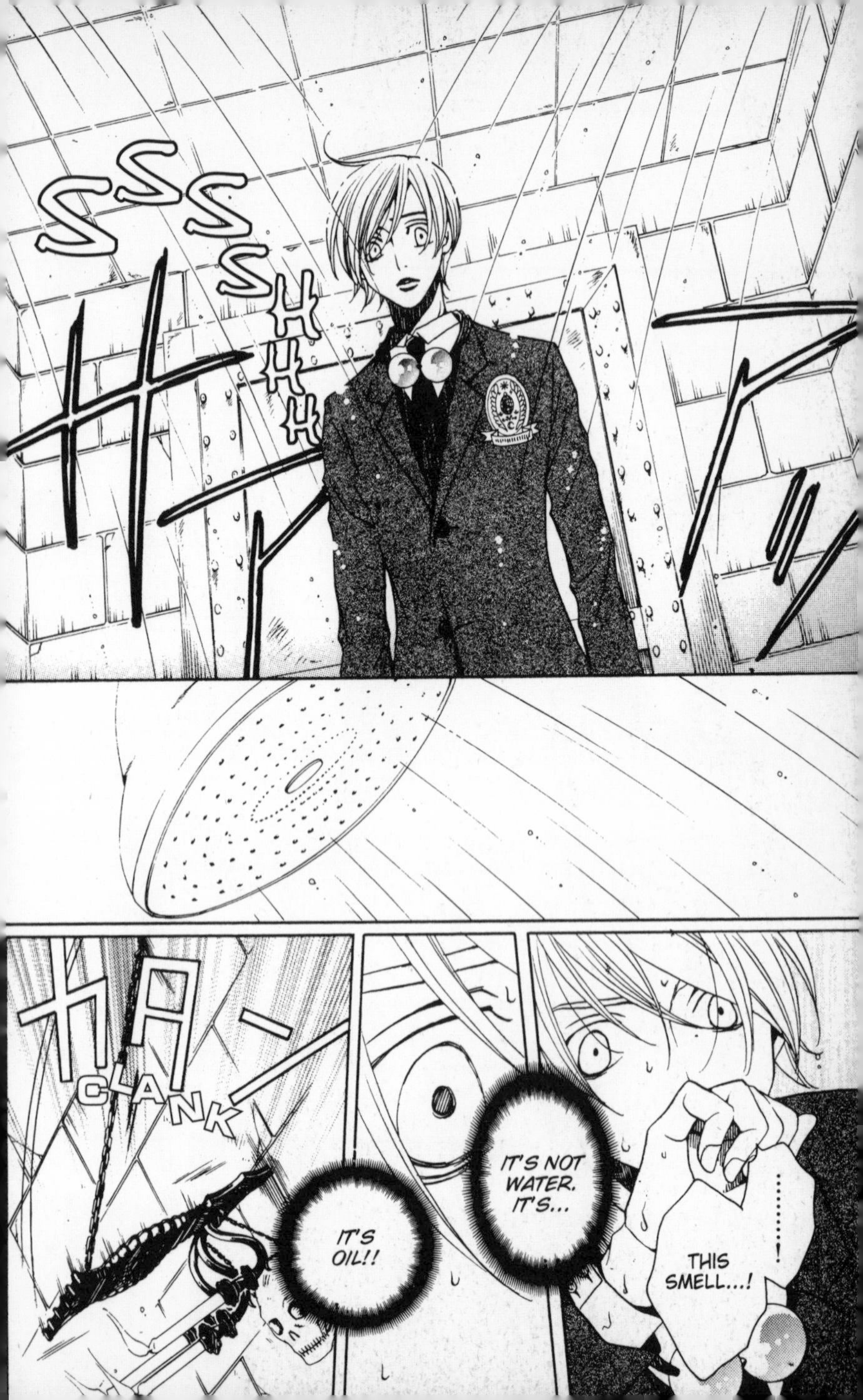
SSSSHHH
...!
THIS SMELL...!
IT'S NOT WATER. IT'S...
IT'S OIL!!
HA-
CLANK

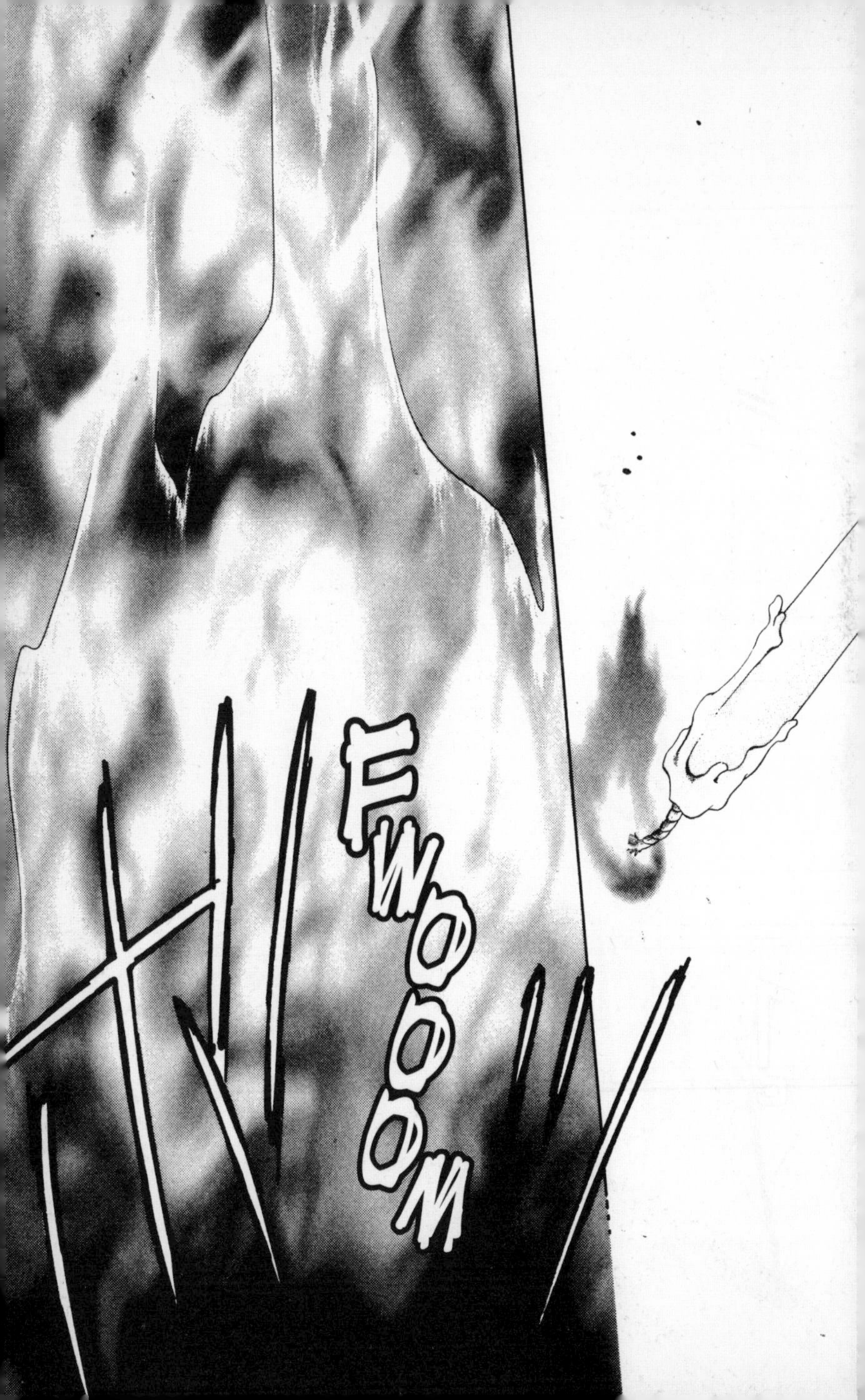
FWOOOOM

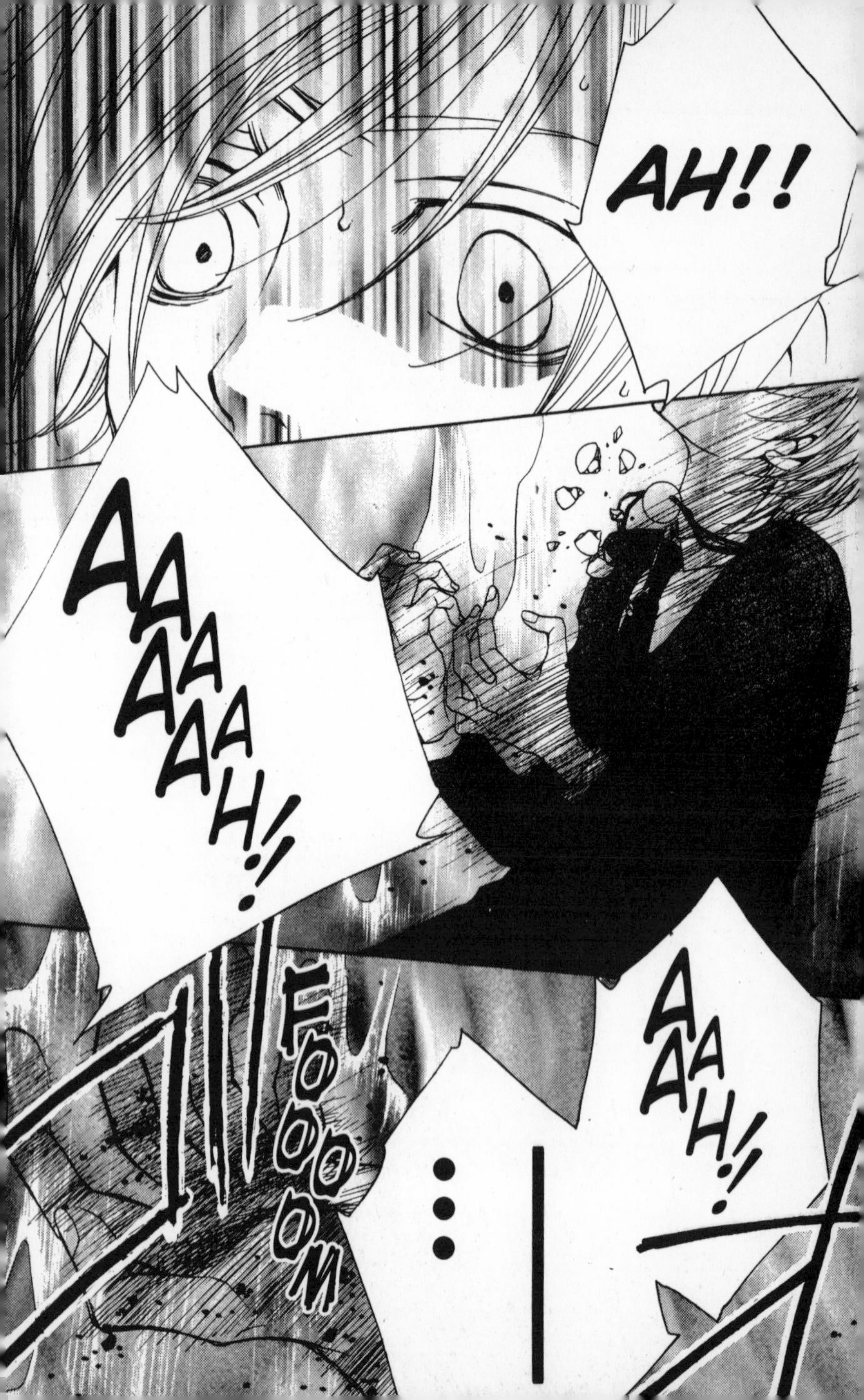
AH!!
AAAAAAAH!!
FOOOOOM
AAAH!!
...

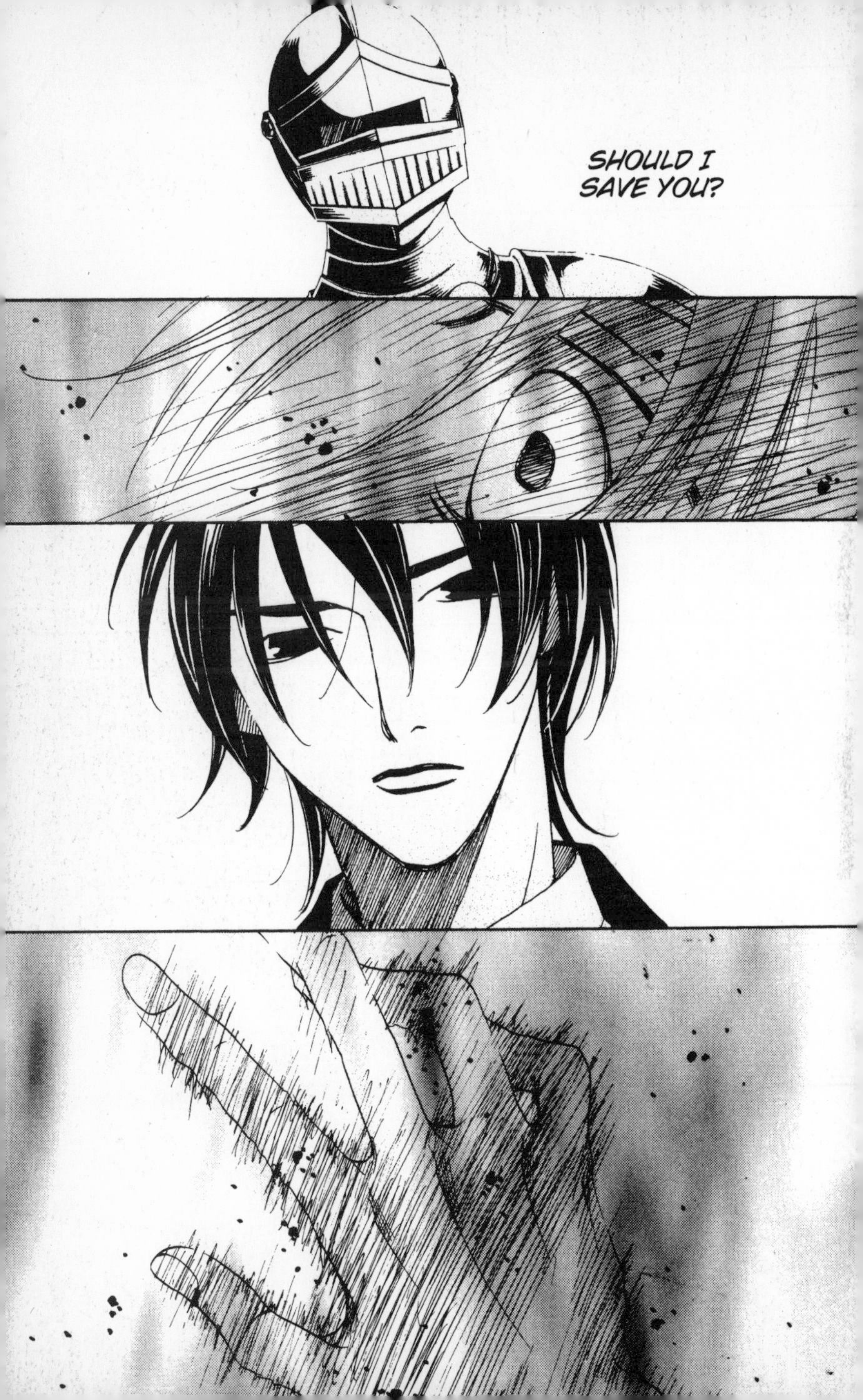
SHOULD I SAVE YOU?

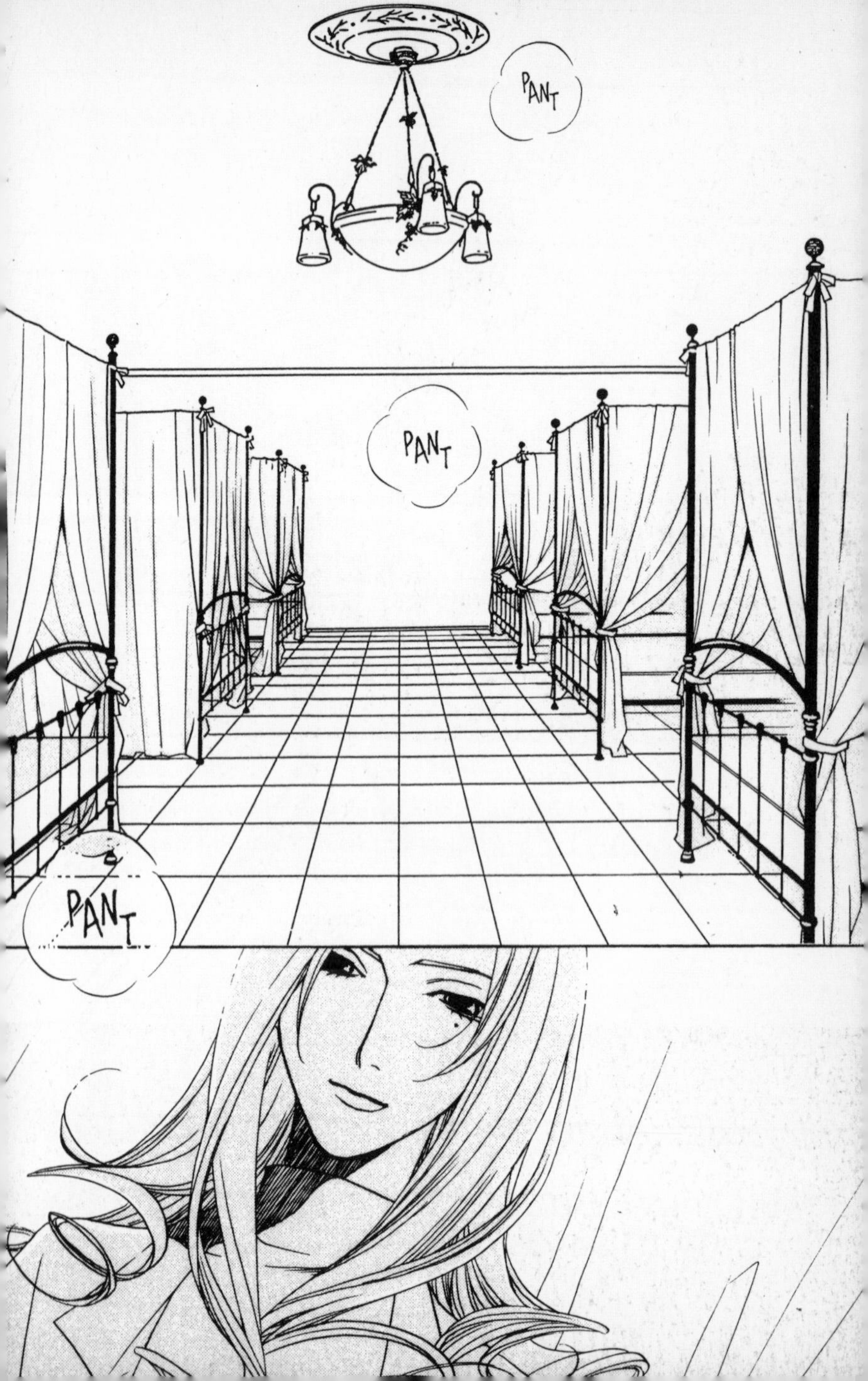
PANT
PANT
PANT

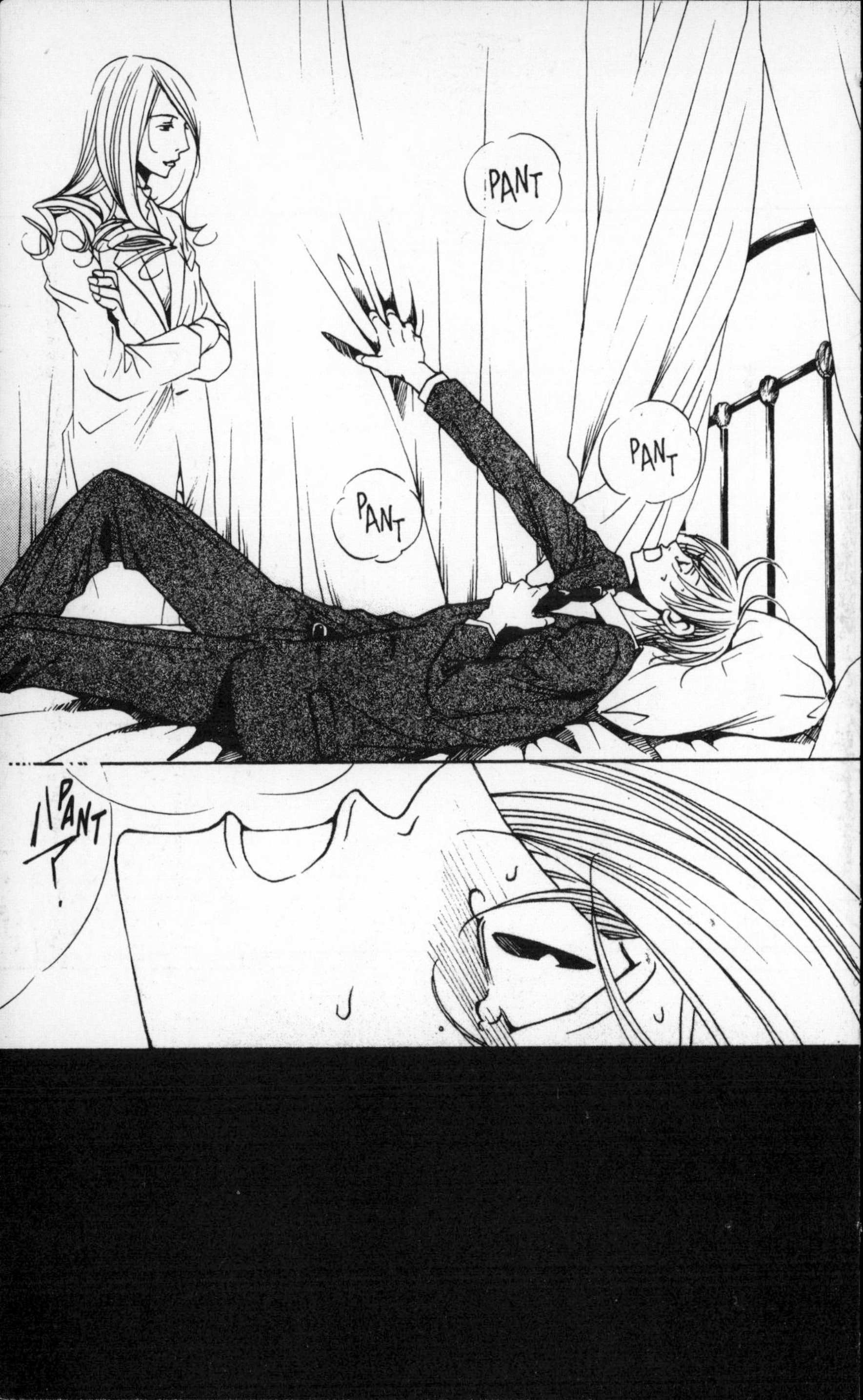
PANT
PANT
PANT
PANT

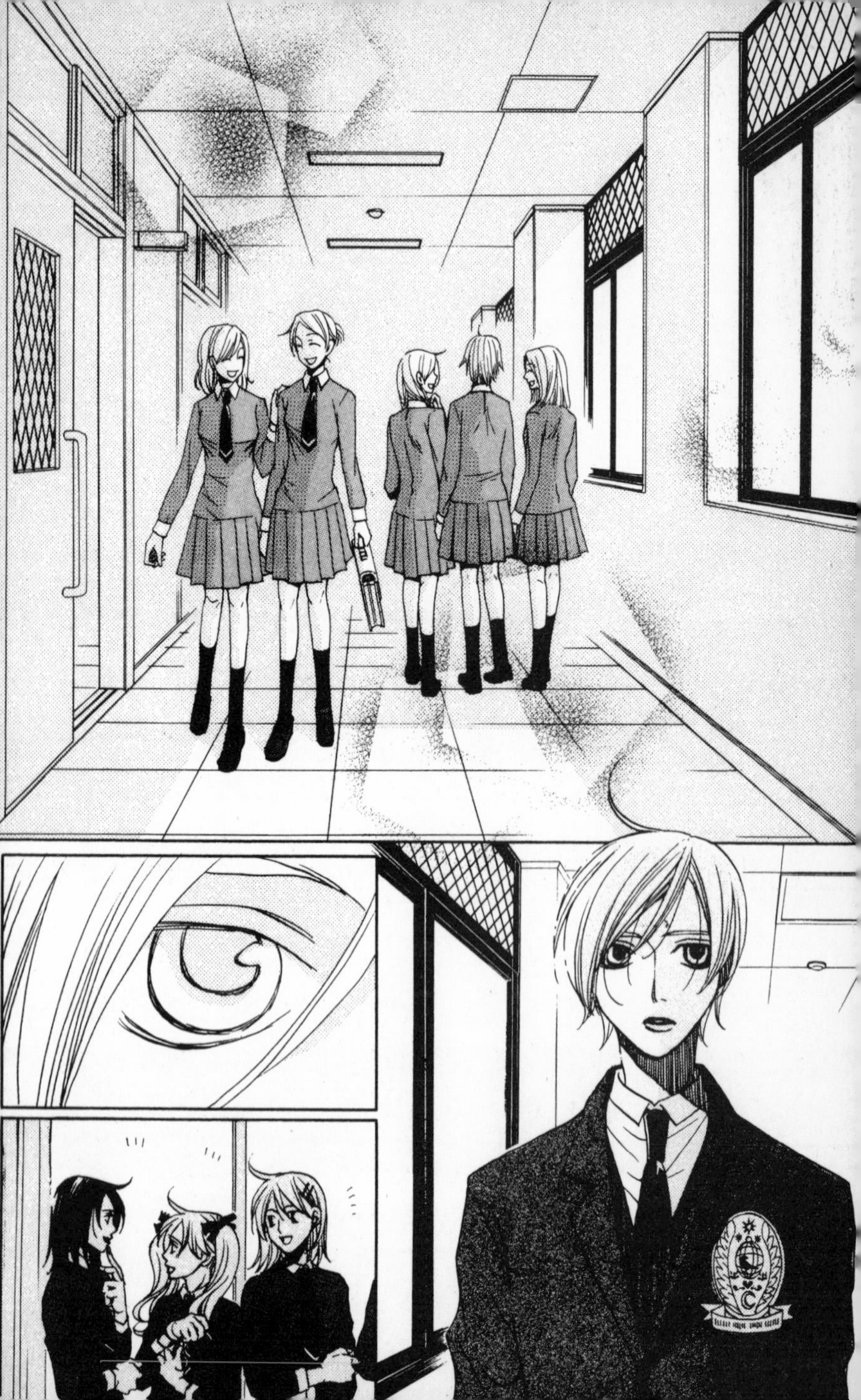

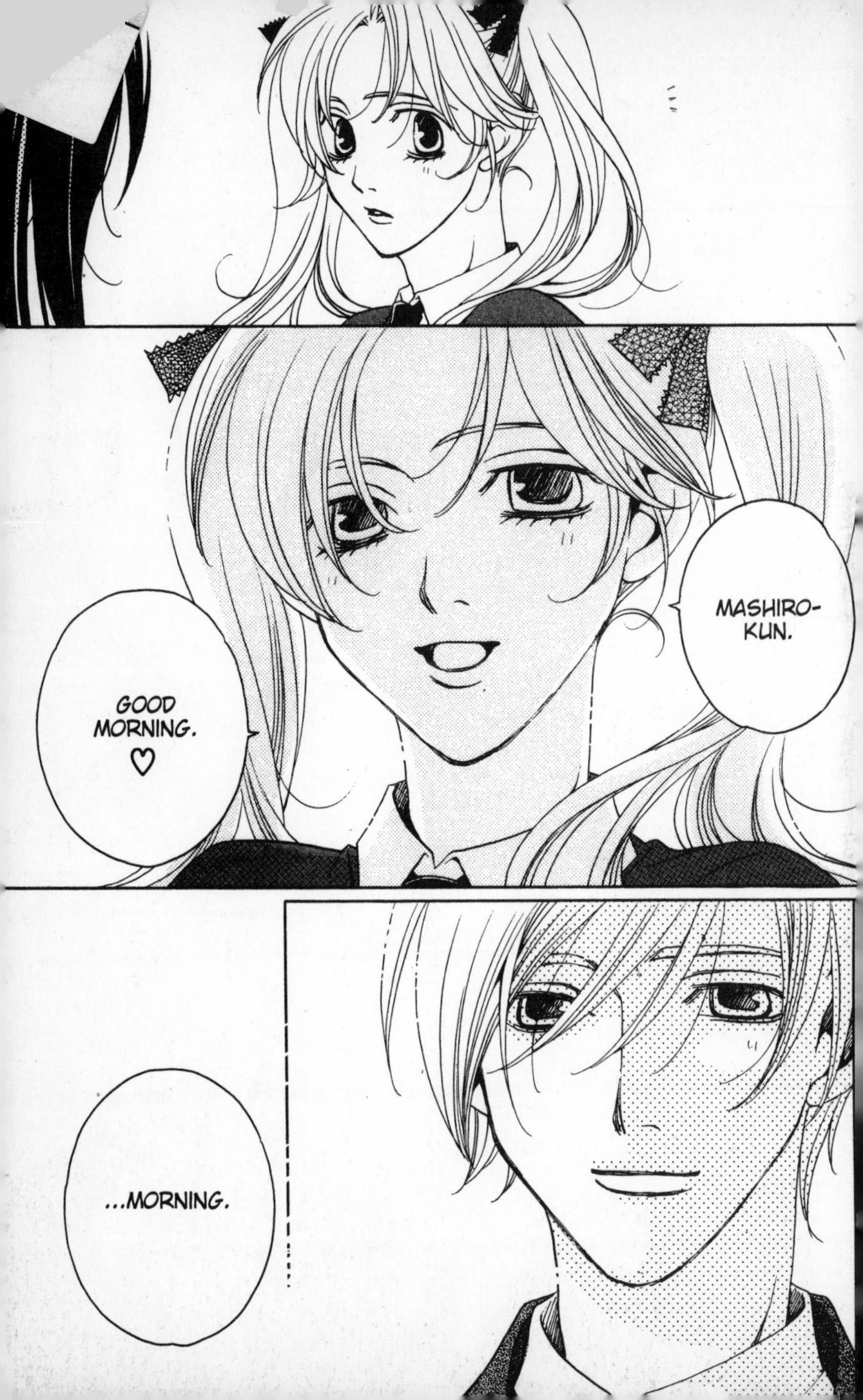
MASHIRO-KUN.
GOOD MORNING. ♡
...MORNING.

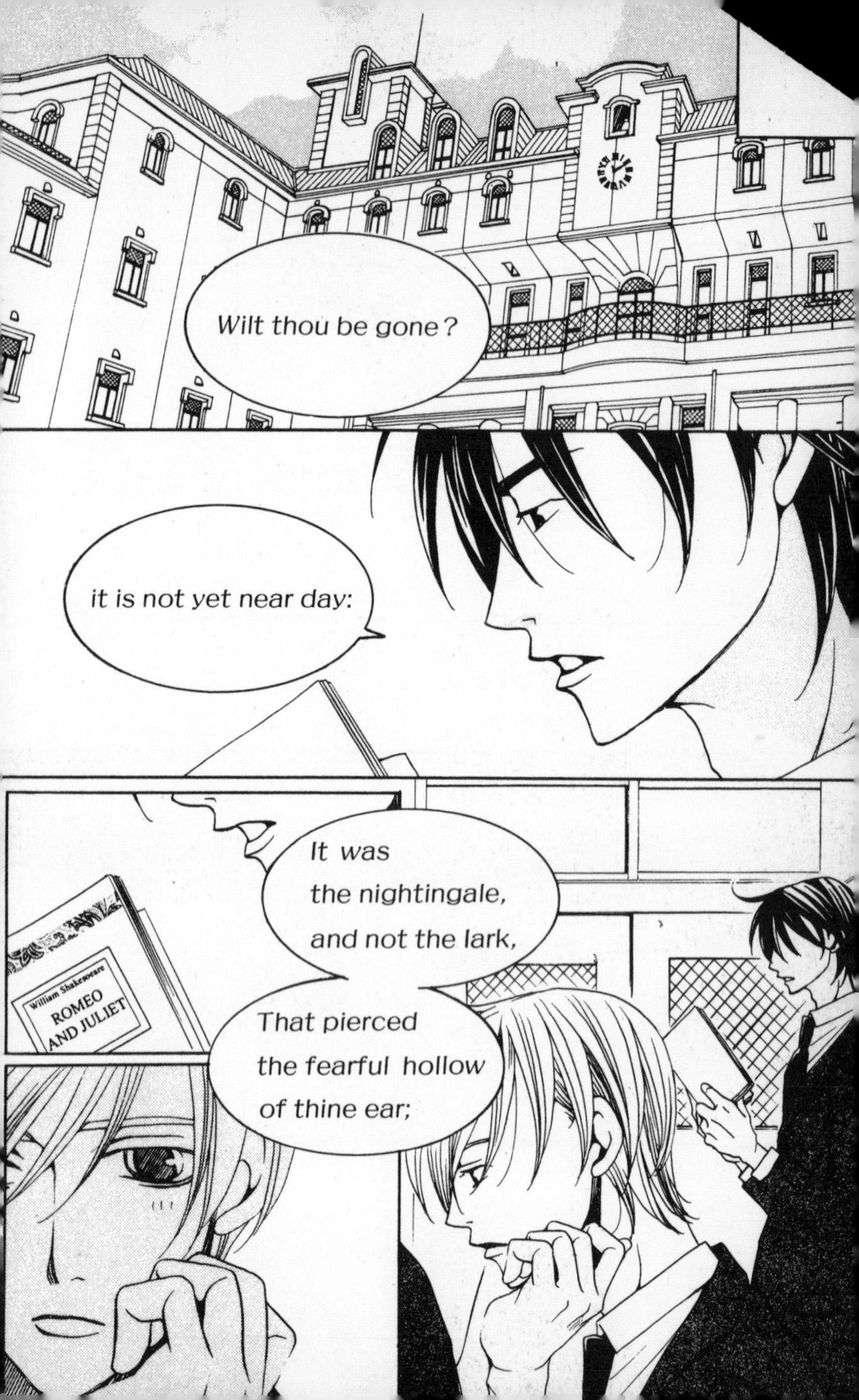
Wilt thou be gone?
it is not yet near day:
It was the nightingale, and not the lark,
That pierced the fearful hollow of thine ear;
William Shakespeare
ROMEO AND JULIET

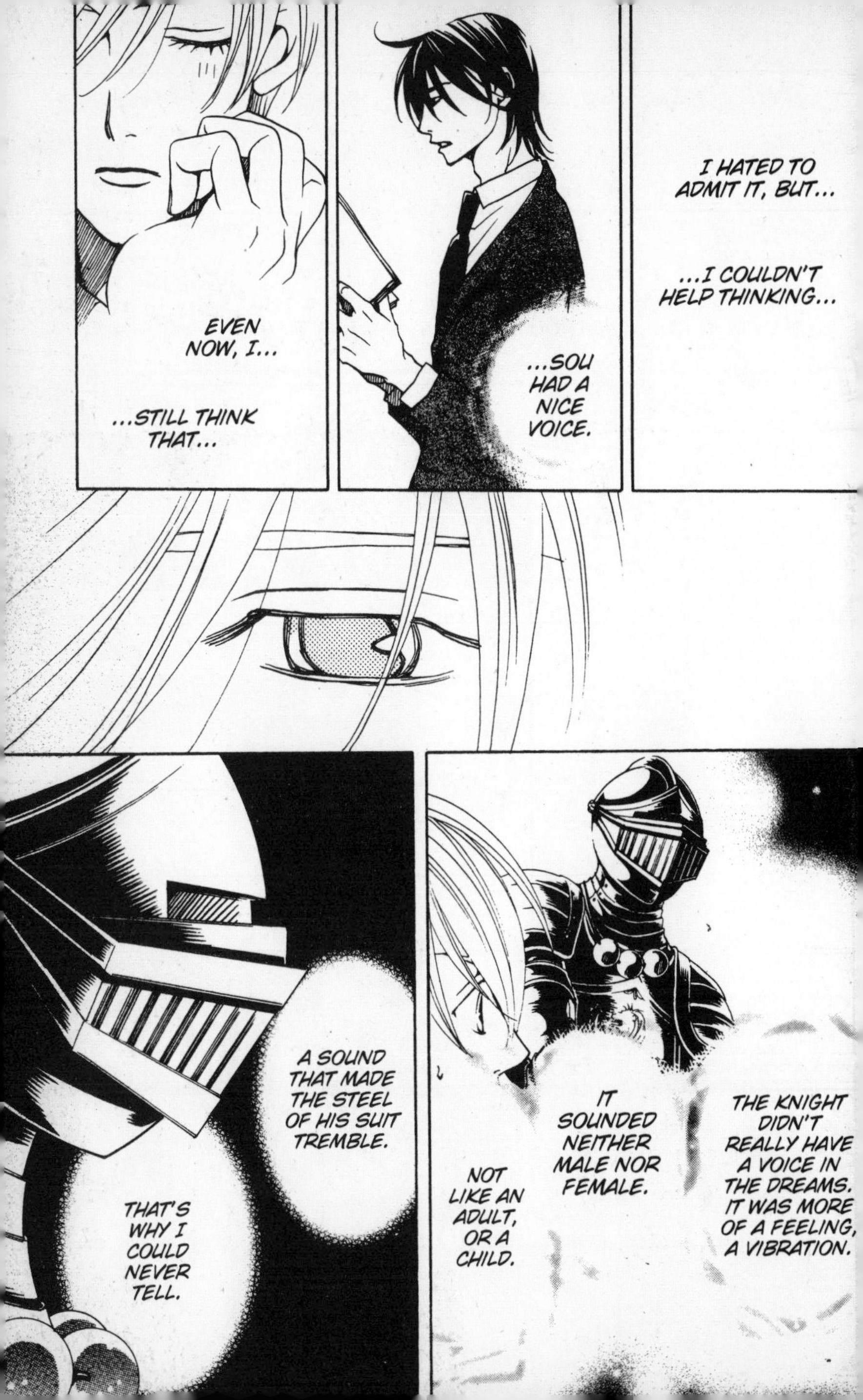
I HATED TO ADMIT IT, BUT...
...I COULDN'T HELP THINKING...
...SOU HAD A NICE VOICE.
EVEN NOW, I...
...STILL THINK THAT...
THE KNIGHT DIDN'T REALLY HAVE A VOICE IN THE DREAMS. IT WAS MORE OF A FEELING, A VIBRATION.
IT SOUNDED NEITHER MALE NOR FEMALE.
NOT LIKE AN ADULT, OR A CHILD.
A SOUND THAT MADE THE STEEL OF HIS SUIT TREMBLE.
THAT'S WHY I COULD NEVER TELL.

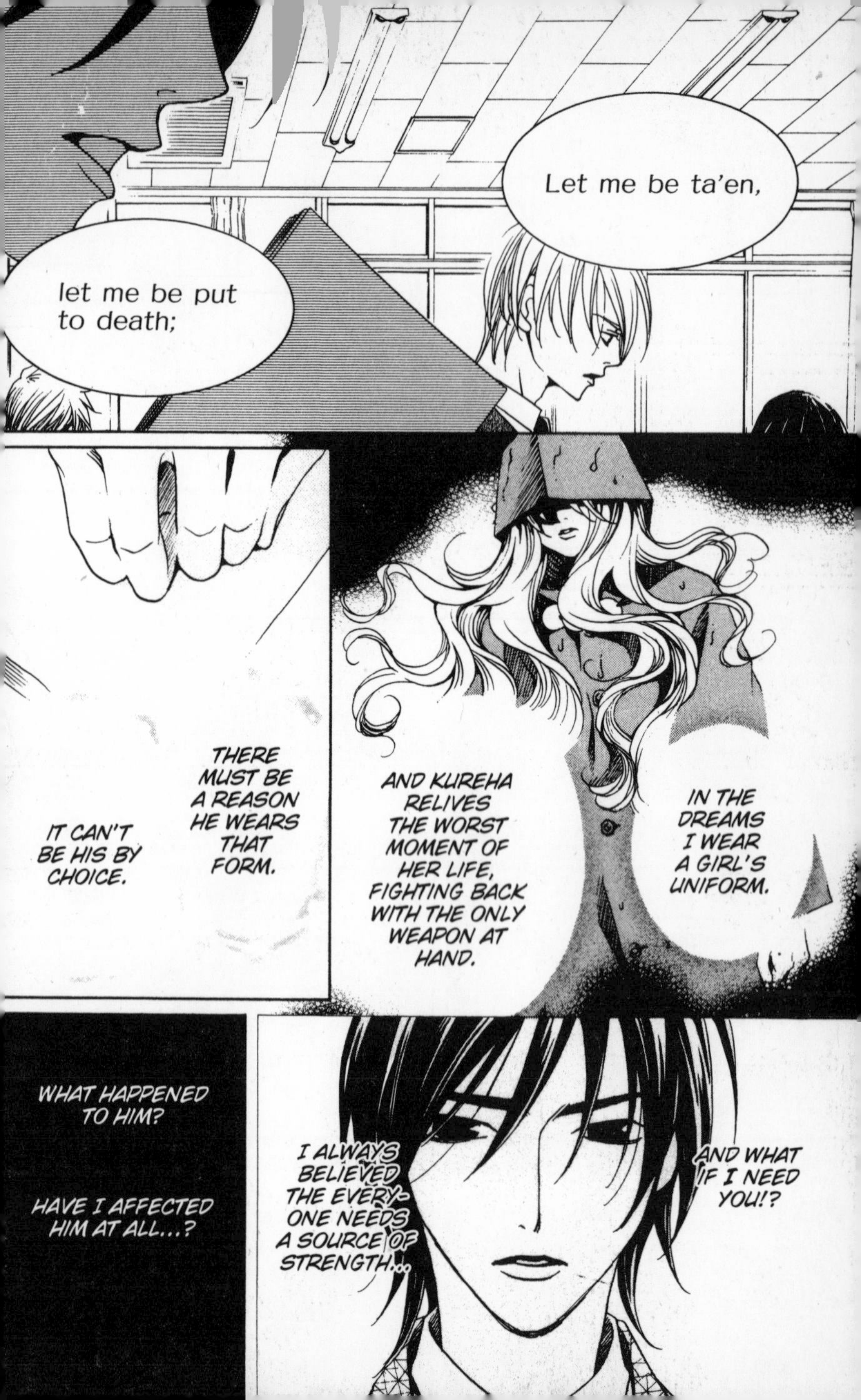
Let me be ta'en,
let me be put to death;
IN THE DREAMS I WEAR A GIRL'S UNIFORM.
AND KUREHA RELIVES THE WORST MOMENT OF HER LIFE, FIGHTING BACK WITH THE ONLY WEAPON AT HAND.
THERE MUST BE A REASON HE WEARS THAT FORM.
IT CAN'T BE HIS BY CHOICE.
AND WHAT IF I NEED YOU!?
I ALWAYS BELIEVED THE EVERY-ONE NEEDS A SOURCE OF STRENGTH...
WHAT HAPPENED TO HIM?
HAVE I AFFECTED HIM AT ALL...?

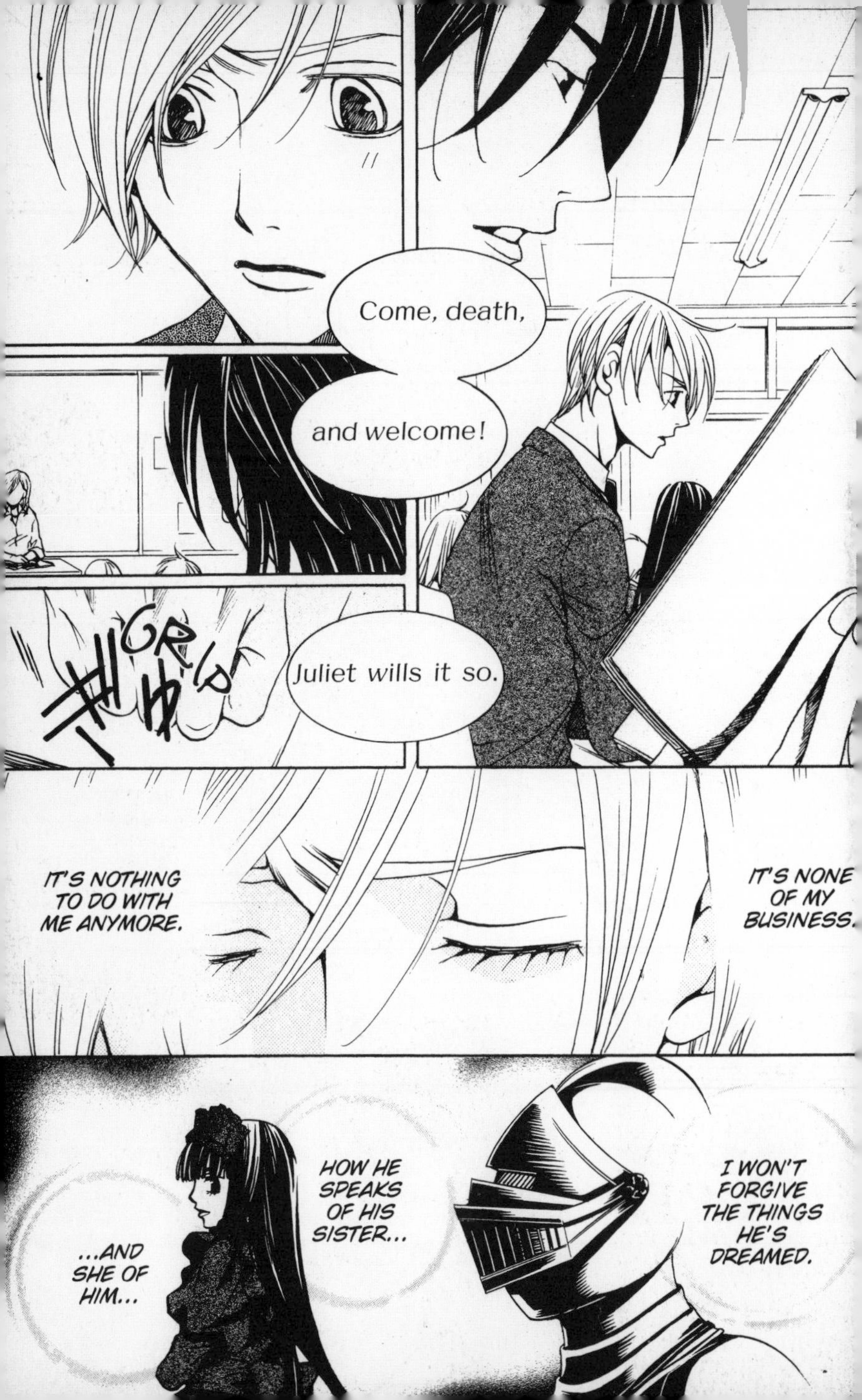
Come, death,
and welcome!
Juliet wills it so.
GRIP
IT'S NONE OF MY BUSINESS.
IT'S NOTHING TO DO WITH ME ANYMORE.
I WON'T FORGIVE THE THINGS HE'S DREAMED.
HOW HE SPEAKS OF HIS SISTER...
...AND SHE OF HIM...

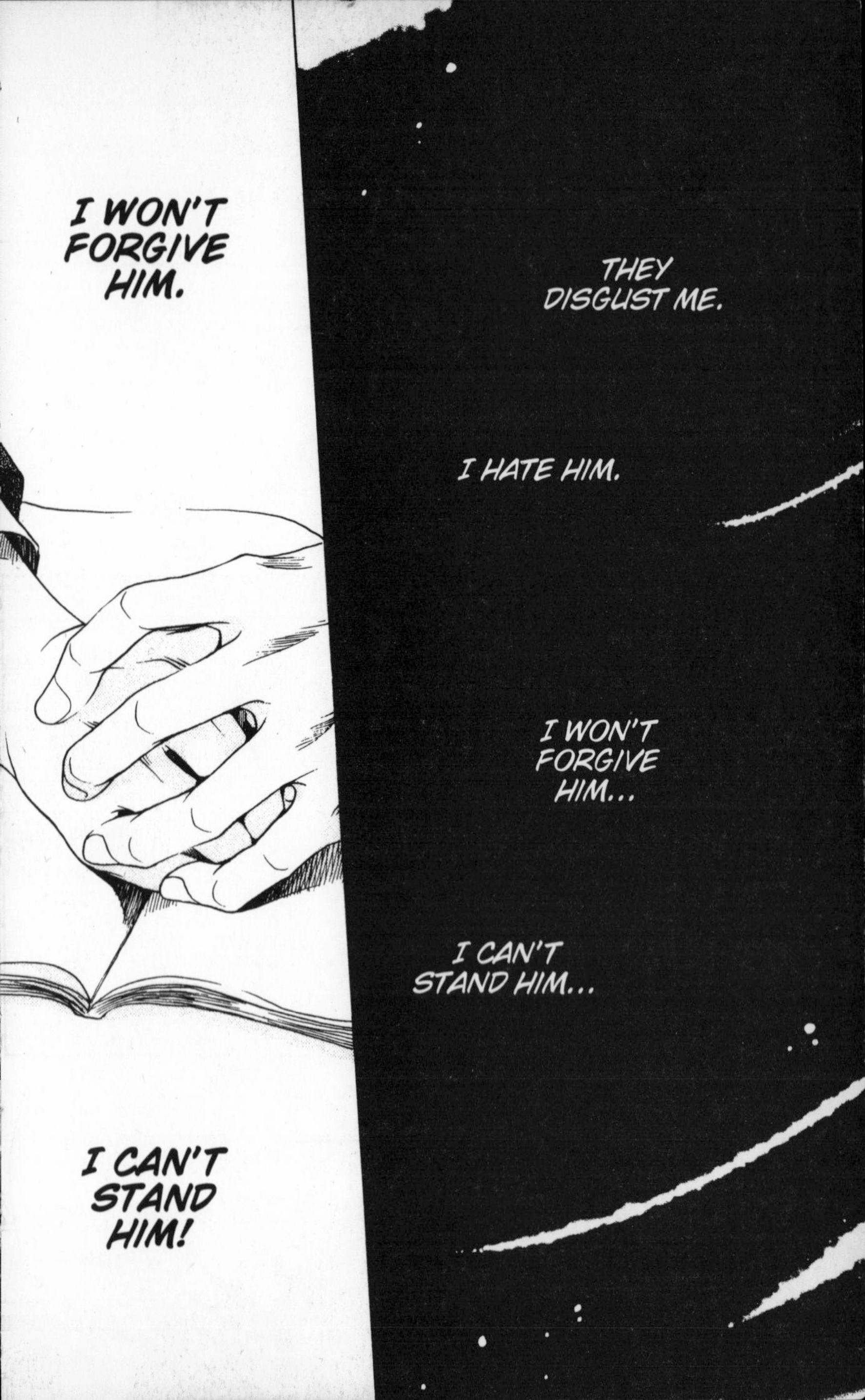
THEY DISGUST ME.
I HATE HIM.
I WON'T FORGIVE HIM...
I CAN'T STAND HIM...
I WON'T FORGIVE HIM.
I CAN'T STAND HIM!

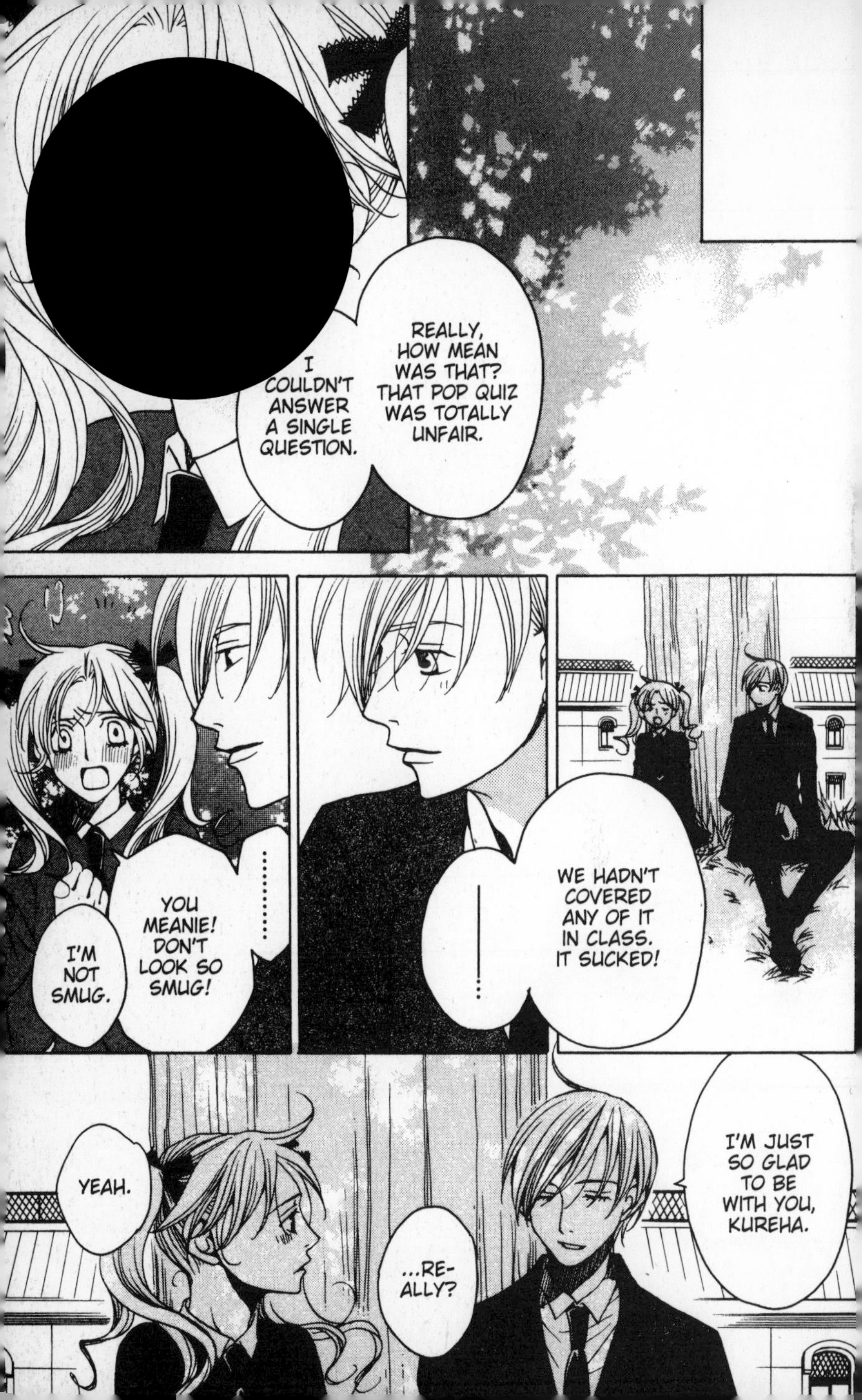
REALLY, HOW MEAN WAS THAT? THAT POP QUIZ WAS TOTALLY UNFAIR.
I COULDN'T ANSWER A SINGLE QUESTION.
WE HADN'T COVERED ANY OF IT IN CLASS. IT SUCKED!
……
……
YOU MEANIE! DON'T LOOK SO SMUG!
I'M NOT SMUG.
I'M JUST SO GLAD TO BE WITH YOU, KUREHA.
...RE-ALLY?
YEAH.

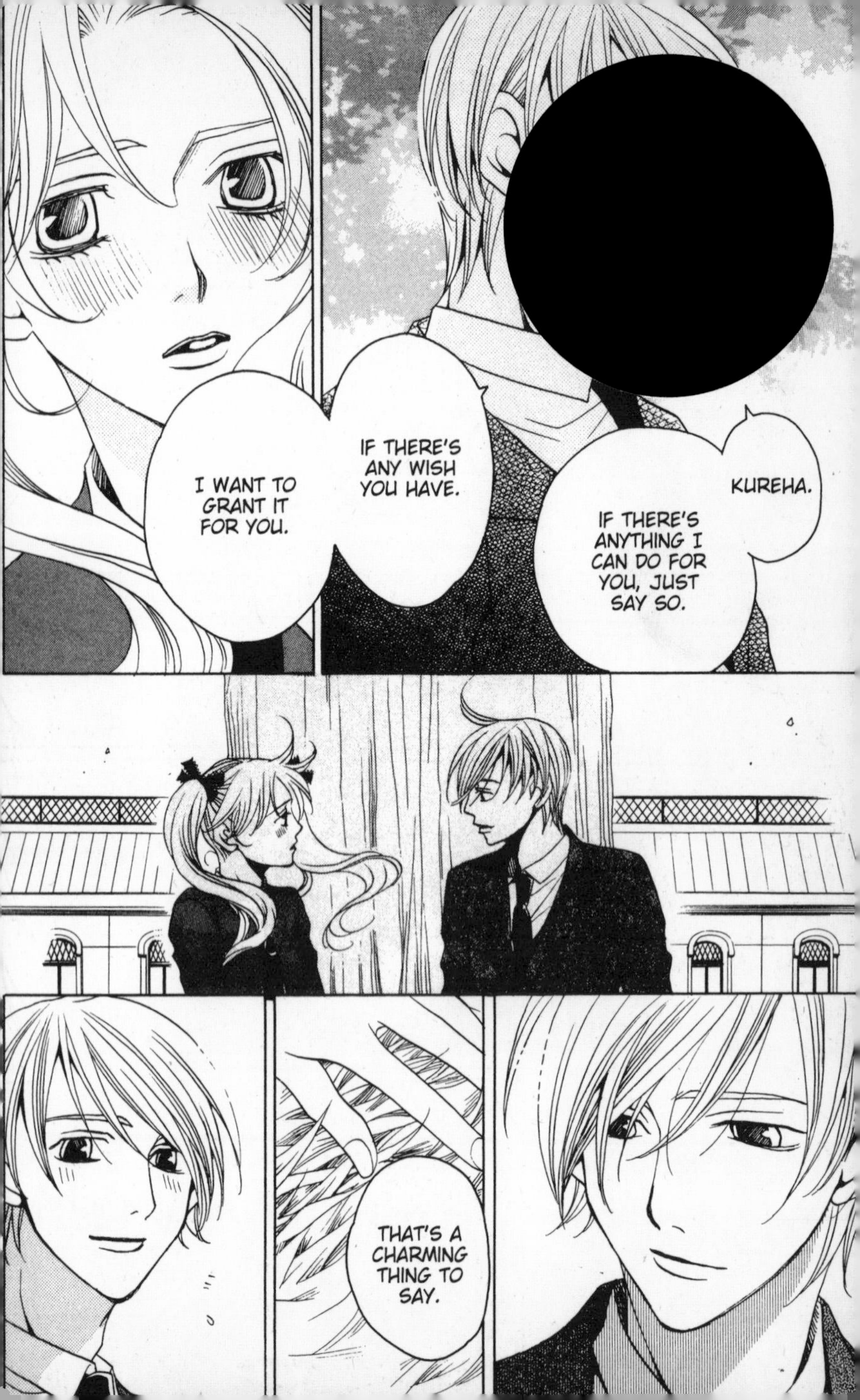
KUREHA.
IF THERE'S ANYTHING I CAN DO FOR YOU, JUST SAY SO.
IF THERE'S ANY WISH YOU HAVE.
I WANT TO GRANT IT FOR YOU.
THAT'S A CHARMING THING TO SAY.

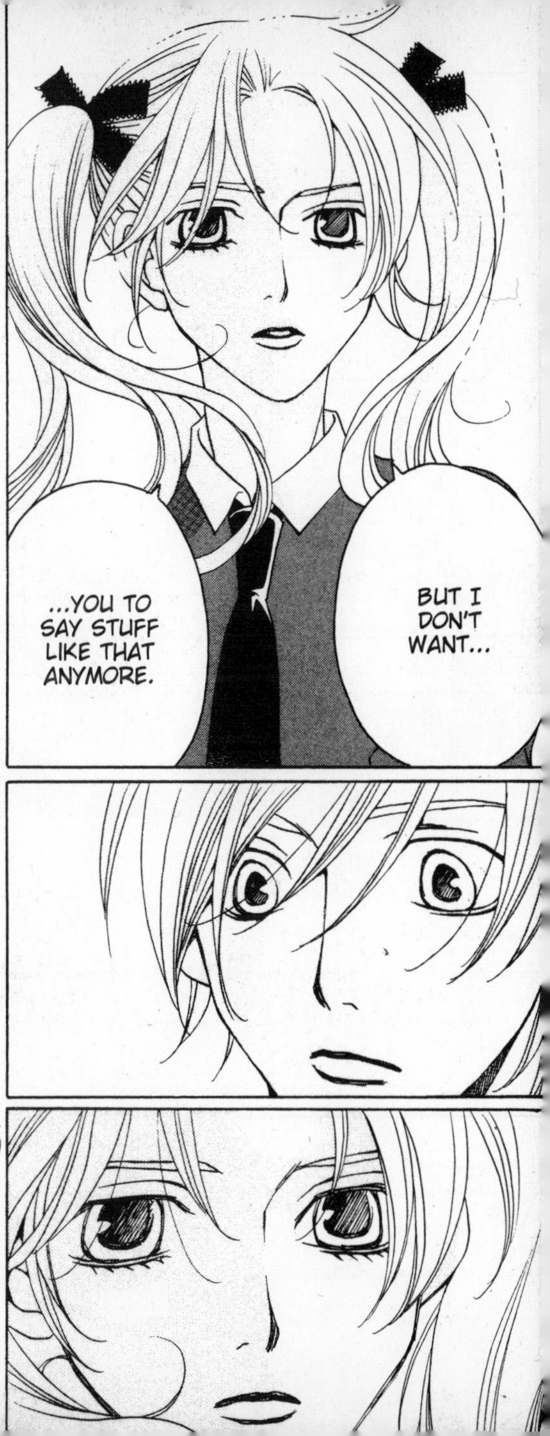
BUT I DON'T WANT...
...YOU TO SAY STUFF LIKE THAT ANYMORE.

This is the original long-haired version of Mashiro. "That picture kind of gives me goose bumps," and "It's hard to imagine a kid who doesn't want to be a girl keeping his hair that long," were the criticisms that came up to make me scrap the design.

There's just something so adult about it...

Also, there was a time while designing the girls' uniforms that I was considering doing a sailor version.

I think a sailor outfit would match this hair style very well.

But it wouldn't be right to have this character look good in a sailor suit, for the storyline at least...

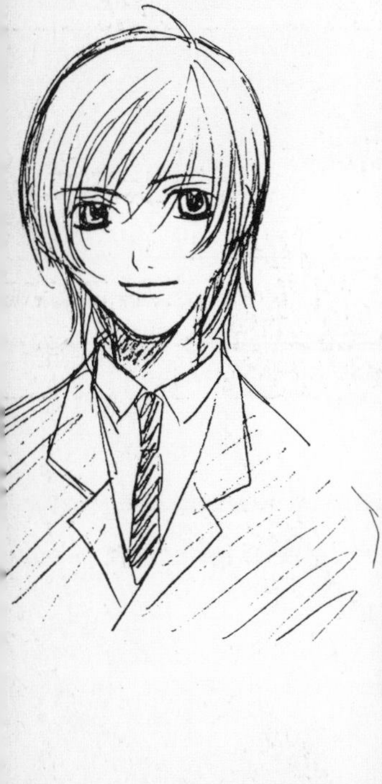

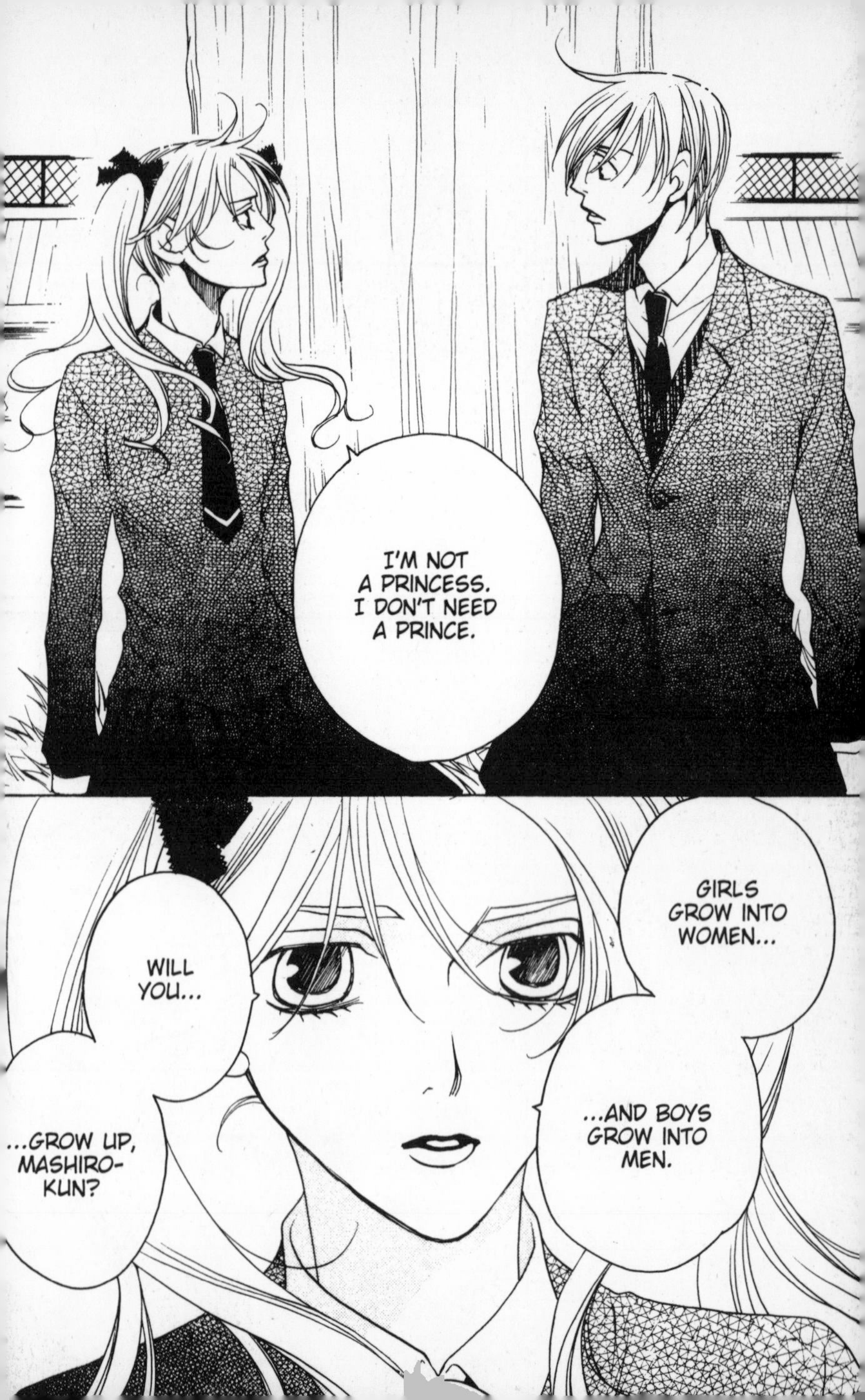
I'M NOT A PRINCESS. I DON'T NEED A PRINCE.
GIRLS GROW INTO WOMEN...
...AND BOYS GROW INTO MEN.
WILL YOU...
...GROW UP, MASHIRO-KUN?

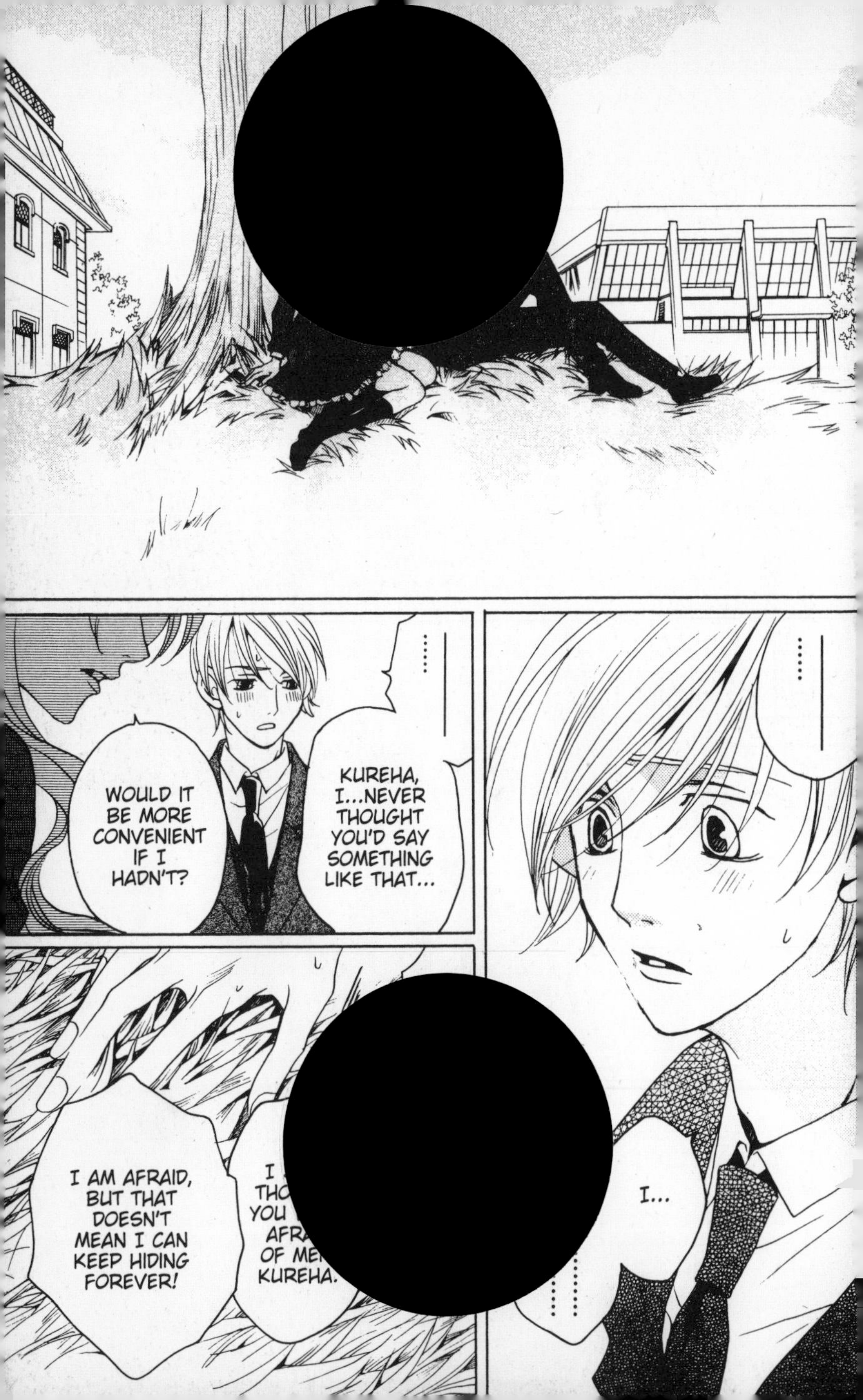
......
I...
......
......
KUREHA, I...NEVER THOUGHT YOU'D SAY SOMETHING LIKE THAT...
WOULD IT BE MORE CONVENIENT IF I HADN'T?
I [redacted] THO[redacted] YOU [redacted] AFRA[redacted] OF ME[redacted] KUREHA.
I AM AFRAID, BUT THAT DOESN'T MEAN I CAN KEEP HIDING FOREVER!

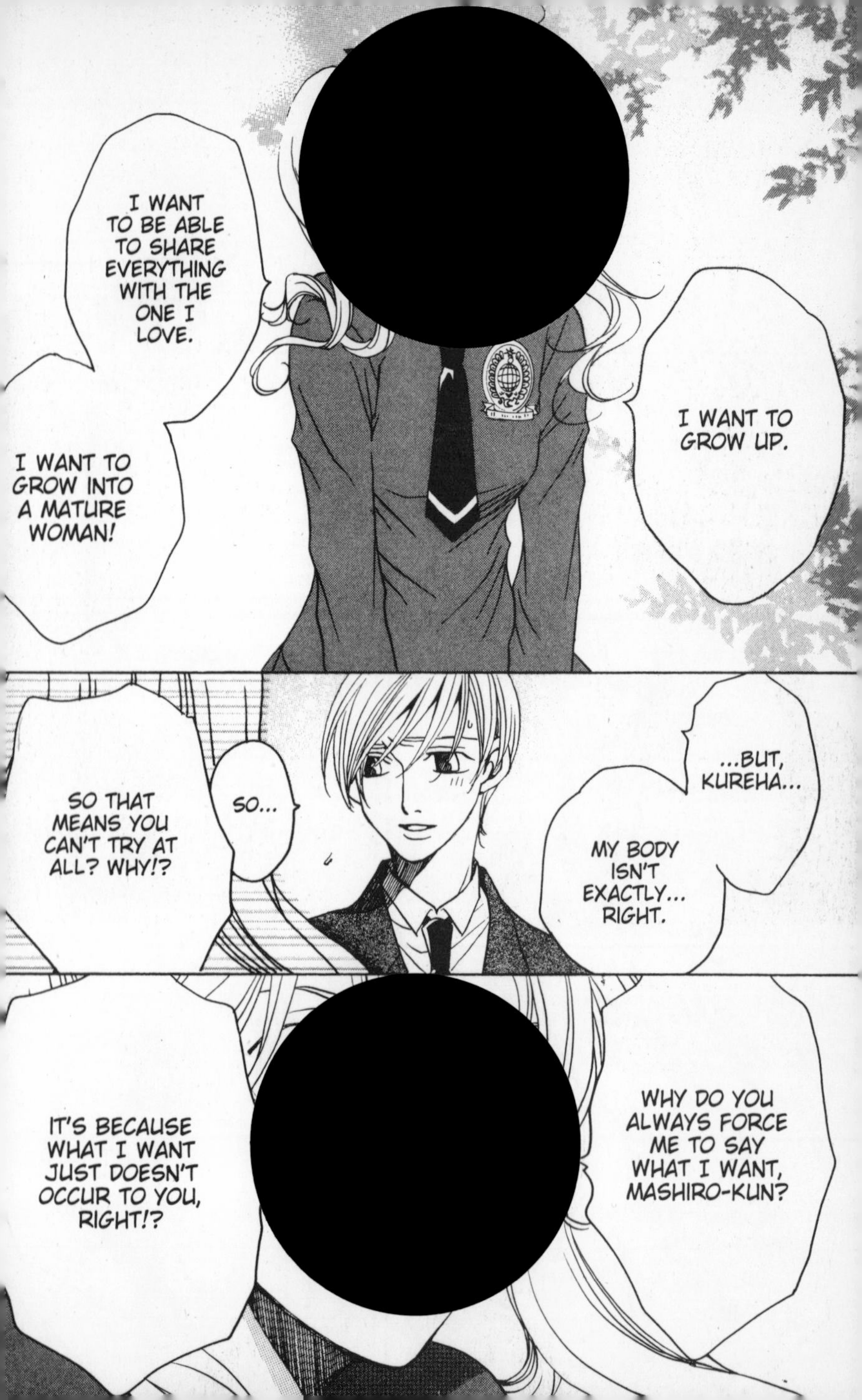
I WANT TO GROW UP.
I WANT TO BE ABLE TO SHARE EVERYTHING WITH THE ONE I LOVE.
I WANT TO GROW INTO A MATURE WOMAN!
...BUT, KUREHA...
MY BODY ISN'T EXACTLY... RIGHT.
SO...
SO THAT MEANS YOU CAN'T TRY AT ALL? WHY!?
WHY DO YOU ALWAYS FORCE ME TO SAY WHAT I WANT, MASHIRO-KUN?
IT'S BECAUSE WHAT I WANT JUST DOESN'T OCCUR TO YOU, RIGHT!?

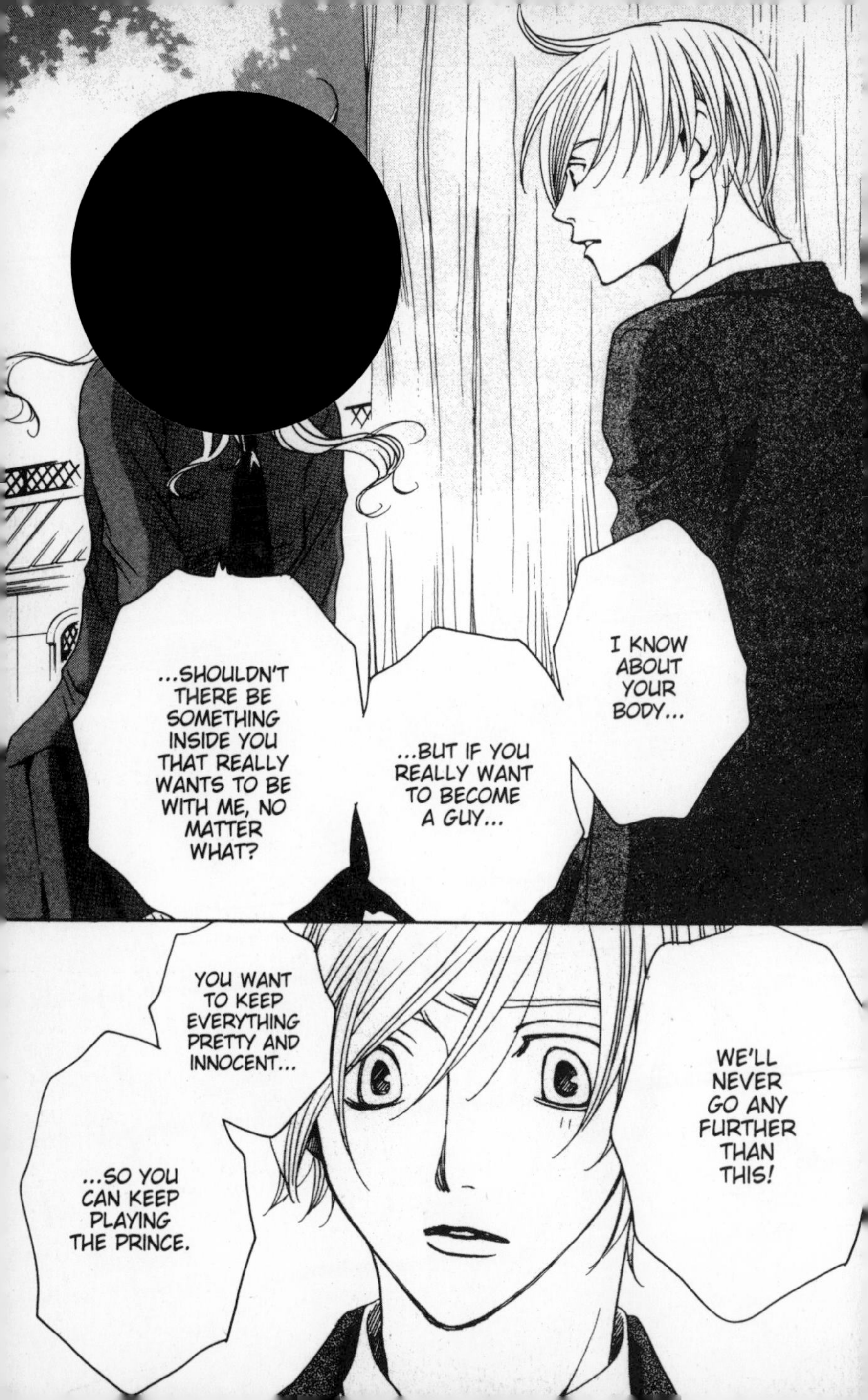
I KNOW ABOUT YOUR BODY...
...BUT IF YOU REALLY WANT TO BECOME A GUY...
...SHOULDN'T THERE BE SOMETHING INSIDE YOU THAT REALLY WANTS TO BE WITH ME, NO MATTER WHAT?
WE'LL NEVER GO ANY FURTHER THAN THIS!
YOU WANT TO KEEP EVERYTHING PRETTY AND INNOCENT...
...SO YOU CAN KEEP PLAYING THE PRINCE.

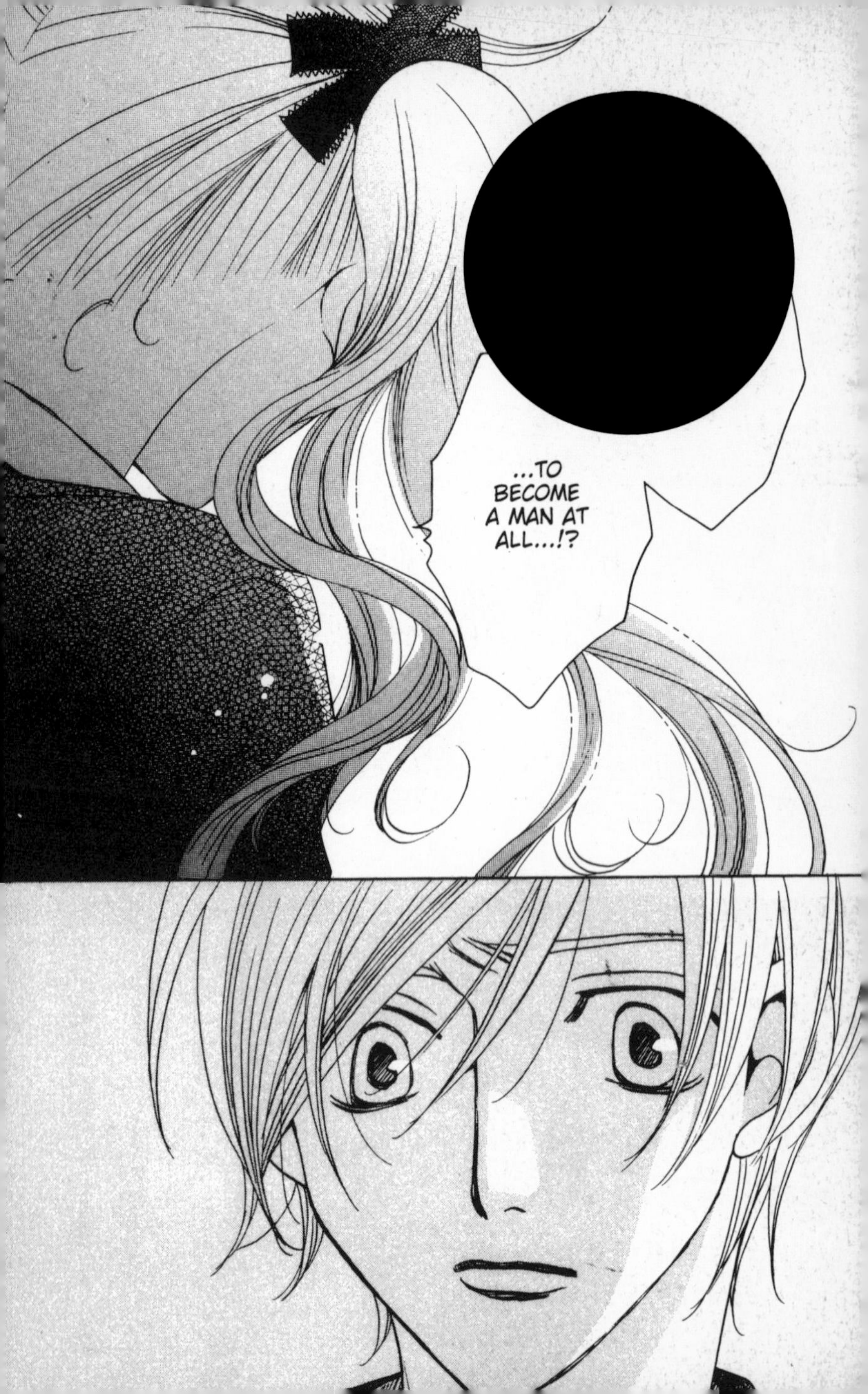
[redacted]
...TO BECOME A MAN AT ALL...!?

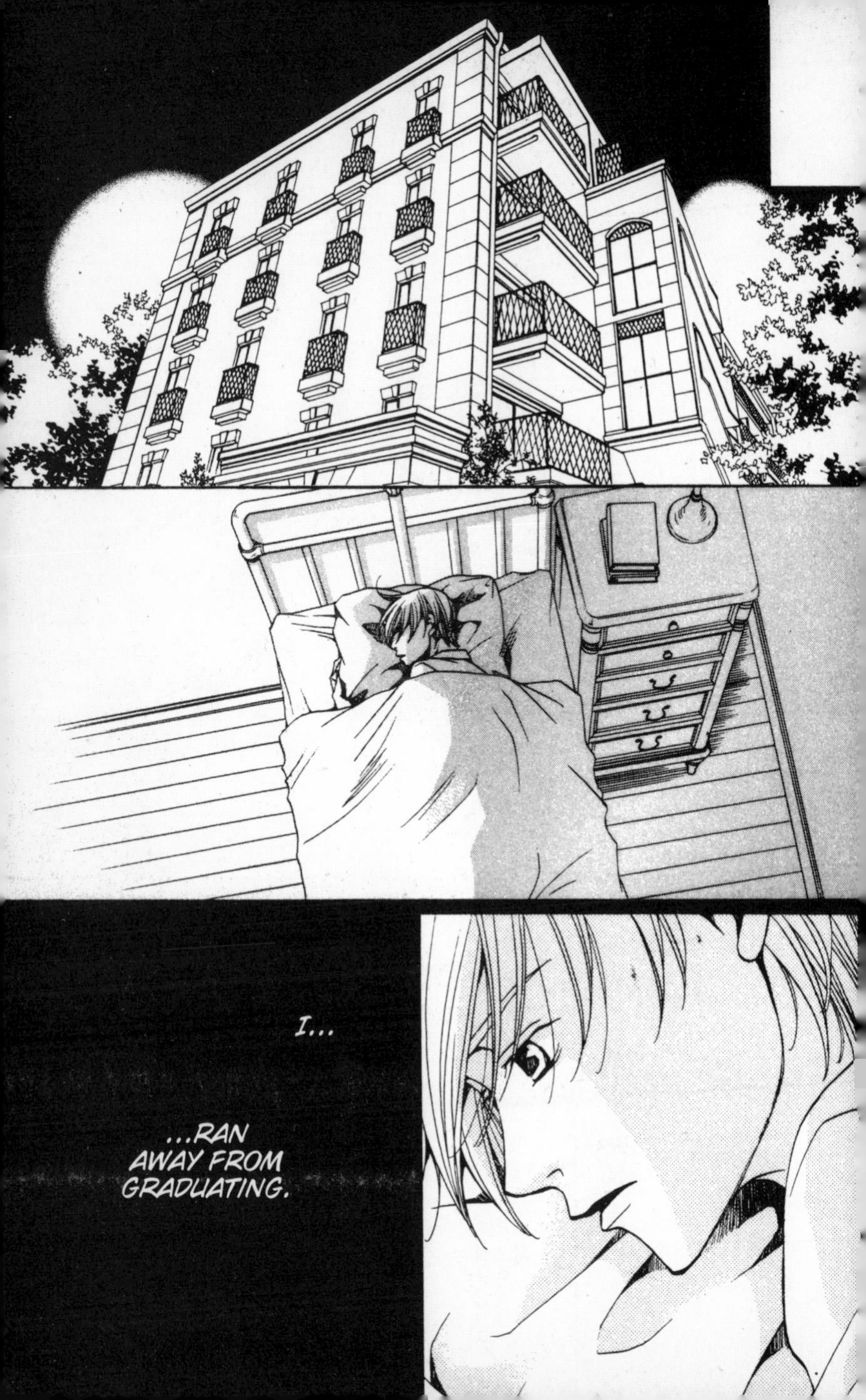
I...
...RAN AWAY FROM GRADUATING.

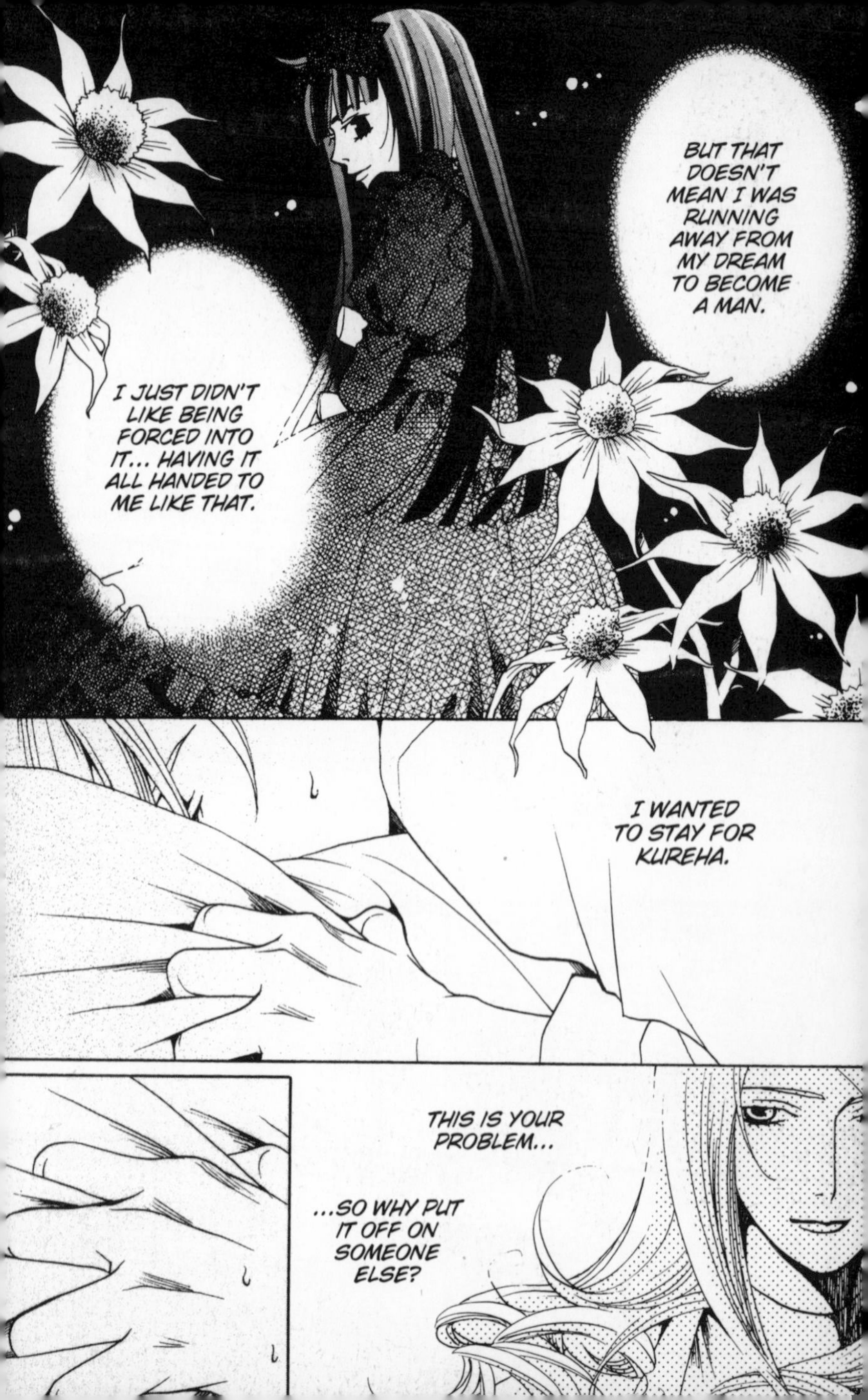
BUT THAT DOESN'T MEAN I WAS RUNNING AWAY FROM MY DREAM TO BECOME A MAN.
I JUST DIDN'T LIKE BEING FORCED INTO IT... HAVING IT ALL HANDED TO ME LIKE THAT.
I WANTED TO STAY FOR KUREHA.
THIS IS YOUR PROBLEM...
...SO WHY PUT IT OFF ON SOMEONE ELSE?

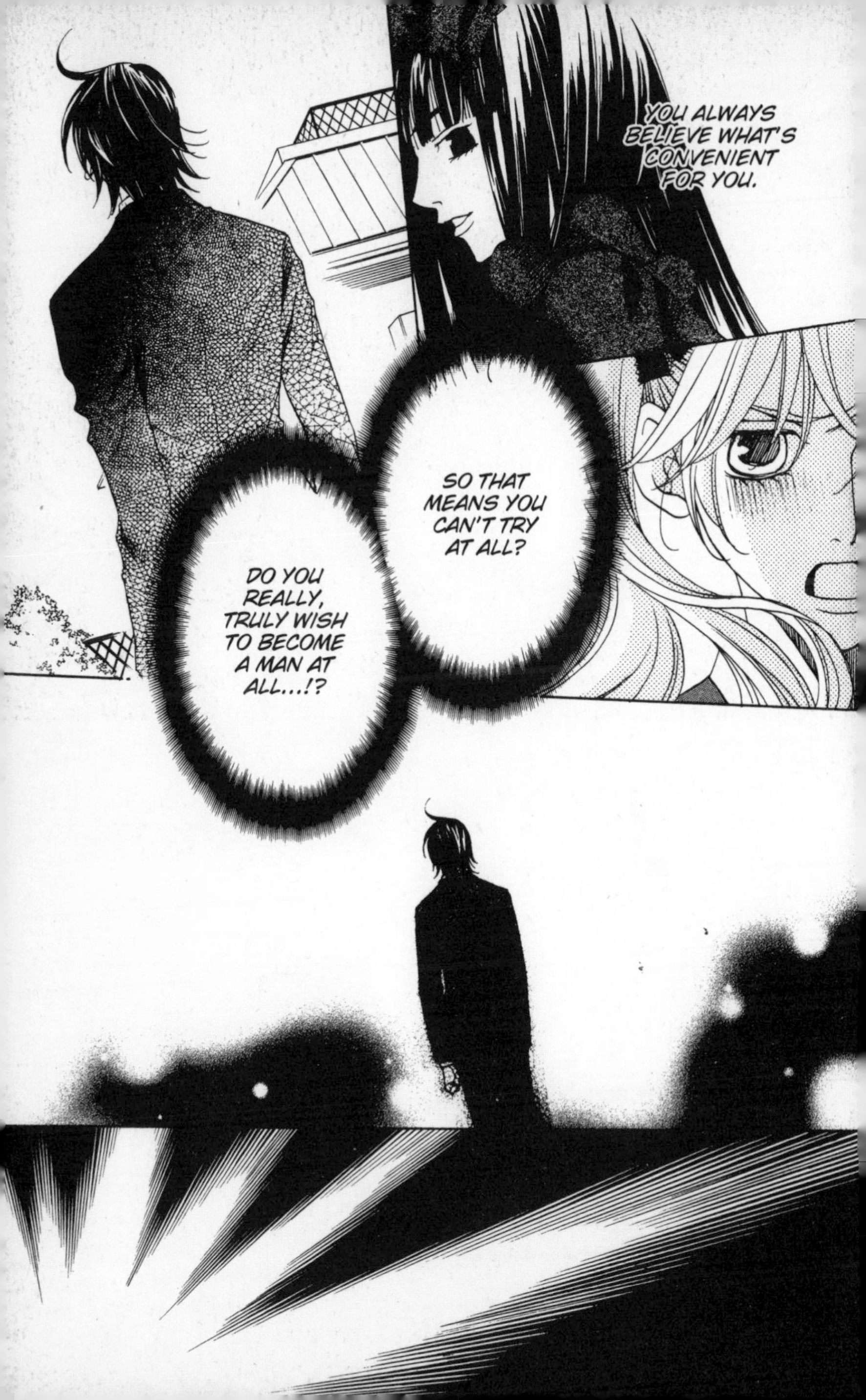
YOU ALWAYS BELIEVE WHAT'S CONVENIENT FOR YOU.
SO THAT MEANS YOU CAN'T TRY AT ALL?
DO YOU REALLY, TRULY WISH TO BECOME A MAN AT ALL...!?

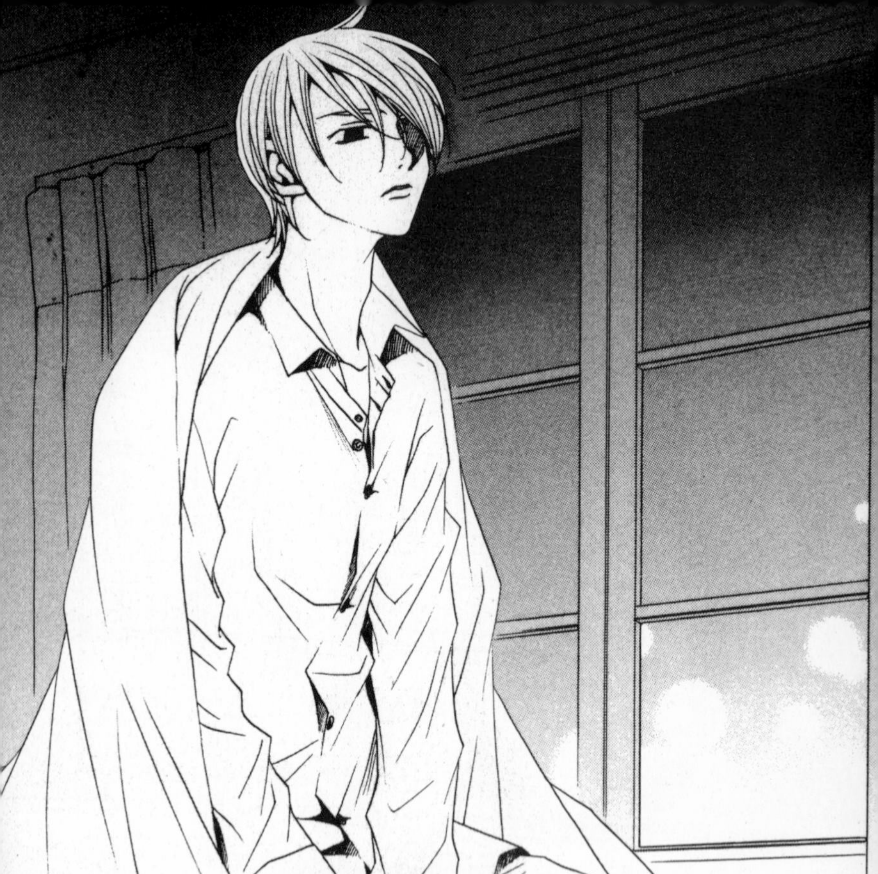
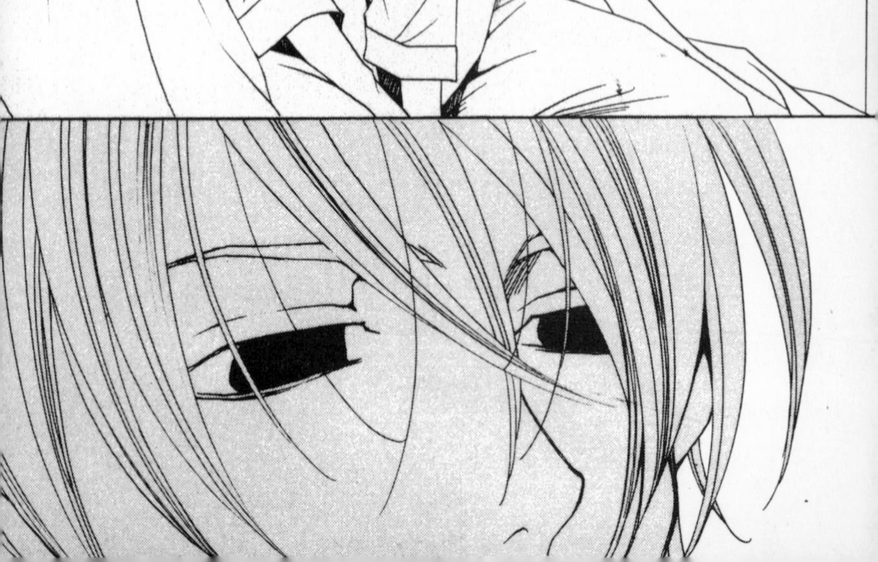

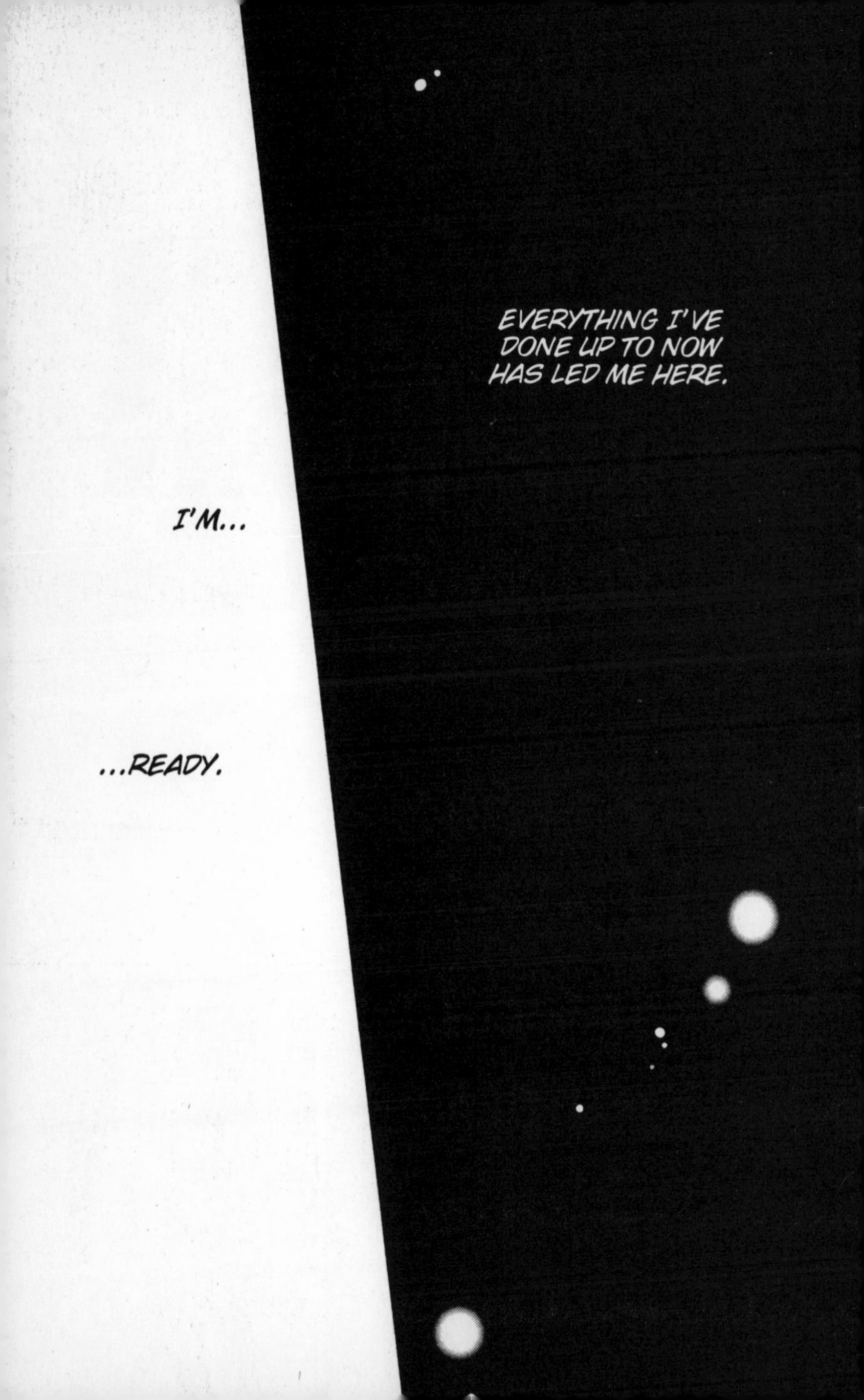
EVERYTHING I'VE DONE UP TO NOW HAS LED ME HERE.
I'M...
...READY.

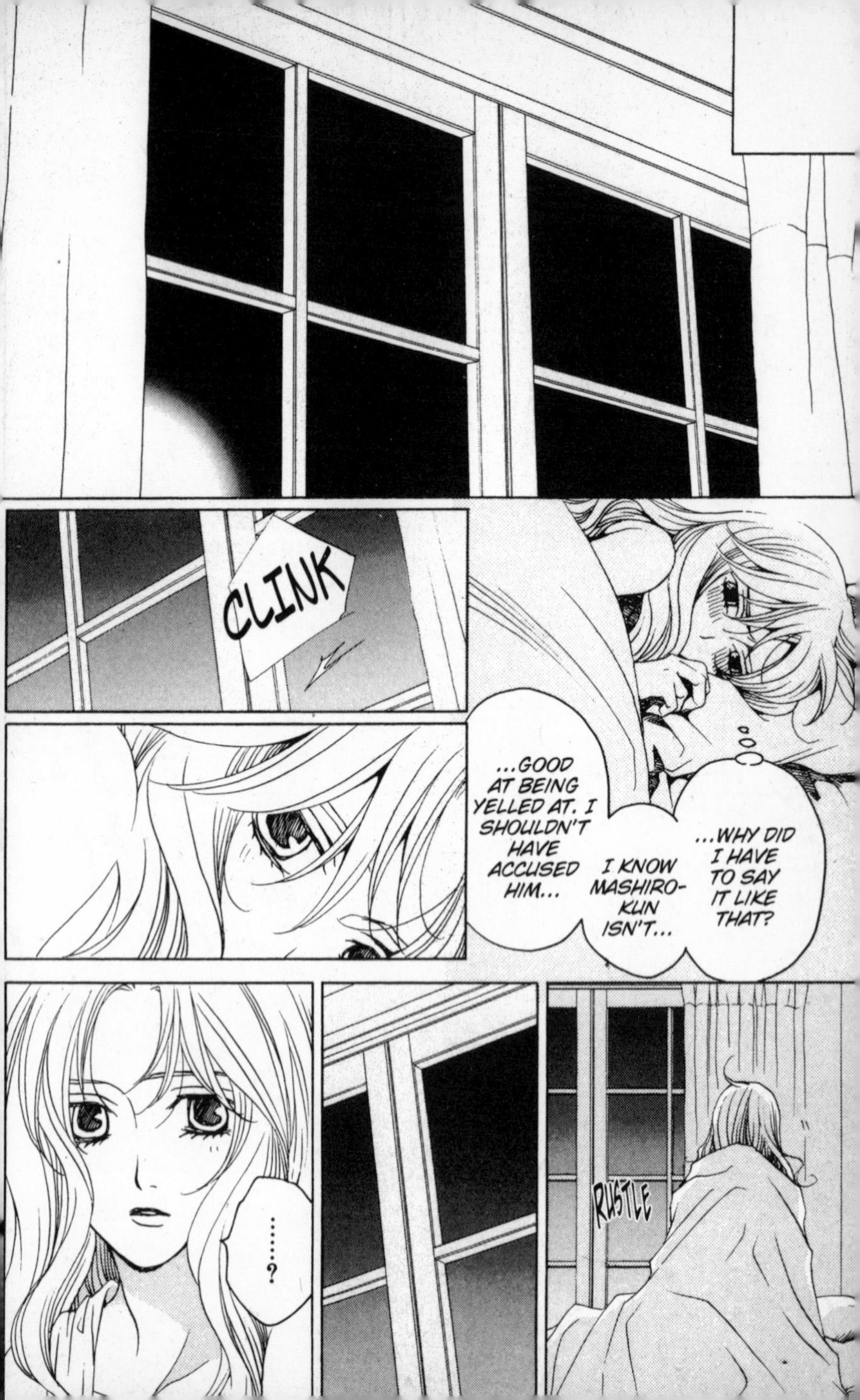
...WHY DID I HAVE TO SAY IT LIKE THAT?
I KNOW MASHIRO-KUN ISN'T...
...GOOD AT BEING YELLED AT. I SHOULDN'T HAVE ACCUSED HIM...
CLINK
RUSTLE
......?

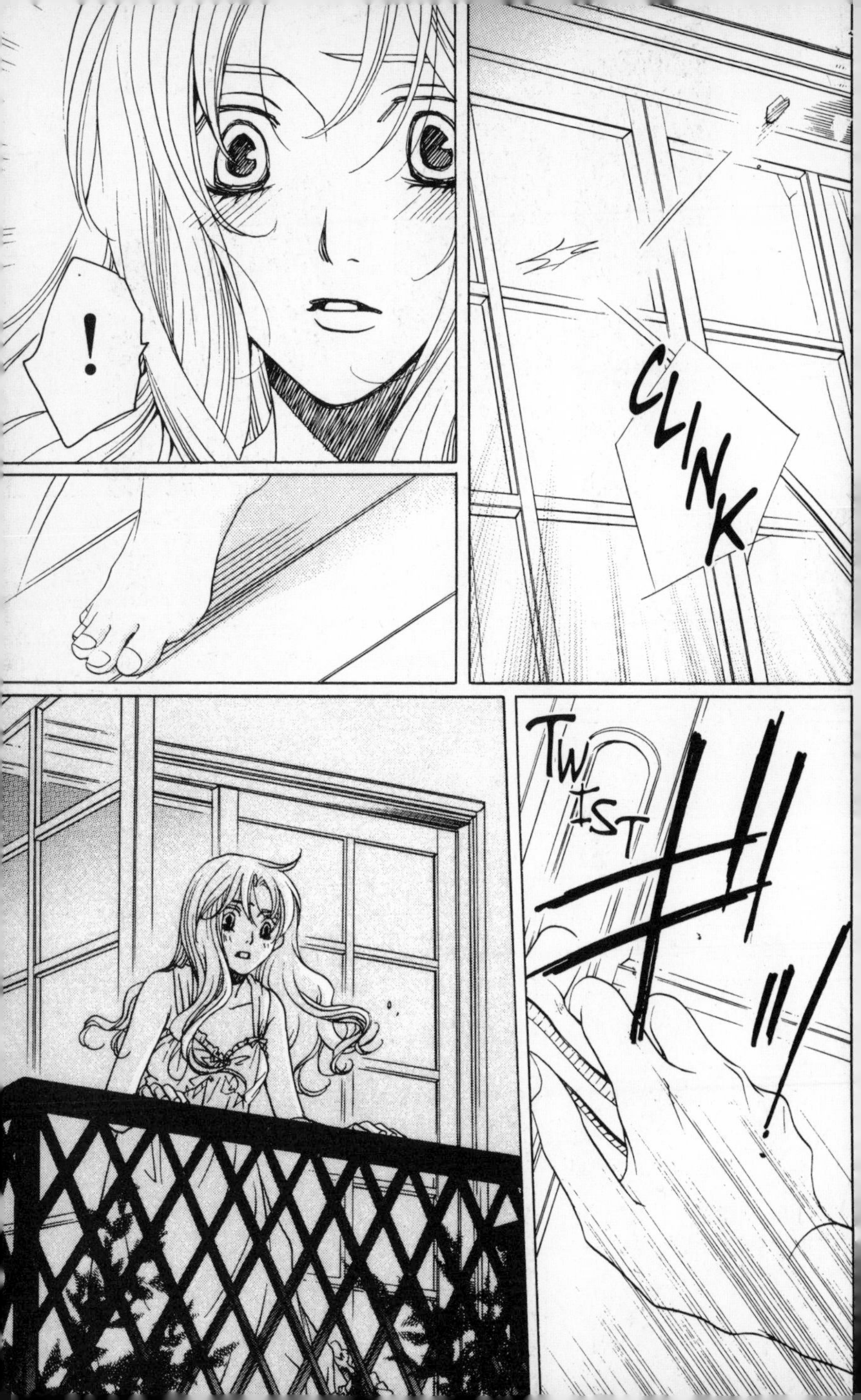
CLINK
!
TWIST

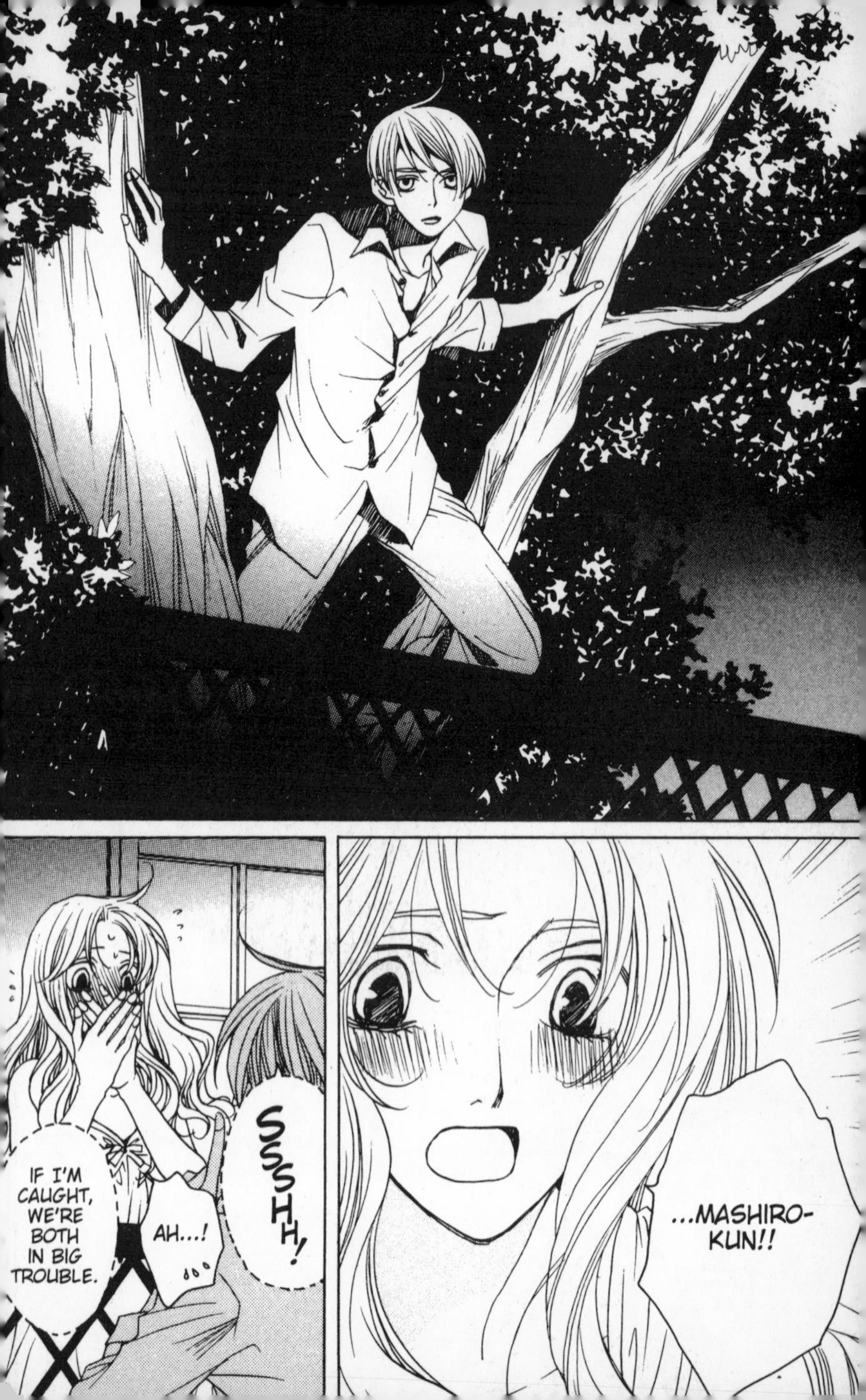
...MASHIRO-KUN!!
SSSHH!
AH...!
IF I'M CAUGHT, WE'RE BOTH IN BIG TROUBLE.

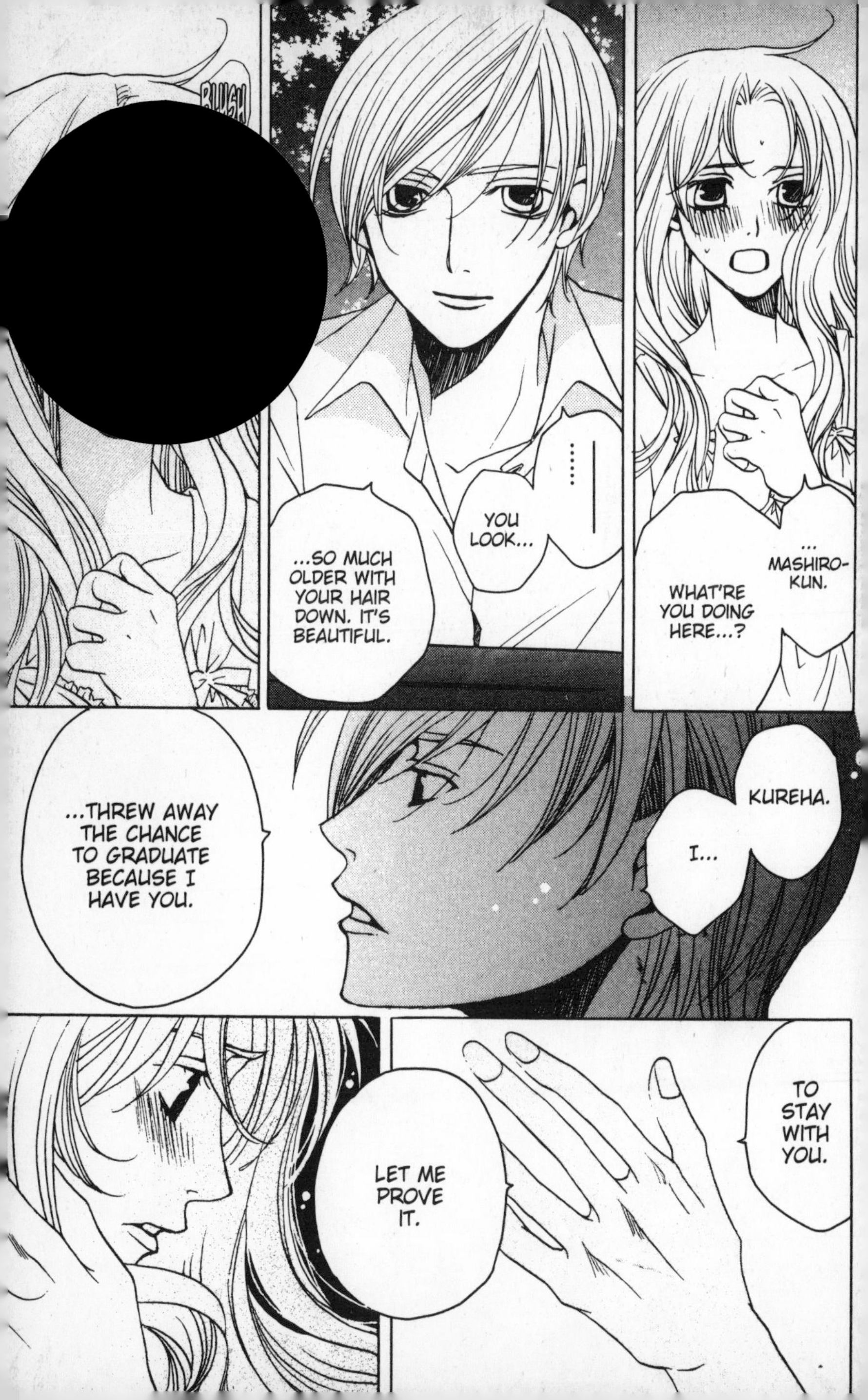
... MASHIRO-KUN.
WHAT'RE YOU DOING HERE...?
......
YOU LOOK...
...SO MUCH OLDER WITH YOUR HAIR DOWN. IT'S BEAUTIFUL.
BLUSH
[redacted]
KUREHA.
I...
...THREW AWAY THE CHANCE TO GRADUATE BECAUSE I HAVE YOU.
TO STAY WITH YOU.
LET ME PROVE IT.

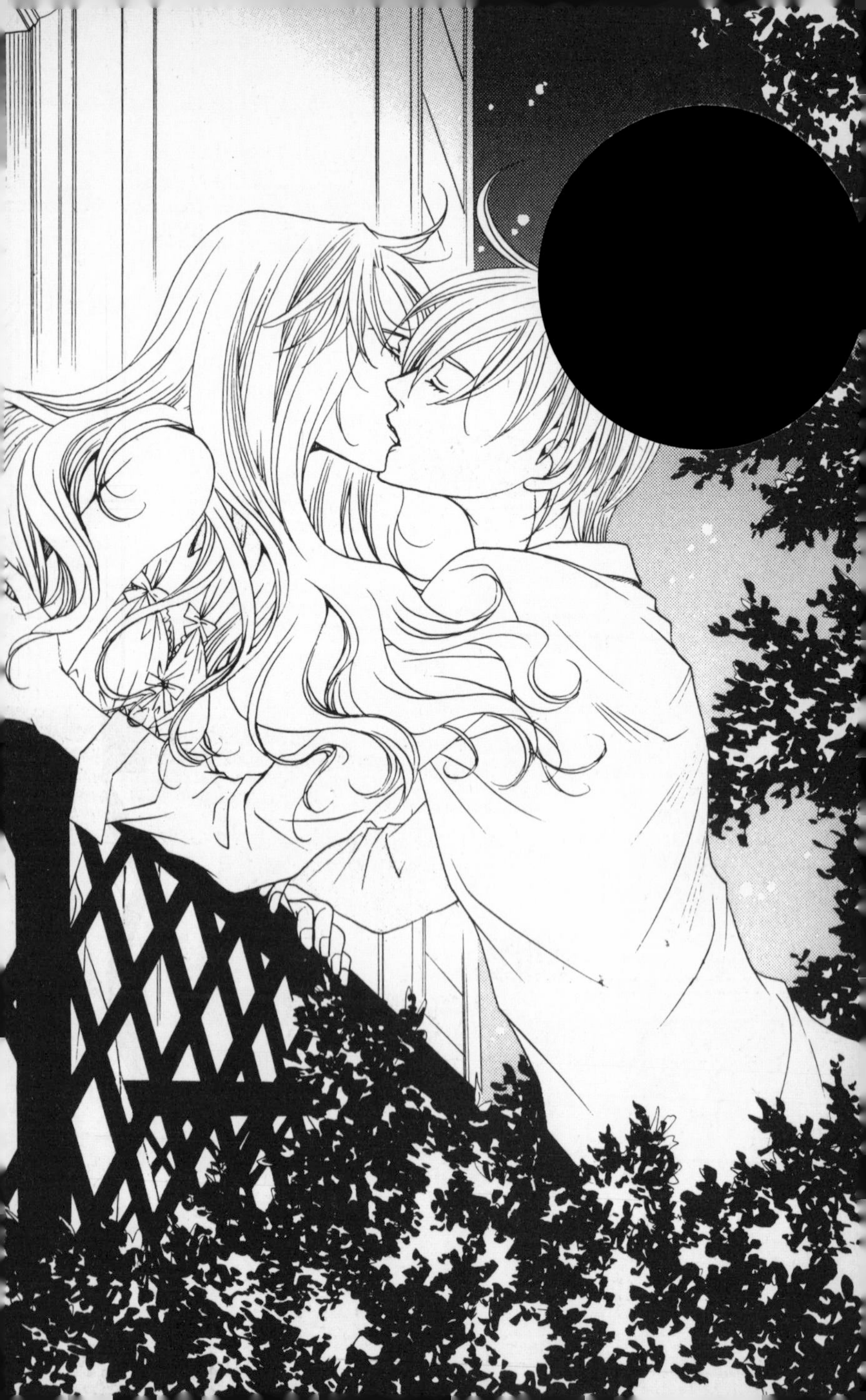

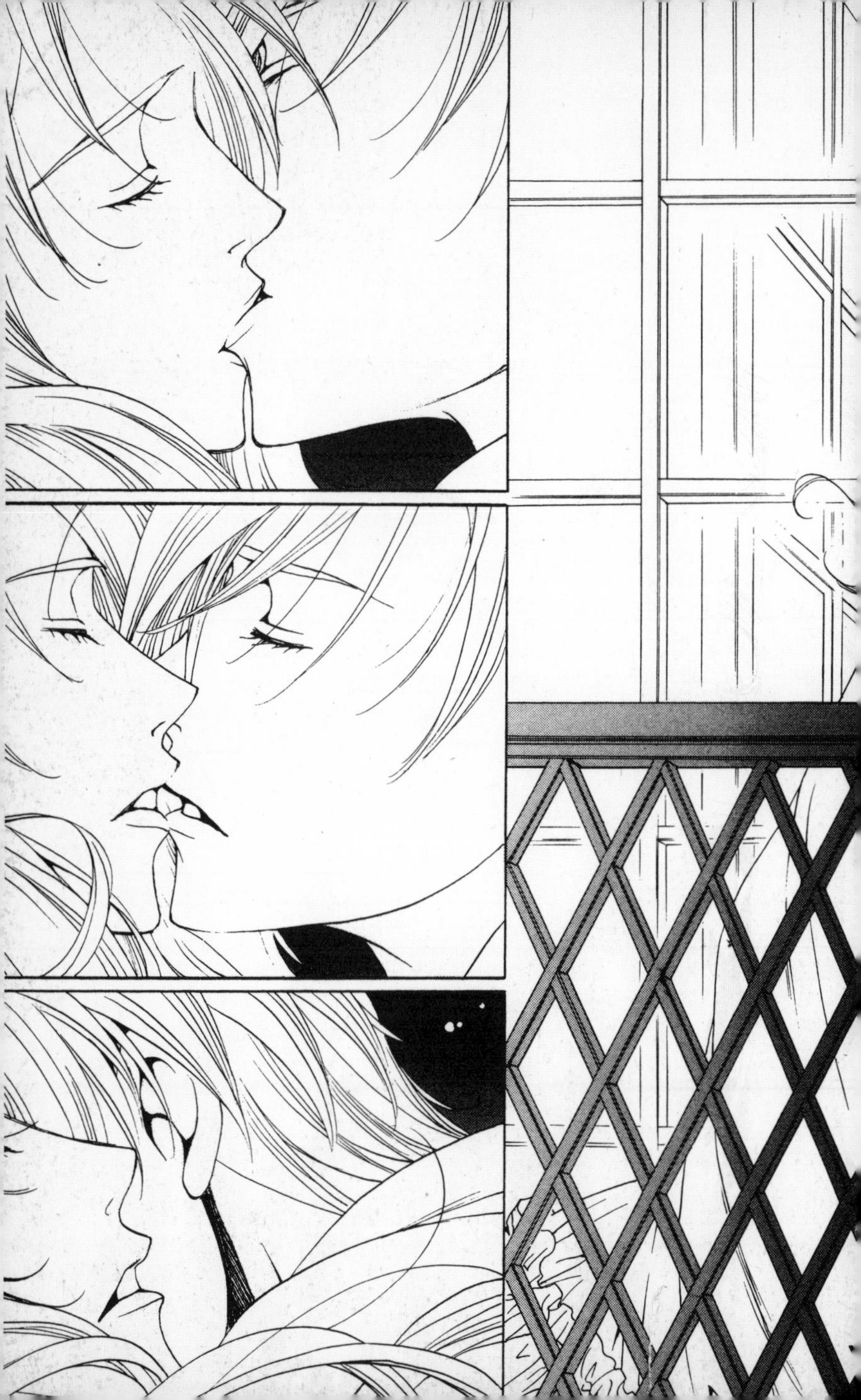

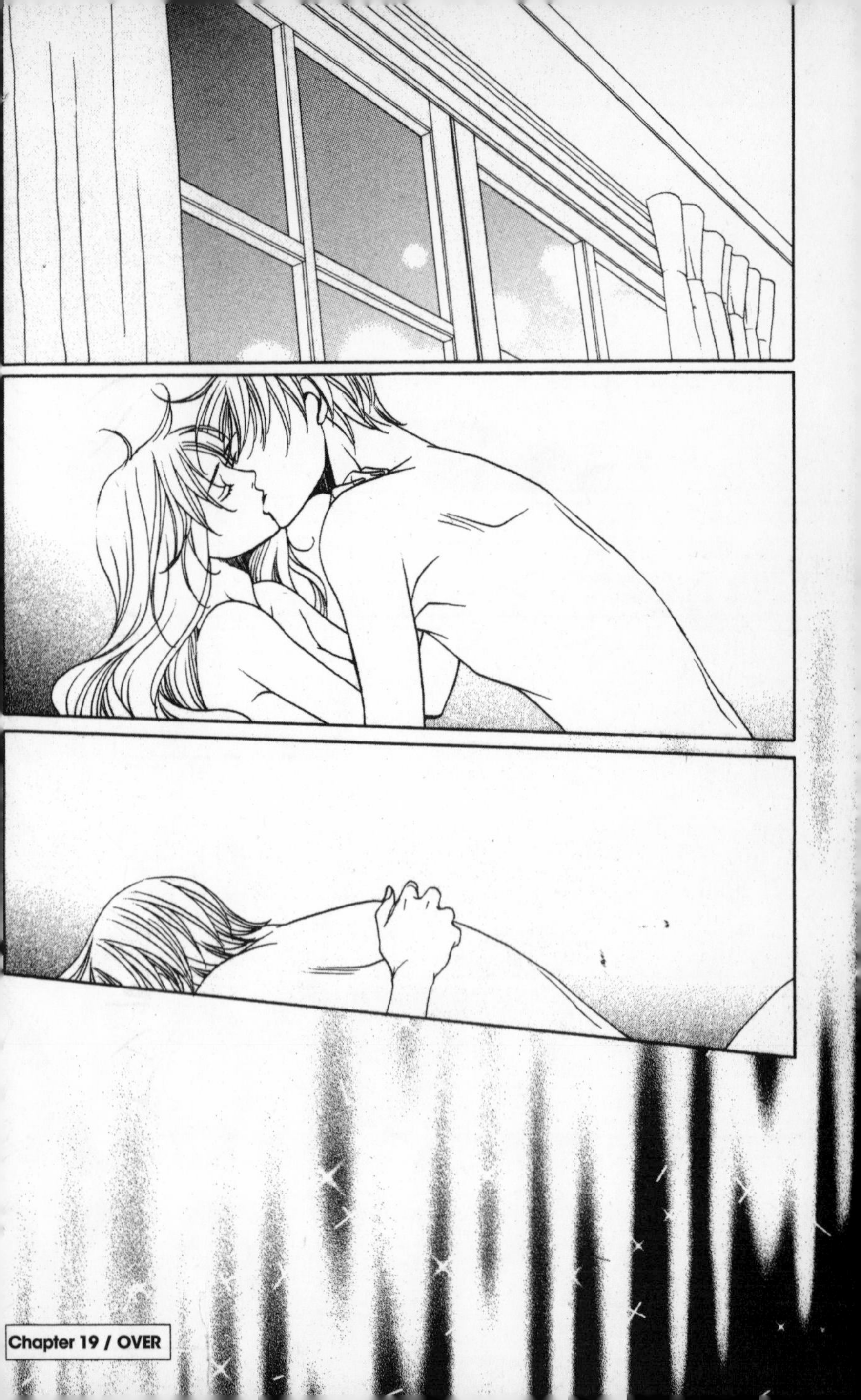
Chapter 19 / OVER

AFTER SCHOOL NIGHTMARE Chapter 20

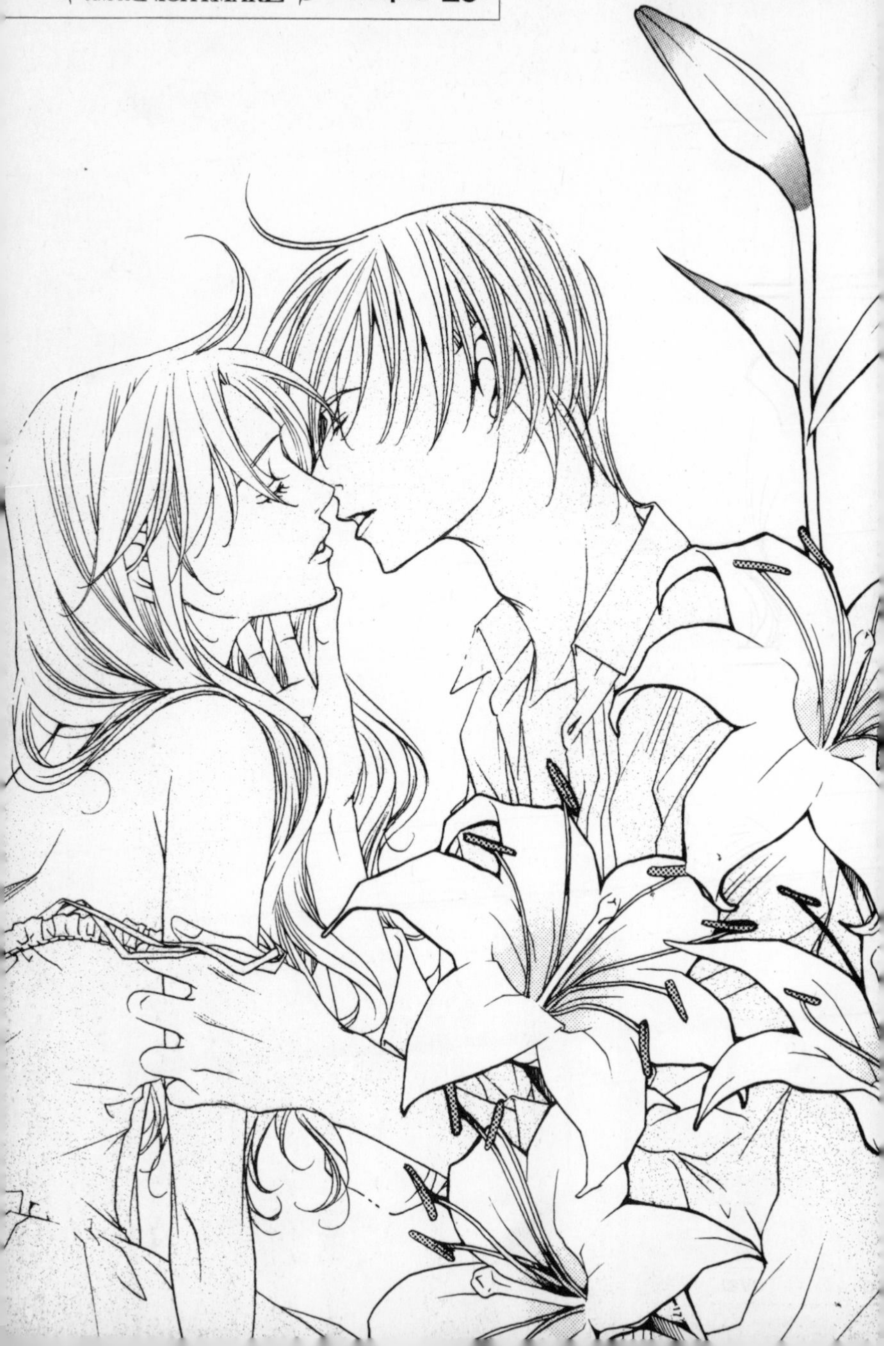

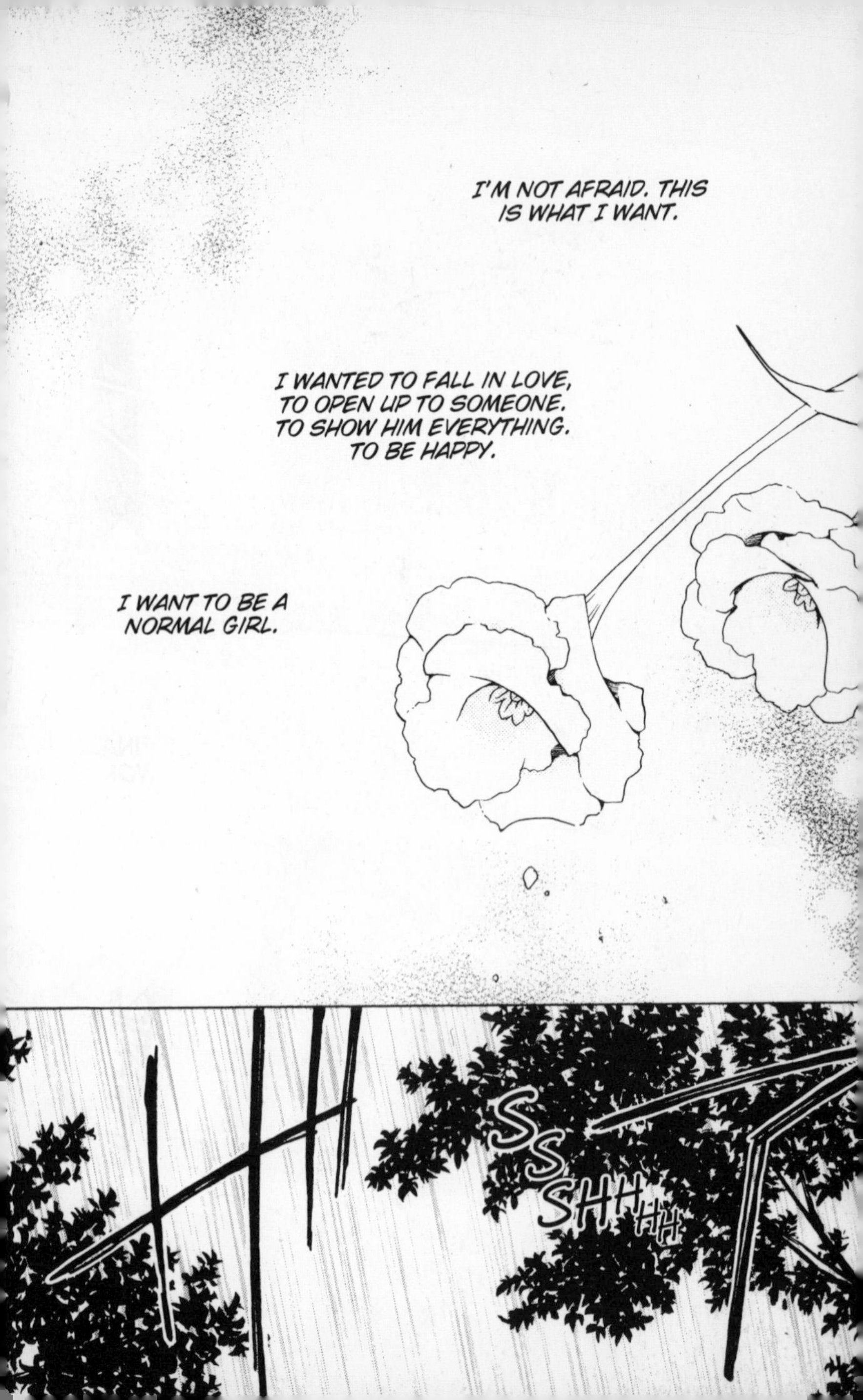
I'M NOT AFRAID. THIS IS WHAT I WANT.
I WANTED TO FALL IN LOVE, TO OPEN UP TO SOMEONE. TO SHOW HIM EVERYTHING. TO BE HAPPY.
I WANT TO BE A NORMAL GIRL.
SSSHHHH

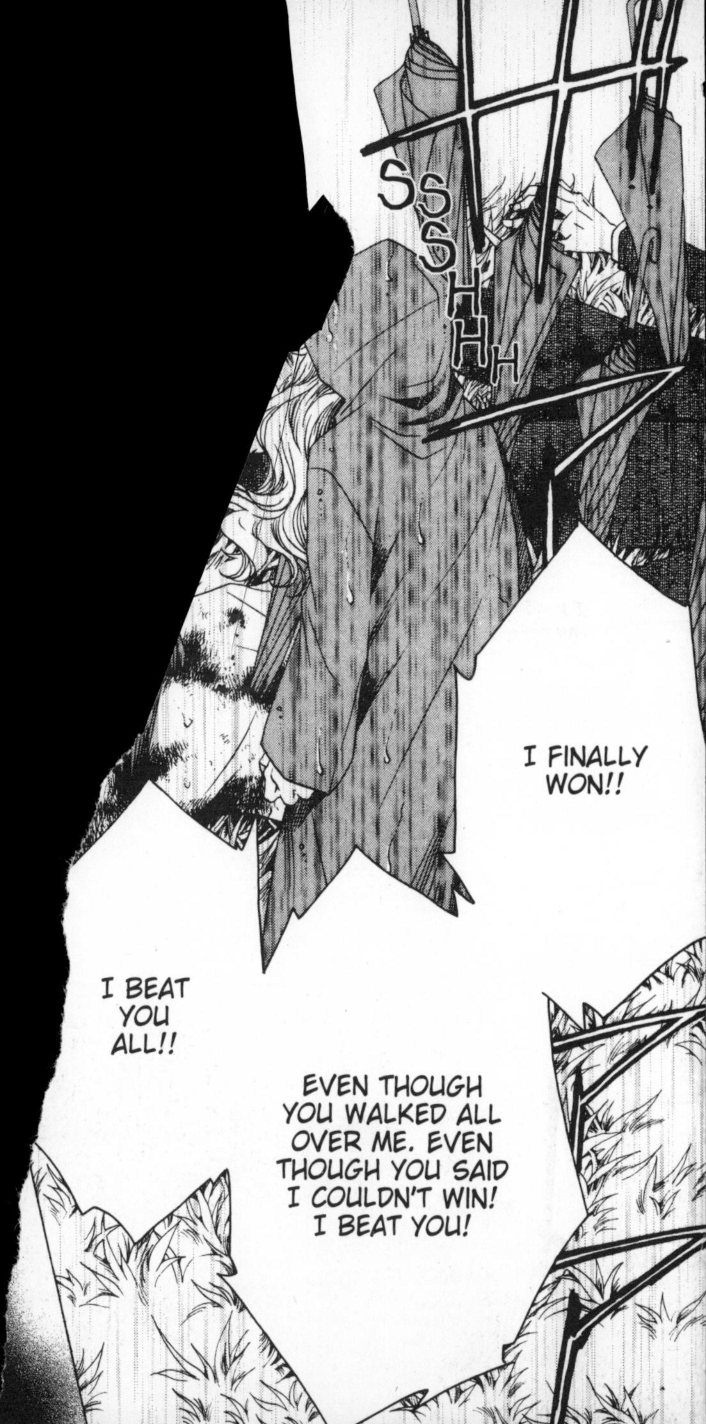
SSSHHH
I FINALLY WON!!
I BEAT YOU ALL!!
EVEN THOUGH YOU WALKED ALL OVER ME. EVEN THOUGH YOU SAID I COULDN'T WIN! I BEAT YOU!

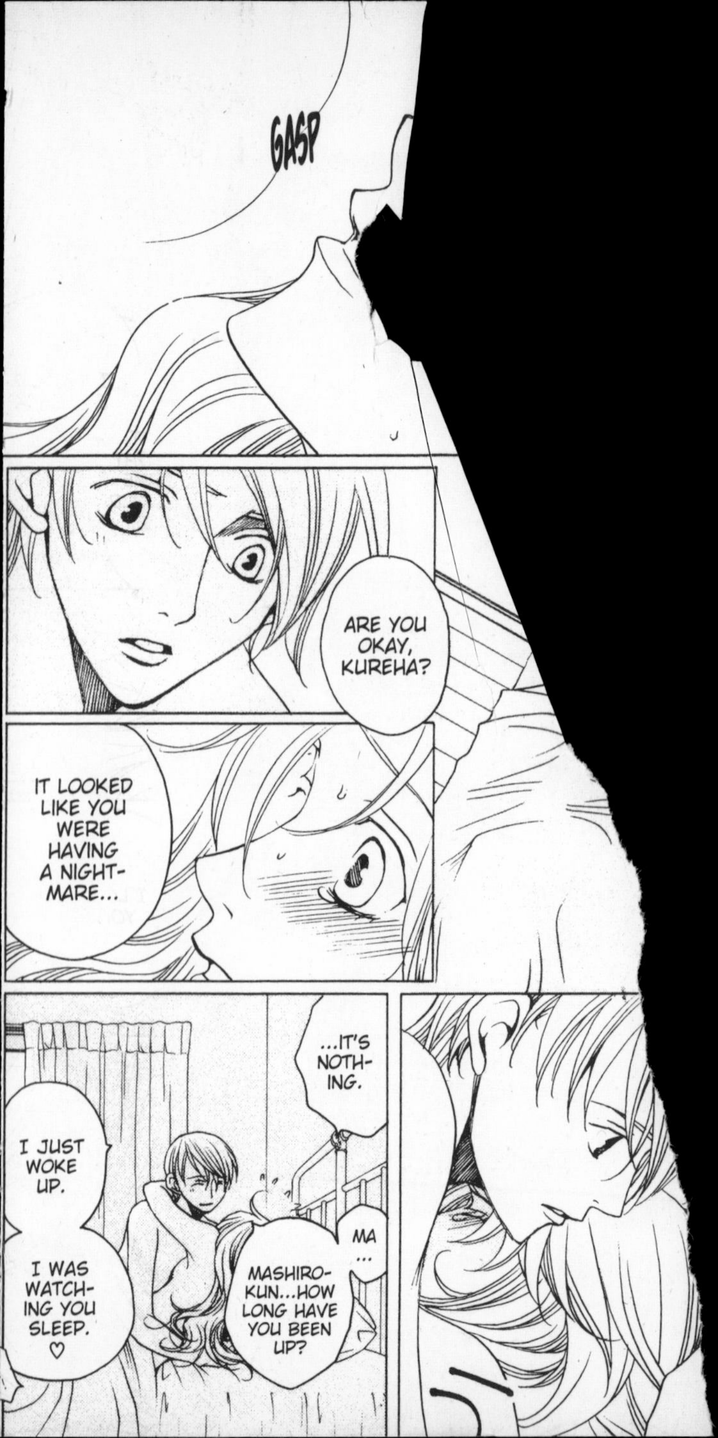
GASP
ARE YOU OKAY, KUREHA?
IT LOOKED LIKE YOU WERE HAVING A NIGHT-MARE...
...IT'S NOTHING.
MA...
MASHIRO-KUN...HOW LONG HAVE YOU BEEN UP?
I JUST WOKE UP.
I WAS WATCHING YOU SLEEP. ♡

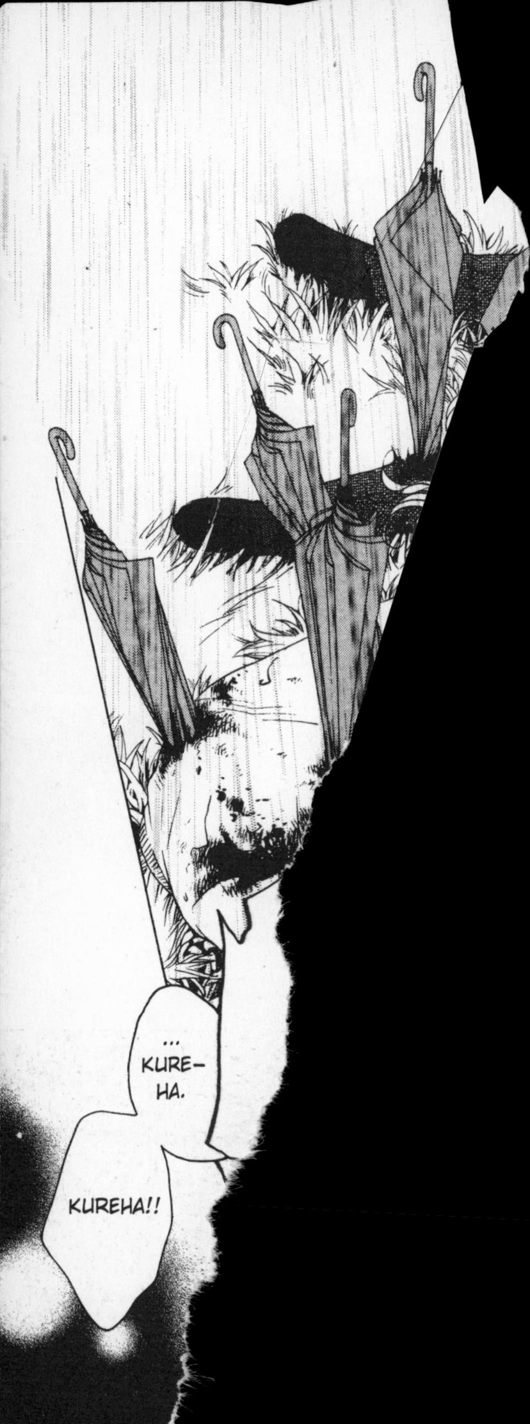
... KURE-HA.
KUREHA!!

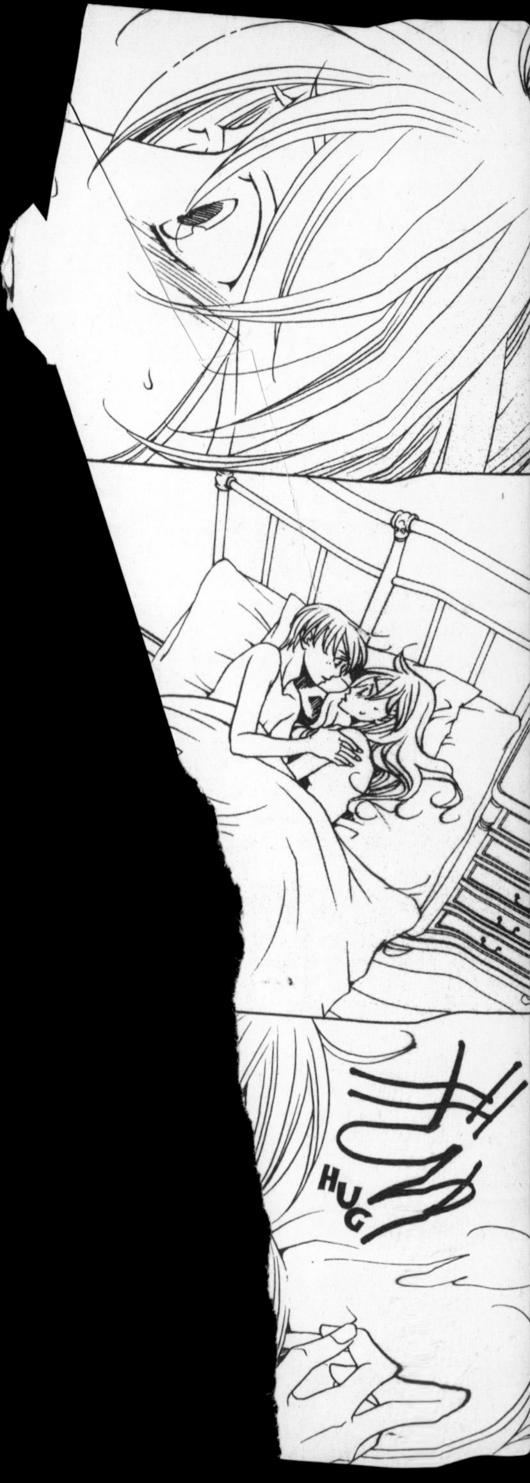
HUG

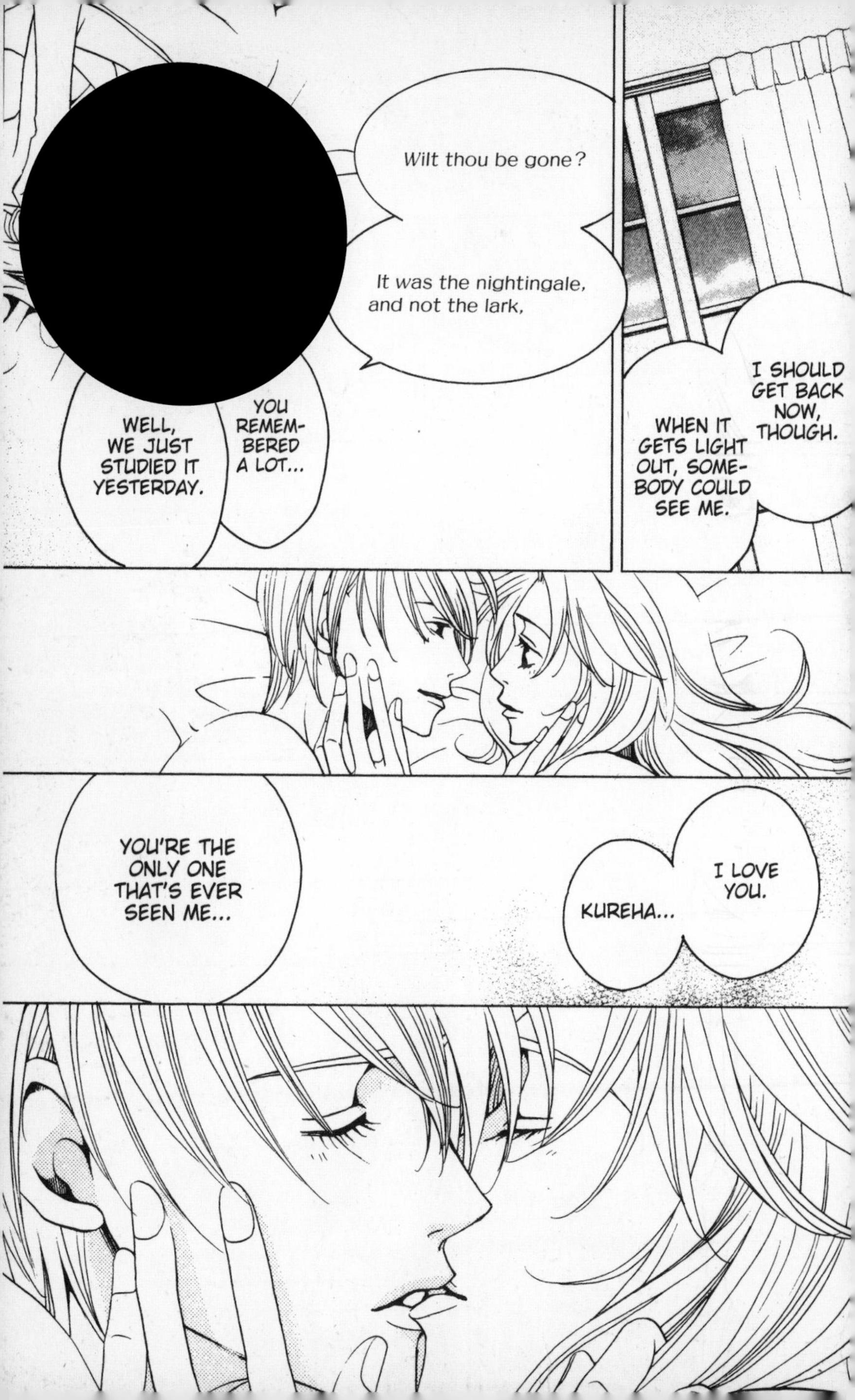
I SHOULD GET BACK NOW, THOUGH.
WHEN IT GETS LIGHT OUT, SOMEBODY COULD SEE ME.
Wilt thou be gone?
It was the nightingale, and not the lark,
YOU REMEMBERED A LOT...
WELL, WE JUST STUDIED IT YESTERDAY.
I LOVE YOU.
KUREHA...
YOU'RE THE ONLY ONE THAT'S EVER SEEN ME...

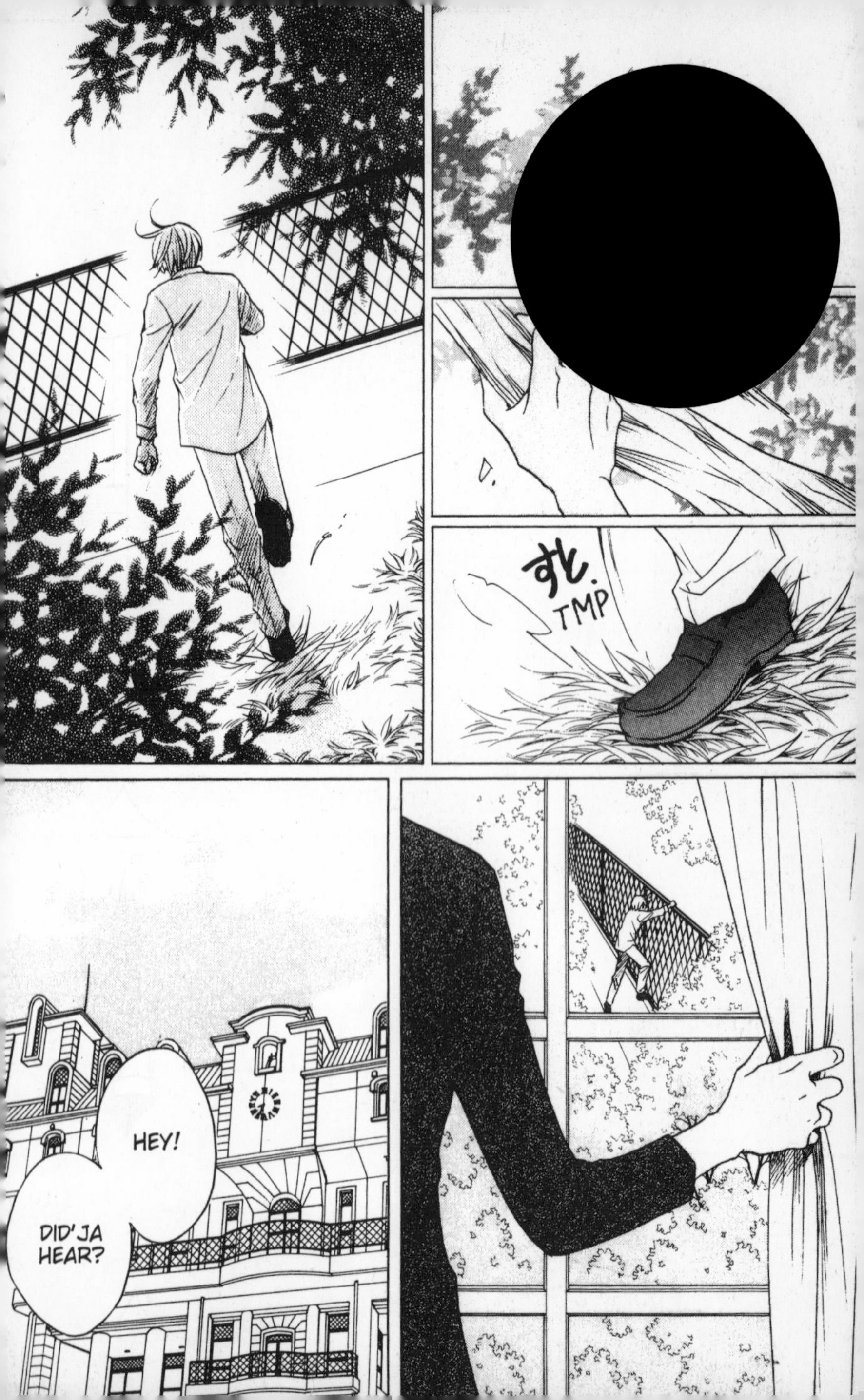
すと.
TMP
HEY!
DID'JA HEAR?

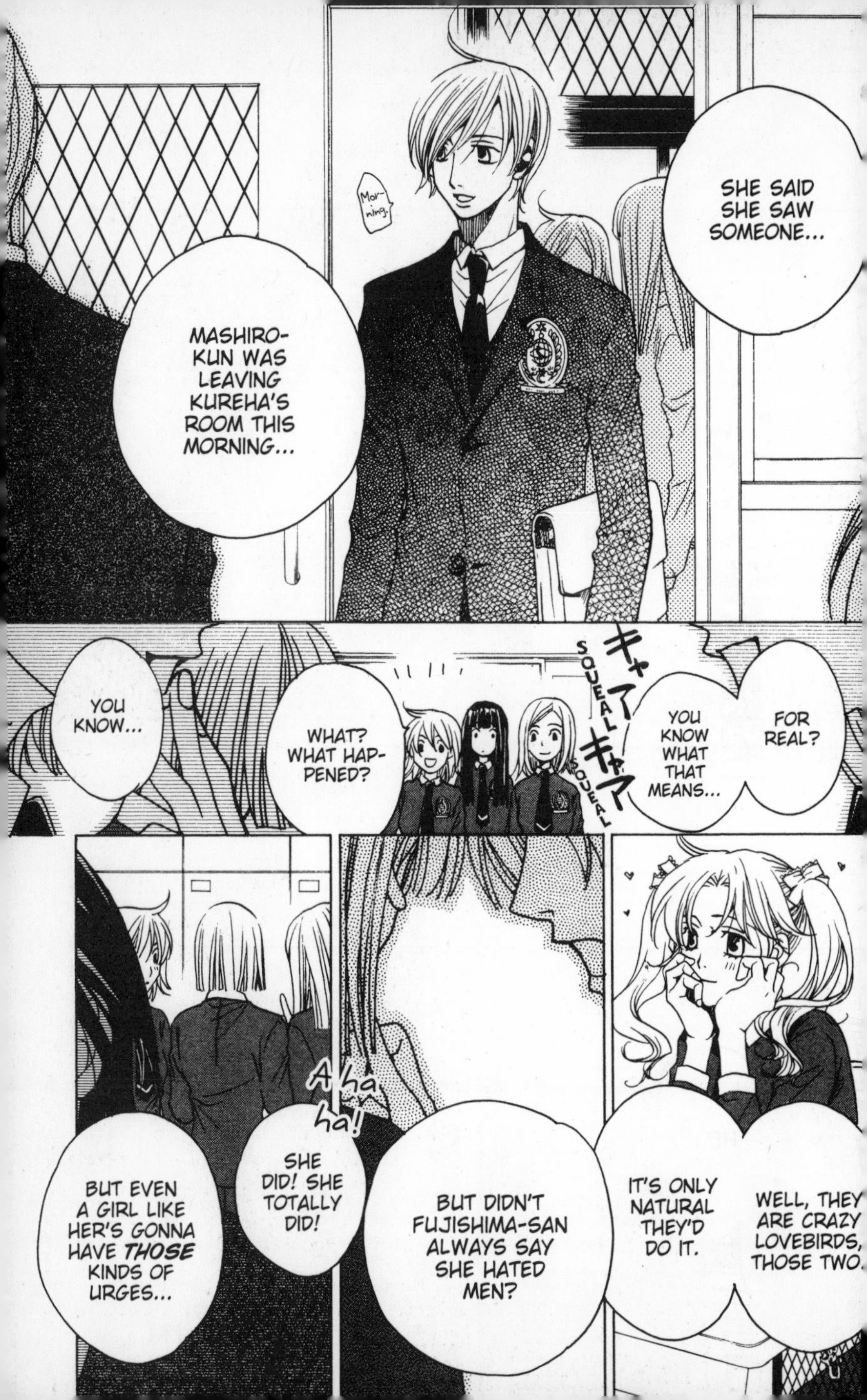
SHE SAID SHE SAW SOMEONE...
Mor-ning.
MASHIRO-KUN WAS LEAVING KUREHA'S ROOM THIS MORNING...
FOR REAL?
YOU KNOW WHAT THAT MEANS...
キャア SQUEAL
キャア SQUEAL
WHAT? WHAT HAP-PENED?
YOU KNOW...
WELL, THEY ARE CRAZY LOVEBIRDS, THOSE TWO.
IT'S ONLY NATURAL THEY'D DO IT.
BUT DIDN'T FUJISHIMA-SAN ALWAYS SAY SHE HATED MEN?
A ha ha!
SHE DID! SHE TOTALLY DID!
BUT EVEN A GIRL LIKE HER'S GONNA HAVE *THOSE* KINDS OF URGES...

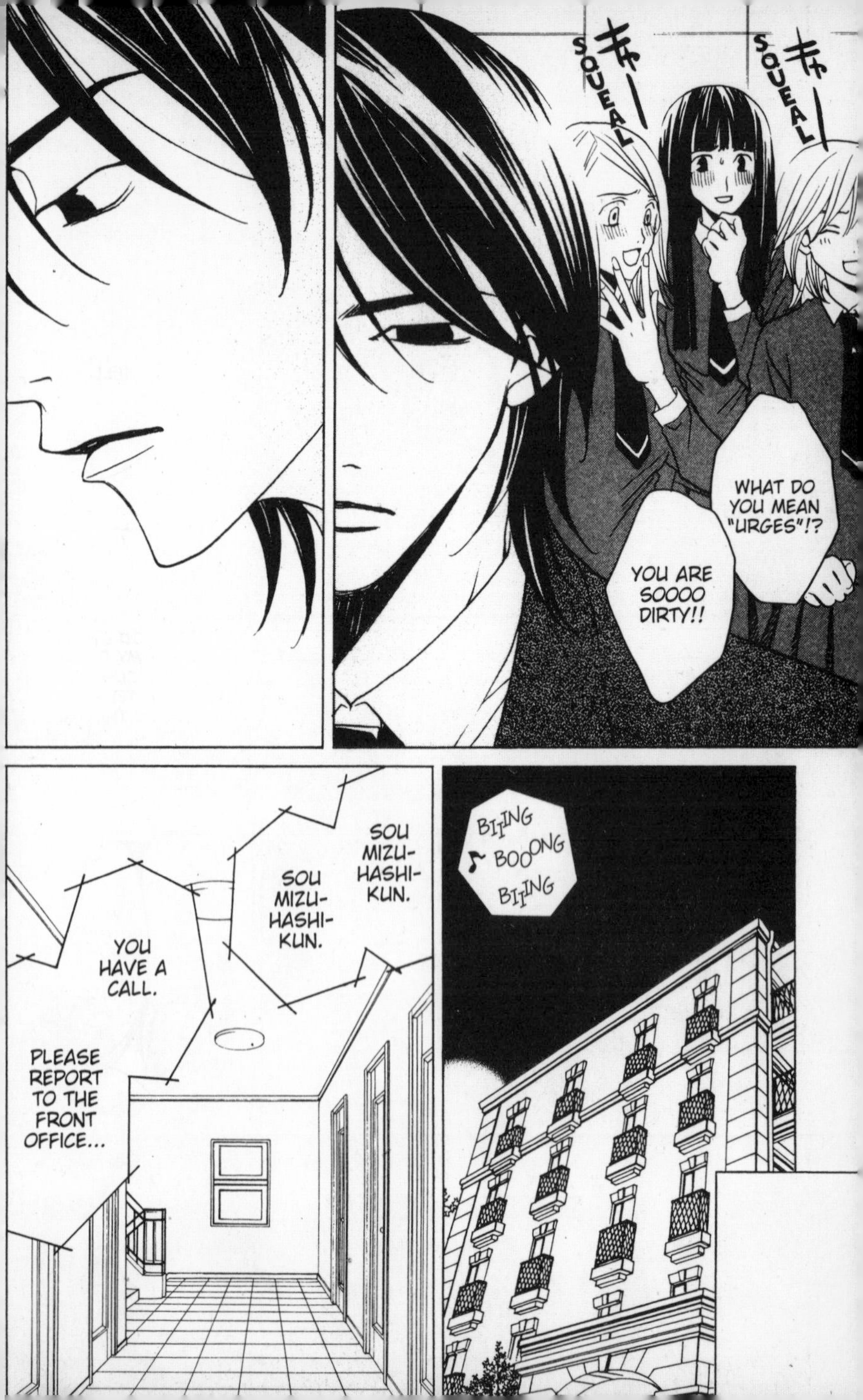
キャー
SQUEAL
キャー
SQUEAL
WHAT DO YOU MEAN "URGES"!?
YOU ARE SOOOO DIRTY!!
BIIING ♪ BOOONG BIIING
SOU MIZU-HASHI-KUN.
SOU MIZU-HASHI-KUN.
YOU HAVE A CALL.
PLEASE REPORT TO THE FRONT OFFICE...

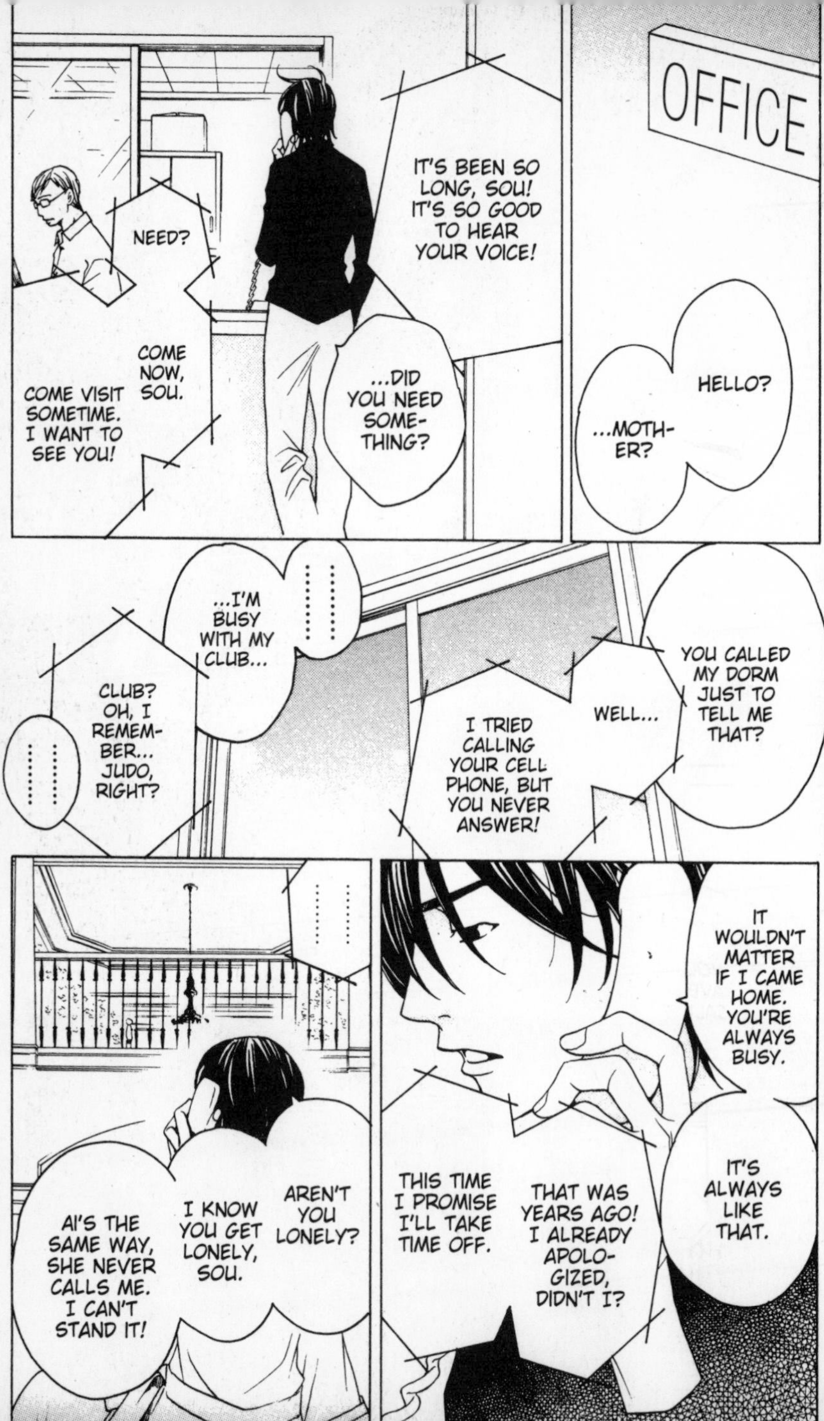
OFFICE
HELLO?
...MOTHER?
IT'S BEEN SO LONG, SOU! IT'S SO GOOD TO HEAR YOUR VOICE!
...DID YOU NEED SOMETHING?
NEED?
COME NOW, SOU.
COME VISIT SOMETIME. I WANT TO SEE YOU!
YOU CALLED MY DORM JUST TO TELL ME THAT?
WELL...
I TRIED CALLING YOUR CELL PHONE, BUT YOU NEVER ANSWER!
......
...I'M BUSY WITH MY CLUB...
CLUB? OH, I REMEMBER... JUDO, RIGHT?
......
IT WOULDN'T MATTER IF I CAME HOME. YOU'RE ALWAYS BUSY.
IT'S ALWAYS LIKE THAT.
THAT WAS YEARS AGO! I ALREADY APOLOGIZED, DIDN'T I?
THIS TIME I PROMISE I'LL TAKE TIME OFF.
......
AREN'T YOU LONELY?
I KNOW YOU GET LONELY, SOU.
AI'S THE SAME WAY, SHE NEVER CALLS ME. I CAN'T STAND IT!

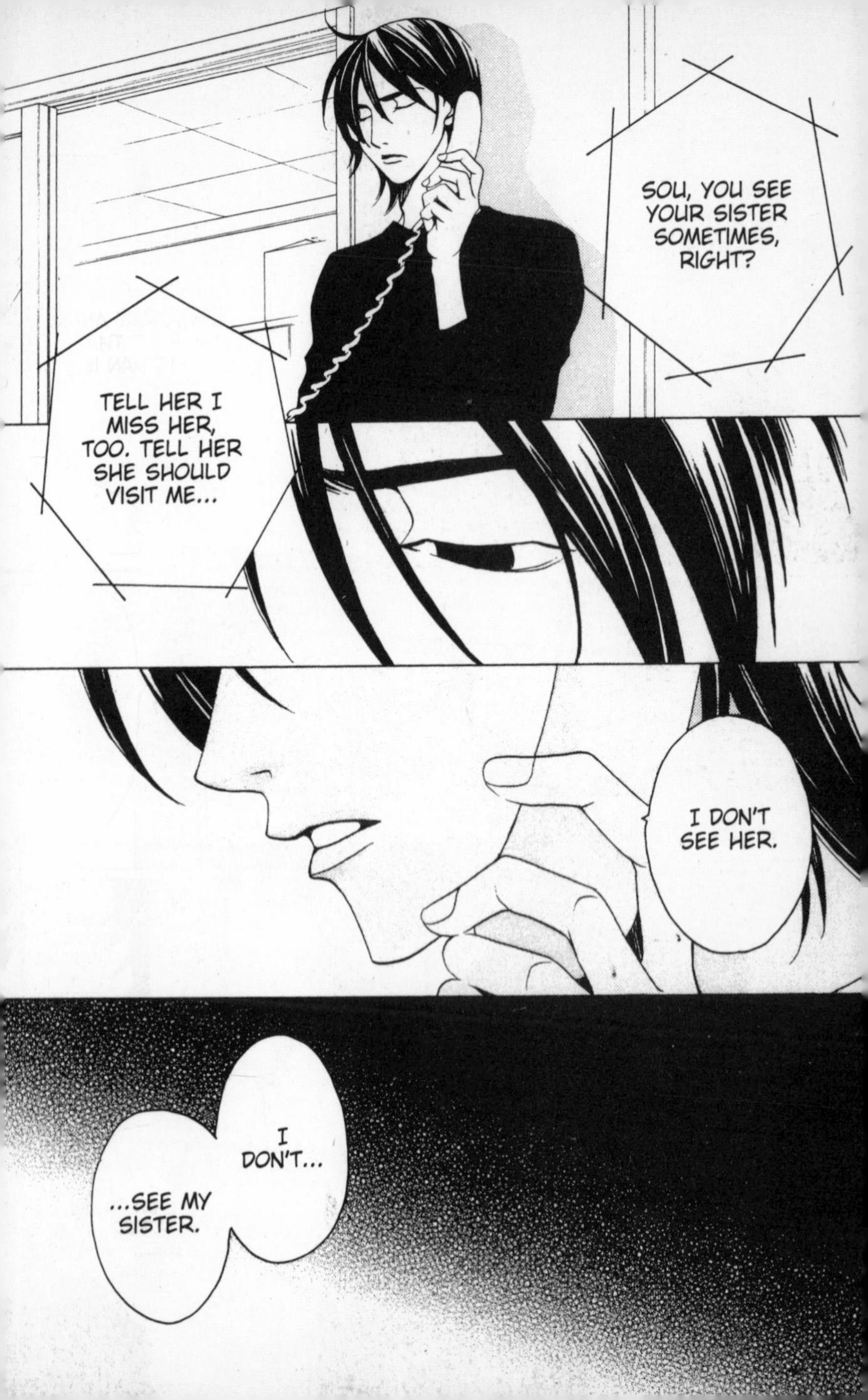
SOU, YOU SEE YOUR SISTER SOMETIMES, RIGHT?
TELL HER I MISS HER, TOO. TELL HER SHE SHOULD VISIT ME...
I DON'T SEE HER.
I DON'T...
...SEE MY SISTER.

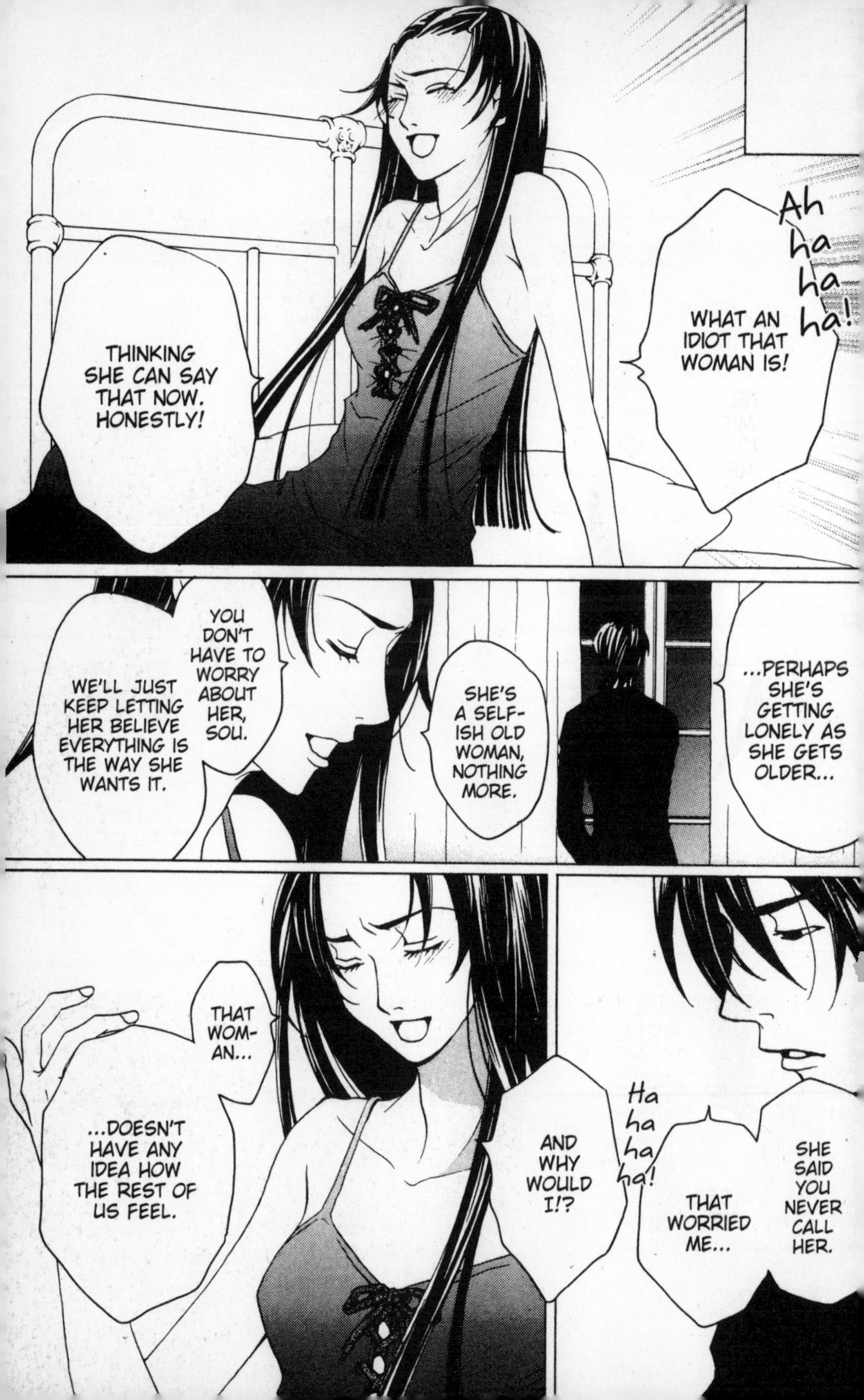
Ah ha ha ha!
WHAT AN IDIOT THAT WOMAN IS!
THINKING SHE CAN SAY THAT NOW. HONESTLY!
...PERHAPS SHE'S GETTING LONELY AS SHE GETS OLDER...
SHE'S A SELF-ISH OLD WOMAN, NOTHING MORE.
YOU DON'T HAVE TO WORRY ABOUT HER, SOU.
WE'LL JUST KEEP LETTING HER BELIEVE EVERYTHING IS THE WAY SHE WANTS IT.
SHE SAID YOU NEVER CALL HER.
THAT WORRIED ME...
Ha ha ha ha!
AND WHY WOULD I!?
THAT WOM-AN...
...DOESN'T HAVE ANY IDEA HOW THE REST OF US FEEL.

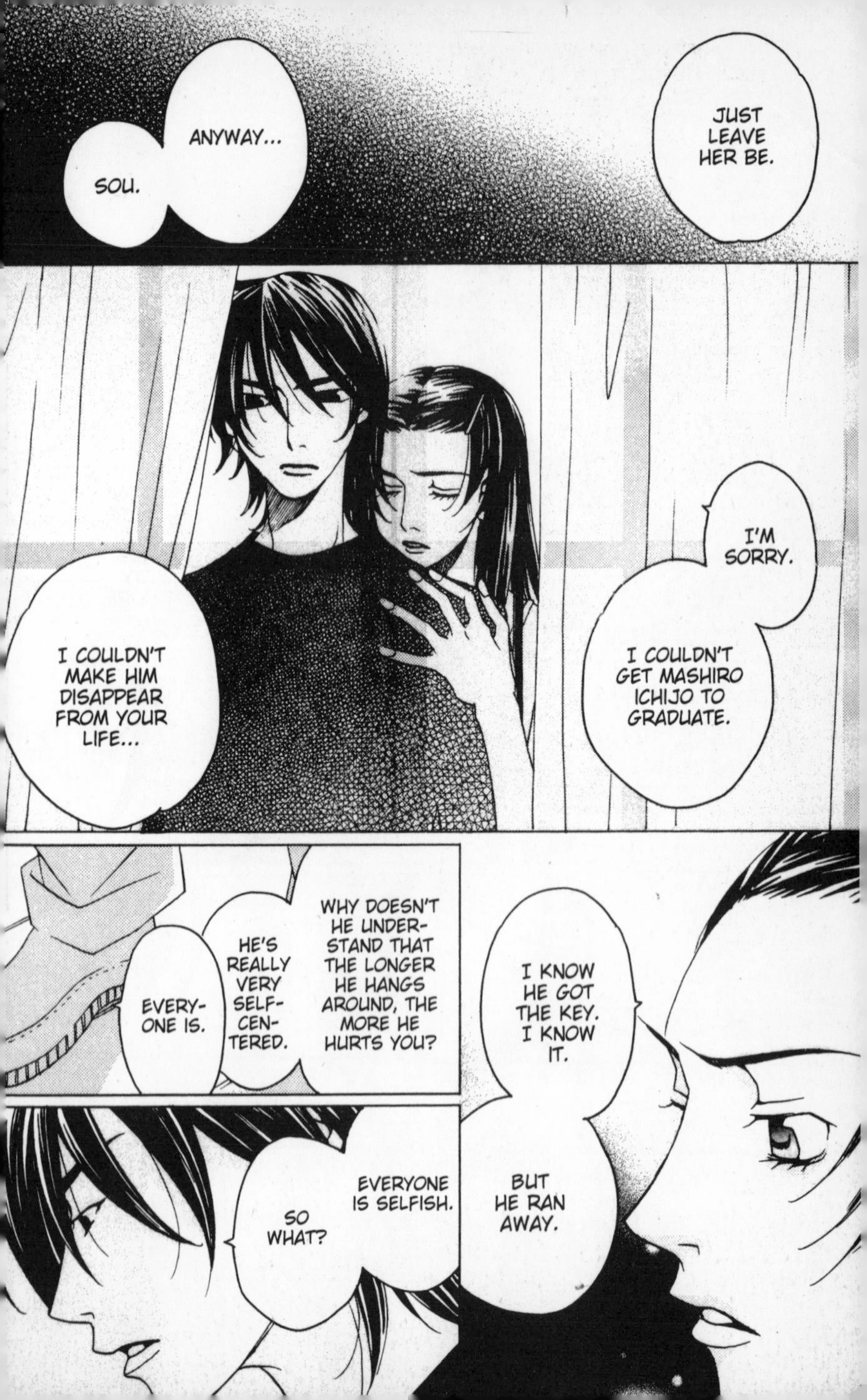
JUST LEAVE HER BE.
ANYWAY...
SOU.
I'M SORRY.
I COULDN'T GET MASHIRO ICHIJO TO GRADUATE.
I COULDN'T MAKE HIM DISAPPEAR FROM YOUR LIFE...
I KNOW HE GOT THE KEY. I KNOW IT.
BUT HE RAN AWAY.
WHY DOESN'T HE UNDER-STAND THAT THE LONGER HE HANGS AROUND, THE MORE HE HURTS YOU?
HE'S REALLY VERY SELF-CEN-TERED.
EVERY-ONE IS.
EVERYONE IS SELFISH.
SO WHAT?

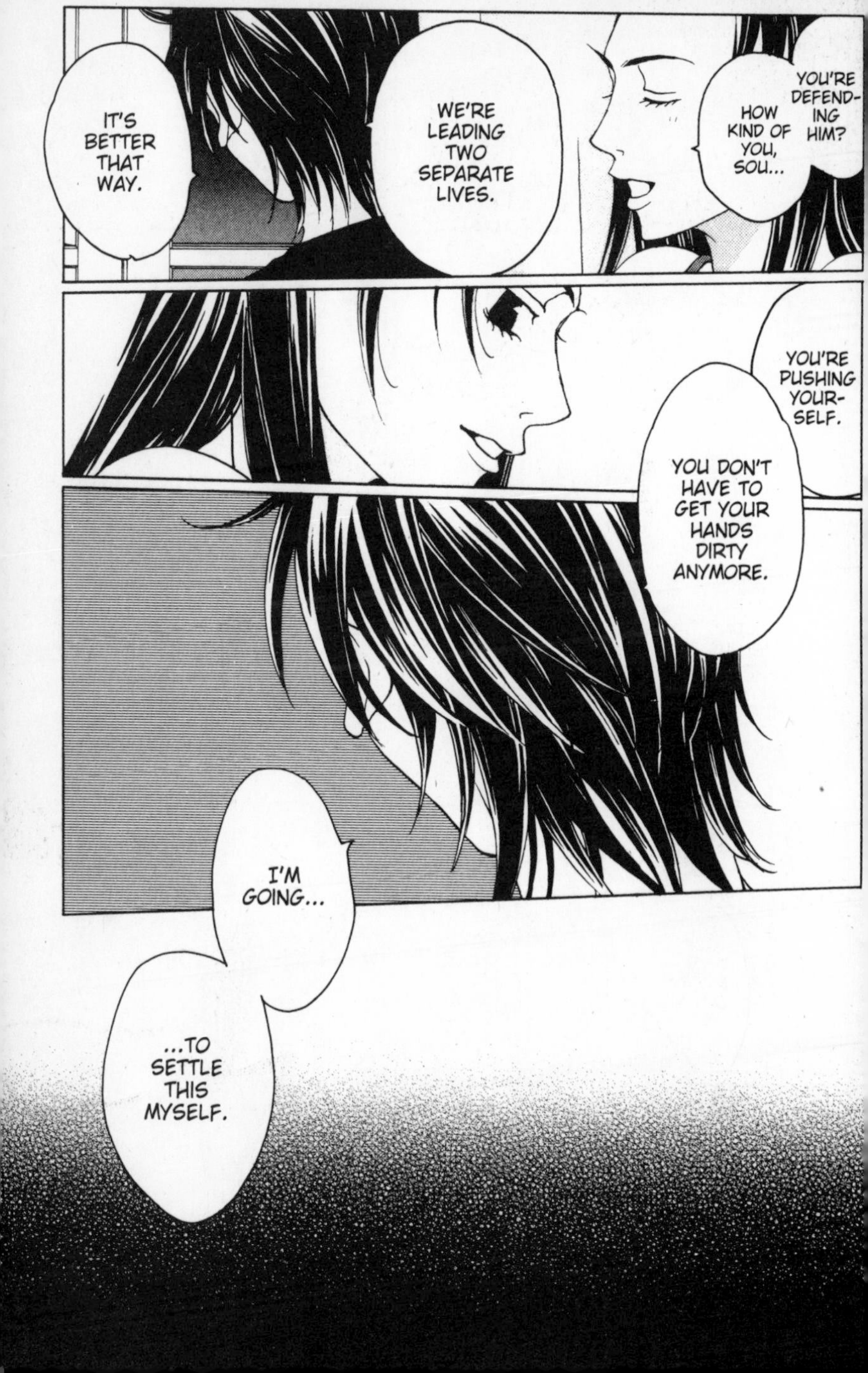
YOU'RE DEFENDING HIM?
HOW KIND OF YOU, SOU...
WE'RE LEADING TWO SEPARATE LIVES.
IT'S BETTER THAT WAY.
YOU'RE PUSHING YOURSELF.
YOU DON'T HAVE TO GET YOUR HANDS DIRTY ANYMORE.
I'M GOING...
...TO SETTLE THIS MYSELF.

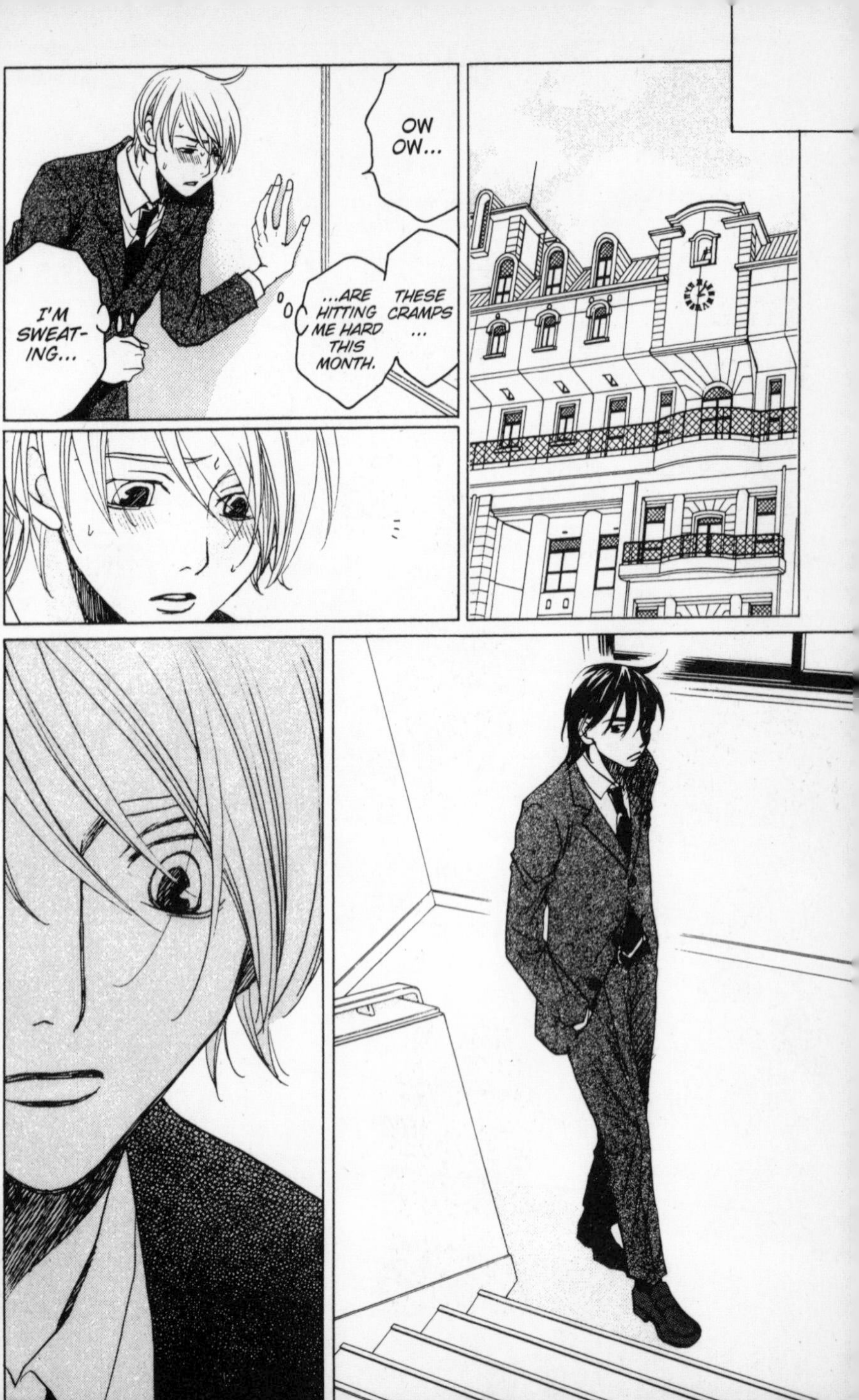
OW OW...
THESE CRAMPS...
...ARE HITTING ME HARD THIS MONTH.
I'M SWEATING...

Sou's visual image was still pretty vague at the start of serialization. I pretty much decided that he'd have black hair, but as for what his expression was like, I had no ideas in mind. At that time, my editor was talking about her favorite actor and then I thought, "Oh, let's try and give him that look." And before you know it, the rest of the image fleshed itself out.

For the splash page announcing the start of the serialization, his design was still not done. I kept thinking, "Who is this?" when I looked at him.

It seems I gave him plenty of forehead and double-fold eyelids before the finalized version.*

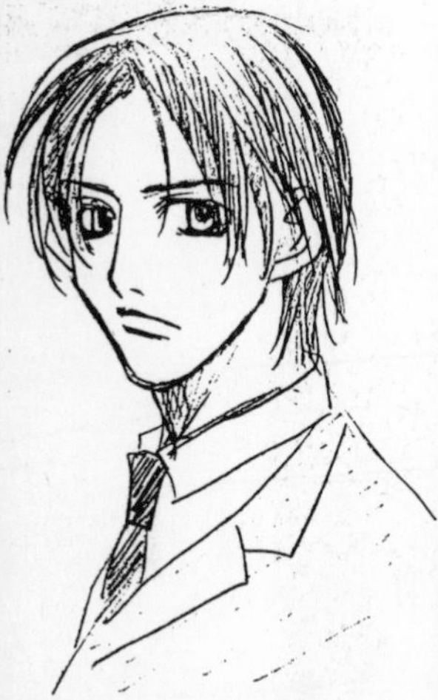

*SEE TRANSLATOR'S NOTES

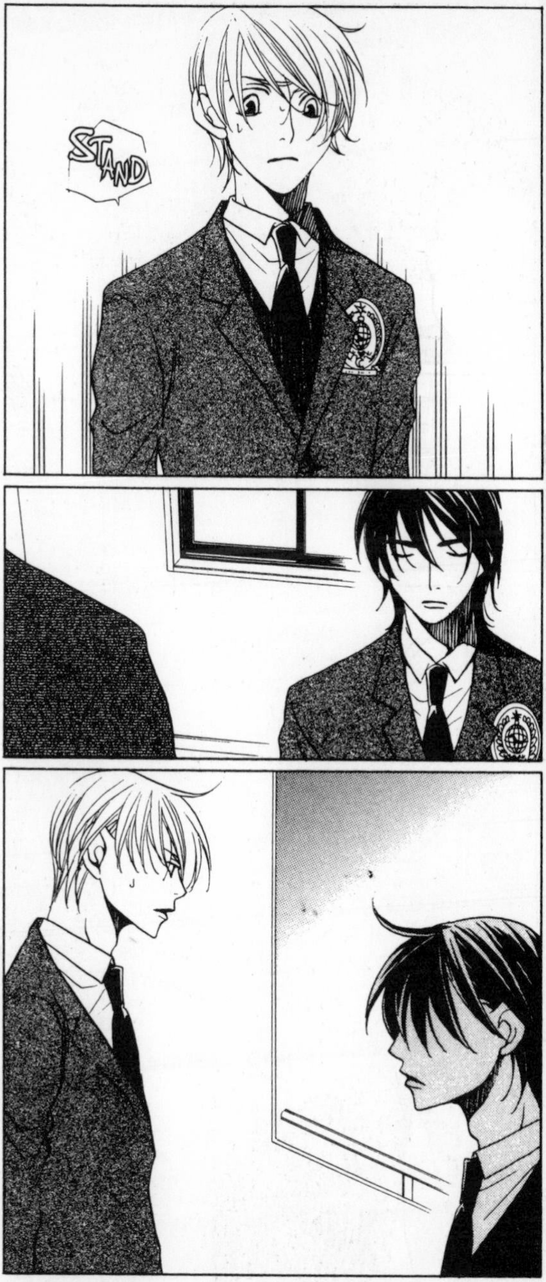
STAND

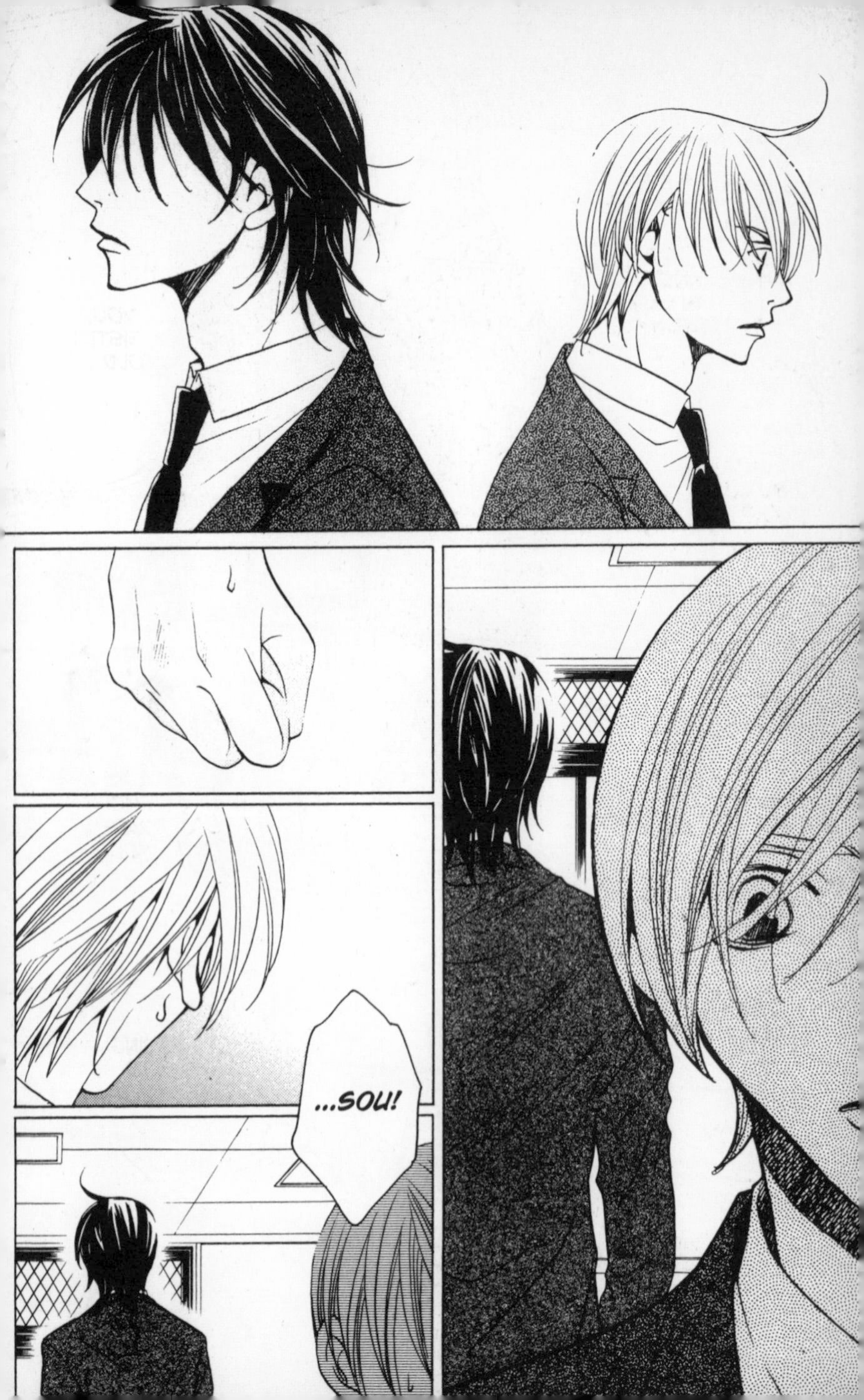
...SOU!

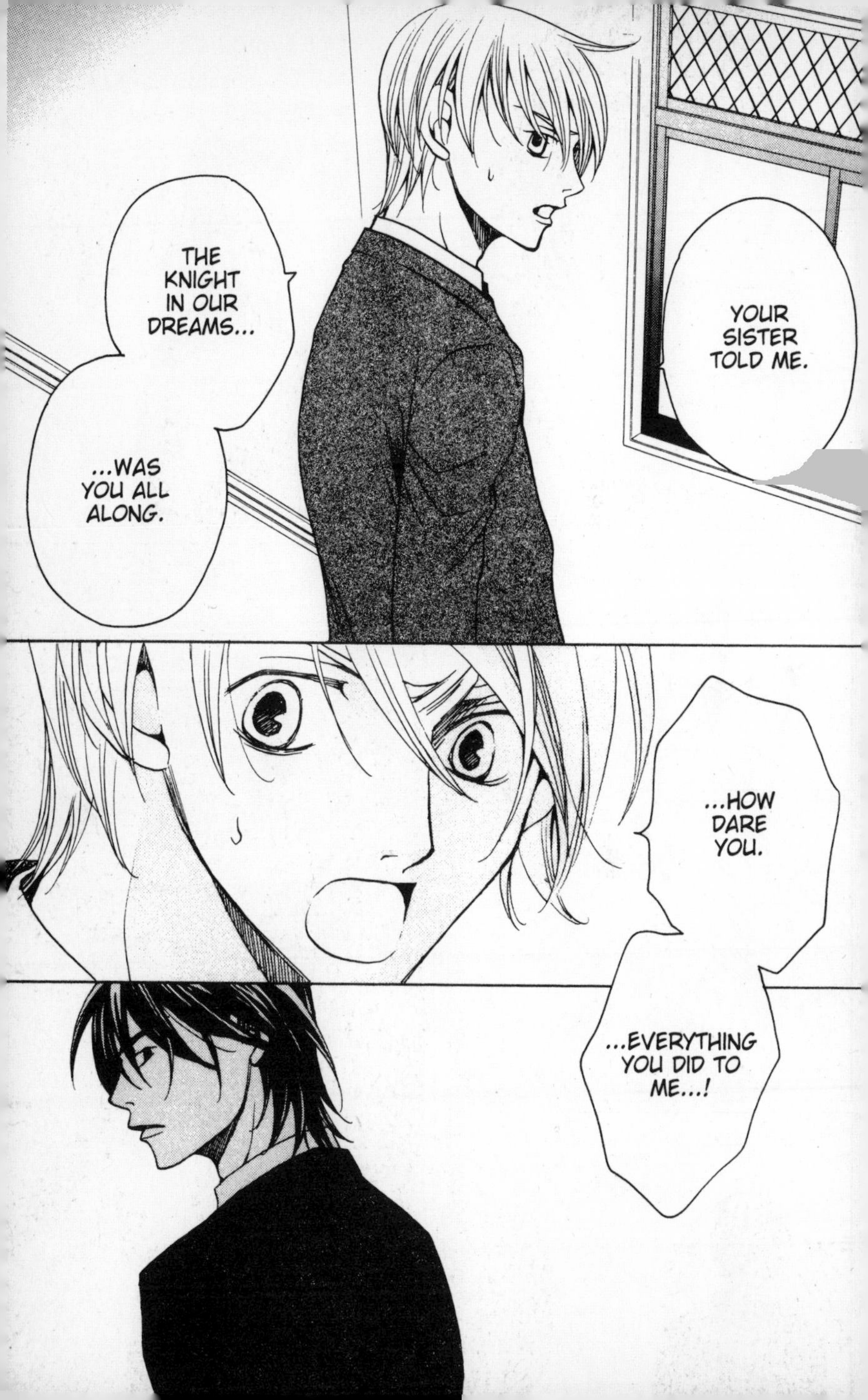
YOUR SISTER TOLD ME.
THE KNIGHT IN OUR DREAMS...
...WAS YOU ALL ALONG.
...HOW DARE YOU.
...EVERYTHING YOU DID TO ME...!

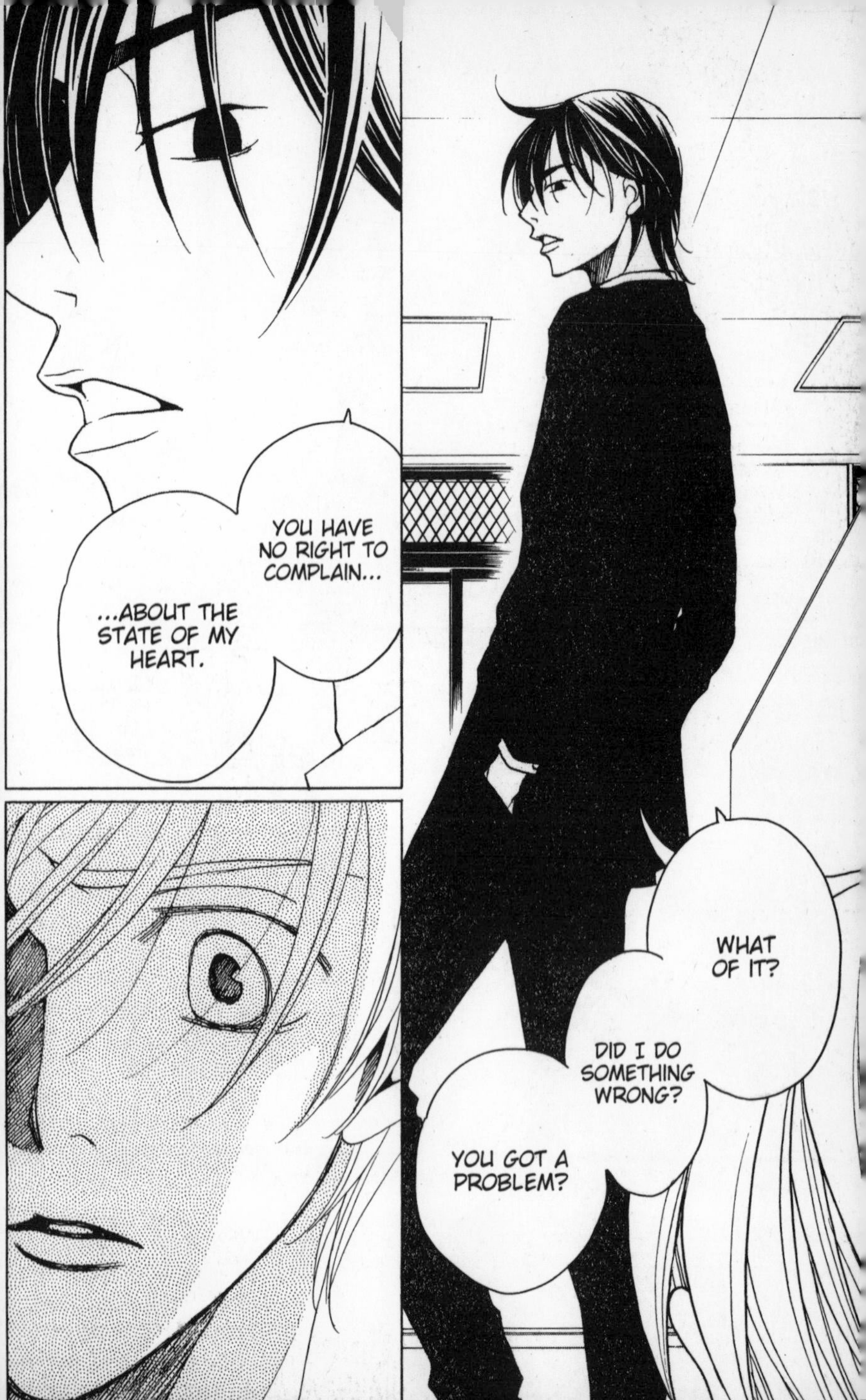
WHAT OF IT?
DID I DO SOMETHING WRONG?
YOU GOT A PROBLEM?
YOU HAVE NO RIGHT TO COMPLAIN...
...ABOUT THE STATE OF MY HEART.

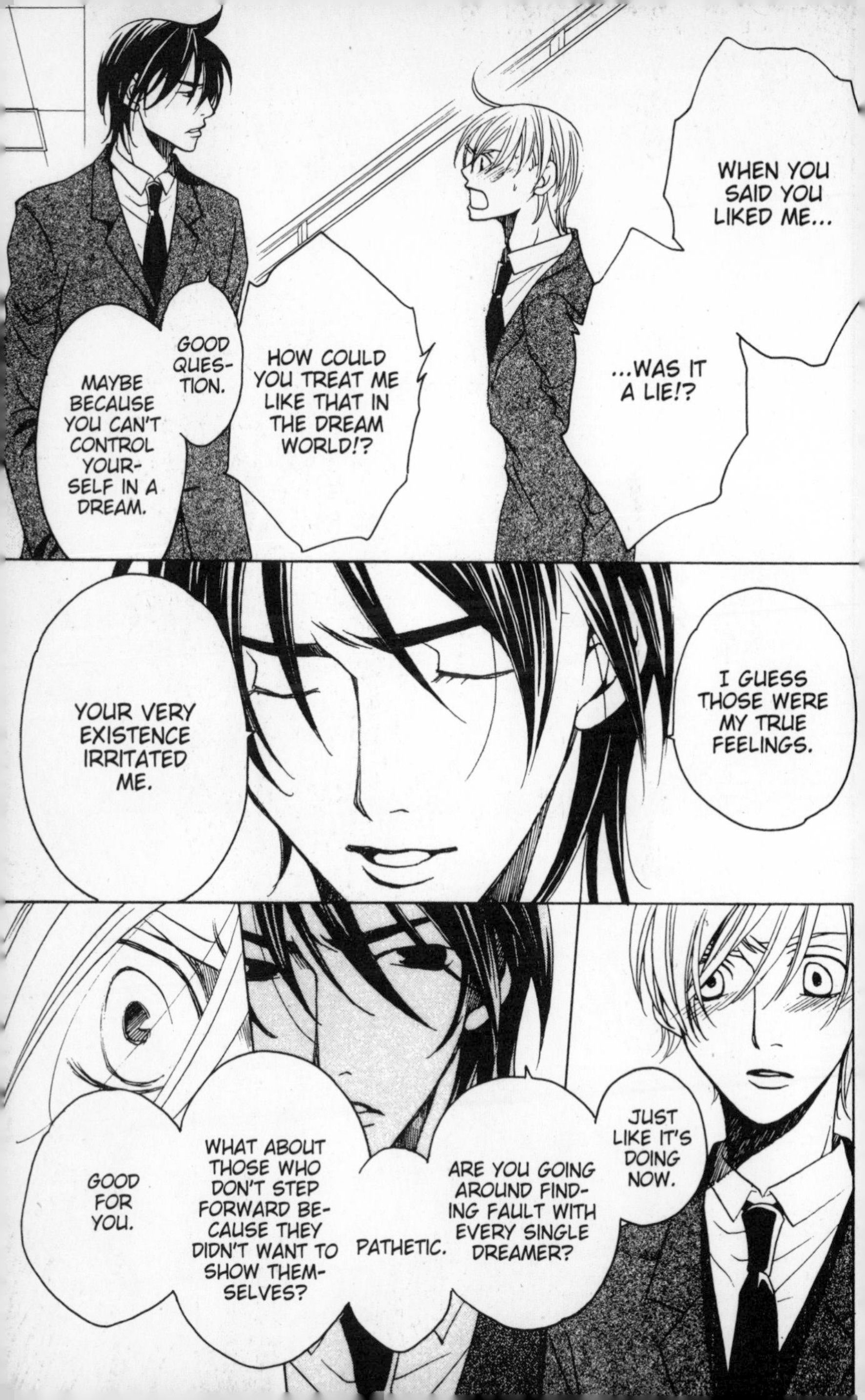
WHEN YOU SAID YOU LIKED ME...
...WAS IT A LIE!?
HOW COULD YOU TREAT ME LIKE THAT IN THE DREAM WORLD!?
GOOD QUES-TION.
MAYBE BECAUSE YOU CAN'T CONTROL YOUR-SELF IN A DREAM.
I GUESS THOSE WERE MY TRUE FEELINGS.
YOUR VERY EXISTENCE IRRITATED ME.
JUST LIKE IT'S DOING NOW.
ARE YOU GOING AROUND FIND-ING FAULT WITH EVERY SINGLE DREAMER?
PATHETIC.
WHAT ABOUT THOSE WHO DON'T STEP FORWARD BE-CAUSE THEY DIDN'T WANT TO SHOW THEM-SELVES?
GOOD FOR YOU.

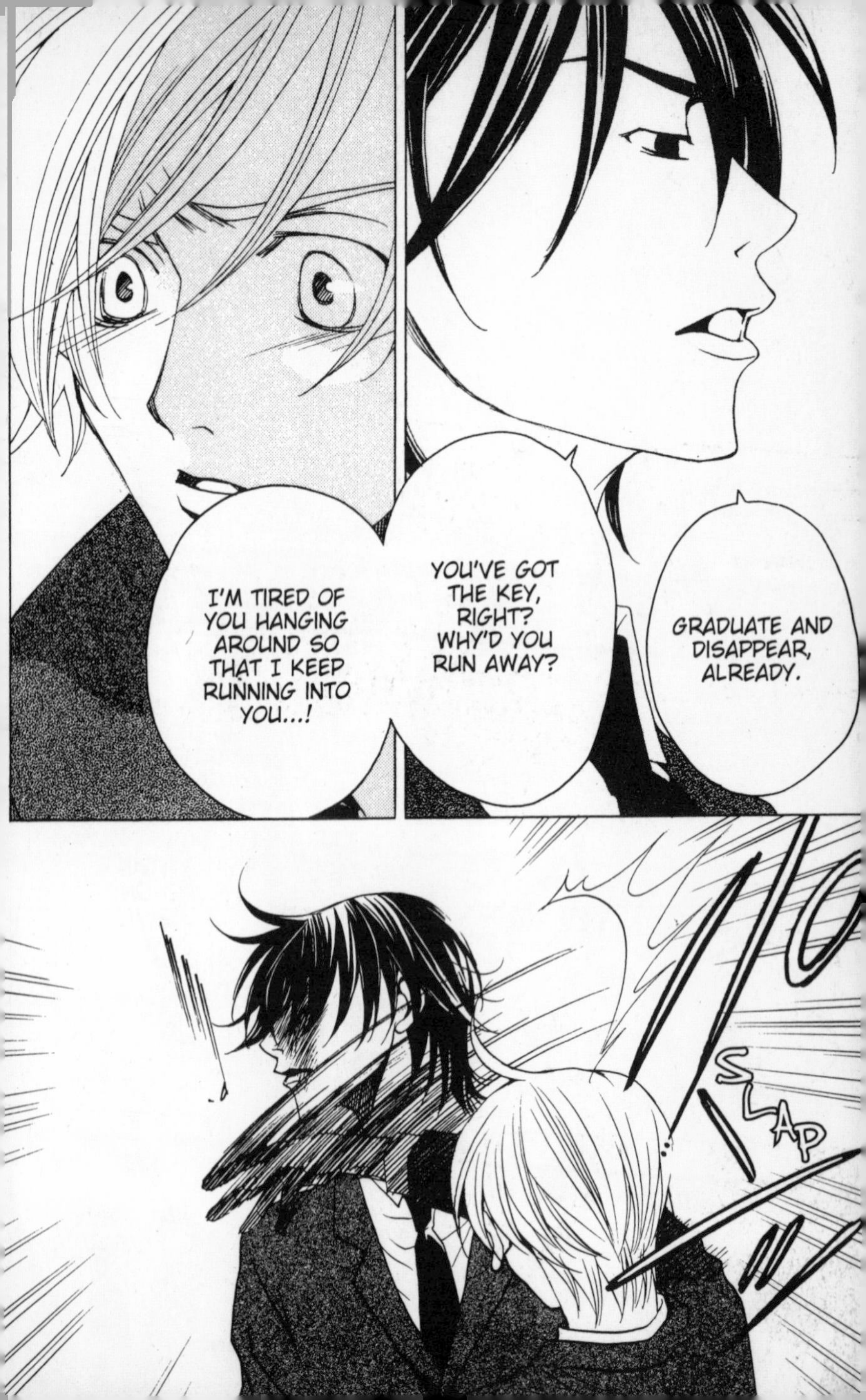
GRADUATE AND DISAPPEAR, ALREADY.
YOU'VE GOT THE KEY, RIGHT? WHY'D YOU RUN AWAY?
I'M TIRED OF YOU HANGING AROUND SO THAT I KEEP RUNNING INTO YOU...!
SLAP

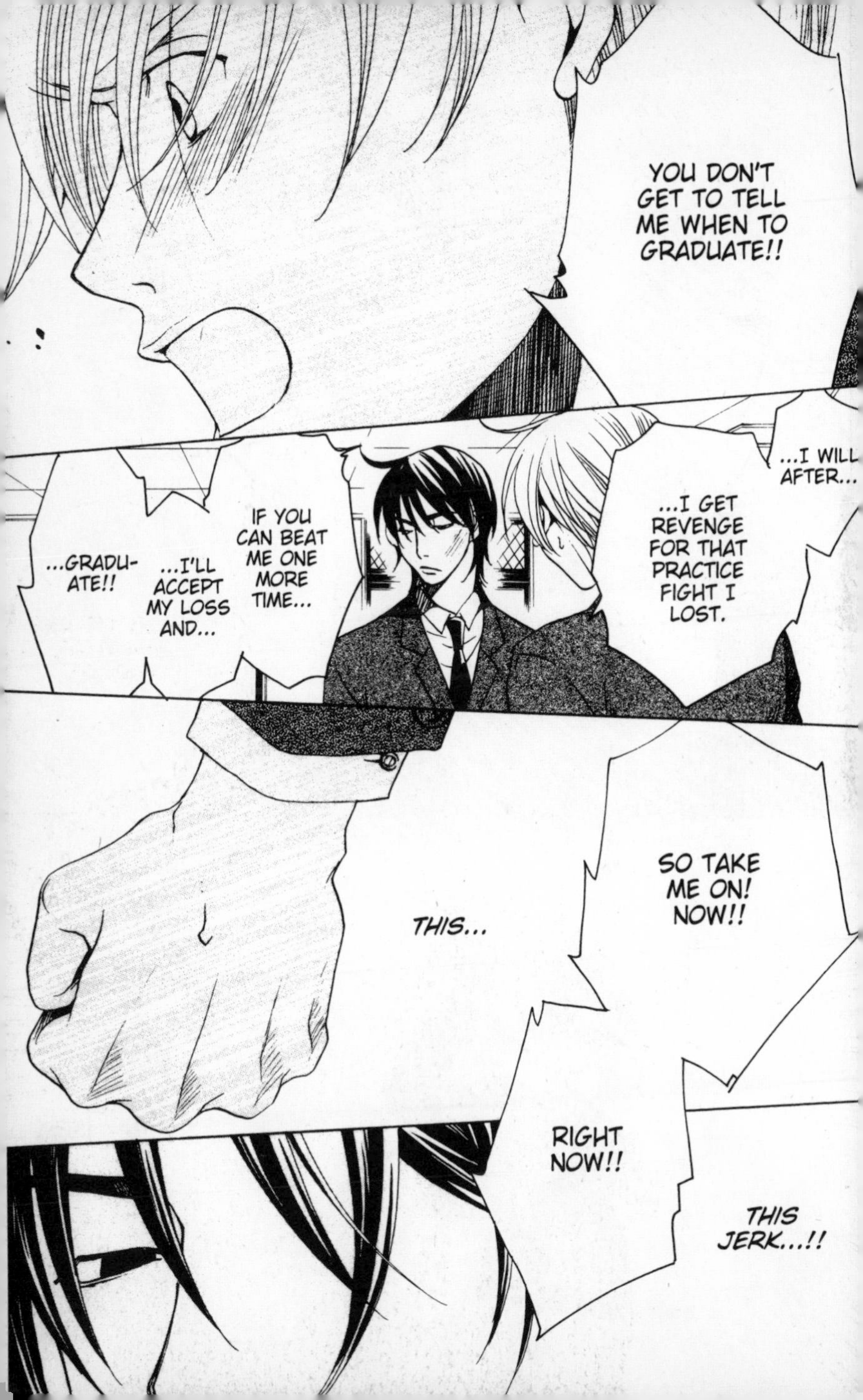
YOU DON'T GET TO TELL ME WHEN TO GRADUATE!!
...I WILL AFTER...
...I GET REVENGE FOR THAT PRACTICE FIGHT I LOST.
IF YOU CAN BEAT ME ONE MORE TIME...
...I'LL ACCEPT MY LOSS AND...
...GRADU-ATE!!
SO TAKE ME ON! NOW!!
THIS...
RIGHT NOW!!
THIS JERK...!!

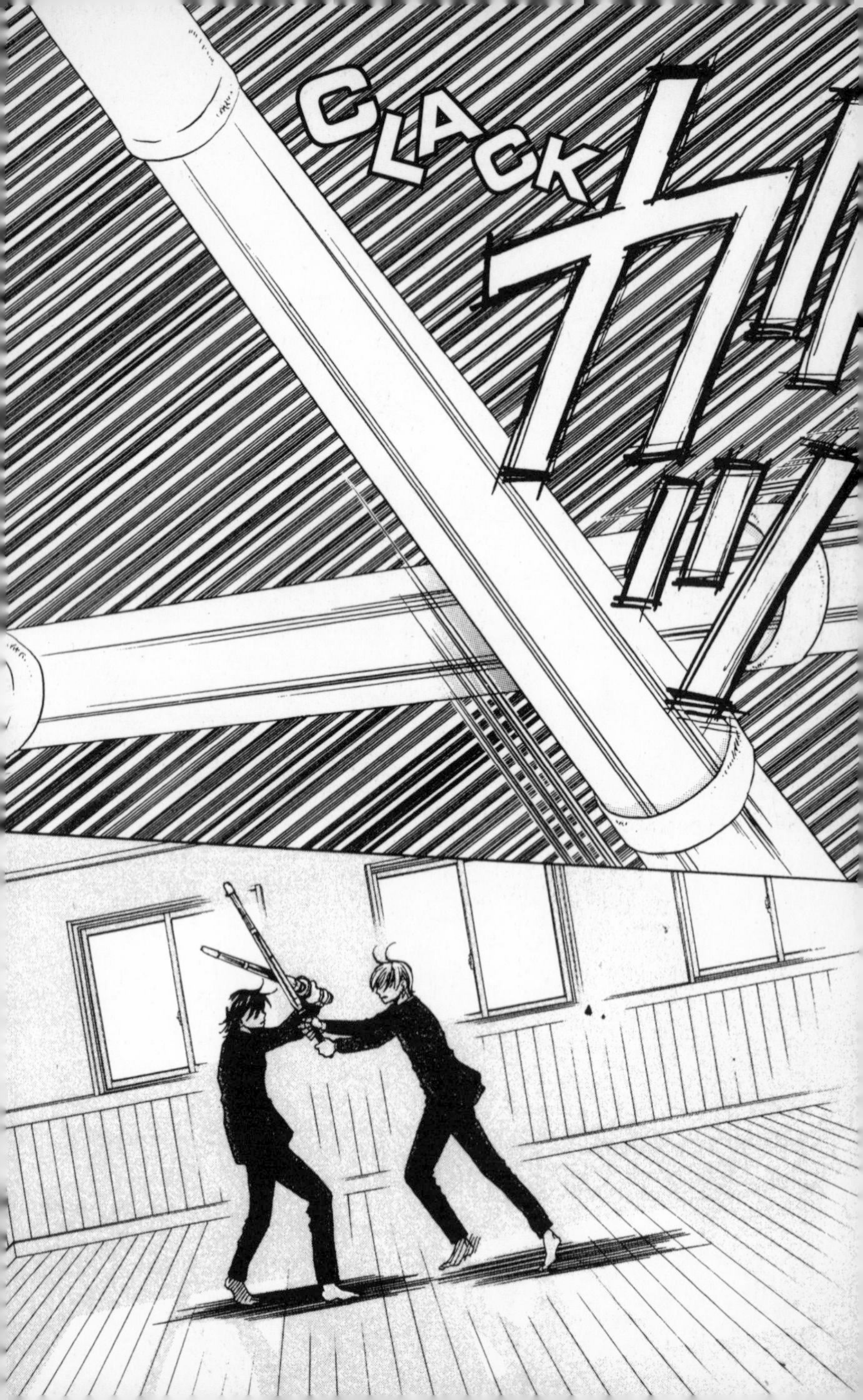
CLACK

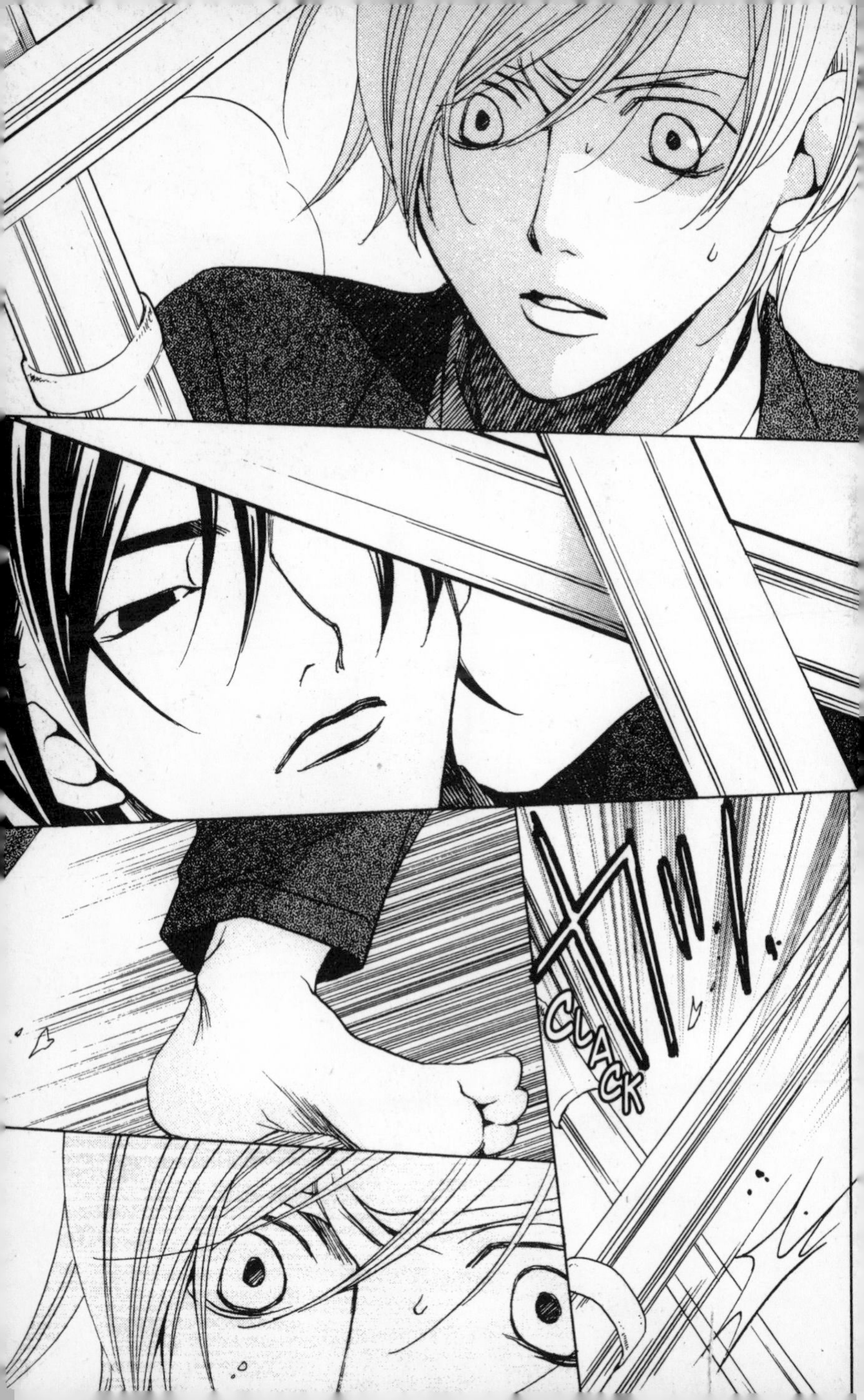
CLACK

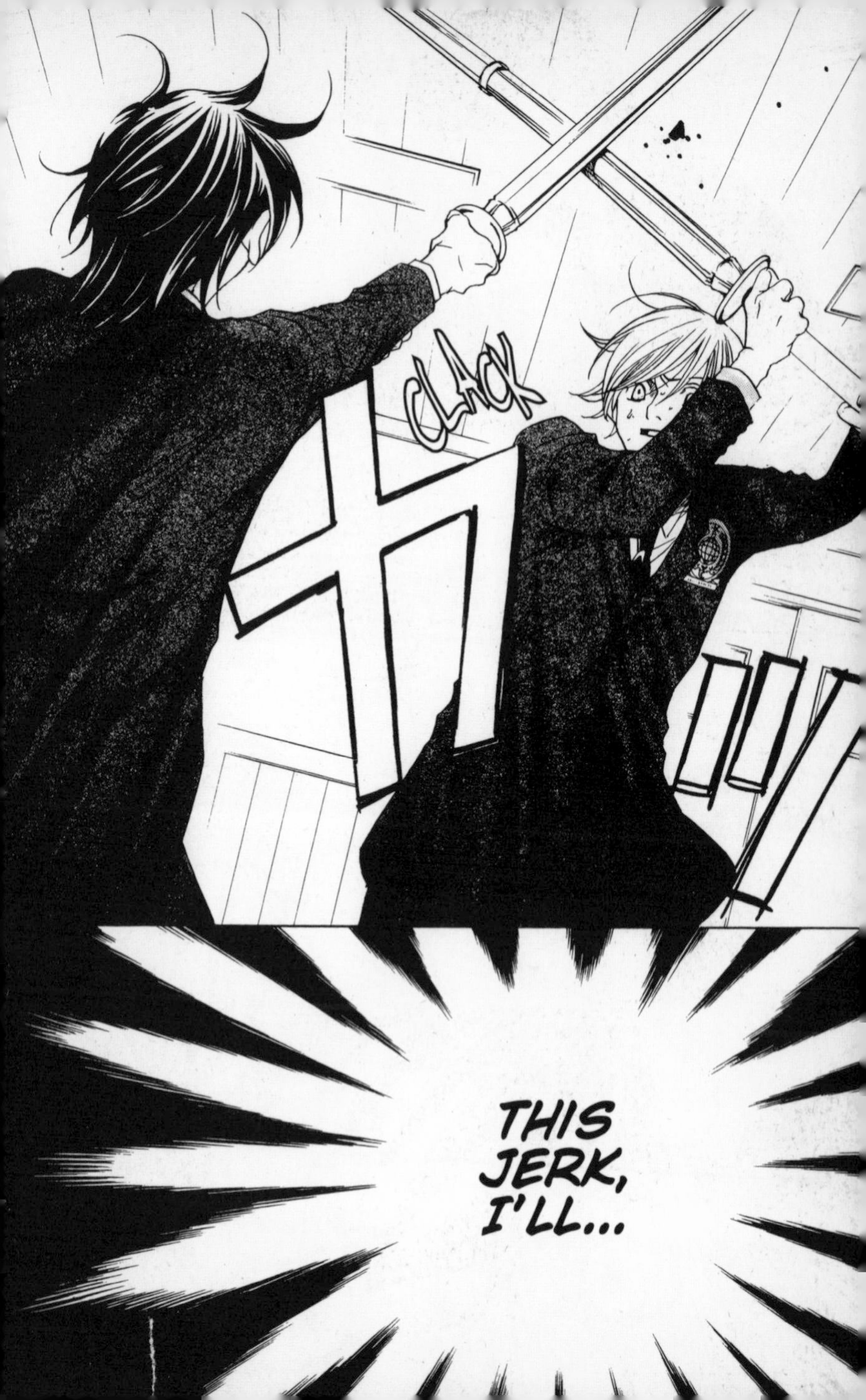
CLACK
THIS JERK, I'LL...

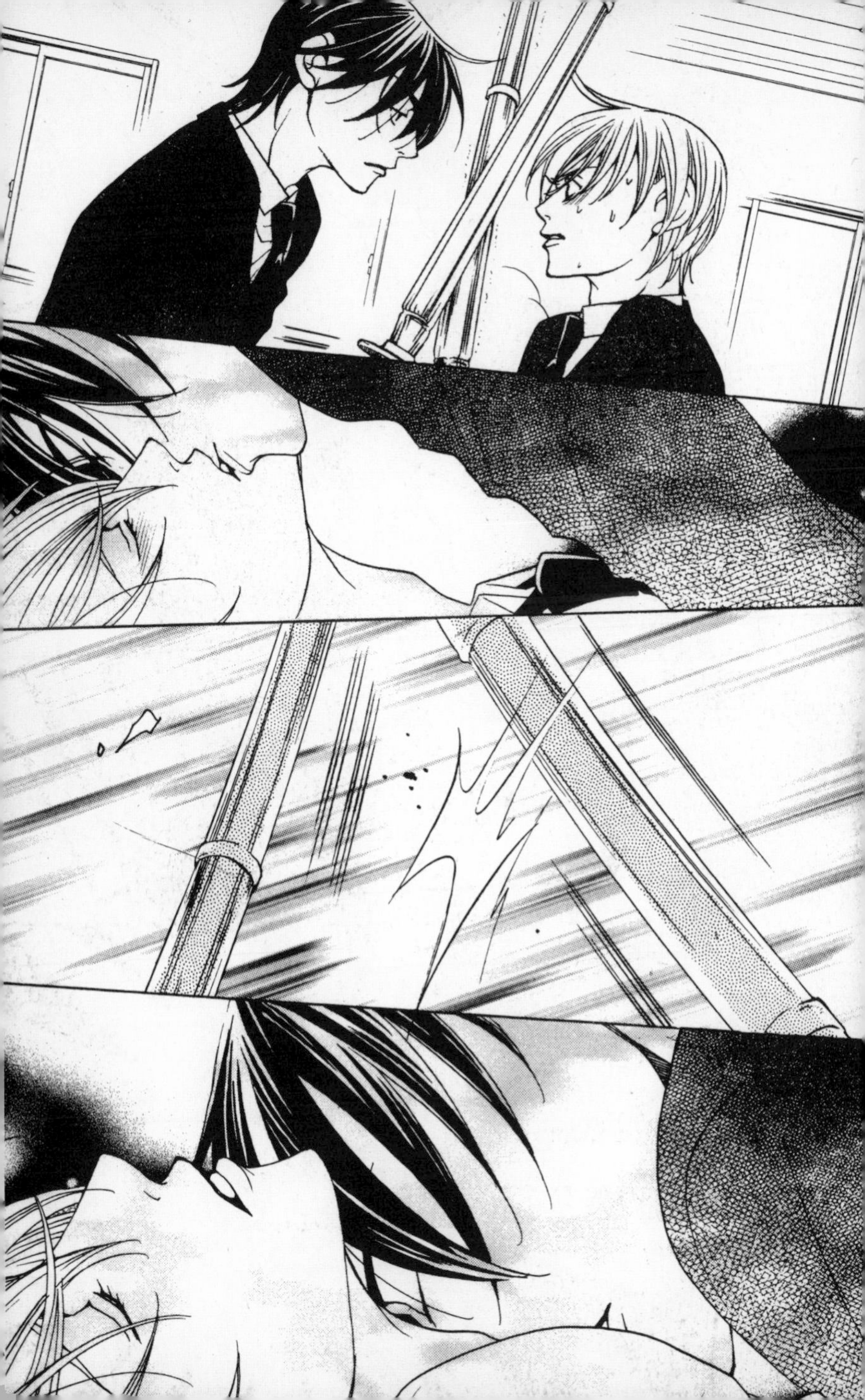

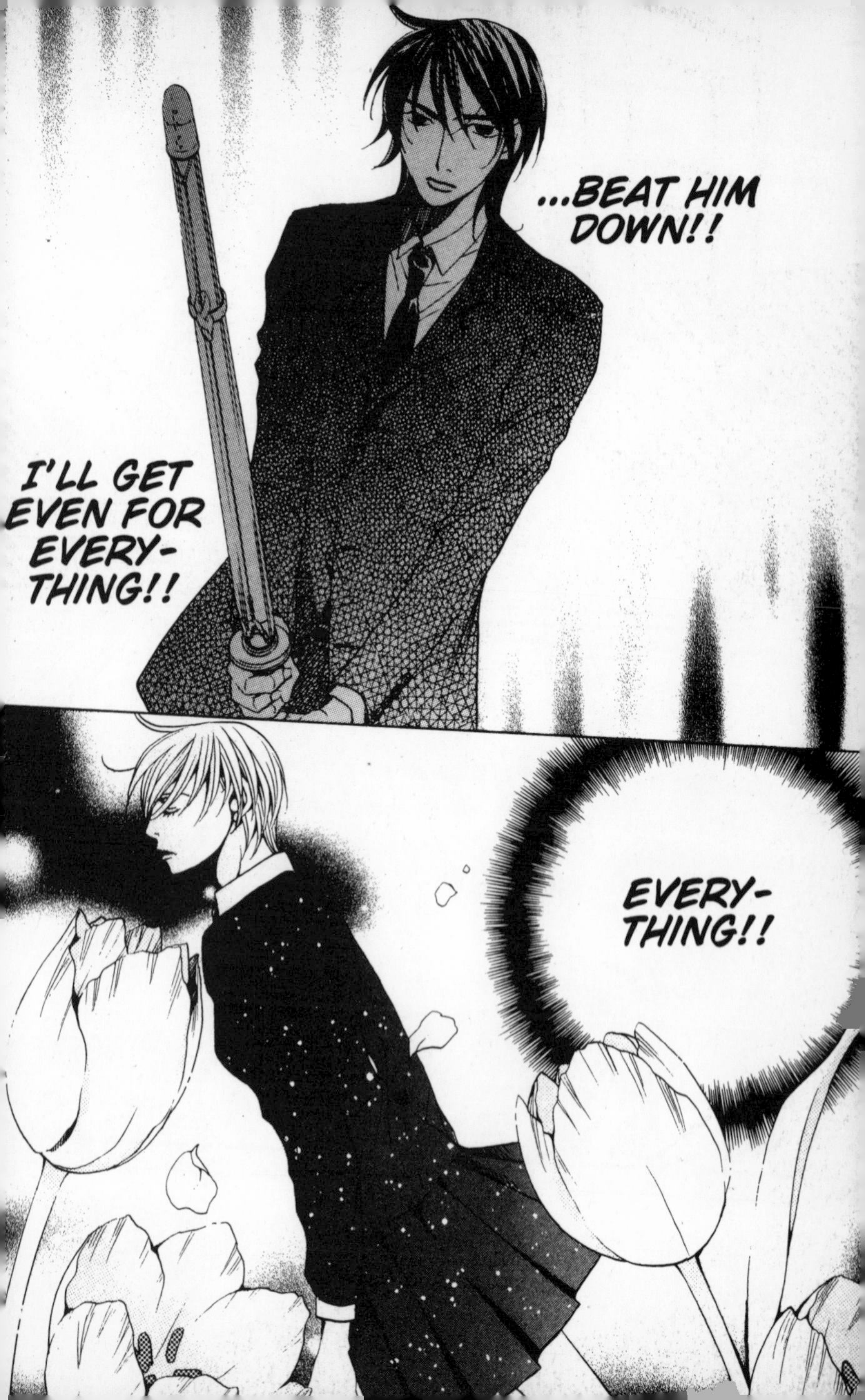
...BEAT HIM DOWN!!
I'LL GET EVEN FOR EVERY-THING!!
EVERY-THING!!

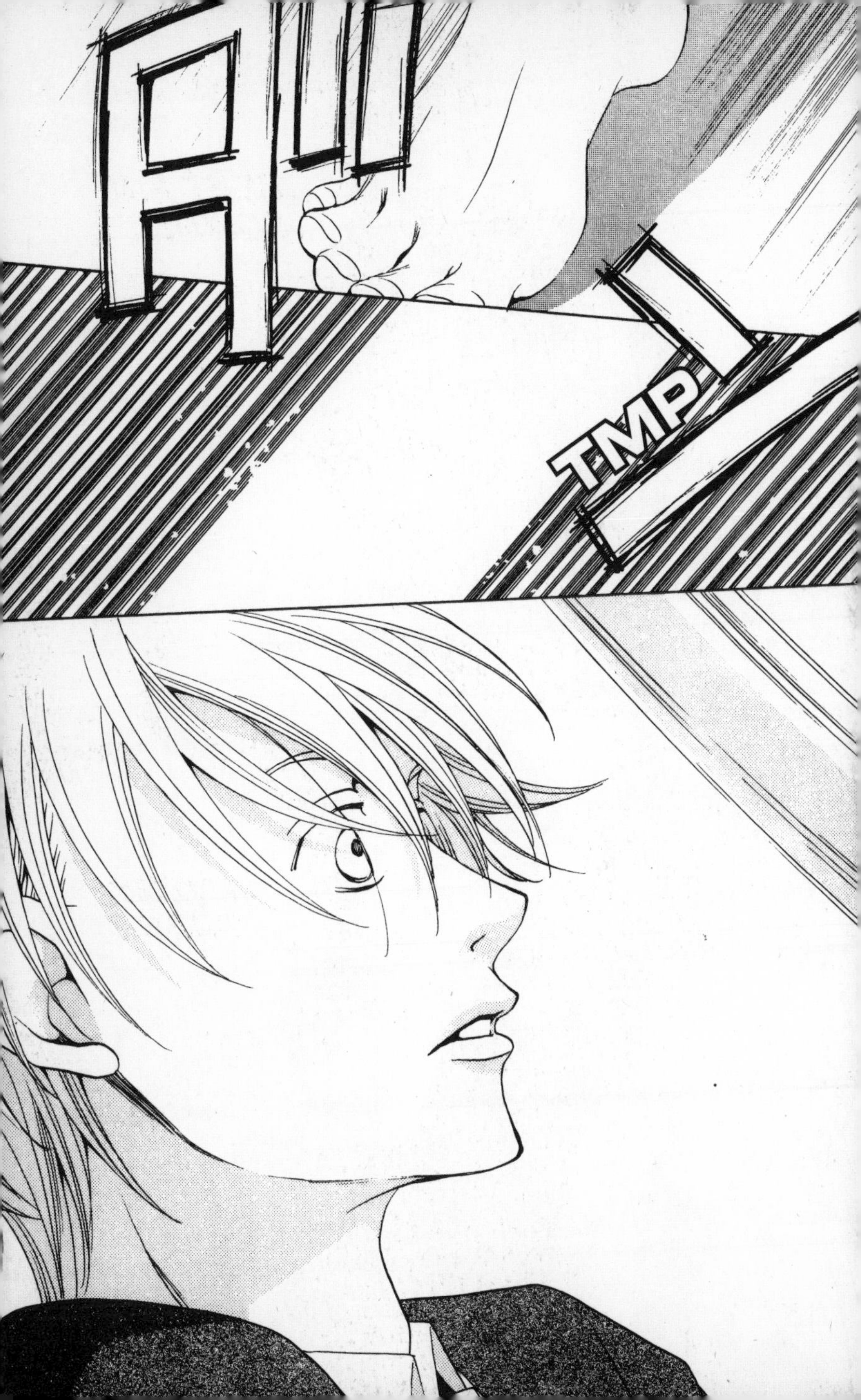
TMP

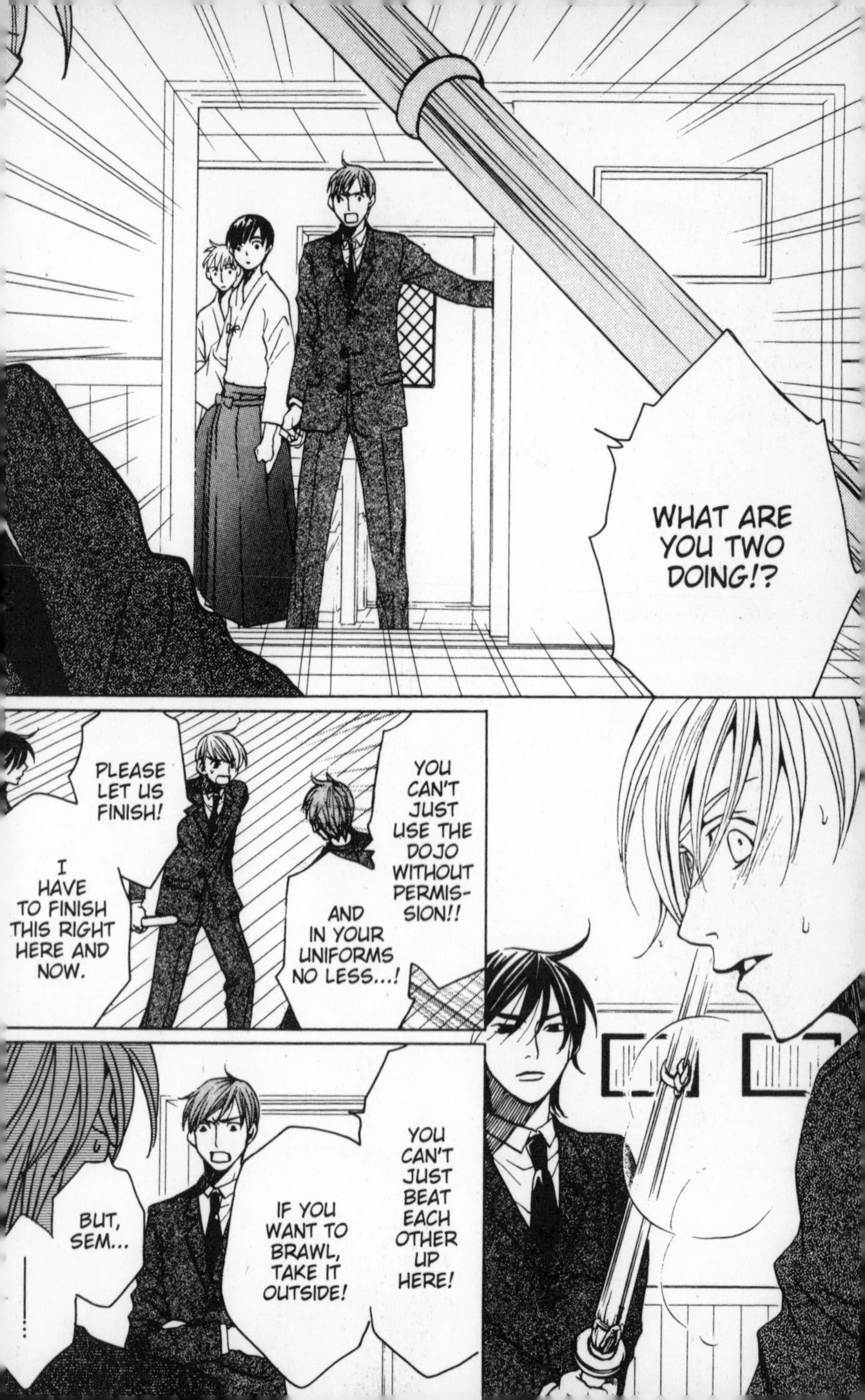
WHAT ARE YOU TWO DOING!?
YOU CAN'T JUST USE THE DOJO WITHOUT PERMIS-SION!!
AND IN YOUR UNIFORMS NO LESS...!
PLEASE LET US FINISH!
I HAVE TO FINISH THIS RIGHT HERE AND NOW.
YOU CAN'T JUST BEAT EACH OTHER UP HERE!
IF YOU WANT TO BRAWL, TAKE IT OUTSIDE!
BUT, SEM...
......

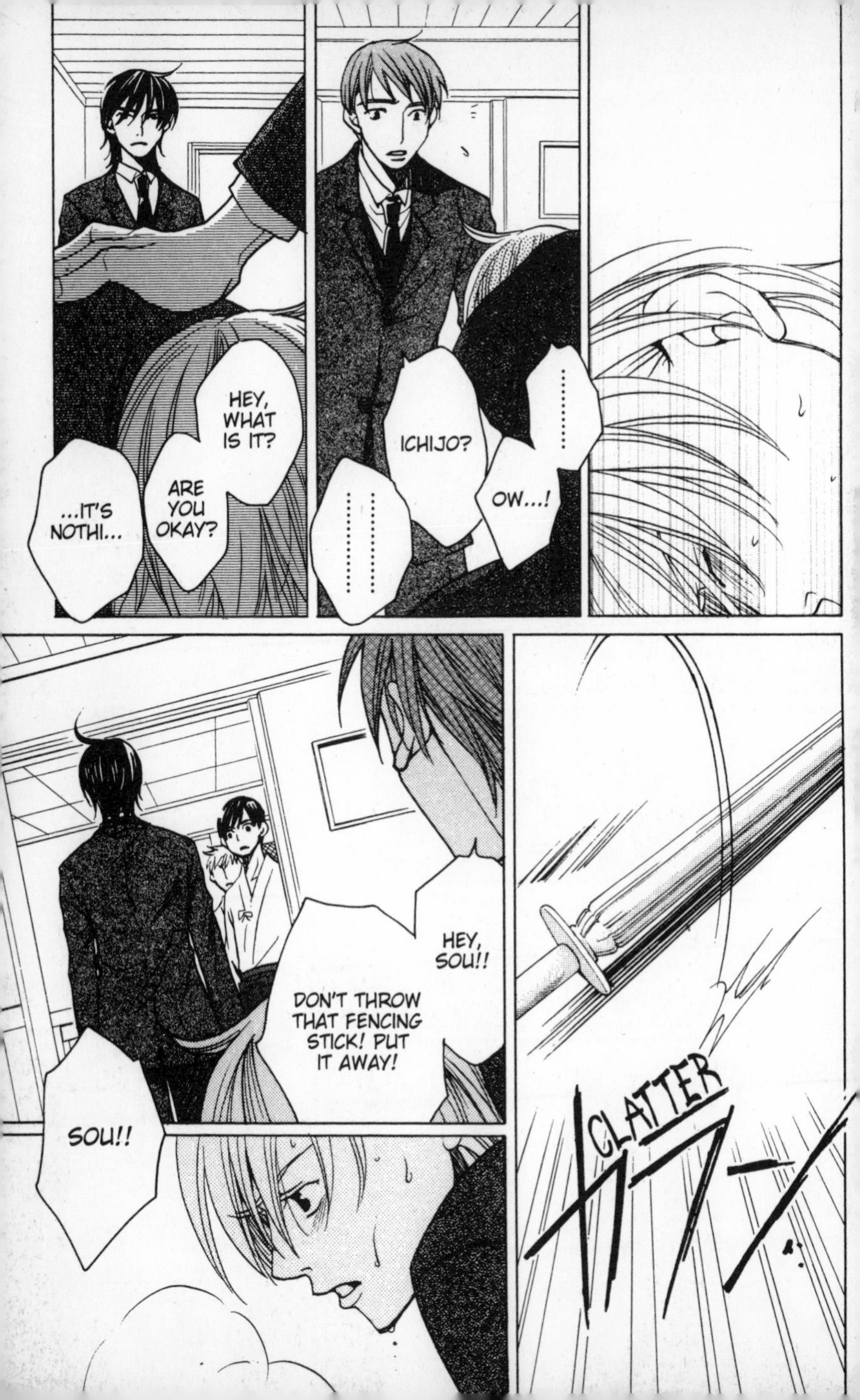
......
ICHIJO?
OW...!
......
HEY, WHAT IS IT?
ARE YOU OKAY?
...IT'S NOTHI...
CLATTER
HEY, SOU!!
DON'T THROW THAT FENCING STICK! PUT IT AWAY!
SOU!!

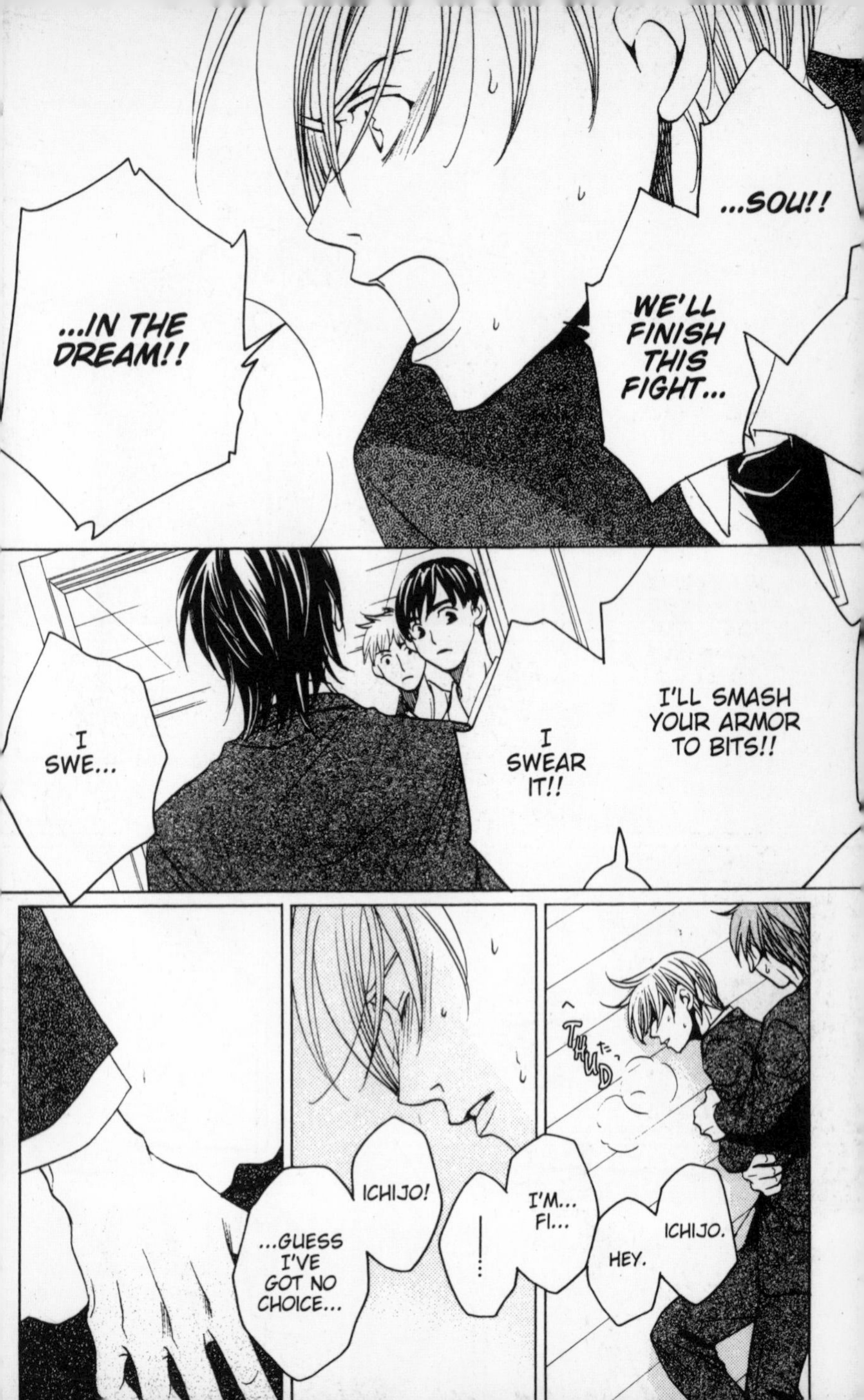
...SOU!!
WE'LL FINISH THIS FIGHT...
...IN THE DREAM!!
I'LL SMASH YOUR ARMOR TO BITS!!
I SWEAR IT!!
I SWE...
ICHIJO.
HEY.
THUD
I'M... FI...
...!
ICHIJO!
...GUESS I'VE GOT NO CHOICE...

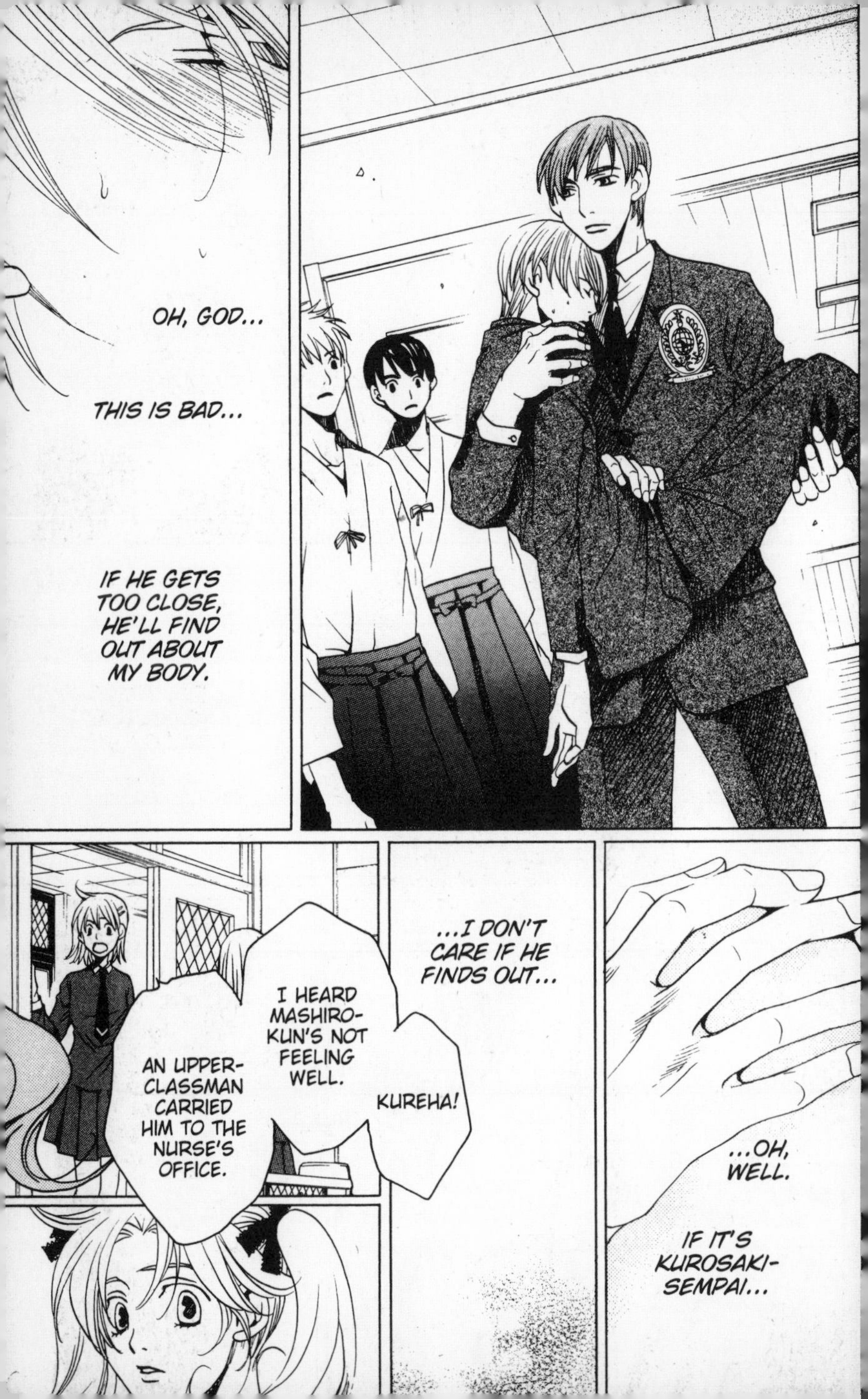
OH, GOD...
THIS IS BAD...
IF HE GETS TOO CLOSE, HE'LL FIND OUT ABOUT MY BODY.
...OH, WELL.
IF IT'S KUROSAKI-SEMPAI...
...I DON'T CARE IF HE FINDS OUT...
KUREHA!
I HEARD MASHIRO-KUN'S NOT FEELING WELL.
AN UPPER-CLASSMAN CARRIED HIM TO THE NURSE'S OFFICE.

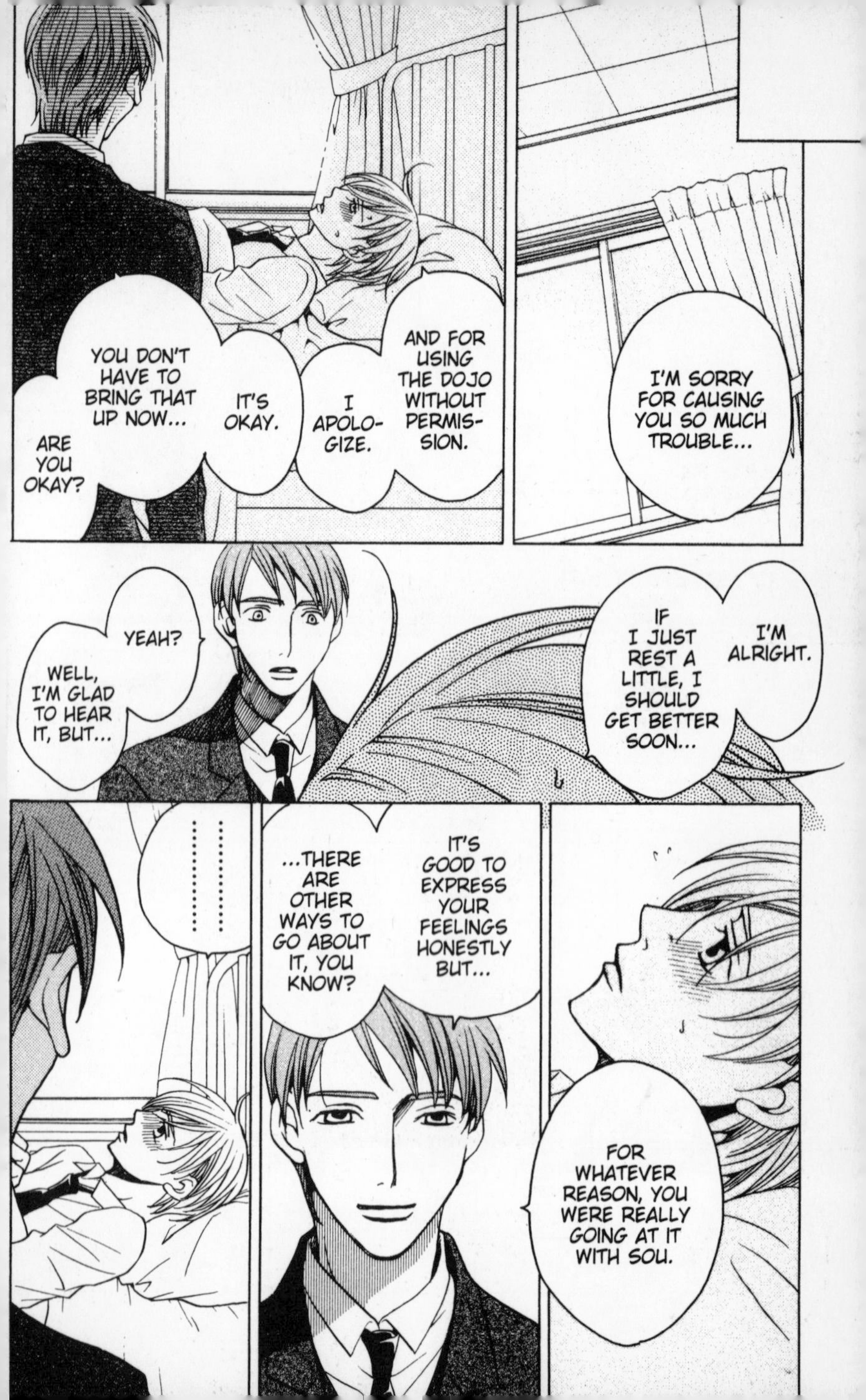
I'M SORRY FOR CAUSING YOU SO MUCH TROUBLE...
AND FOR USING THE DOJO WITHOUT PERMISSION.
I APOLOGIZE.
IT'S OKAY.
YOU DON'T HAVE TO BRING THAT UP NOW...
ARE YOU OKAY?
I'M ALRIGHT.
IF I JUST REST A LITTLE, I SHOULD GET BETTER SOON...
YEAH?
WELL, I'M GLAD TO HEAR IT, BUT...
FOR WHATEVER REASON, YOU WERE REALLY GOING AT IT WITH SOU.
IT'S GOOD TO EXPRESS YOUR FEELINGS HONESTLY BUT...
...THERE ARE OTHER WAYS TO GO ABOUT IT, YOU KNOW?
......

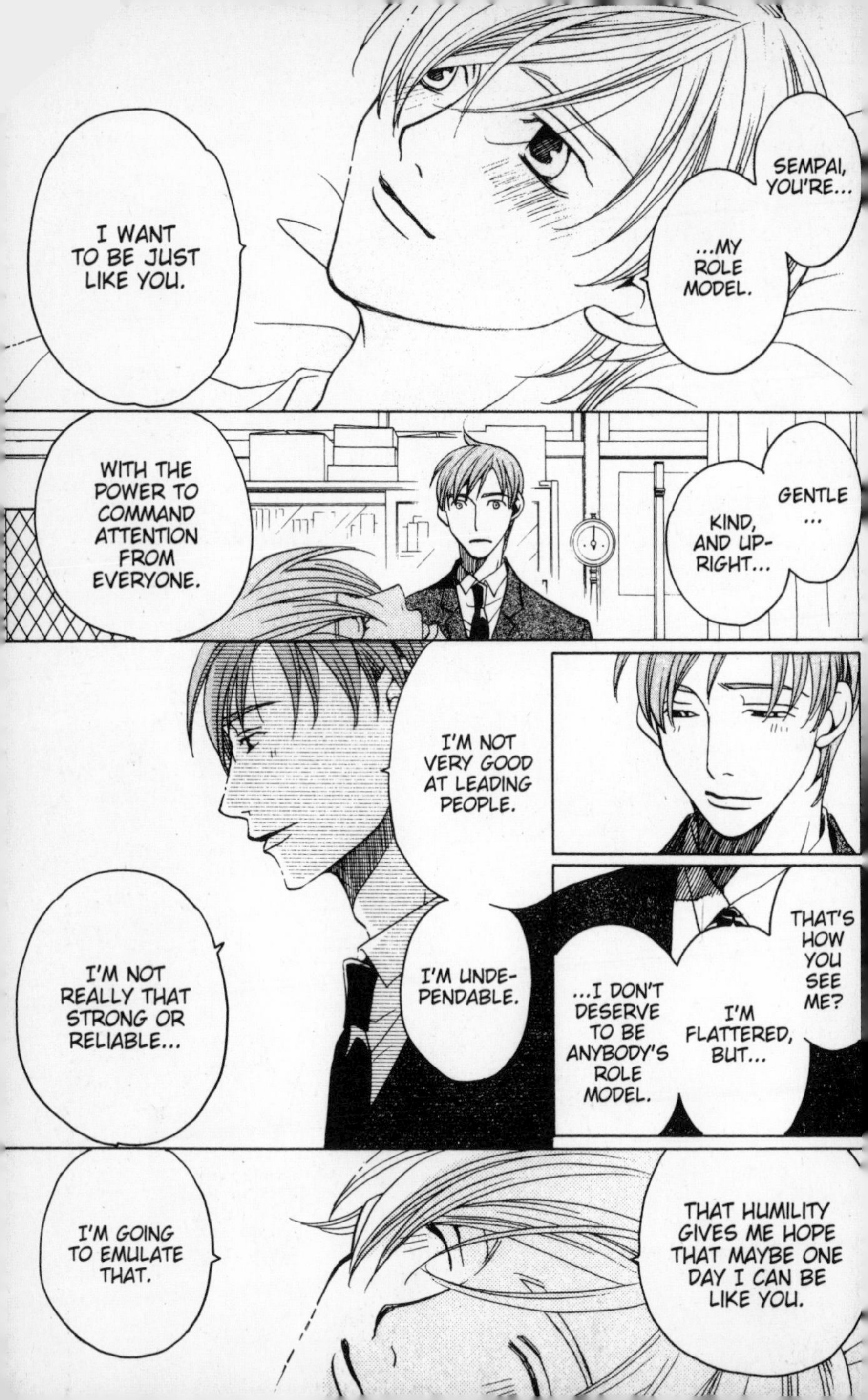
SEMPAI, YOU'RE...
...MY ROLE MODEL.
I WANT TO BE JUST LIKE YOU.
GENTLE...
KIND, AND UP-RIGHT...
WITH THE POWER TO COMMAND ATTENTION FROM EVERYONE.
THAT'S HOW YOU SEE ME?
I'M FLATTERED, BUT...
...I DON'T DESERVE TO BE ANYBODY'S ROLE MODEL.
I'M NOT VERY GOOD AT LEADING PEOPLE.
I'M UNDE-PENDABLE.
I'M NOT REALLY THAT STRONG OR RELIABLE...
THAT HUMILITY GIVES ME HOPE THAT MAYBE ONE DAY I CAN BE LIKE YOU.
I'M GOING TO EMULATE THAT.

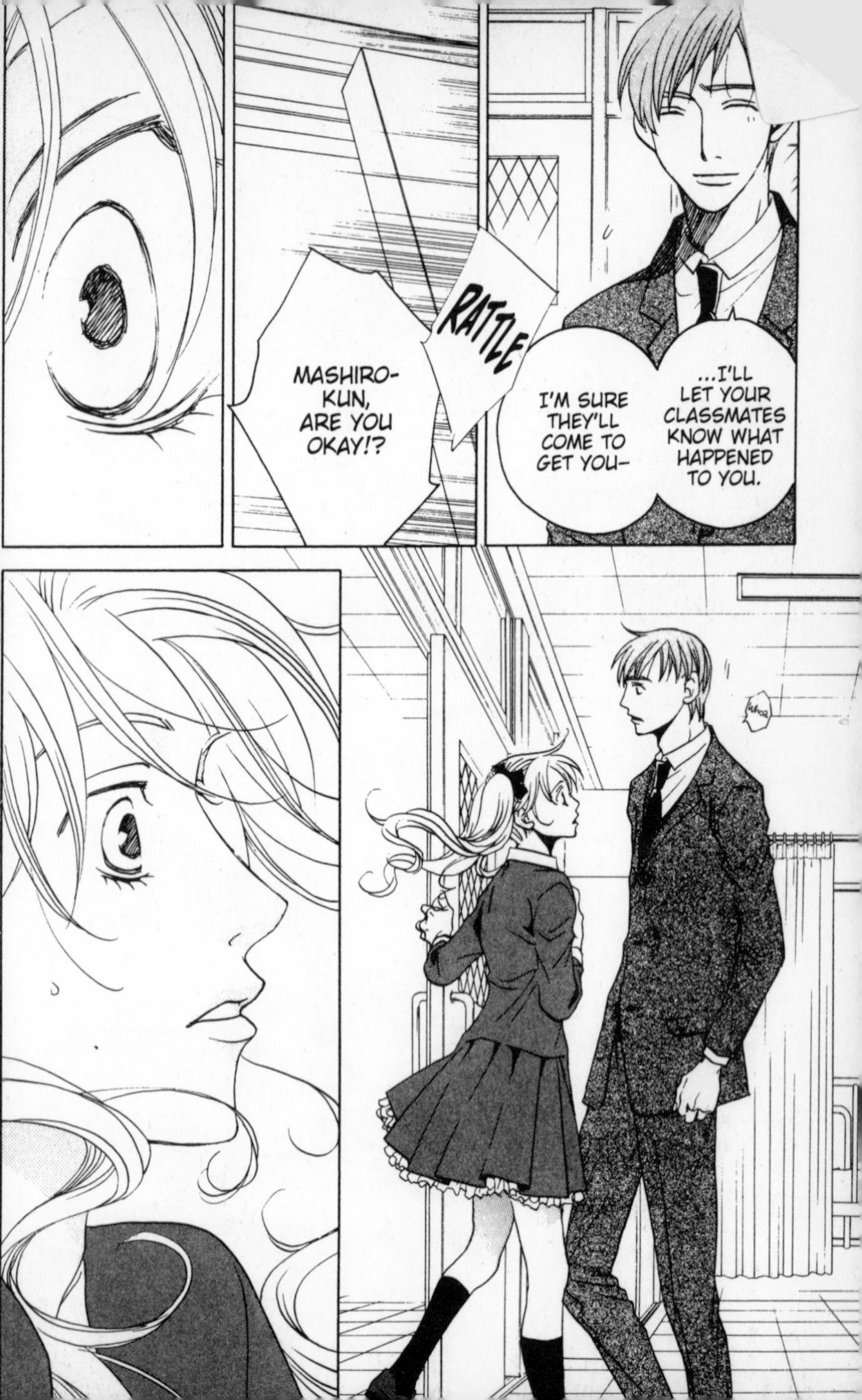
...I'LL LET YOUR CLASSMATES KNOW WHAT HAPPENED TO YOU.
I'M SURE THEY'LL COME TO GET YOU—
RATTLE
MASHIRO-KUN, ARE YOU OKAY!?
Whoa

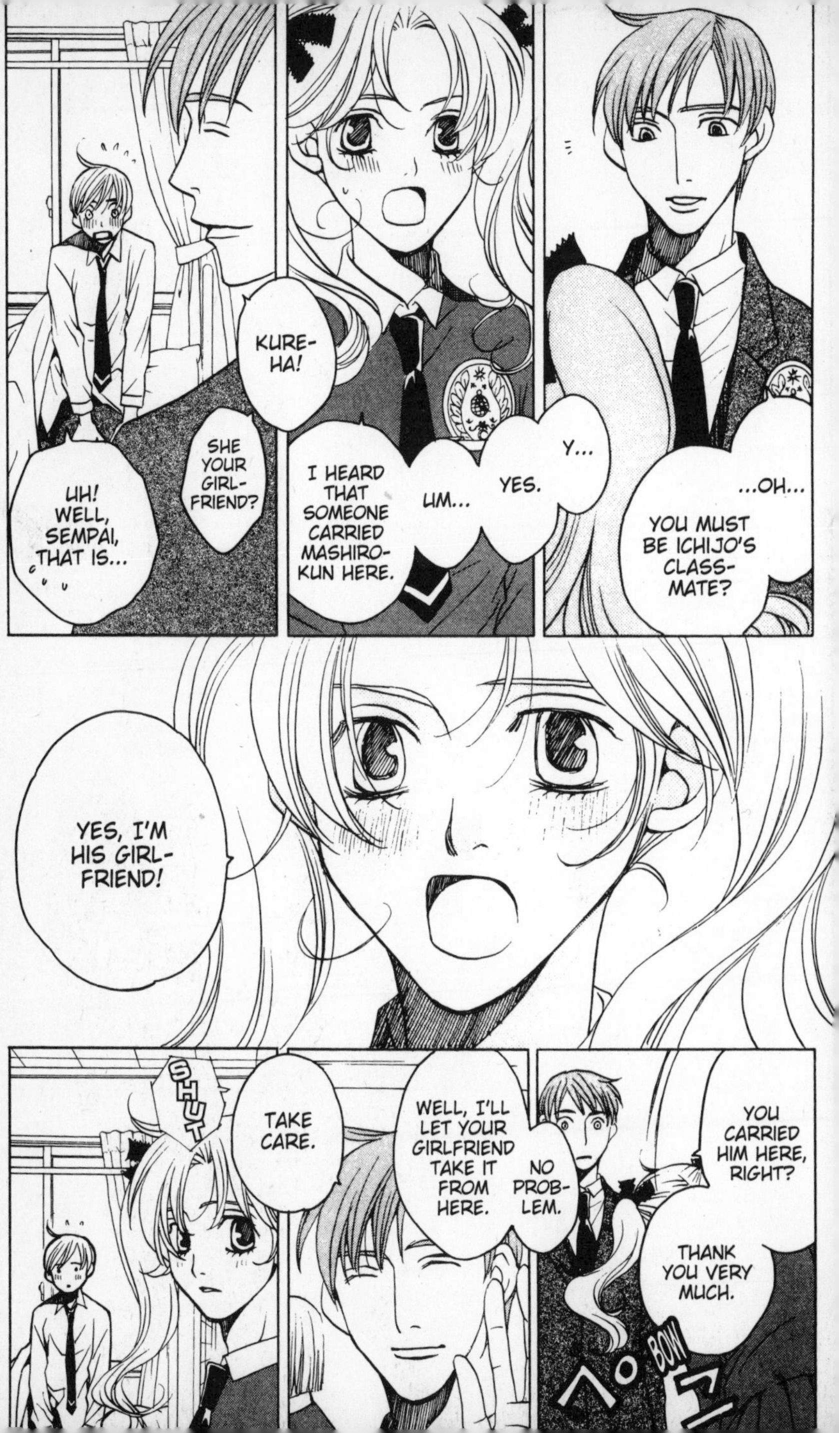
...OH...
YOU MUST BE ICHIJO'S CLASSMATE?
Y...
YES.
UM...
I HEARD THAT SOMEONE CARRIED MASHIRO-KUN HERE.
KURE-HA!
SHE YOUR GIRL-FRIEND?
UH! WELL, SEMPAI, THAT IS...
YES, I'M HIS GIRL-FRIEND!
YOU CARRIED HIM HERE, RIGHT?
THANK YOU VERY MUCH.
BOW
NO PROB-LEM.
WELL, I'LL LET YOUR GIRLFRIEND TAKE IT FROM HERE.
TAKE CARE.
SHUT

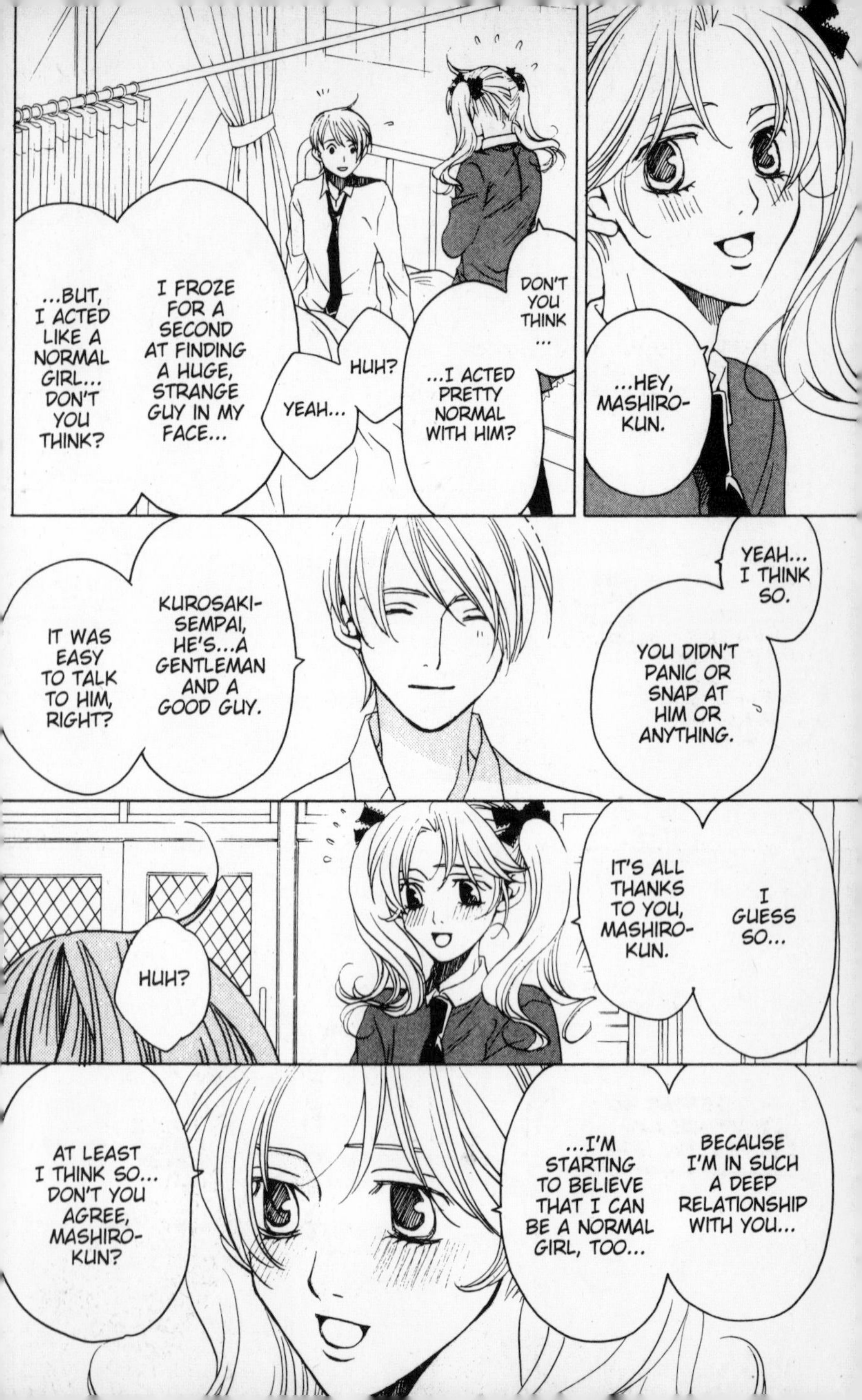
...HEY, MASHIRO-KUN.
DON'T YOU THINK ...
...I ACTED PRETTY NORMAL WITH HIM?
HUH?
YEAH...
I FROZE FOR A SECOND AT FINDING A HUGE, STRANGE GUY IN MY FACE...
...BUT, I ACTED LIKE A NORMAL GIRL... DON'T YOU THINK?
YEAH... I THINK SO.
YOU DIDN'T PANIC OR SNAP AT HIM OR ANYTHING.
KUROSAKI-SEMPAI, HE'S...A GENTLEMAN AND A GOOD GUY.
IT WAS EASY TO TALK TO HIM, RIGHT?
I GUESS SO...
IT'S ALL THANKS TO YOU, MASHIRO-KUN.
HUH?
BECAUSE I'M IN SUCH A DEEP RELATIONSHIP WITH YOU...
...I'M STARTING TO BELIEVE THAT I CAN BE A NORMAL GIRL, TOO...
AT LEAST I THINK SO... DON'T YOU AGREE, MASHIRO-KUN?

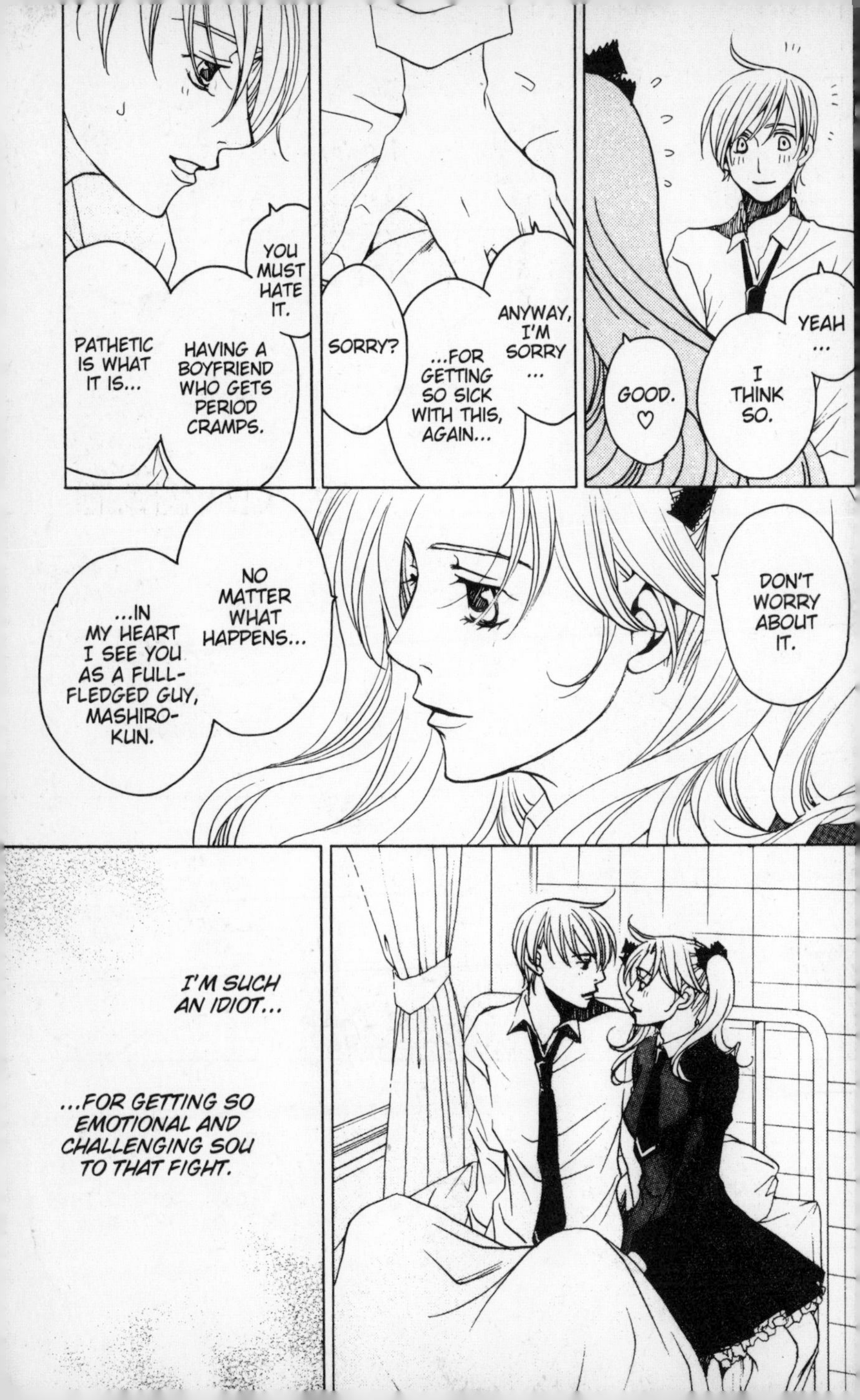
YEAH...
I THINK SO.
GOOD. ♡
ANYWAY, I'M SORRY...
...FOR GETTING SO SICK WITH THIS, AGAIN...
SORRY?
YOU MUST HATE IT.
HAVING A BOYFRIEND WHO GETS PERIOD CRAMPS.
PATHETIC IS WHAT IT IS...
DON'T WORRY ABOUT IT.
NO MATTER WHAT HAPPENS...
...IN MY HEART I SEE YOU AS A FULL-FLEDGED GUY, MASHIRO-KUN.
I'M SUCH AN IDIOT...
...FOR GETTING SO EMOTIONAL AND CHALLENGING SOU TO THAT FIGHT.

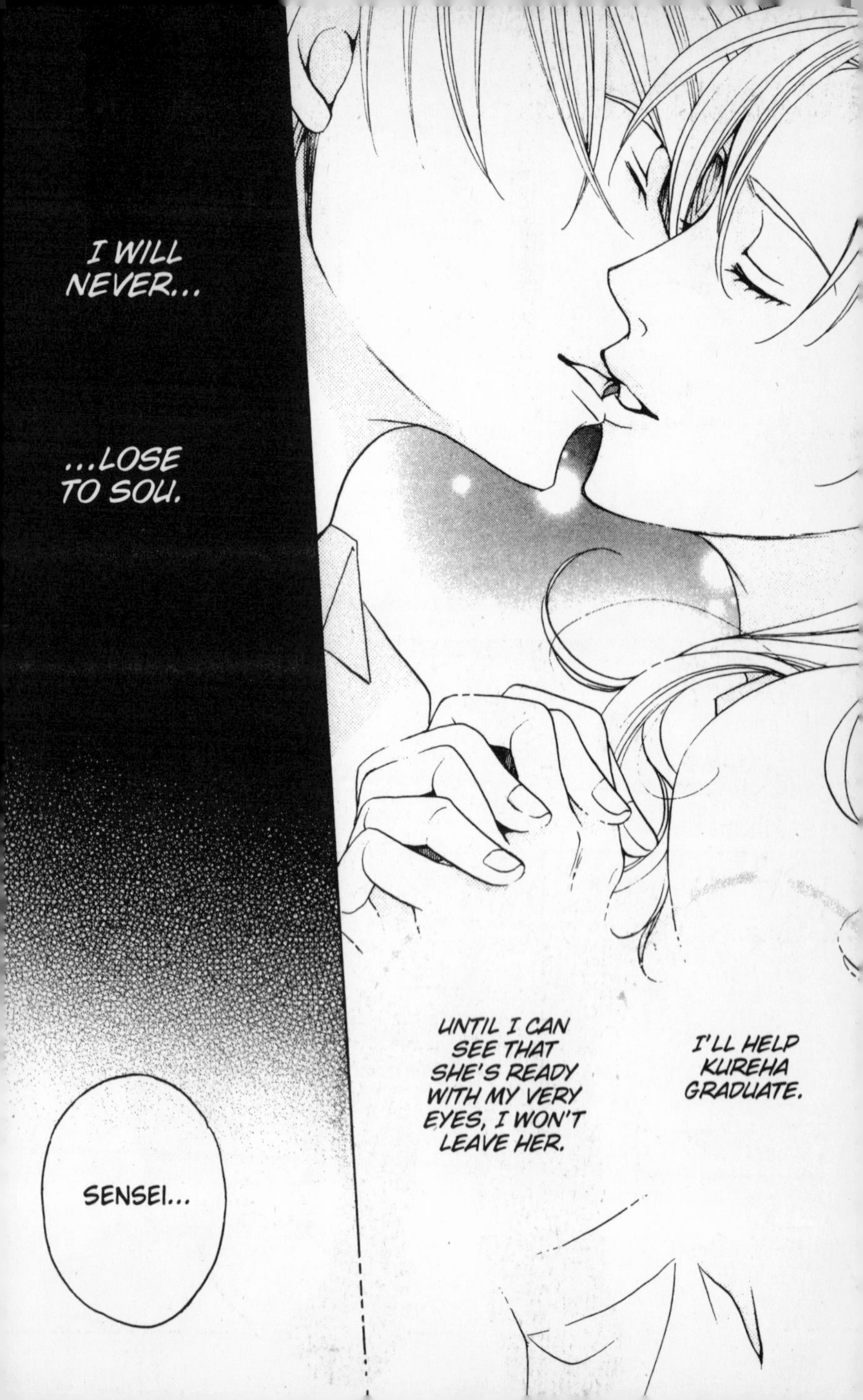
I'LL HELP KUREHA GRADUATE.
UNTIL I CAN SEE THAT SHE'S READY WITH MY VERY EYES, I WON'T LEAVE HER.
I WILL NEVER...
...LOSE TO SOU.
SENSEI...

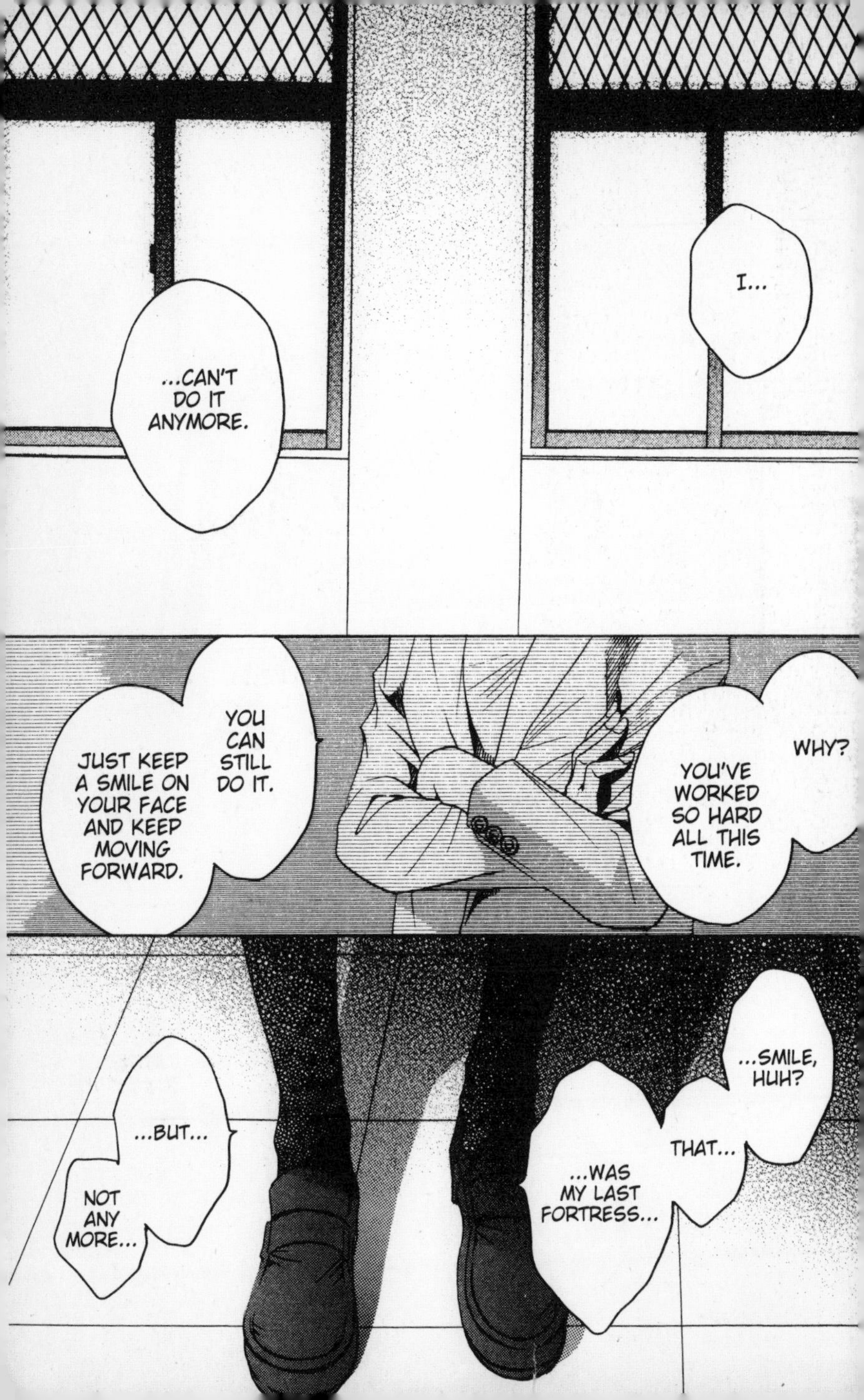
I...
...CAN'T DO IT ANYMORE.
WHY?
YOU'VE WORKED SO HARD ALL THIS TIME.
YOU CAN STILL DO IT.
JUST KEEP A SMILE ON YOUR FACE AND KEEP MOVING FORWARD.
...SMILE, HUH?
THAT...
...WAS MY LAST FORTRESS...
...BUT...
NOT ANY MORE...

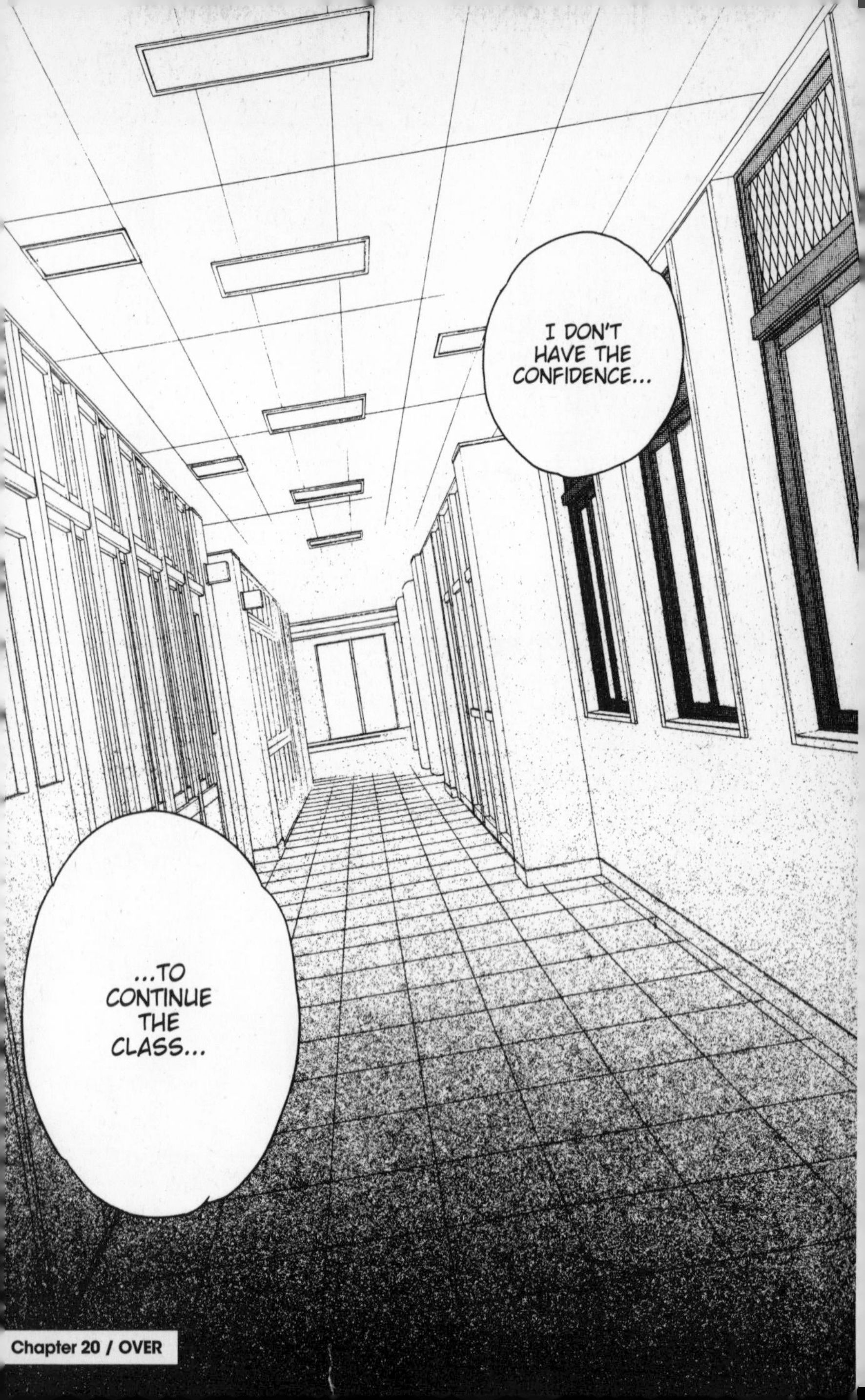
I DON'T HAVE THE CONFIDENCE...
...TO CONTINUE THE CLASS...

Chapter 20 / OVER

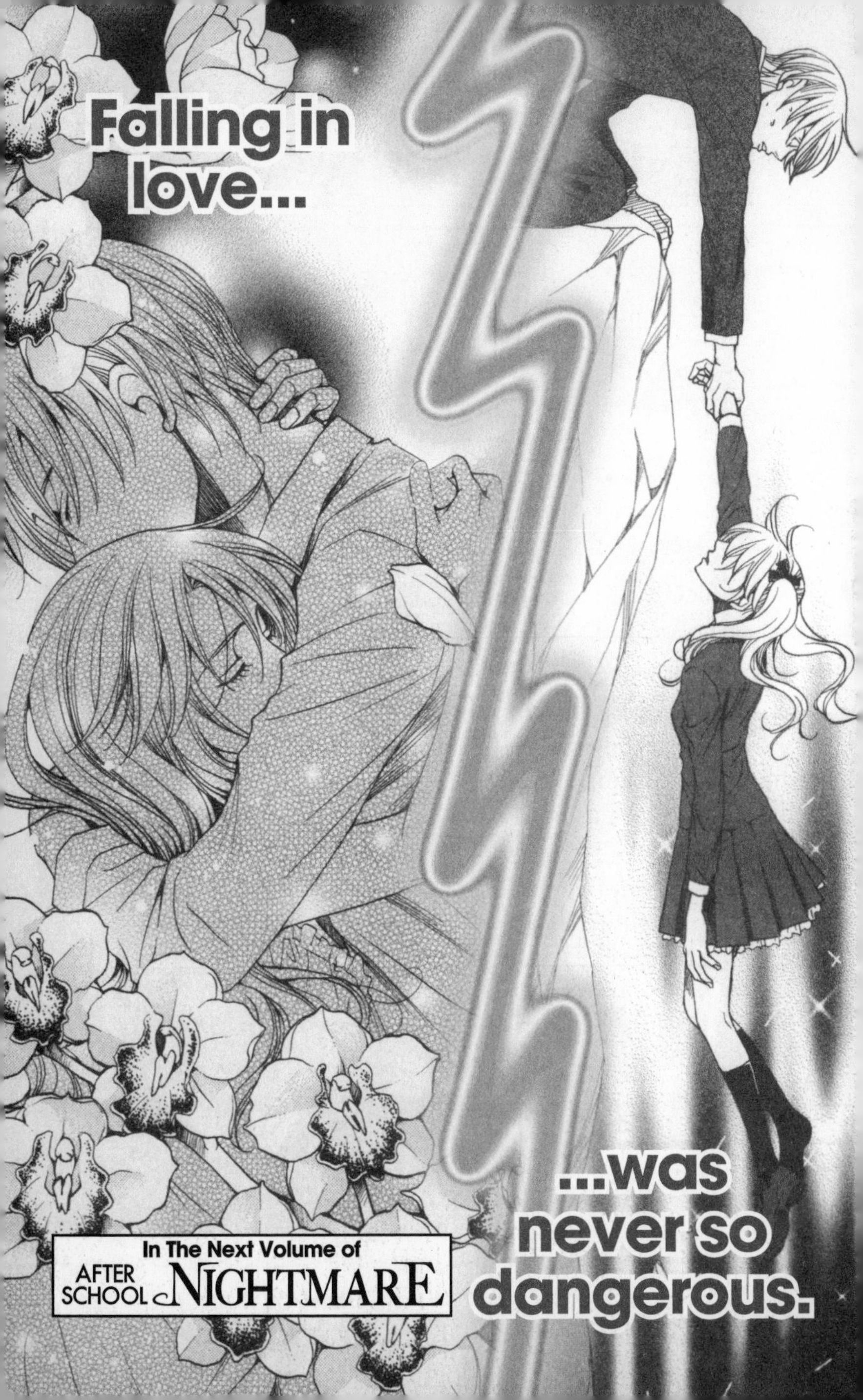
Falling in love...
...was never so dangerous.
In The Next Volume of
AFTER SCHOOL NIGHTMARE

Translator's Notes:

Pg. 32 – Hiwada and Fujikura
Two more color-names. "Hiwada" is a traditional Japanese color derived from the color of bark of the cypress tree. The "fuji" in "Fujikura" means "wisteria" and it denotes a light blue-violet color.

Pg. 66 – *obento*
A boxed lunch very popular with all ages. They usually include rice, fish or meat and pickled vegetables. Fabulous for an easy picnic!

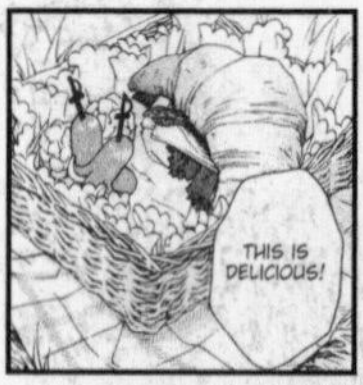
THIS IS DELICIOUS!

Pg. 66 – *korokke*
Korokke are deep-friend snacks closely related to French *croquettes*. They are patty-shaped and can be filled with meat or vegetables in a creamy concoction.

Pg. 163 – double-fold eyelids
Japanese eyes do not usually have the same eyelid fold – called the epicanthic fold – that Caucasians do. It's pretty desired and Asian people sometimes even have surgery to get it put in. The fold-less look is somewhat classic to the Japanese.

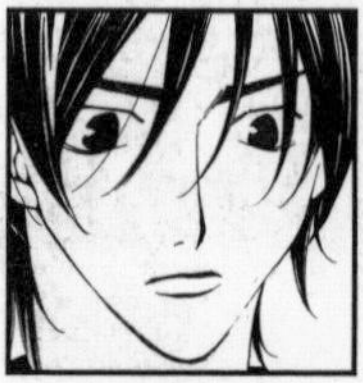
Fold-less

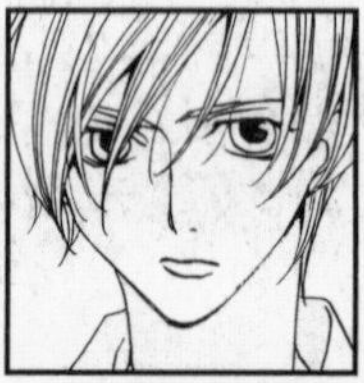
Double-fold